THOUGHTS GALLERY

THOUGHTS GALLERY

Dr. Sunil Gupta

PRABHAT PRAKASHAN

ISO 9001: 2008 Publishers

Published by
PRABHAT PRAKASHAN
4/19 Asaf Ali Road,
New Delhi-110 002 (INDIA)
Tele : +91-11-23289777
e-mail: prabhatbooks@gmail.com

ISBN 978-93-5186-669-5
THOUGHTS GALLERY
by Dr. Sunil Gupta

Edition
First, 2016

Price
₹ 750.00 (Rupees Seven Hundred Fifty only)

Printed at
Yash Printographics, Noida

Advance Praise for 'Thoughts Gallery'

"Love and Blessings for your endeavour, 'Thoughts Gallery'."

—**Sri Sri Ravi Shankar**

Founder, The Art of Living Foundation

❋❋❋

"Articles in this book have thoroughly discussed subjects of internal security, Centre-State relations, financial inclusion of the poor, and socio-economic reforms and also have come up with feasible solutions."

—**Rajnath Singh**

Minister of Home Affairs,
Government of India

❋❋❋

"It was a pleasure to know that your book 'Thoughts Gallery' is being published.

The totality with which you have put across views on social, political, economic and cultural matters deserves to be thought of and followed. The points raised in the book are pertinent and advanced of their times, and their relevancy is self-explanatory.

I whole-heartedly congratulate you on this occasion and have faith that this book will establish its significance for readers in wide-ranging context."

—**Amit Shah**

President, Bharatiya Janata Party (BJP)

❋❋❋

"Having covered almost every corner and aspect of society, politics and economy, the writer has suggested constructive ways that can produce change we have craved for since long."

—**General (Retd.) V.K. Singh**

Minister of State (IC) for Statistics and Programme Implementation, and MoS for External Affairs and Overseas Indian Affairs

❋❋❋

"Small changes can lead to social and economic revolution, words of this book substantiate this fact. Very true, participants in country's development have to be all Indians."

—**Dr. Mahesh Sharma**

Minister of State (IC) for Culture and Tourism, and MoS for Civil Aviation

❋❋❋

"It is really thought provoking and fascinating work. I recommend that all workers engaged in national services and policy makers should read this book. My all congratulations to the learned writer."

—**Dr. Bajranglal Gupta**

Kshetra Sanghchalak, RSS

❋❋❋

"Had there been a true sense of devotion in all countrymen, our country would have been more tolerant and just. Writer's suggestions come out as inspiring all Indians recognise their national duties and serve the country with utmost 'sewa'."

—**Rakesh Jain**

Akhil Bhartiya Sangathan Mantri, Sewa Bharti

❋❋❋

"Dr. Sunil Gupta's book, 'Thoughts Gallery', is a compilation of articles on different issues of society and economy. The book contains 125 articles on subjects ranging from Indian political and economic milieu to environmental and social state of affairs. These articles are worth reading for students and researchers in the field of social sciences since Dr. Gupta has digested the issues and placed it for the readers in a simple language and sharply focused. For example he correctly brings out that more than Article 370 of the Constitution it is Article 35A that is pernicious for national integration. He also gives crisp advice in his essays such as on the economy to the people: 'Stop Expecting. Start Participating'.

Thus, I warmly welcome this book and recommend that all interested in socio-economic issues read the book."

—Dr. Subramanian Swamy
Former Union Cabinet Minister
for Commerce, Law & Justice

❋❋❋

"Public opinion is the bedrock on which democracy is anchored. It implies that many citizens should take the lead in moulding public opinion to focus on issues which impact society. Dr. Sunil Gupta has, over the years, written extensively on very many issues in an analytic and scholarly manner. This book, a collection of his writings, now collated under various topics, carries forward our debates for the greater common good."

—T.V. Mohandas Pai
Chairman, Manipal Global Education
and Ex-director, Infosys

❋❋❋

"Dr. Sunil Gupta's Thoughts Gallery is a book that came out timely. His eclectic collection of essays is riveting and highlights on issues which are current and pertinent for our democracy. A must read book for those interested in the social, economic, political, and other aspects of our nation."

—Dr. D.P. Tripathi
Member of Parliament (Rajya Sabha)

❋❋❋

"Dr. Gupta's book carries facts and their analysis hand-in-hand, and the subjects are related to both traditions as well as modernism."

—Dainik Jagran
Daily Hindi-language Newspaper, India

❋❋❋

"Dr. Sunil Gupta, in his book, has touched every of the aspects needed to comprehend present day socio-economic scenarios, and the book has been effective in grasping and making the readers diagnose these subjects."

—Hindustan
Daily Hindi-language Newspaper, India

❋❋❋

"This book is a powerful testament about those issues which need to be discussed today. From the little on the cover to last page, I found it written very well. Sure, Dr. Gupta has done a remarkable job."

—Sudhir Chaudhary
Editor, Zee News

❋❋❋

"Renowned chartered accountant and financial services advisor Dr. Sunil Gupta has authored a book titled Thoughts Gallery which is a compilation of most of his blogs on a variety of subjects containing facts, impressions and opinions, concerning various national and international problems and issues that modern India is currently facing. The author refers the mandate of the General Elections 2014 as the turning point for India heightening expectations that the current Government will enable this country to realise its massive potential and make rapid progress."

—The Pioneer
Daily English-language Newspaper, India

❋❋❋

"The book is thought-provoking and should ignite every thinking person ponder on its merits and demerits."

—The Statesman
Daily English-language Newspaper, India

This book is dedicated to my Mother and Father, Smt. Dayawati and Shri Ram Niwas Gupta

You gave all your children, including myself, the best childhood that we could have ever asked for and made us what we are today. Without both of you, none of our successes would have been possible. Your continuous guidance and veteran advice on day-to-day living aspects, even today, has been and will always be the chief source of inspiration for all your children.

You imparted in us the right set of values, the fundamentals of ethics, unambiguous ideas about the paradoxes of life and a pristine perception about the role of an individual in life for the collective good of the society. You convinced us there is no way an individual can truly thrive without carrying the rest of the society along. From your lives, we learned how to set about accomplishing onerous tasks. Such were the nuggets of wisdom that your children imbibed from the first lessons at home in the course of acquisition of crucial knowledge!

Even now, I can recall how life in the part of the town where we lived was fraught with impediments, such as severe constraints of sources of quality education and income. We are grateful that both of you ceaselessly put up valiant struggles to provide all of us quality education and the right conditions to get along, without being the least affected by the flipside of life in our surroundings and neighbourhood.

Your lessons on ethics were quite precise and practical. For instance, answers to questions like 'Why we cannot thrive individually without the betterment of society?', 'How actions of one person can lead to the economic growth of the entire country?' and 'Where to start from, so as to reach the ultimate goal?' were best given by you. And these answers have helped us construe events with morality and righteousness.

From you, we came to know that without motivating and inspiring the common man, no good can be achieved in any nation's socio-economic sphere. We learned that our society is what we make it. Just blaming politicians, bureaucrats, leaders or anyone else without taking individual responsibility or contributing to the society's betterment is not going to serve any purpose. Every single rupee counts, even a piece of bread holds worth, and one enlightened and committed person can bring about revolutions were some of the key chunks of your lessons. Given the above, my writings reflect the journey of my life of which you have been the most central part.

To tell you honestly, we can't ever thank you enough for your selflessness, kindness, devotion, endless support and other contributions in our lives. Hence, we shall do our best to follow the path you have expounded. Meanwhile, I humbly dedicate this book to both of you.

—Sunil
Your Devoted Son

Acknowledgements

This book is a labour of love and I would like to express my gratitude and indebtedness to all those who inspired me for this work and contributed towards making the dream of this book a reality.

To my parents who offered me fundamental lessons in morality and righteousness and thus enriched my life. The two of them laid the foundation of whatever I am today, and for that I will remain indebted to them forever. Moreover, I have immensely benefited from their unconditional love, something that I have always treasured and will eternally cherish. Both of them are the central pillars of support for me. As such, I am indeed very blessed to have their continued love and guidance even today.

To my wife, Mamta, who has been a constant source of unwavering support and encouragement for me throughout my personal and professional life. My daughter, CA Shruti, and son, Mayank, who gave all the required inputs to keep me updated with the latest technological revolutions and thereby make a vital difference in my life. I feel blessed to be the father of these two wonderful, supportive, ethical and truthful children.

To my brothers, Dr. Anil and Sushil; sister, Usha; and other family members and friends who chipped in with very pertinent observations and clear-headed counsel. They also helped me identify diverse and interesting subjects, thereby enhancing the scope and reach of my writings. Thus, they have all been enthusiastic supporters of this project.

To all my teachers during the phase of my academic pursuits and even after that, who transformed a novice like me into a well-informed professional who could construe the developments around and become a part of the process of nation-building, to whatever extent I have been able to, until today. My ideas about our society, our country and the world around us have been greatly influenced by them.

Then there are so many others to thank. First and foremost being the publishers of the book. Then I am also immensely grateful to CA Vini Sharma; and S/Shri D.K. Pandey, Ankit Sethi, Suresh Menon, Bharat Bhushan, Nitin Agarwal, Mayank Goel, R.V. Deshpandey, Deepak Rath and Vibhav Kant Upadhyay. This list embraces many more unstated names associated with my attainments till date.

Meanwhile, Dr. Krishna Gopal, Sahasarakaryavah, Rashtriya Swayamsevak Sangh and Shri Rakesh Jain, Akhil Bhartiya Sangathan Mantri, Sewa Bharti deserve a special mention. Their invaluable inputs on how to interpret and contribute towards the social betterment of our country have reshaped my thought process. Many of my articles are a reflection of their judicious ideology and wisdom of inclusive growth.

Finally, I am extremely grateful to the readers of my articles that were regularly posted on my blog www.drsunilgupta.com, and also to the readers who will generously set aside their valuable time for reading this book – because without them this entire endeavour will remains inadequate and incomplete. And in case I have missed out anyone, I hereby express my sincere apologies.

Foreword

Before ancient civilisations like Indian, Chinese, Minoan, Grecian, Egyptian, Roman and Maya of Mexico grew and blossomed from time to time, there was ***a great legendary figure in Indian civilisation, Manu,*** who gave the world all laws and jurisprudential philosophy to govern for ensuring basic human urges, firstly to live, secondly to live better, thirdly to live longer, healthily, purposefully and happily, and fourthly to die peacefully on this planet earth.

Prophetically, he observed:

"Etath desa prasutasya, saakasaat agra janmanah swam swam sevabhi sikheran priithivyam sarva manavah" Manu Smriti

(Those that are born in this land would be considered to be elders under the sun to teach service-based values to humans on this planet)

In the West, the mighty Roman emperor Julius Caesar said: "You can kill a man, but you cannot kill an idea." Later Marcus Aurelius, the well-known Roman emperor-philosopher said in his meditation: "Our life is what our thoughts make it."

Thought is mother of idea, which is mother of imagination, which is mother of vision, which is mother of intention, which is mother of action, which is mother of result, in every sphere of human existence and endeavour. All over the world, ***thought masters*** swayed civilisations, which in turn swayed wings of progress and prosperity of human race. That is why ***thought is considered to be the most important.***

Here is a book by Dr. Sunil Gupta, titled "Thoughts Gallery", a purposeful compilation of most of his blogs on a variety of subjects containing facts, impressions and opinions, concerning various national and international problems and issues that modern India is currently facing.

The book is divided neatly into 12 chapters, namely Ameliorating Indian Politics, Fostering Governance, Momentous to Economy, Pushing the Industry, Real Development, Base of India: Agriculture, Nourishing Health and Education, Roots: Women and Children, Religion and India, India Together with the World, The Common Indian, and Dexterous Electoral Process.

Obviously, the copyright on the mentioned facts, opinions and inferences and all contents of the book exclusively rests with the author.

This is a strenuous effort and the sweep is wide and varied.

Some may agree or disagree with different contents in the book, but the contents are bound to make honest and conscious citizens think, think and think. In one word, the book is thought-provoking and should ignite every thinking person ponder on its merits and demerits.

I wish author all the best

—Dr. G.V.G. Krishnamurty
Former Election Commissioner of India

Preface

India, a country pompously referred to as the world's largest democracy, is home to not just the most ancient tribes but also to people from diverse descents. The inhabitants of this great country in its days of glory were seekers of truth. Their prayer was encapsulated in the following verse from Brihadaranyaka Upanishad: *'Tamaso mâ jyotir gamaya'*. (From darkness, lead me to light). In keeping with the theme of this prayer, ancient Indians kept their mind and heart open for truth from different directions to trickle in because they always believed in the following adage propounded by the seers of the hoary past, 'The truth is one, but wise men know it as many' (Rig Veda).

Consequently, visitors from different countries were welcomed as Guests of Honour – true to the dictum *'Atithi Devo Bhava'* (Guest is equivalent to God) – and were allowed to practise their belief system and faith without restraint. The Parsis were a case in point. The consequent blossoming of different ideological concepts and doctrines over thousands of years of relative peace and serenity culminated in the metamorphosis of the Indian society, which was living in perfect harmony in a nation that made a mark for itself as a land of spiritual sublimity and bliss. Rather than wilting under the glare of alien faiths, the native wisdom of our ancestors shone brightly like a beacon of truth.

The peace and prosperity of the country gave it the sobriquet *'Sone ki Chidiya'* (Golden Bird). This and the added charm of the liberal and universal outlook of the people in spiritual matters and their traditional hospitality led to an unapprehended situation, leading to marauding fortune hunters from the monolithic killing fields of Arabia and Central Asia, invading the land of peace and spiritual bliss; and putting it to waste by trying to change the value system and mental outlook of the original inhabitants who were forced under the threat of death and dishonour to don a religious straightjacket and wear blinkers.

Even before the survivors of unspeakable atrocities could regain their wits, there was a washing down of the remnants of the self-esteem and pride in their ancient way of life, by European traders who tricked, with the support of their armies, the native rulers into accepting, over a period of time, the suzerainty of the British Empire. What followed was a seamless transition from a 1,000-year occupation of the land by the proponents of one alien faith into a 200-year rule by the proponents of yet another.

A country subjugated, mauled, brutalized and vandalized beyond recognition, survived the atrocities by the invaders to emerge more united and politically stronger than ever in the past albeit for the partition of the country enforced by a clever conspiracy hatched by the outgoing colonial powers and forces inimical to the unity of the Indian nation. The spiritual and cultural ethos of the nation was left in tatters, but it still held together. What made this possible? It was the *'Bharatiya'* ethos that presented itself as a source of inspiration and hope. The Indian Tricolour symbolizes the *'Bharatiya'* ethos, inspires the people to join the nation's march, stride by stride, to progress and prosperity and hope for a bright future for the country.

Thankfully, with all those painful ups and downs behind us, India now stands at the dawn of a new era. The collection of articles in this book represents my thoughts about various issues currently facing our country. They reflect the state of affairs in various fields ranging from politics to social welfare, arts to sports, economy to judiciary, and agriculture to industry, to name a few. On going through the pages of this book, one can easily get an overview of what India is today and also make a fair assessment of the various challenges that our country faces. The readers will also know that the prevailing conditions are neither too bright for complacency nor too dismal for despair.

While everything has not been lost, there is no time to be lost either in the nation's endeavour for regaining the lost glory. The overall situation for India's advancement in the right direction is brighter now than till recently during the indifferent and lackluster governance of the country by ragtag outfits of political opportunism. This turning point for India came after the general election 2014 when the new government was elected to rule with an overwhelming mandate, heightening expectations that the current government will enable this country to realize its massive potential and make rapid progress.

The country is, at last, on its course from darkness to light, in deference to the prayer of every Indian, past and present. That is the core spirit which this book tries to capture.

—Dr. Sunil Gupta

Contents

FOSTERING GOVERNANCE

MOMENTOUS TO ECONOMY

PUSHING THE INDUSTRY

REAL DEVELOPMENT

INDIA, TOGETHER WITH THE WORLD

THE 'COMMON' INDIAN

DEXTEROUS ELECTORAL PROCESS

Ameliorating Indian Politics

Is Returning Awards a New Addition to Pseudo-secularism

Dear eminent awardees, your capabilities and competence to comprehend issues are much more than the common man of the country. Your works are cherished by the society, your views followed and your verdicts noted. Then isn't any act of insulting the country and renowned institutions by returning souvenirs of applause a defamation of the jury and of the countrymen? The aim of this writing is to bring a slight variation in your perusal of present happenings. Also, being from the same community and having pursued writing for long, I should not blame you of being politically driven against an established and reformist union government, after all liberty of speech and expression is what that makes us free in true sense; however the debates in this context are more or less being diverted to politics, which is a strong reason to give your stand a second thought. I may breach my limits in the following paragraphs by making you remember that the awards aren't just the money associated with them or the plagues, citations and mementos, they are hopes that the society and the nation have from persons of your caliber and excellence. Isn't the return of awards an outright murder of this hope?

History of the Republic of India isn't unknown. The Vedic period, rise of the Maurya and Guptas, followed by the ferocious Delhi Sultanate, Mughal era and the colonial rule are the chapters of academic books, and notable writers and other awardees are more familiar with times past than a common Indian. Post-independence era, when the notions of democracy, secularism, equality and freedom gained utmost prominence, the exploitation of these, which we expected to bring Ram-Rajya, by political parties did not allow India to advance in the way envisaged by the makers of the Constitution. Cases of oppression of

Dalit, communal appeasement, ignorance of women and child rights, and breach of internal security by extremist forces have been more than what a nation could sustain. Now the question which shoots up is that weren't these awardees aware of the globally known and many a time criticized Indian social state of affairs at the time of accepting awards from eminent Indian institutions?

Communal violence, or the so-called 'vitiated atmosphere', has prevailed in India for a long now. Mentioning the Muslim sovereignty that began with the founding of the Delhi Sultanate by the ruler of Slave Dynasty, Iltutmish and subsequent conquests by Timur, Nader Shah and others makes sense to let the protagonists of secularism in modern India know that today's India is way more stable and tolerant than pre-independence times. It is also true that the Republic of India hasn't been out-and-out prolific in delivering concepts of equality and freedom as treasured in the supreme law of the land, for which mischievous interpretation of 'freedom of religion' and 'secular nation' can be widely held liable. Here, it is also vital to note that if the call for banning of cow slaughter is viewed as an outright strategy or 'propaganda' of right groups to make India a pro-Hindu country then any pacific and meaningful solution would remain out of reach. Isn't it quite uncomplicated that considering the faith of Hindus, who unluckily form a majority in the so-called secular India, with respect to cows, outlawing acts of cow slaughter is not a sin and nothing that can promote intolerance?

It is expected out of learned writers and the honourable awardees of Sahitya Akademy that they interpret present happenings in a wider parlance and in a way that promotes communal harmony instead of igniting the feelings of discord and insecurity among the minorities. Film-makers, who have earned accolades from the government for their endeavors to promote art and creativity, are looked upon by the nation as promoters of social congruence; their returning the awards for alleged intolerance against minority is more like letting your presence felt by 'exploiting a timely opportunity'. At a time when India is excelling towards technological and scientific advancements, a veteran scientist's step to return his Padma Bhushan award is a clear deviation from setting upright examples for the future generation; holding the present central government responsible for any and every acts of intolerance, for which governments of respective states are liable, is an unfounded excuse that can hardly justify returning of awards.

It is afraid to note that instances like ethnic cleansing of Kashmiri Pandits, Mumbai and Delhi bombings, 1984 anti-Sikh riots, the Godhra train burning and never-ending suppression of Dalit, women and children could not create a feeling of anxiety among scholars who today see no other option than insulting the decision of the distinguished panels that honoured their works. Have we become so insensitive when it comes to overpowering of the rights of Hindus, women and children, or does secularism hold value in the Indian context only when minority group is devoid of some special rights, even when under the doctrine of equality? Lynching of a man in the state of UP over alleged consumption of cow meat is in no sense a justifiable act and condemning the same is the duty of every government, state or central. In the light of this, however, questioning the intentions of central government with respect to Indian secular setup is exceedingly imprudent, corrupt. It is the state government's duty to maintain a law and order situation that permits relishing of fundamental rights; declaring the so-called propaganda of the Modi-led government to spread Hindu supremacy as a cause is nothing else than politicizing the matter.

When a Chief Minister of an Indian state dares the centrally ruling government to act against him for eating beef, when a senior leader from an opposition party declares that RSS holds the remote control of country's administration and when a minister from the UP state government talks of his plan to write to the United Nations about lynching of a man over beef row, the political milieu of our country that revolves around appeasing separate communities and castes for votes stands blamable. However, intellectual personalities, awarded for their notable works, when 'use' such events as a motivation to protest, their objective and timing becomes questionable. Suicides by Indian farmers, rapes of minor girls, violence against women and thousands of street children on the roads of metropolis demand courtesy of writers, activists, film makers and others associated directly or indirectly with the social sphere. But this as well, does not seek return of awards as a means to protest inefficiency of the government. In their respective domains, these people hold enough authority and influence to express their worries, resorting to defaming the elected central government and its representatives is senseless and infertile.

In the states of UP, Bihar and Bengal, politics of communalism and appeasement has been the most reliable means to rise to the echelons of being an MP, MLA or a CM. Now when the same has led to troubles, which you must agree is a reciprocal occurrence, nervousness has found its place among pseudo-seculars. Though no one can be held accountable unless an unbiased investigation reveals findings, one side of the coin foretells that communal forces would not mind harming the members of the vote-bank they rely upon during polls so that the meritoriously functioning union government can be stopped from gaining support in legislative elections. The other side is shady; no one from the general public or the writers and scholars returning their accolades can give a clear verdict. Then why accuse the BJP government just on grounds that RSS is their ideological mentor and this voluntary organization does not find a reputable standing in the eyes of pseudo-seculars? Barbarism against any community holds no place in the Indian democratic and secular setup, in the wake of this expression, however, politics should not be permitted to thrive illicitly.

From where has the question of infringement of right to free speech and expression has arisen is hard to understand. In the past one year, more so since the BJP has been elected to power, freedom of speech has thrived extraordinarily; the awardees, opposition political parties, religious leaders and others have not only criticized the BJP of being biased against the minority, they have also halted the process of much-needed social and economic reforms. The massacre of free speech during national emergency of 1975, during anti-Sikh riots of 1984 and on many such occasions is to be compared with what the state of affairs India is experiencing today. News debates, press conferences and one-on-one discussions are filled with free expressions, some in support and many against the government of the day. The leader of the country talks about and advocates harmony among communities and inclusive development then isn't halting the process of growth and reforms the most forbidden use of freedom of expression?

What this entire episode has boiled down to is just an attack against the Modi-led government; manufactured or not, but this is the bitter truth and awardees returning their accolades ought to realize this. When Moody's, World Bank and IMF are bullish on India's prospects, a sudden turmoil is washing away all the hard work. Also, the incessant pain of Kashmiri Pandits, their exodus from own houses, now seems a trivial issue owing to awardees sudden anxiety just for a few atrocities, planned or unplanned, against people from minority groups. Indeed, this raises a question mark on the acumen of eminent people who opted for silence all through the time which was adverse for the Hindus and now doubt the intentions of the central government. Very bitter this may sound but the 'Grand Alliance' of Bihar against the lone BJP is supplemented by a cartel of national awardees. While they are alleging 'enhanced intolerance', politically stable government of the country is being burdened. One such attempt in Gujarat has recently been busted by the investigation agency, which validates scrupulous measures against the government. Needless to say, returning award can be anyone's personal choice, but unverified accusations, which can arouse communal tension, by deliberately making minority groups feel insecure, against a democratically elected government is a plain act of sedition, a novel addition to pseudo-secularism.

(Posted on blog on 31 October, 2015)
(Posted on Bharat Niti portal on 3 November, 2015)

□

Politics and Accountability

By virtue of the tremendous responsibility vested in them, politicians in a democratic nation like India are expected to be as much responsible for their speeches as for their actions. It is especially so concerning the speeches made by them before the elections because it is primarily on the strength of these speeches that they get elected. The pre-poll speeches made by politicians are generally in the nature of propagation of the policies and programs of their parties; the action plan contained in their party's election manifesto and objective criticism of the rival parties. In reality, however, much of the time is spent by them, while electioneering, in unceremoniously castigating the rival parties and tarnishing the image of their candidates in a no-holds-barred attack, rather than on explaining their own party's policies and programs or action plan for the next five years that are of crucial importance to the public.

This is primarily because, an unscrupulous and unprincipled party in power very often misuses its position, power, and other resources by twisting the facts related to its own misrule and by fabricating false statistics about development and misleading announcements through the state machinery. Furthermore, it does not have any qualms about garnering vast sums of money from corporate houses and money making enterprises that are at the mercy of the government for ensuring hassle-free operation of their activities. Besides, black marketeers, tax dodgers and anti-national elements who stash away hordes of black money in overseas tax havens, tend to take great pains to remain in the good books of the government by financing the costs of electioneering of the ruling party.

Slanging Matches

Consequently, the ruling party ends up with having so much to hide from the public glare, apart from its own law-enforcing agencies. In a bid to divert the attention of the public, it hits out at the Opposition parties, which try to unearth the misdoings and misdemeanors of the ruling party. The electioneering then ends up as a slanging match between the two sides, with the electorate looking for a comparative analysis of the roadmaps of the two sides for evaluating the right party for their votes. Sometimes they are left high and dry. What is particularly distressing is the fact that many a politician refuses to enter into a meaningful debate with the rival candidate on how their party proposes to develop the nation and serve the people. Instead, they settle down to the easier option of flinging baseless charges of corruption, allegations of moral turpitude and accusations of lack of integrity on the part of their rivals.

Their bravado and braggadocio, are neither thought-provoking nor are their speeches made with the welfare of the public in mind. They constitute mere gimmickry aimed at the gullible masses that tend to get carried away by the show of sound and fury instead of light and substance. Listening to the demagogue whose speeches are full of fire and brimstone but no substance, an impartial observer cannot help wondering as to why such spiteful behaviour comprising vile language and insidious but unsubstantiated charges against the rival candidate is allowed to go, more often than not, unnoticed by the law and a benign public with a mere smirk and oodles of philosophical detachment! Normally, such speeches can easily land the speaker in prison if it were not made on a public platform and involved two persons in their individual capacities. Matters have come to such a sorry pass in our country, not because of political immaturity on the part of the public but entirely on account of lack of accountability on the part of the rabble-rousers for making slanderous speeches.

Why the Accountability?

In the long run, an absence of accountability would most definitely derail democracy and lead to the emergence of an autocratic or totalitarian form of governance and eventually to dictatorship. Any person in a position of power could potentially be as fickle-minded as the man next to him and his decisions capricious if he is not answerable to higher authority or accountable for his actions. Who could wield more power in a democracy than politicians that get elected as people's representatives and become lawmakers of the nation? As their decisions and follow-up actions in the service of the nation are supposed to be in the best interests of the people whom they represent and are intended to bring greater good to the greater number of people, it is absolutely necessary that they be accountable to the lawmaking bodies, namely legislatures, and through them, answerable to the people.

This is precisely the reason why debates and discussions taking place in Parliament and State Legislative Assemblies are directly telecast for view by the public who have a right to know how a law is passed and convince themselves that a law is not unilaterally or whimsically passed by a single erring politician or a group of politicians with vested interests. The legislative bodies are the most powerful and sovereign organ of the democratic form of governance. Members of the legislative bodies are not answerable for their speeches and actions made on the floor of the House, either to the executive or the judiciary. Nor are they accountable to the Media, which spares no opportunity to ruthlessly address and criticize their decisions and actions. They are solely answerable to the people who have elected them. This enables them to fearlessly participate in debates and discussions on issues that impinge on the lives of the people and the course of progress of the nation.

Right to Recall

However, the voting public in India does not have the right to recall a legislator no matter how irresponsible or ineffective he is found. Bad policies and non-implementation of good policies can only be criticized by the people in the public fora like the Social Media, with the Mainstream Media (MSM) that has its own agenda, often failing to objectively report the mood swings and pulse of the people. Spontaneous protest marches and rallies held by the public to demonstrate their displeasure with the powers that be over matters of national interest often degenerate into unruly gatherings thanks to the agents provocateur of an unscrupulous ruling party and sometimes even by the machinations of some Opposition party or other with vested interests, aiming to bring discredit to the government.

In the circumstances, only political parties are in a position to successfully organize and hold such events. Even then, protest marches and rallies if frequently held disrupt the smooth flow of business and cause tremendous inconvenience to the people. Moreover, such gatherings of crowds could become a convenient opportunity for anti-national or anti-social elements bent on sabotaging peace and tranquility and instilling in the minds of the people a fear psychosis. Protest marches and rallies held by members of the public or political parties should, therefore, be allowed by the authorities only in exceptional circumstances like when there is a tremendous and sudden spontaneous surge of emotions on the part of the people.

Such events should be allowed only on the basis of a mandatory undertaking from the organizers that they would be personally responsible for the maintenance of law and order during the event. What is of still more importance is the putting in place of a badly-needed Right to Recall, which would allow the people of any constituency to recall their legislator under certain conditions like when he fails to fulfill out his pre-poll promises or has flagrantly misled the people into electing him.

Freedom of Expression Misused

The Right to Freedom of Expression guaranteed by the Constitution is quite frequently misused by the motor mouths among the politicians. There have been many instances in the living memory when important leaders of some political outfits that are, in reality, nothing more than communal organizations, targeted certain sections and communities for launching virulent verbal attacks on communal lines; apart from making flagrantly provocative and venomous speeches against the targeted community and hurting their religious sentiments. Such politicians have even dared to challenge the authority of the law-enforcing agencies – all in the name of Right to Freedom of Expression! As of now, these politicos who are, in reality, nothing more than agent provocateurs of anti-national forces from across the border, merely have cases registered against them by the police for making inflammatory speeches and causing a potentially explosive situation between different communities.

Peace-loving people of the community that come under the insidious and unwarranted verbal attack by a bunch of rabid communal elements given to fits of bigotry and attack of verbal diarrhea, easily become vexed with the mild nature of action initiated by the authorities. Such actions are restricted to mere registering of cases. Furthermore, disposal of such cases gets inordinately delayed because of the slow pace of progress of judicial action albeit due to genuine problems. A clear case of breach of the spirit of democracy is when a rabid speaker of a measly communal outfit attacks a numerically stronger community along communal lines. This not only hurts their religious sentiments but sometimes tend to remain out of the clutches of the Law!

Such situations are fraught with danger of getting out of control and degenerating into avoidable communal conflagrations between communities living thus far in peace. It is sometimes observed that the law-enforcing agencies do not push the envelope beyond a limit by way of bringing the guilty to book, nor the erring politico is reined in by the leadership of his party. In fact, such politicos are allowed to roam around freely and make with impunity more and more hate speeches, every one of which is a shade more sinister than the previous one.

Aside from the helplessness of the law enforcing agencies, and the growing sense of despondency on the part of the peace-loving people, some politicians belonging to the rival camp, who do not want to lag behind, retaliate by making counter attacks in the form of speeches. Though such reactions may be justified in the context of the provocative speech made earlier or may even be a kneejerk reaction by a few individual politicians, some mischievous elements project it as the official line and a sign of arrogance on the part of the party that tries to protect the interests of the community attacked. Sections of the Mainstream Media, given to sensationalism, often play up such instances and cause further rifts between communities.

Vote Bank Politics

It would be too naive to expect the rabble rousers to be punished and trounced at the next round of polls by the peace-loving people. This is because such errant politicians usually contest from what are considered 'safe constituencies,' a misnomer for pocket boroughs of influential persons, where people of certain communities allow themselves to play into the hands of politicians of communal proclivity that encourage vote bank politics, and vote on communal lines. In such cases, gross misuse of the Right to Freedom of Expression should be made punishable under charges of sedition. Moreover, other punishments, including disqualification from contesting elections or making speeches in the public, should be meted out.

Religious Congregations and Places of Worship Misused

Religious congregations and places of worship are often misused by the rabid clergy and communal political leaders for making hate speeches and provoking people into mounting physical assault and attacks against members of other communities. The persons in charge of such places should be asked to give a mandatory periodical undertaking that they will be personally responsible for maintaining and upholding the religious sanctity of the places and that they would not allow the premises for anti-national and insidious purposes on pain of exemplary punishment in the case of default.

Performance and Action Plan

One of the first things that politicians do after coming to power is to take advantage of the short span of the voting people's collective memory and let their party's election manifesto die a natural death by completely ignoring it. They settle down to a comfortable life of reacting to day-to-day situations, problems, and crises. The Opposition parties, on their part, get to the busy mode of shoring up the way of the government, any number of day-to-day situations, problems, and crises. Besides, much of the time of the government is spent in exposing more and more scams and corruptions involving the previous government.

The Opposition parties are too hard put to defend themselves from the government's allegations and accusations to get down to the real work of pricking the government's conscience on delivering on its pre-poll promises. Such a paradoxical situation leads to the roadmap and action plan for the ruling party becoming more and more irrelevant and infructuous with the passage of time. The people, on their part, are too preoccupied with the availability or non-availability of the essential commodities, cost of living, rate of inflation and continuous dents and knocks to their quality of life in general, to be bothered about the glories or disgrace of the government or its lambasting by a peevish Opposition trying to justify its existence with shifting stances on eminently forgettable issues like Communalism and Secularism vis-a-vis crucial issues of development and inclusive growth of the nation.

In the circumstances, it would be in the fitness of things to create an autonomous rating agency as a part of the legislative bodies both at the Central and State levels to monitor not only the performance of the political parties in terms of their election manifesto but also that of their elected representatives in terms of their attendance and participation in the activities of the legislatures. There should be a constant and continuous updating of the ratings, which should be accessible to the public desirous of knowing about the output of their representatives and their parties. Such a course of action would not only be reflective of the performance of the politicians but also make them truly accountable to the people of the nation.

(Posted on blog on 5 November, 2015)

□

Patriotism versus Populism

Patriotism is a noble virtue and supreme quality that every proud and law-abiding citizen of a nation wears like a medal of honour. An article of faith, patriotism is an ingrained trait that gives those living in a country a national identity. It binds people into a cohesive body and coalesce them into a unified driving force for the survival and development of a nation. It occupies pride of place in an array of qualities of an honourable citizen like integrity, pride and love for the state and collective self-esteem of people over and above all other commonalities such as religion, language or affinity to customs and traditions spread worldwide. The lack of patriotism in people would reduce a nation to a mere geographical landmass of zombies, distinct from living and breathing people whose patriotism is in sync with their readiness to live and die for their country.

Opportunist Politicians and Populism

In contrast, populism is tactical gimmickry adopted by wily politicians, who are desperate for power, popularity or narrow personal gains and espouse the cause of the common man who they say is exploited by the rich and the elite. Patriotism would be conspicuous by its absence in such persons for whom the larger interests of the nation or society are secondary. Even though they espouse noble aims and objectives like ridding the nation of corruption, improving the law and order situation or augmenting the standards and quality of the people, they have no vision or strategy and lack a road map and action plan. In the quest for power, they make compromises with forces interested in destabilizing the country, creating anarchy and conditions congenial for their selfish ends and purposes. Financed by evil forces with sinister designs like thwarting the Constitution or abetting communal and divisive forces for the ultimate destruction of the nation, they need a launching pad to catapult themselves to positions of political power. Populism is the Trojan horse that carries them to the highest echelons of power.

The Allure of Populism

Populism undoubtedly has a niche space in politics, whether it is regional or national. It is capable of carrying politicians on its steely wings to positions of power at dizzying heights but has no feet of credibility to stand on. The political landscape of our country has a surfeit of corrupt and unscrupulous politicians who try to quench their polydipsia for power at the fountainhead of all political authority, namely elections. Bereft of ideology and principles, such candidates try to appease the common man and promise freebies, sops, subsidies, improbable concessions and outlandish quotas for entry into government jobs and promotions in service and educational institutions for different segments of the society including on communal lines. Pandering to the demands of casteist and communal forces to grant undeserved concessions and quotas is fraught with the danger of fragmenting the society if and when such schemes are implemented. The speeches of demagogues are replete with catchy phrases and crispy slogans. Attractive promises are bandied about, sounding deceptively alluring, as well as viable and within the realm of political and administrative feasibility. Thus, they capture the imagination of the easily-swayed sections of the electorate who are gullible and naive and have them eating out of their hand. When electioneering is thus reduced to the level of a contest between unprincipled politicians who resort to the gimmick of populism on the one hand and parties and individuals who fight on the strength of political ideology and personal integrity on the other, the die is heavily loaded in favour of the former category. The electorate, weighed down with the harsh realities of the day-to-day life and yearning for immediate relief, no matter how interim, could tend to get carried away by flights of fancy induced by the speeches of the demagogue. In such circumstances, the elections could be no more than a case of the people being led up the garden path by opportunist politicos, the electorate being none the wiser.

Opportunist Politicians Exposed

Having deposited the position seekers, who had solely banked on its appeal, in high offices of profits at stupendous heights, which are notoriously fragile and unstable amid the whirlwinds of political turbulence, populism takes a backseat. Then it waits in the wings for the next set of opportunist politicians to come by and succumb to its seduction. Left now on their own, the power grabbers are precariously perched in high offices and come under the harsh scrutiny of the media and discerning people, the same ones who had voted for them on the basis of the promises and the slew of populist measures that the politicos had bandied about before the polls. Now they feel threatened and tend to get panicky about their political survival. With nary a roadmap nor an action plan to deliver on the promises made, the persons in the hot seat are exposed, and their real identity revealed – crass political opportunism, unvarnished. This tends to assume scary connotations in the post-poll scenario, in terms of economic viability, budgeting, pre and post-auditing and, above all, the compulsions of priority spending on more urgent projects and programs.

Still More Populism

Desperate to retain their offices of profit at any cost, the political opportunists, left denuded of the fig leaf of credibility and integrity, look to populism for their rescue once again. They announce more and more populist measures, freebies, sops and subsidies at enormous costs, with absolutely no qualms or compunction to explain to the intended beneficiaries as to how they propose to finance the schemes they are about to splurge on. No matter how politically well-informed, the less-than-modestly-enlightened segments of the public fall for the sweet talks of the crafty politicians. And apart from putting up with their political shenanigans, very often they keep returning the wrong ones to power time and again, hoping against hopes that the tide would turn. However, the situation keeps worsening before the bitter truth of bad governance hits the people and they look for the alternative – not any alternative, but the real one.

The Real Alternative

What is the real alternative? A party with sound political ideology, a clear roadmap for a bright future, a viable action plan, and a strong leadership with a vision and determination to succeed, tempered with the spirit of patriotism. The course and drift of the electioneering such as a campaign free from fake promises and false assurances, hate speeches along communal lines and polarization of the society are evidently indicative of a healthy trend in the course correctness of alternative governance. The speeches delivered during such campaigns are often based on developmental issues and inclusive growth.

The Virtue of Patriotism

Patriotism presupposes the evil of dividing people along the rich-poor lines and the virtue of inclusive growth. At the best of times, like during peace and economic stability, it lies dormant as a spark in the heart of every law-abiding and proud citizen of the country. The spark of honour and love for the nation flares into a torch of patriotism, more often than not, in times of trials and tribulations in the course of the country's history, like during external threat or wars. On such occasions, spurred on by the patriotic fervour every citizen pitches in for the nation's unity and integrity. During times of peace, however, patriotism remains shrouded in the psyche and sub-conscience of the individual. While electing the government or evaluating its performance, patriotism becomes the touchstone. The patriotism of the individual citizen does not brook wrong doings on the part of the symbols of authority, political or bureaucratic, just as the government or bureaucratic machinery does not condone anti-national activities by the individual citizen.

Patriotism is a fire of river that everyone must swim and cross for redeeming his honour and pride when his integrity is challenged. This is especially so in the case of political parties and individual candidates fighting elections. Allegations of anti-people or anti-national stances leave a slur or stigma on a candidate to his utter detriment. This is the reason why election campaigns are full of speeches surcharged with pop patriotism to vindicate one's own integrity and all sorts of allegations against rival candidates to besmirch their reputation.

Party of Principles and Patriotism

Political parties that get elected to office on the strength of their development programs, economic policies, inclusive growth and non-divisive approach to a multilingual, multi-religious and multicultural society, cannot but be guided by patriotism in all their policies and actions. Their policies and actions are bound to be in stark contrast to those of the opportunist politicians who ride the wings of populism to power and hold offices of profit solely on the strength of their populist policies that are counterproductive to sustained economic growth. Some of their actions based on the hard options available to the government like taxation, stopping or curtailing of subsidies, withholding of concessions that cause an excessive drain on resources, etc are like bitter pills for a healthy economic growth. In such cases, the Opposition parties do not miss an opportunity to criticize the government for taking measures that are described by them as anti-people.

All the same, even a party of lofty policies and noble principles, with a highly motivated leadership, endowed with a vision, determination and will to succeed in its mission for the restoration of the nation's lost glory and the upliftment of the society, cannot afford to abruptly scrap or withdraw, while in power, certain populist measures that have been already introduced by the previous governments. This is because of the apprehension that such a course correction will draw avoidable flak. For the people such tightening of belt hurts; more so when decreed by law. Such a predicament does not, however, make the party any less principled than when it started off in power and definitely no less patriotic. Thus, the party of principles in power is saddled with the twin responsibility of providing good governance and also convincing the people about the course correctness of the non-perfect alignment of its policies and actions owing to the prevailing political conditions taken with the larger interests of the nation in mind. This situation is exploited by the Opposition parties by projecting it as a sign of weakness, if not a downright failure, on the part of the ruling party in implementing its policies and programs. Beyond a limit, the party has to be reconciled to grinning and bearing the accusations, leaving it all to the better judgment of the thinking public.

The Poll Scenario

While contesting bitter polls, participated in by mealy-mouthed politicians who stoop to mudslinging and casting aspersions on the integrity of the representatives of the party with principles, politicians whose strongest asset is patriotism and the most effective poll plank developmental programs and inclusive growth, are hard put to fight their case on what is evidently not a level playing field. In pockets of constituencies that are economically lagging behind in comparative terms, focusing on long-term projects, programs or goals for the development of the State's economy is a hard sell. Where there are crunching poverty, rampant unemployment, deep-rooted communal divide and deplorable rates of literacy, midterm and long-term economic programs do not resonate with the people as much as populist schemes and announcements of freebies and sops, which have immense appeal in the short term. As such, the people who trade their invaluable votes for cheap material gains cannot be faulted for lacking patriotism in the discharge of their fundamental democratic duty of electing their representatives to the legislature. However, the opportunist politicians who exploit the miserable conditions of the people should most certainly not escape the charge of compromising on their patriotism.

Patriotism Flourishes, Populism Flounders

While populism has feet of clay, patriotism is deep-rooted. While one vacillates, the other is resolute and unyielding. Populism survives on the crutches of falsehood, tall talks and empty promises, whereas patriotism thrives and flourishes on honesty and truth. When the immediate appeal of populism wears off, the crafty politicians are exposed for the men of straw that they are. The true leaders of the people whose hallmark is their unwavering patriotism, bide their time. And by the sheer dint of determination and uncompromising stand on their policies, they prevail over all sorts of odds and adversities to emerge as farsighted visionaries or courageous statesmen.

Judicious Choice

On their part, people realize that patriotism and populism are as different as cheese and chalk. Political maturity and sagacity gained over a period, combined with hindsight, enable them to ward off the spurious stuff and settle for the genuine option in the service of the nation. In short, individual members of the society should put the collective welfare and development of the country above their personal interests. Ultimately, voting judiciously and electing politicians known for their patriotism and dedication to the service of the nation is the collective responsibility of the people in the interests of the nation as well as in their own interest.

(Posted on blog on 10 November, 2015)

□

Fishing in the Troubled Waters of Bihar

Winds of Change

With the crucial assembly elections in Bihar scheduled to take place in October-November, a large section of people are looking forward to a change of guard and hoping for a positive and refreshing change to sweep across the state in the coming years. Meanwhile, Prime Minister Narendra Modi in his speech at the first Parivartan rally in Muzaffarpur on July 25 sounded BJP's bugle call for the transformation of Bihar from an under-rated actor, waiting in the wings, into a lead character on the centre-stage in the dramatic political events about to pan out shortly. After that, he addressed three more Parivartan Rallies – in Gaya on August 9, in Arrah and Saharasa on August 18 and in Bhagalpur on September 1.

Breaking the Mould

Meanwhile, the voters of Bihar are currently on a roll, taking pride in being accorded by the nationalist forces a break to emerge at last from the shadows and constricted contours of regional politics to take their rightful place in the national politics. They are also enthralled at the prospects of aligning the State's political destiny with the engine of development that appeared on the national scene last year and has since been chugging on in its inexorable march to the country's ultimate goal of emerging as the 'Vishwa Guru'.

Bihar has never lagged behind in playing its part in the process of shaping or moulding of the country's destiny right from the pre-independence days. Nor is it likely to do so this time around either. For the State and the people of Bihar, the elections due later this year provide a windfall opportunity to sever their connection with the State's dubious past of caste and communal politics and usher in a brave new world of mainstream politics and pan-Indian model.

Windfall Offer

Of particular importance in the course of the developments leading to the present stage was Prime Minister Modi's landmark announcement of a stupendous special package of ₹ 1.25 lakh crore for the State, which he said had been "yearning for development and progress". The package, which covers a wide range of development sectors such as roads, highways, petroleum refineries, gas, airports, rural electrification, education, health, farmers' welfare, digitalization of Bihar, etc, is expected to change the economic landscape of the State tremendously.

One would, therefore, have thought that the package would be whole-heartedly welcomed by the entire spectrum of political parties and stakeholders in the State's development and progress. But that is not what transpired! While the Centre's special package is bound to act as a catalyst for the accelerated growth of the State's economy and the people of Bihar would undoubtedly be the beneficiaries, Modi's political rivals feel outwitted and threatened and are bitter over the introduction of a 'game changer' by the Prime Minister. Not surprisingly, Chief Minister Nitish Kumar gave vent to his disappointment and sense of helplessness when he reacted by lashing out at Narendra Modi for 'bidding' for Bihar. He exhibited his characteristic braggadocio when he called the special package a trumped-up one and threatened to expose the 'real truth' behind the package soon. It was indeed a splendid display of a remarkably narrow mindset that would not allow the regional politician to rise above the usual antics of a mere powerbroker!

Being neither a sop nor a mere promise, the package was a windfall offer of a badly needed economic assistance by the Centre on an unprecedented scale. It was a wonderful opportunity for the State to shore a much-needed breakthrough up the alley of its beleaguered economy. However, the occasion turned out to be yet another case in point, which proves that it takes as large a heart to appreciate a real crackerjack of an act of goodwill as the one that conceives and delivers it. And again, notwithstanding how the people of the State feel about the economic benefits expected to accrue, thanks to the special package, the politicians of the back alleys of Bihar are hardly likely to grow out of the caste and communal mould that has kept the State tied to the shackles of laggardness in the first place. And yet, Nitish Kumar has been demanding special category status for the State to place its economy, which is in tatters, on an even keel.

Casteism and Communalism

It is a matter of abiding shame and embarrassment that political battles have traditionally been fought in Bihar, as in several other Indian States, on the lines of casteist or communal politics. It would appear by implication that those politicians who had vote bank politics for strategy had the only aim of winning polls on the unquestioning support of an entire community or caste whose narrow interests they were espousing on the basis of sops, freebies and populist schemes, with absolutely no concern about the development and progress of the State as a whole. For the self-serving practitioners of the fine art of vote bank politics in Bihar, the forthcoming elections present yet another opportunity to hone their skills and put them to good use for the purpose of perpetuating their hold on the levers of power in the State.

On the one hand, the RJD-JD (U)-Congress coalition has been bitterly complaining against the special package that helps bolster the development plank of NDA's poll strategy. On the other hand, RJD Chief Lalu Yadav has accused the NDA of trying to split the Yadav-Muslim vote bank by helping Asaduddin Owaisi's All India Majlis-e-Ittehadul Muslimeen (AIMIM) contest the elections and garner Muslim votes to the detriment of the RJD-JD(U)-Congress coalition. Fear of a split in the Muslim vote bank owing to the Owaisi factor, and the apprehension that the Yadav segment of the electorate may also not vote for them en masse this time around owing to the presence of Yadav leaders in NDA, have sent tremors down the ranks of the RJD-JD(U)-Congress grand alliance.

The camp opposing NDA would much rather have the Muslim segment of the electorate believe that BJP is and has always been a party of Muslim-baiters and is, therefore, against Secularism. Likewise, they do not favour the idea of the splitting of the Yadav votes. They are keen on keeping the flock of the Muslim-Yadav vote bank in their stranglehold by operationalizing their tried-and-tested strategy of playing the Communalism card against NDA and offering the vote bank constituents sops and populist schemes.

The hypocrisy of extending unabashed support to a particular religion or a community in the name of promoting Secularism or warding off casteism does not in the least make them feel queasy. Such is the audacity of political rivals of the NDA of arrogating to themselves the mantle of champions and protectors of the interests of these groups! It shows the ugly underbelly of vote-bank politics practised with such ease and aplomb against the development agenda of NDA! It is time for Bihar to choose between the progressive and development agenda of the NDA and the regressive vote bank politics of the RJD-JD (U)-Congress combine.

Hollow Speeches

The RJD-JD (U) coalition has no economic agenda whatsoever. Lalu has made it clear that his coalition is fighting against 'fascist and communal forces'. There is nothing more to his agenda. The champions of pseudo-Secularism have no intention of being ever concerned about the State's economy and have apparently been 'dedicating' and periodically 're-dedicating' their lives every time there is an election, to fighting 'fascist and communal forces'. How they propose to do the fighting is by identifying the BJP with Communalism and entering into a grand coalition against that party with whosoever is ready for such collaboration.

When the BJP or the NDA, of which it is a partner, talks of development politics, the RJD-JD (U)-Congress clique counters it with the talk of Communalism and Secularism. As Lalu once famously said, development projects do not fetch votes, but talking of the bugbear of Communalism and Secularism does! Lalu has further dared the Prime Minister to bring back black money stashed away at overseas tax havens in keeping with BJP'S poll promise of 2014. Conveniently overlooking all the good work already initiated by the NDA government in this regard, he went ahead and taunted Modi by stating that the latter was incapable of vindicating his promise of unearthing black money.

Referring to onion prices shooting up across the country, albeit due to shortage of production, he made a jibe at Modi about the latter's 'inability' to unearth stocks of onion hoarded by black marketeers, let alone unearth black money, thereby making a facetious charge over a matter of great national importance. Such flippant quips and facetious comments made in casual reference to matters of national importance do get a moronic claps and guffaws from his roadside audience who are out for a good time and even endear this clown to the mainstream media (MSM), which is all the time on the lookout for sound bites (the nastier the better). Whether his antics and buffoonery are capable of translating the amusement and titillation of the audience into votes in this age of right to information and vibrant social media, which have transformed the common man into less gullible and more knowledgeable and discerning a voter, is a foregone conclusion.

Fight against Corruption

Never the one to shy away from fishing in troubled political waters, Delhi Chief Minister Arvind Kejriwal has thrown his hat in the ring by agreeing to campaign for the RJD-JD(U)-Congress coalition. The plank of his campaign? Why, corruption, of course! There was a time when he called every political party in the country corrupt and declared that all politicians were crooks and guilty of complicity. Today, his ire is exclusively targeted at Prime Minister Narendra Modi and the BJP. In the name of fighting corruption, he is campaigning for the defeat of the BJP and its NDA allies in Bihar. What is more, he is working hard for the success of some of the most discredited and corrupt political leaders and ideologically bankrupt and irrelevant political parties in the country.

As recently as a few days ago, the Supreme Court had issued a notice to Lalu Yadav on a plea by the CBI against the dropping of certain charges in one of the FIRs by Jharkhand High Court in the multi-crore fodder scam in which Lalu had been convicted and is currently out on bail. As regards Nitish Kumar, he has no reservation or compunction about working with a fellow politician of Bihar with whom he has a love-hate relationship and who is convicted on multi-crore corruption charges.

Besides, he had no qualms either about being egoistic while turning down point blank an aid of ₹ 5 crore from the Government of Gujarat for the people of Bihar who had been affected by floods in Kosi river in 2008. This he did without caring a whit about the distress of the people of his own State and their need for relief or the sentiments of the people of Gujarat who had contributed the amount, making a prestige issue of accepting the aid from his political rival. Why accept the aid and let Modi, the then Chief Minister of Gujarat, hog the credit for coming to the rescue of the people of Bihar, earn their goodwill and make political mileage out of it, was his line of reasoning. He had no conflict with his conscience about placing a false pride and prestige before the distress and sentiments of people. In short, politics before people!

Furthermore, now Arvind Kejriwal is all set to wage a war against corruption by joining hands with Lalu Yadav, who is convicted on multi-crore corruption charges, Nitish Kumar who puts politics before people in distress and in need of assistance, and the Congress which is neck deep in numerous cases of scams and corruption charges and is under investigation and litigation! A unique way indeed of fighting corruption! Having fought and won elections for the Delhi Assembly twice, both the times on the plank of fight against corruption, and formed the government both the times, he has so far failed to introduce his much promised Jan Lokpal Bill and Swaraj Bill in the Assembly.

If he could not accomplish the task of passing the two anti-corruption Bills to which his Aam Aadmi Party owes its existence, despite having a steamroller majority in the Assembly, how does he hope to win over corruption in Bihar by campaigning for tainted and convicted parochial politicians who lack an economic agenda and a pan-Indian vision and are preoccupied with perpetuating family rule?

Cradle of Political Corruption

Bihar, one of the poorest States in India, is about to go to polls that are, according to media reports, expected to be the costliest ever. The exact dates of the election will be announced soon, and the campaigning has already commenced. Having to stagger the publicity and campaigning over a period of more than two months, the candidates are already bewildered by the huge cost of electioneering.

The estimated expenditure of each candidate on campaigning is expected to cross the ₹ 1-crore mark. However, the expenditures admissible in terms of the ceiling fixed by the Election Commission (EC) are in the range of ₹ 20-28 lakh. In this context, would it sound too cynical an observation if one called India's elections the cradle of political corruption and fountainhead of black money? Given the candidates and their parties have to resort to plying enormous amounts of unaccounted money into their campaigns, these undoubtedly seem to be very apt observations.

Momentous Occasion

The forthcoming elections are of tremendous significance for the voters of Bihar. Standing at a crossroads, they now have two different paths diverging in front of them. And since they cannot travel both, they have to choose one of them. They may either take the much-treaded path of Pseudo Secularism, or they may choose the unfamiliar road of issue-based politics and development agenda.

Here they just need to remember that if they go for the first option, it will lead their beloved state to the murky world of regional politics – a veritable 'Jungle Raj,' stalked by ideological dwarfs and political pygmies with arrows tipped with the poison of casteism and communalism.

On the other hand, if they opt for the second alternative it will open up for them a brave new world of social development and economic progress like never before. It will also enable them to finish an important task of seeking out and identifying the politicos who are out to fish in the troubled waters of Bihar and eliminate this scourge from their State forever.

(Published in weekly magazine Uday India in Vol. VI, No, 42, 20-26 September, 2015 edition)

□

States to Back the Centre in Honest Endeavors

The Republic of India has a federal parliamentary setup and follows dual polity system of governance, with a supreme set of laws, the Constitution, outlining the powers and limitations of both the union as well as state governments. The Upper House represents the states and the Lower House the people of India. Inclusive growth, improvement of social and physical infrastructure, and taking the pluses of success towards the most underprivileged households is the responsibility of both states and the Centre. Can any Indian state survive in isolation? Then why not participate in the best possible manner in the furtherance of the nation? Obsolete laws, uncooperative plans and unjustifiable contradiction with the measures of the central government on the part of states have held back real development. Subsidy, for instance, is a way of giving some added perks to the poor so as to augment their growth, but unless states provide unambiguous facts about the number of such families and unless they have procedures in place that can assure of authentic movement of funds to the poor, for which adequate supervision and apt monitoring and reporting mechanism is a must, circumstances will rarely recover. One of the most annoying points of contradiction is when any probable shift in present laws is proposed by the union government, which though has the caliber to add pluses, does not get the obligatory support in the houses of parliament.

Let me quote some examples that would reveal how redundant laws in some states are totally in contrast with development. In the state of Tamil Nadu, prosopis, which can be converted into high grade charcoal, isn't allowed to be converted so. A marginal farmer cannot easily sell his/her land in the state of Delhi, therefore needs to employ every of the illicit means to fetch some benefits from the rising price of land. In Maharashtra, one cannot purchase agricultural land except if is an agriculturist, which means that the industry is deprived of acquiring farmland. To move paddy from one zone to the other in the state of U.P. one needs a certificate, implying that to move grains from one point to the other, located only a few km away, however in separate zones, one has to abide by the law and get disgusting clearances from the officials. This list is lengthy and has many concerns that are detrimental to the pace of progression in the present economic scenario. Three lists, enumerating the items that fall under the purview of the Centre, the states and both (concurrent list), as are in the Constitution carry the notion that few subjects have a local bearing and as such states should be well positioned to deal with them, but this cannot be at the stake of people's development owing to conceptual and ideological clashes between the political parties ruling in the states and the one with majority at the Centre.

Another such issue can be seen with the land acquisition subject-matter that falls in the concurrent list. The Rajasthan State Highways Act isn't in sync with the central law on land acquisition. The state's Act avoids some crucial steps, such as the social impact analysis and need to obtain consent of land owners; the compensation to be paid is less when compared to what is mandated under the central law. Misrepresenting and under-reporting of facts related to healthcare, malnutrition, unemployment, and such other social infrastructure minuses by states and regions has held the speed of all-inclusive development. On the issue of toilets, the U.P. government's report suggested that more than 90 percent of households in the rural parts had toilets; however the Census data reported that the figure was mere 25 percent. How MGNREGA scheme is being handled at the ground level is known to all, dummy employees are paid the government's money and those actually working at the sites are underpaid. States need to understand that Centre cannot have an eye at the last person for whom schemes are launched; this has to be the indisputable duty of the state governments and gram panchayats. It has been pointed out in a study that of all working under the gram panchayats in Jharkhand, only 18 percent get paid in time. Same is the case with mid-day meal programmes and other schemes taken care of at the state or district levels.

To bring in what we have termed as 'Inclusive Growth', India needs a robust monitoring and reporting system, and then it is to be assured that the benefits, without cuts, flow to the most disadvantaged ones, which asks for fair participation of states. Governance will be the key, but unless states rise above the notions of communal and caste-based politics, we can hardly dream of success. For instance, half of the collectors in the state of U.P. are transferred within a year of their posting. Policemen fear suspensions and transfers, which results in lesser attention towards public grievances and more towards the orders of the ruling men. Right from the way the Centre provides funds to states to placement of men in administrative jobs; India now needs a creative and out-of-the-box approach. The Rajya Sabha, representing the states of India, shall play its role in such a manner that central government's measure of passing even one ordinance stands truly unjustifiable. The Constitution has to be respected in every manner, and when the same outlines the ways how states and Centre shall work separately, yet in co-ordination and sync to take forward the nation and its residents, partaking of states in the growth of India becomes a must. Along with, implementing an effective monitoring and reporting system, obsolete and contradictory laws are to be amended/repealed. Ease of doing business, improvement in social infrastructure (health, education, sanitation etc.) and in physical infrastructure (roads, power, water etc.), and reaching the poor is the aim.

Stability, security and economic development of the country rest on the shoulders of all representatives of public, be it in the Lok Sabha or state legislative assembly. Provisions according superiority to laws passed by the Parliament over state laws, keeping the residuary powers with the Centre and imposition of emergency rule by the Centre in extreme situations are in the Constitution with a view to safeguarding India's integrity and making the union of states stronger than individual states. The other side of the coin is harsh as well with respect to central governments misusing provisions of Article 356 of Constitution to dismiss state governments, appointment and role of governors, and intrusion of the Centre into the state list. These, however, have been the instances in the past while the present leaders at the central level have talked much about co-ordination and consensus between states and the Centre. While on one hand, the functioning of the Inter-State Council has to be fortified so as to help the Centre understand the challenges faced by the states; members of the Rajya Sabha and state legislative assemblies will have to respect productive labors of the

Centre, keeping aside the ill politics of vote-bank and appeasement of some sections. All in all, harmony between the states and the Centre, as has been reached for GST and newly-formed NITI Ayog, is to be achieved by talks, explanations, understanding, and above all, by way of substantial backing for all constructive endeavors.

(Posted on blog on 2 February, 2015)

□

Congress Under Rahul Gandhi

The Indian National Congress (INC) is desperately in need of reinventing itself. Its ideological bastions of democratic socialism, non-alignment and peaceful coexistence with neighbouring countries have all been dashed to the ground long ago by the shifting geo-political tectonic plates. Utterly bereft of ideological moorings and rendered short of a niche space in Indian politics to make it a distinct identity as in the past vis-a-vis other political parties, especially its arch-rival, the Bharatiya Janata Party (BJP), it is as of now, just another political outfit of power brokers and wheeler-dealers like the innumerable parties hankering for a piece of the power pie at the Centre.

With a mother-son duo leading it like a family enterprise and loyal foot-soldiers hanging on like limpets, a serious problem of crisis of identity is staring the party in the face. Unless the Congress gets a firm grip on itself and handles the situation imaginatively in the context of changing political realities, this situation may worsen in the course of time and lead the party to face an existential crisis. However, if one takes into account the peevish antics enacted by Rahul Gandhi recently, he seems to be in a hurry to accelerate the process of wall papering the fissures and bringing it all to an abrupt end sooner rather than later.

Here it is worth recalling that Rahul forayed into active politics in 2004 when he contested for and won the Lok Sabha election and became a Member of Parliament from Amethi in Uttar Pradesh. In 2007, he was made the General Secretary of the Congress Party. Then in 2013, he was elected as its Vice President and was given the charge of spearheading the campaign of the INC for the approaching 2014 Lok Sabha elections, in which his party suffered its worst electoral defeat in its entire history winning only 44 seats in a House of 540, as against 206 won in the earlier 2009 general elections. If one is generous enough to grant that ups and downs are part of the political scenario, then consider the following.

Voice of Dissent

In a recent letter to Congress President Sonia Gandhi, Shashi Tharoor, a one-time party spokesperson and former Minister of State for External Affairs, expressed dismay that his years of sincere service to the party has not been recognized or appreciated and that he was suspected by the party President of leaking information regarding party affairs to the Press. Categorically denying a leakage on his part, he referred to leaking as a habit of cowards and conspirators. Conceding that he had earlier voiced, in a meeting of Congress MPs, disagreement with the party's strategy of stalling Parliamentary proceedings in the monsoon session, he gave vent to his apprehension of feeling isolated, with all the other party worthies turning against him.

Now, who is the coward and who is the conspirator? Definitely it is not the solitary one who stood his ground on the burning deck and shot off a missive to the President to boot, that could be either! Tharoor went on to state that some people with access to Sonia Gandhi had poisoned her mind by planting conspiracy theories so much so that his loyalty had become a much-suspected commodity. What he did not say, but left to be understood, was that the party had become a den of cowards and conspirators and – here comes the kill – these elements had access to the highest authority in the party and lost no time in branding him a traitor!

Tharoor's letter gives rise to two inevitable questions. First off, what is the party high command going to do concerning his litany of charges – award him with a plum position or elevate him in the party hierarchy? That is hardly likely. The second question is what Tharoor himself is going to do about his grievance. Having already stripped him of the party spokes person's post, Sonia Gandhi has heaped on him the ignominy of severe castigation time and again for 'always' towing an anti-party line. To drive home her point, she alluded to instances that had brought him appreciation from Prime Minister Narendra Modi, like participating in the Swachh Bharat Abhiyan and his recent address at the Oxford University, highlighting the reparations that Britain owed India.

What remains to be done with a recalcitrant foot-soldier who dared mutiny? Caught in a bind over the personal tragedy that had entailed his wife's murder and the political brinkmanship that put his nerve to test, does he have the cojones to hang on to the status quo for much longer? This is a moot question which, along with the party high command's likely course of action, falls in the realm of speculation.

More Dissidence

It would be foolishness to believe that Tharoor's was a lonely voice in the wilderness. There have been discordant notes from other disgruntled party members as well. Soon after the electoral debacle last year, T.H. Mustafa, a Congress leader from Kerala, sent shock waves among the party by stating that the shaming of the party at the polls was on account of Rahul's behaviour as a 'joker'. He demanded Rahul's ouster from the post of Vice President and induction of Priyanka Gandhi Vadra. Veteran Congress leader Bhanwar Lal Sharma of Rajasthan went a step further and said that the time had come for the party to think beyond Rahul and Priyanka, both of whom wielded clout only on account of their hailing from the Gandhi family.

The five-time Mizoram Chief Minister Lal Thanhawla did not lag far behind and left his party dumbfounded by openly criticizing its leadership. Despite the party high command's diktat to all its chief ministers not to attend the swearing-in of Prime Minister Narendra Modi, he attended the ceremony. Jibes and barbs from dissidents were aimed not only at Rahul or the high command, but also at Rahul's coterie of aides and advisors who had been inducted into his team entirely on account of their proximity to the family despite their lack of support at the grassroots level. Former Minister Milind Deora demanded that it was not only Team Rahul, which gave the high command wrong advice, but also those who had kept quiet that should own responsibility for the failing of the party.

Emergence of Rahul

Notwithstanding the voices of dissent, Rahul seems to have overcome the odds and is inching towards the party President's post by resorting to aggressive posturing after a mysterious two month-vacation at some undisclosed destination earlier this year. Voices of dissidents have been muffled. The idea seems to be to give Rahul another chance to prove his mettle as a leader of all sections of the party and his capability to pull crowds and keep their attention riveted. Referring to reports earlier this year on Rahul Gandhi's proposed elevation to the post of the party President, former Minister Jairam Ramesh, considered close to the scion of the Gandhi family, said Rahul was ready for any responsibility and would not shy away from accountability or responsibility.

Reinvention of Rahul

Rahul who had enjoyed the unsavoury reputation of being an absentee Parliamentarian or one who was a back-bencher that took catnaps when the House was in session on the few-and-far-between occasions that he chose to attend, apparently felt compelled to subject his image to a complete makeover. That seems to have been the motivating factor for his sudden tearing off from the public glare for a two-month sabbatical. When he returned, however, the nation had expected him to wow the public as well as his detractors by taking a headlong plunge into the major political issues awaiting debates and discussions, before and during their introduction in the monsoon session of the Parliament by the government.

What resulted were, however, shock and dismay. Instead of getting under the skin of the subject matters for discussion, Rahul chose to get on the nerves of one and all by resorting to accusatory tactics. His new-found strategy was best described by Union Minister Prakash Javadekar as 'spit-and-run.' This was with specific reference to the vile language used by Rahul to launch a personal attack, by 'crossing all limits of decency' on Prime Minister Narendra Modi over the Land Acquisition Bill which is currently with a House Committee of Lok Sabha.

Logjam of Parliament

When the NDA government was planning to introduce eight new bills and take up other eleven pending bills for consideration and passage during the recently-concluded Monsoon Session in the Lok Sabha, and seven bills pending in the Rajya Sabha, Rahul and his MPs cried hoarse over charges of alleged corruption or impropriety on the part of External Affairs Minister Sushma Swaraj, CM of Rajasthan

Vasundhara Raje and CM of Madhya Pradesh Shivaj Singh Chouhan and demanded their resignation or ouster. When Narendra Modi ruled out any such possibility, the Congress-led Opposition Parties asked for a debate and when the NDA government said it was willing for the debate, Sonia and Rahul Gandhi immediately changed their stance to 'First resignations, then discussions', and insisted that unless Sushma Swaraj, Vasundhara Raje and Shivraj Singh Chouhan resign, they won't be ready for any discussions or debates.

Then, guided by Rahul and Sonia Gandhi, the Opposition MPs resorted to disrupting the proceedings in both the Houses of Parliament without let up, demanding blanket acceptance of their demands. Over the next couple of days, their behavior became more unruly and their protests became more and more shrill and strident. The situation came to such a pass on August 3 that Lok Sabha Speaker Sumitra Mahajan decided to take recourse to Rule 374(A) in Parliament and suspended 25 Congress MPs for five days for unruly behavior and for causing 'grave disorder' in Parliament and for 'persistently and willfully obstructing' the House. This has been the largest such suspension where so many MPs have faced disciplinary action at one go.

While Sonia Gandhi condemned the suspensions and described the Speaker's action as murder of democracy, on his part Rahul asked the Prime Minister to listen to the 'Mann ki baat' of the people of the country. Terming the suspension of the Congress Party MPs undemocratic, on August 5 Rahul Gandhi told media persons that his party won't budge from its stand and there won't be any let up in its pressure on the government as far as issues of corruption, Sushma Swaraj and Vyapam were concerned. He thus made clear his party's intent to carry on with its belligerent posture on the issue of resignations of top BJP leaders whom he had accused of wrongdoing. And eventually the entire Monsoon session between July 21 and August 13, 2015 got completely washed out over the Lalit Modi controversy and the Vyapam scam.

Here it needs to be reiterated that though the NDA government kept saying from day one of the Monsoon session that it was willing to discuss and debate every single issue in Parliament, Sonia and Rahul Gandhi were more comfortable with the disruptions rather than the debate. Even during the Budget session earlier (between February 23 and May 8), there were continuous protests and regular disruptions as the Congress-led Opposition parties were against the passage of the Land Acquisition Bill. This stalling of Parliament's functioning during the past few months at the behest of Sonia Gandhi and her son and party Vice-President Rahul Gandhi, has resulted in the entire monsoon session getting completely washed out, holding up key economic legislations, in addition to an estimated monetary loss of ₹ 260 crore.

Thus, Rahul and his party seem obstinate enough to inflict a major damage on the country in a bid to tarnish the image of the NDA government in the public eye, with scant regard to the nation. Such obduracy and disregard for parliamentary procedures betray the unpreparedness and immaturity of a politician aspiring to become the leader of the oldest political party in the country.

Venom against BJP

Rahul had earlier undertaken visits to different parts of the country like Punjab, Maharashtra and Kerala, purportedly to visit famine-hit farmers. Instead of assuaging the feelings of the distressed farmers, he played politics to the hilt by lashing out at the Prime Minister whom he accused of embarking on a spree of foreign visits and neglecting the farmers. He also visited the Film and Television Institute of India (FTTI) to express support for the students of the Institute who have been on a strike over the election of Gajendra Chauhan as Director of the Institute. Here again, he failed to focus on the students' issue and poured venom on the Prime Minister and his party. He lashed out at BJP and RSS for allegedly promoting mediocrity.

Then on August 14, when Rahul visited Jantar Mantar in New Delhi in an attempted show of solidarity with ex-servicemen at the venue, who were staging a protest demanding implementation of One Rank, One Pension (OROP) scheme, he was embarrassingly greeted by protesters raising slogans of 'Go back Rahul'.

Apprehension over Loss of Power

Meanwhile, Rahul's speeches and statements lack objectivity and focus on the issues involved. Instead, his jibes and barbs are aimed at the Prime Minister and other BJP leaders. His game plan is obviously to malign Narendra Modi and discredit the BJP. Instead of speaking about his own party and its roadmap for the development and progress of the country and welfare of the people, he is gung ho about hurting the government.

Neither he nor his party's President is reconciled to the reality of having been out of power for over fifteen months now. Nor are they inclined to wait for a full five-year hiatus, if not longer, till the next round of elections due in 2019. This may be because they fear if they stay away from the centre of power any longer, the BJP may expose more and more scams and scandals that occurred during the UPA government's misrule, which in turn may help the BJP in its avowed aim of accomplishing a 'Congress-mukht Bharat'.

Meanwhile, the corruption cases which have already been exposed, are at various stages of investigation and litigation and are expected to be pursued by the NDA government in real earnest. The mother-son duo is personally involved in the National Herald case and has so much at stake. Any semblance of weakness or vulnerability on their part is capable of resulting in a revolt by the regional satraps of the party. Besides, the people of the country are not unlikely to get used to the NDA government's rule and give Congress a short shrift.

In short, the longer the Congress party is away from the levers of power at the Centre, the lesser its chances of a comeback to power or even survival in national politics. Hence the desperation of Sonia and Rahul Gandhi to fish in murky political waters by extending support to unprincipled political allies such as Lalu Yadav, Nitish Kumar and Arvind Kejriwal.

Rahul's Handicap

Rahul has already become the butt of ridicule in the social media as well as certain sections of the mainstream media (MSM). His lack of vision, game plan, perspicacity, focus on issues that impinge on national interests and people's welfare, his acts of disappearance, mysterious personal life, lack of objectivity and reverence for the established political norms, non-accountability and opaque style of functioning, have all contributed to a serious erosion of his credibility, image and stature. All these have rendered him woefully short of standards expected of a leader with a pan-Indian appeal. Lately, voters across the country have started realizing that Rahul is not Prime Minister material by any stretch of imagination or yardstick. His party colleagues and he himself should be aware of this more than anybody else. And, last but not least, the people of India have already proved they are quite capable of thinking beyond Congress and they do not want another person from the Gandhi family as a default Prime Minister.

(Published in weekly magazine Uday India in Vol. VI, No. 40, 6-12 September, 2015 edition)

□

The FTII Brouhaha and Politicking

The Film and Television Institute of India (FTII) at Pune, which is the premier institute for learning film making and allied matters in Asia, has lately been on a slide. Film making has been edged out by theatrics and the congeniality in the atmosphere of the campus by vexation. The students as well as the officials have also started trading charges and resorting to unprecedented and unconventional methods and means to prove their respective points. And the institute has now become a scene of action where battle lines have been clearly drawn and positions taken by these two warring factions.

With the ongoing battle of wits and nerves showing no signs of abating and neither side displaying willingness to take the extra step to resolve the issues to mutual satisfaction, no end to the acrimony and animosity is in sight. While the student representatives claim that they are ready to have talks with the government, they are insistent on their demands and have ruled out any compromise. The reputation of the FTII has become the first casualty, especially with some of the dubious goings on in the campus among the student community having been brought to light by the glaring attention that the developments have attracted.

The Outbreak of Trouble

Trouble started with the appointment of actor Gajendra Chauhan as Chairman of the Institute. Students protested against this appointment, calling Chauhan a candidate lacking 'vision and artistic credentials'. He was derided as someone incapable of leading an institute of the stature and prominence of FTII. His selection was attributed to his perceived proclivity to the RSS ideology and alleged proximity to the BJP leadership at the Centre. Selection of other candidates chosen to fill the vacancies in the FTII Society was also condemned on account of the candidates' allegiance to the Saffron ideology. Casting aspersions on the appointments on account of alleged political overtones, the students have been vociferous and unequivocal about their demand for revocation of the appointments. They vented spleen and went on strike, which has been continuing since then, without letup.

Roping in Celebrity Support

Not wanting their protest against the government's actions, described as unilateral and far from being objective, to go ignored or forgotten, the students roped in celebrity support and even staged a morcha in Delhi. An array of film industry personalities and politicos came to the fore to enjoy their two-minute of publicity in the process of expressing solidarity with the student community and their 'horror' at the 'insensitive' and 'unimaginative' manner in which the matter was handled by the officials of the Institute and the Central government.

Meanwhile, the student representatives and alumni of the Institute claimed that they held 'positive interactions' with their counterparts from quite a few universities across the country like Jawaharlal Nehru University, Delhi University, Jamia Milia Islamia in Delhi, Jadhavpur University and the Satyajit Ray Film and Television Institute in Kolkata as well as colleges in Ahmedabad and Pune, to enlist their support. Apparently, their idea was to explore the possibility of mobilizing sympathy and solidarity from the student bodies across the country to be used to force the authorities into acceding to their demands.

Entry of Politicos

Congress Vice President Rahul Gandhi, who had been touring States like Rajasthan, Maharashtra and UP to meet famine and drought-hit farmers for the purpose of vilifying the National Democratic Alliance (NDA) government's Land Acquisition Bill and turning the farmers against it, readily joined the fray by visiting FTII on an invitation from the protestors and expressed his and his party's solidarity with the students. He also seized the opportunity to wax eloquent about what he called the RSS ideology of promoting mediocrity in the country. This was followed by a retort by the Union Minister of State for Information and Broadcasting, Rajyavardhan Singh, who tweeted about the politicization of a students' issue by the Congress Party. The student representatives also had a meeting with Finance Minister

Arun Jaitley, which failed to break the deadlock. At the meeting, Jaitley reportedly hinted at the eventual privatization of the FTII, but assured the students that they would continue to enjoy academic freedom.

Dubious Activities

The issue at the core of the movement became much larger and murkier by the day when incidents of some recalcitrant student leaders and elements with vested interest hanging around in the campus even years after completion of the duration of their courses were reported in the Main Stream Media (MSM) as well as the Social Media. Incidents of abuse of drugs and alcohol as well as involvement in political activities of the extreme kind on the part of these elements who were well past their student life and academic career were brought to light. These elements were reported to have a vested interest in prolonging the confrontation to make political mileage out of the resultant fluid situation.

The authorities of the Institute who wanted to cleanse the campus of such undesirable elements started issuing notice to them for vacating the accommodation on the campus occupied by them, on receipt of instructions from the Ministry of Information and Broadcasting. Continued occupation by the hangers-on of the accommodation on the campus, which is heavily subsidized by the government, makes it difficult and even impossible for bonafide new students to get inexpensive accommodation on the campus. The newly-appointed Director of FTII, Prashant Pathrabe, announced the Institute's decision to assess the incomplete diploma film projects of the 2008 batch with a view to weeding out the hangers-on.

This move was denounced as 'irrational, unjustified and unfair' and was resisted by the affected students and their sympathizers among the students fraternity. They wanted the status-quo to continue as they feared that post-assessment those with incomplete projects may be declared failed and would have to leave the Institute. The students contested the admissibility of the decision to assess in the absence of the approval of the Institute's academic council, which had allegedly been bypassed. The Ministry of I&B had earlier raised the question of non-completion of diploma film projects by the 2008 batch and non-conduct of convocation for the past 17 years that prompted the crackdown by the Institute.

Midnight Arrests

The crackdown led to precipitation of an ugly incident with unpleasant fallout. The FTII Director reported on August 17 a case of his being manhandled, harassed and herded into his office when he tried to leave for home at the end of the day. He was then held captive for about seven hours. All the time, the unruly student mob raised slogans against him, shouted he was unfit for the post and demanded withdrawal of the decision to take up the incomplete diploma film projects by the 2008 batch for assessment. On receipt of an SOS, the Police rescued the Director from the unlawful custody of the students. The Police raided the campus around midnight. Although they had warrants against fifteen, they arrested only five students, all male, and booked cases against all of them. They were then charged with obstructing a public servant from performing his duty besides criminal intimidation, destruction of property, voluntarily causing hurt and rioting.

The arrested students were later let out on bail. The FTII Students Association has predictably put down the arrests as an act of spite arising out of an ulterior motive of weakening the students' stir by ejecting some of its active participants. They have questioned the absence of the Registrar at the time of the arrests carried out at midnight, alleging that it drives home the point that the welfare or fate of the students figured nowhere in the scheme of things of the Institute's administration. The youth wing of Shiv Sena and several student outfits in Pune have denounced the midnight arrests and stressed on the need for the government to find an amicable solution to the logjam.

Kejriwal Chips In

Whenever there is a controversy, can Arvind Kejriwal be far behind? He muscled his way through and reminded all concerned that he had a pebble or two of his own too to throw in and make the muddy waters still murkier. He received a delegation of FTII students in Delhi and assured them of his support. He went to the extent of offering them temporary space in Delhi where they could hold their classes and have their studies continue uninterrupted. He also offered to set up an institute in Delhi on a regular basis in the event of the fracas not being resolved by the Union Government to the satisfaction of the students. In short, he prodded the students to continue with their confrontationist attitude and not to scale down their demands or not to score a note of reconciliation while talking with the government!

Chauhan's Response

On his part, Gajendra Chauhan denied all the charges against him and expressed regret that he was being denied an opportunity to perform despite the appointment made by the Union government. He said he was unable to comprehend why the students of the Institute were being judgmental without giving him a chance to prove himself. If given an opportunity, he will do everything possible to address their problems and grievances, Chauhan added.

Emphasizing that the FTII Chairman's job profile is administrative in nature, Chauhan said he has ample experience to fit into this position as he was BJP's national convener, culture, and had promoted ideology of the party through cultural activities. "I was also a part of the Cine and TV Artistes Association, first as an executive committee member and then as the vice-president for four years. Furthermore, I was its president for a year, " he elaborated.

Wondering why should the students be questioning his credentials and how was the FTII Chairman answerable to them, he asked, "Why should the FTII be heading towards a future where students get to decide who their teacher will be? "

Meanwhile, noted filmmaker Shyam Benegal said it was incorrect on the part of FTII students to assume that Gajendra Chauhan was incapable of leading FTII without knowing his exact plans. To find out his credentials, the students should first meet Chauhan, have a dialogue with him and understand his plans. They should protest only if they find that Chauhan is trying to impose his ideology.

Emphasizing that students should not get provoked by opinion makers at this point in time, Benegal said it is they who would be the losers in terms of studies and training. As such, there is no point in politicizing the issue further, he pointed out.

Politicization

Notwithstanding the merits and demerits of their demands, the way students have gone about politicizing the issue speaks volume about their deplorable attitude and confrontationist approach concerning the core issue involved. Thus, a local issue has got blown out of proportions!

In other words, a storm, nay, a tsunami in a teacup! Was it the idea of the students to apprise the authorities of their genuine grievances for possible redressal or to bring a mighty government to its knees? If it was all about genuine grievances and possible redressal, then the motions they have gone through hardly constitute the right way. If, on the other hand, the idea was to enact a David versus Goliath docu-drama in true filmy style, the protesting students should be congratulated for attempting a great job. But, then, that was exactly what Rahul Gandhi and Arvind Kejriwal and the sundry politicos had done when they cheered up and feted the protestors. Wasn't it? A rather nice script and stellar enactment! How exactly the student community has benefited from allowing politicization of their movement, with the exception of the hangers-on and the ones with the ulterior motive of making political mileage out of the protests, is for the student community to ponder over.

Authorities to Act

As regards the authorities, where do they stand? It is high time the Institute's administrative authorities took the instructions of the Information and Broadcasting Ministry seriously and initiated appropriate actions to clear up the backlog of diploma film projects. It is equally important to clear up the mess of the hangers-on who seem to be out on the campus for a good time with their inadmissible behaviour and illegal activities, making conditions increasingly difficult for bonafide students. Film making should be allowed to take once again its rightful place, which currently seems to have been replaced by theatrics.

Muddling by the Media

On their part, the self-proclaimed liberal thinkers and self-styled secular media had gone gaga over the ugly developments and their unpleasant fallout. They went to town with the story that the government's 'high-handed' action in the matter of appointments was on account of its susceptibility to instructions from the RSS. Nobody seems to be in a hurry to refute the imputation as it is for the umpteenth time that the government's detractors had come up with the sensational invention that the ubiquitous RSS hand was behind the decision-making process of the BJP-led NDA government!

Reckless Charge

Here it needs to be noted that the process of selection of candidates for appointment and ensuring selection of the best candidates is a matter for objective discussion among all the parties and stakeholders concerned. However, deriding an appointment by branding it an act of rewarding of a party loyalist is tantamount to a wanton and reckless act reflective of irresponsible behaviour and absence of objectivity on the part of the critique. As Gajendra Chauhan has rightly pointed out, career achievement cannot be the sole criterion for appointment to such posts.

For that matter, even if every authority and official of FTII were a carefully handpicked dye-in-the-wool loyalist of RSS or BJP, how would that result in the dreaded saffronization of the Institute? So long as the students enjoy academic freedom to craft the kind of films they aspire to make, how would the selection of officials affect their presentation? The FTII is no Censor Board! Nor is it an institution for indoctrination. And, on a different note, party loyalists do not necessarily have to be starved of consideration for appointments so long as the government takes care to act by the laid-down and established norms!

Furthermore, the Indian Constitution gives everyone the freedom to have a political affiliation of his liking. Hence, singling out Gajendra Chauhan saying he has been hired because of his political affiliation does not cut much ice. And if one looks back, FTII Chairman has always been appointed by the Union government. In other words, it is always the political party in power that gets to decide who would be the FTII Chairman.

Moreover, the latter is only a figurative head because ultimately the FTII Society is an autonomous body under the Ministry of Information and Broadcasting. As such, it enjoys full functional autonomy, and all its policies are determined by the Governing Council. So what exactly is bothering the students so much is something that is difficult to comprehend. This leads one to conclude that the striking FTII students are either making reckless charges or they are being misled by some vested interests keen to cash in at their expense in a bid to create problems for the Central government.

(Posted on blog on 26 August, 2015)

□

Why are the Opposition and Media Picking on Female Leaders of the BJP?

What better way for a government to complete its first full year in office than by ensuring clean and scam-free governance? That is exactly how the Narendra Modi-led government at the Centre marked its first anniversary in May this year. Even as the rejoicing over the landmark occasion had barely subsided and the government rededicated itself to the service of the nation and welfare of the people, four of the party's important female leaders came under scathing attack from the Opposition and the Main Stream Media (MSM) for their 'alleged involvement' in cases of corruption, financial irregularities and impropriety.

External Affairs Minister Sushma Swaraj was falsely blamed for helping Lalit Modi, former Commissioner of IPL, who had been erroneously accused by the Opposition and Media as 'fugitive', get his travel documents from UK by writing in her official capacity to a British Labour MP stating that grant of travel documents would not affect India-UK bilateral relations. Meanwhile, it was alleged that Rajasthan Chief Minister Vasundhara Rajewas also involved in a scam relating to Lalit Modi. The media and the Opposition contended that she had supported the former IPL boss in migrating to the UK. It was also alleged that Lalit Modi was a business partner of her son and had invested in the latter's company, resulting in financial impropriety on the part of Raje.

In the meantime, the Congress Party revived its long-forgotten complaint against HRD Minister Smriti Irani, which it had made some time last year immediately after her induction into the Narendra Modi Cabinet, regarding her alleged attempt to mislead the Election Commission by falsifying her educational qualifications. Then Pankaja

Munde, young and upcoming BJP leader and key minister in the BJP-Shiv Sena coalition government in Maharashtra, was accused of clearing contracts worth ₹ 206 crore on a single day for the purchase of a host of items under the Integrated Child Development Scheme, casting procurement procedures to the winds. Since 'chikki', a groundnut-based sweet highly popular in Maharashtra – is one of the major items in the said purchase list, some journalists have termed this scandal 'Chikkigate'.

Media in the Fray

In a bid to be sensational and gain TRP ratings, the Media went gaga over the allegations and carried out a shrill and strident campaign, replete with a swelling number of 'breaking news' and 'exposes' seeking the scalps of the targeted ministers. Both the Opposition and the Media, which have been starved of scams and scandals during the past one year, gratefully seized the opportunity to make up for the lost time by working overtime on a long drawn out campaign against BJP in general and the four targeted ministers and Prime Minister Modi in particular.

Not a day passed without the Electronic Media coming up with a regular feed of updates on 'Lalitgate' and 'Chikkigate'. A large posse of news reporters was deployed exclusively for hunting vignettes of the scams-related developments. At least one news anchor flew all the way to Montenegro to interview Lalit Modi, the man in the eye of the storm. In their programs of high decibel noise power, which passed for panel discussions, visibly tired and harried anchors dutifully kept reminding BJP leaders that the nation wanted to know answers to their questions and how Prime Minister Modi's silence in the matter would only hurt the party and the government.

The Aam Aadmi Party (AAP), whose Law Minister in the Delhi Government, Jitender Singh Tomar, had recently been arrested and thrown in jail for obtaining and possessing two fake degree certificates, joined Congress in targeting Smriti Irani and sought a probe against her claim of higher educational qualifications than she actually possessed.

Congress and the Scams

Prima facie, the charges appeared serious enough to make the people of the nation sit up and wonder in amazement about the veracity of the allegations. Congress spokesmen who had gone into hibernation over sheer exhaustion, and who were desperately waiting in vain for a goofup, gaffe or faux pas by some BJP leader or the other, got a fresh lease of life and were seen waxing eloquent about the 'duplicity' and 'hypocrisy' of BJP vis-a-vis Congress party's 'high moral and ethical standards' and wondering why Prime Minister Modi had been a picture of silence with regard to his 'errant' party colleagues.

They stooped to new lows by insinuating that Bada Modi (Narendra Modi) was trying to help Chhota Modi (Lalit Modi). All this without a shred of evidence to support their claim that there had been foul play or quid pro quo! They commiserated with the "people of the nation who had been conned into reposing faith" in a party which claimed moral high grounds by the day and committed acts of betrayal of people's faith on the sly! The Congress Party cadres brought up the rear by carrying out protest rallies and demonstrations outside the residences of the ministers and party offices of BJP.

Charges Fail to Stick

Notwithstanding all the rolling up of sleeves and flexing of muscles by the Opposition and a high octane presentation by the Media of the terrible 'assault' on democracy by the 'errant' ministers, the concerned BJP ministers stoutly defended their own integrity. With the support they received from their party leadership and failure of the allegations to stick in the absence of substantial evidence or proof on legal or technical grounds, it became increasingly evident that the charges did not add up to merit either the gusto and aggression with which these were pushed forward by Congress or the sensation whipped up by the Media to tarnish the images of the accused leaders and their party.

Support by Party Leadership

On its part, the BJP leadership announced that none of its leaders was tainted and that in the case of Vasundhara Raje, the documents produced against her had not been verified. Sushma Swaraj had acted in good faith and had extended help on humanitarian grounds. Smriti Irani's position had already been cleared in 2014 itself, when she dared her detractors to move the court of law regarding the complaint against her. Pankaja Munde had, on her part, stated that 'Chikkigate' was a scam of words; she had done no wrong and was, in any case, ready for a probe. In view of the above, the party asserted there was no question of any of the ministers resigning. Furthermore, the whole scenario of the ministers being axed was imaginary, it elaborated.

Pressure Tactics

The unflinching solidarity of the BJP with its ministers under attack foiled the efforts of the Congress Party, which had been feeling a bit too pleased with the work of its Dirty Tricks Department in coming up with what it considered was invaluable information pertaining to the 'indiscretions' and 'impropriety' of the BJP ministers. With the attempts of the Opposition to besmirch the images of the ministers coming to naught inspite of the many unruly protests and rallies by its cadres and huge ruckus raised by the Media, Congress Party nearly ran out of steam and started desperately shooting arrows in the dark with the aim of further discrediting BJP.

It went about flagrantly bullying BJP with its plans to stall the proceedings of the forthcoming monsoon session of Parliament. When BJP did not acquiesce to the demands of the Congress on pain of a washed-out Parliament, the latter adopted yet another tactic of its by wooing BJP with an interesting proposal – it would not block the Goods and Services Tax (GST) Bill despite its strong reservations, if it got the scalps of Sushma Swaraj and Vasundhara Raje.

The proposal was, however, stonewalled by BJP by taking the principled stand of not yielding to strong-arm tactics of the Congress. The decision of the BJP to stand by its flock and call the bluff of Congress flummoxed the latter, which had been looking for an opportunity to make a mark for itself ever since it was trounced in the 2014 Lok Sabha polls.

Why Women Leaders

That all the targets of the vilification campaign are women is the lowest common denominator in the calculations of the Congress that has been trying hard to besmirch the image of BJP, which has provided corruption-free governance at the Centre during the last one year. Is it a coincidence or is there a design to this interesting commonality?

One would be a bit too naive to believe that it is a sheer coincidence that all the ministers who are sought to be discredited are women or that they constituted the low hanging fruits for a Congress on the offensive. It is interesting to note that all the four ministers are known for their high profile approach to politics. They are outspoken, hard hitting and harsh critics of the Congress Party. They have bolstered the glory of their party by their individual track records and fiercely defended the party against attacks by their rivals.

Their role in the landslide victory of BJP at the Centre and the States of Rajasthan and Maharashtra were inestimable. Their oratorical skill, eloquence and ability to systematically demolish the arguments and cases of their detractors, are highly commendable qualities and are indicative of the shaping up of the next generation of party leaders in the making. Sushma Swaraj had been applauded for the exemplary handling of the External Affairs portfolio, when the news of the scam broke out.

She was profusely praised for the manner in which she had managed to steer the Indo-Bangla land boundary agreement through the Parliament earlier this year. Furthermore, the unstinting support that these women ministers received from their own party leadership as well as from the RSS in the face of the intimidatory tactics of their arch rival and political tormentor, amply demonstrates their importance quotient in their party's strategic quest for a Congress-mukht Bharat.

How Rahul Gandhi prattled about his faith in women power on the eve of the Lok Sabha polls of 2014 and kept harping about how he planned to empower women when the Congress Party is returned to power at the Centre, provided comic relief and sounded a pathetic ruse or ploy that it was, on the part of a political greenhorn who dreamt of being catapulted to the highest office of the land (barring that of Honourable President) by default.

In a curious turn of events, the Congress was decimated not only at the Centre but also in the states of Rajasthan and Maharashtra, which had been in its stranglehold for quite some time. Five years of life without power at the Centre and the crucial states of Rajasthan and Maharashtra are both unthinkable and unbearable for the Congress, which had never reconciled in the past to the idea of joining the Opposition ranks.

Walking the corridors of power came naturally to the dynastic family. Life was a breeze, when all one had to do was to call the shots from behind the scene without being answerable to anybody or accountable for one's actions, walk briskly enough to convince the onlookers that one had not a moment to lose, wave vigorously at the multitudes of crowds waiting out in the open for hours on end to have a glimpse of the so-called 'beloved leader', parrot some soulless written-down speeches authored by people who do it for a living, do a brisk pirouette and make the most of photo-ops with visiting foreign dignitaries, and, in general, keep the mystique and sheen of democracy's answer to a monarchy's royal family on.

The misery of being lost in the political wilderness, that too for five long years, is indeed painful! The ignominy of not being able to secure the status of Leader of Opposition in the Lok Sabha is really unbearable! Congress had to figure out a raison d'être. And all that the grey eminences in the oldest political party of the nation could think was to discredit the ruling party and thereby score some brownie points. This would be an easy way out for the party desperately on the lookout for a breath of fresh life rather than having to reinvent itself, which would involve a long-drawn and monotonous exercise! Woman power being a matter of pride for the BJP, why not deride the women leaders and expose the chinks in the armour?

On the one hand, the Congress Vice President waxes eloquent about empowerment of women, and on the other, his party loses no opportunity to put women politicians doing good work down! What a paradox! Besides, there were old political scores to be settled. In Congress, there is a clear red line that is not to be crossed by anyone, whatever the circumstances. The Nehru-Gandhi family is the holy cow, beyond reproach both by the members of the party and its rivals. Nor are its members to be contested against in elections. They have to be extended the courtesy of being returned to the Parliament, totally unopposed.

History is full of wistful moments which beg answer to the question 'If only...?' For instance, if only late Raj Narain had not trounced former Prime Minister Indira Gandhi in the 1977 polls at Rae Bareli, would India's history have remained the same? In 1999, Sushma Swaraj had contested from Bellary constituency, where she had styled herself as the 'Beti' of the people against the foreign-born 'Bahu' Sonia Gandhi. Despite a spirited performance, she had lost by a 7% margin.

To make matters worse, she had publicly declared in 2004 that she would shave her head if Sonia Gandhi became India's Prime Minister – a statement that did not go down too well within the Congress circles.

Fifteen years down the line, history repeated itself when Smriti Irani was locked in a head-on battle with Rahul Gandhi at Amethi, the pocket borough of the Nehru-Gandhi family. Although she lost the battle, she had put up a very valiant fight, which drew tremendous accolade for her spirited performance.

She was also rewarded with a berth in the Narendra Modi Cabinet. At 38, she is currently the youngest among all the women ministers in the NDA government. Her post-poll visits to Amethi, despite her defeat in the election, during which she exposed Rahul Gandhi's hollow claims of «revenge politics» by the Modi government have won her high praise from the party leadership, much to the chagrin of the Congress Party.

Sweet Revenge

Sushma Swaraj's and Smriti Irani's performances causing a halt in the Nehru-Gandhi family's hitherto cosy sojourn in politics, constituted not mere breaches of the red line but major blitzkrieg, in acts both inadmissible and unacceptable, having much in common with late Raj Narain's derring-do! For the Congress Party, it was time for a repeat of the infamous state of Emergency – which it was lamentably in no position to impose this time around!

Having waited long enough in the cases of Sushma Swaraj and Smriti Irani since 1999 and 2014 respectively, it was time for revenge – adish best served cold! Desperate times for the Congress, which called for desperate measures! Add to the unpardonable acts of indiscretion against the First Family, the trouncing of the party's impregnable bastions of Rajasthan and Maharashtra, for a good measure. Hey, presto! You got the perfect plan for the so called scams of the four formidable female leaders of the BJP!

(Posted on blog on 7 July, 2015)

□

Can India Succeed Without State-union Collaboration?

Can you recall the last occasion when a leader of one political group appreciated the works of the other political party? Or, can we even remember when for the last time the union and the state government/s had a consensus? Though the Constitution of India is federal in nature with exclusive powers to the states and UTs; distinct parts of the nation are inseparable and combine to form 'India'. This means that the unitary character of our democratic and political setup cannot be denied. Sad to notice, however, that the politicians representing separate groups and the governments representing different Indian states are rarely united.

With the formation and rise of countless political groups, politics has become an arena of competition, hatred, lust, and arrogance. It is depressing to note that the social service drive has absolutely disappeared, and the politicians have regarded politics as the way to get hold of money and power. The flow of funds during polls, use of illicit measures, and unethical ways to accomplish goals substantiate the underlying fact that politics is no longer a way to serve humanity; rather this is an uncomplicated and powerful method of attaining whatever one desires. The makers of the Constitution would never have anticipated such a downfall.

It was impressive, and above all, satisfying to hear the strong words of the President, Mr. Pranab Mukherjee, while he was addressing the combined session of the Parliament. Though Mr. Mukherjee has a lasting relationship with the Congress, he seemed unbiased and visionary. His words reflected the potential of the present union government in delivering all that has been promised in the manifesto. He honestly counted the letdowns of the UPA and UPA-2 reign and indicated the probable re-election of the Modi-led BJP in 2019. The

President is surely positive and assured of the competence of Mr. Modi and his team of cabinet ministers.

The Prime Minister's visionary goals and prosperity-oriented motives can rarely bring in the much-needed reformation until the state governments participate comprehensively in the evolution of the nation. Though Mr. Modi has the unbeaten capability of putting things in place on his own; with the support of the states and leaders of distinct political groups, the target can be attained swiftly and more effectively. The five T's of Mr. Modi viz. Tradition, Talent, Tourism, Trade, and Technology would surely work towards strengthening the roots; however states will have to contribute with real aims and above personal greediness.

Even Mr. Modi realizes the vital role of the states in the process of nation-building. Working towards the sole aim of betterment of India, prosperity of the underprivileged, women and youth, and transparency and efficiency in the working of the government, Mr. Modi needs firm cooperation from every part of the society. Plus, the general public will too have to apprehend the need of the hour and will have to part with the laid back attitude. Every public servant, representative, and guardian will have to think of the nation prior to looking for personal gains. Remember, the path to India's glory passes through every state, every town, and every house.

(Posted on blog on 11 June, 2014)

□

Independence of Judiciary vs. the NJAC

Independence of judiciary is in the very essence of our Constitution, this also is a pre-requisite for safeguarding the democracy against not-always-just political intentions, which many a time are driven by the greed to extract maximum out the Constitutional setup, even if that demands arbitrary amendments to this supreme of the land. Had there been a political/executive touch in the judiciary, the forty-second amendment to the Constitution that struck down powers of the Supreme Court to a catastrophic extent and such other politically motivated stands would have stripped us of our fundamental rights and shifted the sovereignty exclusively to the parliament. Now that the fight of justifying the National Judicial Appointments Commissions Act 2014 and the ills of the collegium system has landed up in the Apex Court, it is more than warranted that the parties to the case consider this as not being 'exclusive judiciary' or 'exclusive legislature', but from the perspective of the makers of the Constitution.

This isn't for the first time that appointment of Constitutional courts' judges through the creation of the collegium has become a victim of unwanted controversy. To steer clear of the executive and legislature with respect to appointments in the judiciary, the court evolved this system, which however, does not find place in the Constitution of 1950 or any subsequent amendments; we all know how the weapon of 'partially rigid and partially flexible' system for amending the Constitution was exploited by previous governments from time to time, placing supremacy of the original Constitution at stake. Ever since the 'opinion' of the Supreme Court given in the Third Judges Case, the system has been criticized by jurists and legal experts, even by the then President of India. It is often claimed that lobbying has become an inevitable part of the judiciary in post-collegium era, and judges, rather than lessening the burden of ever-high pending cases, secure a position by winning over the collegium members; let us not then also question the evident lobbying deep-rooted in all government functioning, from selection and transfer of ministers to placement of bureaucrats; should then the judiciary not step in to curb such 'biased decisions', would then the governments accept such infringement of their 'exclusive' rights as are in the Constitution?

But the defending of the NJAC in the ongoing Supreme Court hearings has turned into a bitter fight where the hearing bench of five judges has presumed the role of a party to the case, more because they have been compelled so, and the Attorney General has been asked to put up evidences that show inadequacy of collegium. The opaque collegium, as is named by its sheer opponents, certainly has some flaws as far as it allows 'judges appointing judges', which in the very verbatim tone indicates prevalence of favor in some if not all appointments. This, however, cannot render righteousness to the NJAC where the executive and even persons from outside the field of judiciary and legislature may relish the opportunity of appointing judges. It can be agreed that the concept of collegium appointments in its entirety may not be exceedingly transparent; hence the composition of collegium to make it more transparent and the consultation broad-based, as advocated by former CJI Justice Sathasivam, can be deliberated upon, putting this ongoing and unwanted ruckus to a shrewd end.

As said earlier, why not peruse this subject with the eyes and intent of Constitution makers who made 'independence of judiciary' the spirit of this supreme law, and even we, having preserved our rights by timely interventions of courts and through doctrine of basic structure that enables judicial review of any of the government's move, must advocate stringent non-interference of legislature and executive in judicial machinery. Let not a day arrive when the courts of India become a power in the hands of political men, who are free to exploit it for their own good, let not the era of 'Indira Constitution' be resuscitated. Powers to executive, though with eminent jurists, will defeat the soul of the Constitution; also, we do not want delays in the appointment of judges as is seen in crucial appointments, for say heads of PSUs and CPSEs and of CVC and CIC.

'Appointment', be it of the judge of the Constitutional court, or of ministers assisting the Prime Minister/Chief Minister, or in any other office, which is directly or indirectly accountable to the public at large, shall not be the prerogative of an individual/cluster that can be influenced. But, putting this system to end is improbable, since any agency/system in place for appointments will comprise of persons and such persons, whether independent or from within the cluster, can never be immune from influences. Nevertheless, what happens with bureaucrats and the CBI cannot be made a scenario in the Indian judicial setup, which is the savior of our Constitutional setup. Many High Courts are awaiting appointment of Chief Justice and also worrying is the vacancy in offices of high court judges; resolution of NJAC vs. Collegium issue will not only pave way for such appointments but will also speed up justice for the common man. Fight must be brought to such an end that neither the independence of judiciary gets compromised nor does this become an ego conflict between judiciary and government; most judicious is to rework flaws of the collegium and let the judiciary remain a sovereign domain.

(Posted on blog on 16 June, 2015)

□

Upcoming Bill Must Uphold the Independence and Impartiality of Indian Judiciary

As the judiciary is a major pillar that ensures proper enforcement of laws in any country and also safeguards the fundamental rights of its citizens, the success of any democracy is directly dependent on the robustness of the shoulders of its judicial system. Even the power, independence and effectiveness of the other three pillars of a democracy – namely the legislature, the executive and the media – depend on the uprightness, independence and impartiality of its judicial system.

However, if one takes into account the recent public utterances of Justice Markandey Katju about the distortions in appointing judges and the political pressures that often come into play, then it appears that the legislature and the executive have hijacked the judiciary in our country. Furthermore, anyone who has had any experience of the Indian courts is fully aware that our judicial system is beset with many flaws that need to be addressed on a war footing.

The assertions of Justice Katju, who is the current Chairperson of the Press Council of India (PCI), alleging that political pressure during the previous UPA regime had led to elevation of a district judge in Tamil Nadu to an additional judge of the Madras High Court despite charges of corruption against him, have not been the only instance that has damaged the reputation of the prevailing system of selection of High Court and Supreme Court judges.

Who can forget the case of Justice Hans Raj Khanna, a legendary Judge of the Supreme Court of India during 1967-77? He was prevented in January 1977 from being appointed as the Chief Justice of India (CJI) by the then Prime Minister Indira Gandhi owing to the fact that he was honest enough to give a dissenting judgment, against the then Union government, on the right to life and liberty during the internal emergency. Instead, his junior, Justice MH Beg was appointed as the CJI. Though Justice H.R. Khanna's dissent cost him the job of CJI, he became immortal in the annals of Indian history, as also amongst the legal fraternity.

Justice H.R. Khanna's dissenting opinion against the government stating that the Indian Constitution did not permit the right to life and liberty to be subject to any kind of executive decree, is widely regarded as a landmark judgment in Indian democracy. Since then our entire country, including the political leaders, the social activists and even the common man, have been aspiring for an arrangement that could permanently abolish all kinds of political meddling in the judiciary. To achieve this objective and to eliminate political interference in judicial appointments and end the practice of judges being appointed by the government, the existing collegium system was started.

Under the collegium system, which was implemented following a judgment of the apex court in 1993, judges appoint judges to the High Courts and the Supreme Court. Though the said collegium system was supposed to insulate the judiciary from the influence and pressure of the legislature and executive, the recent assertions of Justice Katju reveal it has not happened as expected.

There is a general perception that the collegium system has not performed well and should be radically changed. Some of the worrying concerns relate to appointment of unsuitable candidates, selections based on favouritism and influential connections as well as personal likes and dislikes. Furthermore, the present appointment process adopted by the collegium of judges is plagued with problems of opacity and non-accountability.

In view of the aforesaid flaws and with the aim of eliminating the culture of secrecy and nepotism that envelops the current process of selection of judges by the collegium, the BJP-led NDA government is contemplating to bring in the Judicial Appointments Commission Bill (JACB) providing for the constitution of a National Judicial Commission (NJC) for appointment of judges to the High Courts and the Supreme Court. The NJC will seek to replace the present collegium system with the aim of establishing judicial accountability, upholding the independence and impartiality of the judiciary as well as checking corruption in our judicial system. Thus, the JACB is expected to dilute the lingering bad faith and tug-of-war between the government and the judiciary.

The proposed NJC will be a statutory commission consisting of the Chief Justice of India, the Union Law Minister, two senior-most judges of the Supreme Court and two 'eminent' persons who would be selected for a non-renewable tenure of three years by a collegium of the Prime Minister, the Leader of the Opposition in the Lok Sabha and the CJI. The proposed bill, currently awaiting approval from the Rajya Sabha, will take away the power to transfer High Court judges from the government, and vest that power with the NJC, thereby ensuring total freedom to the judiciary from political interference and political domination.

Over and above bringing in transparency and openness in the appointments of the High Court and Supreme Court judges, the proposed Judicial Appointments Commission Bill should also strive to ensure total freedom from political interference and political domination. It should also address concerns with respect to the nomination of retired judges as the heads of various Tribunals and Commissions. The bill should also accord comprehensive freedom to the National Judicial Commission so as to ensure that only eminent, worthy, impartial and incorruptible judges with impeccable track record are selected for appointments in top positions of the Indian judiciary.

(Posted on blog on 8 August, 2014)

□

The Land Bill Row-Both BJP and Farmers to Re-think

The long-standing and tested saying goes as 'A bend in the storm can help, standing rigid can make the tree collapse'. Devising policies is not an easy task, many a time, in the wake of unforeseen changes in prevailing circumstances, managements do re-think their policies; also make amendments so as not to fall prey to unfavorable conditions. It becomes far more crucial to bend than to fail when your policy is to have a bearing on a vast section of the community, socially as well as economically. The BJP, ruling party in the Lok Sabha, may be heading in the most productive direction that is sure to fetch viable outcomes in terms of foreign investment, employment prospects for Indians and the restoration of Indian manufacturing sector, but if it is clearly visible that one of your endeavors is not able to gather the requisite backing of Indian peasants, shouldn't the scheme be re-considered; a judicious option is to either get the sanctioning of hostile cluster by infusing confidence in them or to drop the policy for the time-being.

Indian farmers have always remained dejected, overlooked, vulnerable and untouchable for most of the past governments. Private moneylenders, banks, government strategies and the discourteous weather conditions collectively have hit the peasants from every possible corner, and the group, which plays the most key role in our social and financial growth, is left with just diverse options to end life voluntarily. More than 16, 000 farmers opt for suicide every year; the figure was 18, 241 in 2004 and between 1995 and 2013, almost 3 lakh farmer suicides have been reported. These figures are mentioned in many reports and writings, mutilation of crops due to recent unseasonal rain and hailstorms is also a known fact and the forecast of a bad monsoon in the upcoming days isn't hidden. The bottom line is that our peasants are in the grip of unendurable conditions, and this may not be the most appropriate time for the BJP to come up with variations that could deprive farmers of their exclusive right to approve/reject any proposed acquisition bids.

Dear PM, the suggested amendments to the UPA's The Right to Fair Compensation and Transparency in Land Acquisition, Rehabilitation and Resettlement Act, 2013, which say that the consent of 70 per cent farmers in case of five categories shall be taken off, are in true terms a well-planned measure to kick-start essential reforms in the country and may be termed a long-term win-win situation for the Indian society as whole, but what happened to the CPM-led government in the West Bengal post the offense of farmers in Singur and Nandigram are the incidents that cannot be under-valued. While traditional vote-bank of the BJP embraces the middle class and industrialists, in the 2014 polls, the wave of Narendra Modi was equally buoyed by small and marginal peasants, along with the sharecroppers. The lower class, especially from the rural parts, is yet to overcome the episodes of cheap acquisition of farmland backed by political corruption and selling of the same to industries at sky-high rates; they are also yet to overcome the fear of development-induced dislodgment of the impoverished and subsequent injuries.

Politics in India is not the numbers that you present, i.e. the GDP growth rate, interest rates or the fiscal deficit; it is how you are interpreted by the stakeholders, and this is where Indira Gandhi failed owing to the forced mass-sterilization led by her son, Sanjay Gandhi during the emergency, and also the Rajiv Gandhi-led government collapsed on the allegations of Bofors scandal. And the same sentimental up and downs of the voters pave the way for smaller political groups that comprehend the pulse of the public, and the same in turn disturbs the efficiency and effectiveness of the political party ruling at the center. BJP may send party-workers and even its legislators to exchange thoughts directly with the likely-to-be-affected farmers; however, damage to the image of the PM as well the party is underway. The most apt code of conduct for the BJP is to diagnose and have compassion with the pain of farmers, and the same asks for identifying with basic concerns like lack of irrigation facilities and sheer dependence on borrowing from private lenders. Acquisition of land and resulting evolution of rural India can, indeed, follow the corrections to fundamental flaws, but cannot supersede them.

Pro-rich, Pro-industries, Pro-urban and such other tags, accorded to the Modi-led union government by the opposition and even many of the farmers' associations, are though not be eliminated, but are to be complemented with labels, Pro-poor, Pro-rural and Pro-agriculture. If the administrators are looking for a country with smart cities, digitalized services, smart phone-equipped citizens and a flourishing industrial sector, alike perusal of the concerns of the rural India, home to farmers and employer to more than half of our workforce, is also obligatory. Acquiring land of peasants is more than a transaction and underlying is the uprooting of dwellers from their social tie-ups, controversies in the title of the land, discretion of government officials in determining market rates and most rough, the loss of livelihood. On the contrary are the projects that are awaiting land for their commencement and PM's dreams for a developed nation, just for all; however the opposition would never consider these while defaming your authentic endeavors.

Elections in key states of Bihar, WB and Tamil Nadu are anytime to ring the bells, which mean that the BJP cannot afford anything like its present portrayal as anti-farmer and anti-poor. Modinomics, the buzz created by economic gurus and even by foreign media, calls for systematic and in-depth analysis of the issues related to Indian agriculture and acquisition of land. It is quite very obvious that lakhs of crores of subsidy flowing to the rural India in the name of fertilizers, food security, and also as compensation for loss of produce and the minimum support price haven't resulted in any betterment of farmers. The past governments were severely weak in terms of analyzing the rural economy and improving the share of agriculture in GDP. While average holding of farmers has dipped consistently and plentiful land has been acquired in the past at exorbitant rates, neither rural nor the industrial sector has delivered optimistic outcomes.

And for the corporates and governments, the alarm wasn't felt the way it actually upset the lives of rural inhabitants. The present government is expected to pay heed to the problems of farmers; the way things are turning out with respect to the land acquisition law, I fear that the prediction of above-7 per cent GDP growth or the positive revision in India's outlook by Moody's may not be able to add to the number of BJP MPs in the Rajya Sabha, a requisite for the Modi-government to revive Indian economy by way of passing key legislations well within time. UP, Bihar, Rajasthan, Punjab, Maharashtra and Madhya Pradesh, states that backed the NDA colossally in the 2014 general elections, are the ones with substantial farmer population; any mutilation to the coalition's image in this regard would let opposition parties revive themselves. PM Modi and his astute ministers are to re-assess their stand in light of latest advancements, and if this asks for holding the planned changes to the land bill for the time-being, the party must bend itself, rather than be uprooted.

I cannot conclude without analyzing the impact, actual and not alleged impact, of the land bill proposed by the government on the lives of rural inhabitants. Believe me, the entire opposition is adamant not to let the bill get the nod of the RS only and only for a simple reason that this is their golden moment to provide some oxygen to their fading parties. Buzz is being created that land owners would lose the opportunity to move the court and no complaint could be registered against the official, which are a fabrication of real intentions of the bill. Also, rural inhabitants are to realize that with more than 65 per cent Indians dependent on farming, agriculture is still a liability on Indian economy and it's high time that alternative livelihood for rural residents is brought to reality, and this isn't conceivable without electrification, industrial corridors and affordable housing. For the same, the government needs land, and justifiable compensation in return is a win-win condition for land owners. Making farming sustainable and providing alternative occupation to farmers will go hand in hand; hence farmers are to re-think their stand.

The government seeks farmers' share in upright and effective governance and in revival of the Indian economy that is to benefit all Indians, farmers and opposition are to know their sense of duty, sooner than later.

(Posted on blog on 7 May, 2015)

□

Opposition's Fake Anxiety, RS Disruption is Nation's Loss

Countries like Greece, New Zealand, Sri Lanka, Singapore and Denmark have adopted the unicameralism setup in their legislative domains, a practice where only one house/chamber takes decisions pertaining to lawmaking. In India, the concept of bicameralism subsists, as enshrined in the Constitution. At first instance, this appears essential so as not to let the lower house of the parliament take hasty and unapprised decisions, and also the vast and heterogeneous demography calls for wide representation of people in the process of lawmaking. But does this allow the upper house to undertake cunning and imprudent political advantage over the ruling party in the lower house? Makers of Indian Constitution considered the British political and legislative setup at the back of their minds while framing this supreme piece of law. But even in the British setup now, the legislations promulgated by the lower house twice in one year are binding on the upper house. Rajya Sabha was always to be a house of shrewd and veteran politicians who can serve the role of a guide; however in the present state of affairs they are not only subsiding their basic duties, but are also suppressing public's mandate to the party chosen in the Lok Sabha. BJP won 282 seats in the 2014 general elections with 31 per cent vote share, and it is their obligation as well as right to take shrewd decisions and implement them without hassles.

The functioning of both the houses of parliament in the Budget session so far has come with some pluses and many minuses. While the lower house delivered productivity of about 123 per cent owing to extra sitting by our legislators, the upper house could not match this optimum pace and restored to sheer politics, aggression and intrusions. On one hand, PM Narendra Modi cautioned absent MPs, on the other,

Rajya Sabha's mighty parties exhibited lack of professional maturity and infringed the mandate of public that backs their strength in the house. It is promising to note that TMC, SP, BJD and others extended much-needed support to the central government with respect to Mines and Minerals (Development and Regulation) Amendment Bill and the Coal Mines (Special Provisions) Bill; passing of the Bills by both houses will open new venues of commerce and employment. In the wake of such competence from the upper house, dominated by Congress and regional political parties, row over the Land Acquisition Bill was uncalled for and completely in contrast with the awaited industrial evolution of the country.

Let us see if at all the revisions proposed by the BJP to the Right to Fair Compensation and Transparency in Land Acquisition, Rehabilitation and Resettlement Act are anti-farmers and pro-industrialists. The amendments favor 'no consent' from stakeholders, but do not overlook the underlying benefits in these special cases which range from defense and national security to affordable housing for underprivileged and village electrification. There exists a fundamental dream of housing for all by 2022, and if you believe that the same will be possible without land acquisition, you need extensive lessons on fiscal administration and policy implementation. The UPA's concerned land legislation of 2013 identified tenant farmers and landless workers as stakeholders under the Social Impact Assessment, and made it rather impossible for sincere development projects to obtain necessary sanctions. Shall I not remind you that the bulldozers and cranes Congress is talking about as the killers of farmers will only result in infrastructure growth, employment for world's largest inhabited youth population and extension of basis amenities like roads, power and sanitation to the rural parts of India?

Madhya Pradesh has seen a number of natural calamities in past years, at times when the UPA was in-charge of nation's furtherance, as being the party with majority in the parliament. Flood and droughts have hit almost the entire of North India as well as other parts, but this is one of those rare occasions that Congress is anxious, moved and highly restless for the loss of Indian farmers. The president of the party is to visit the state of MP where unseasonal rain has hit the produce of farmers; however they had no such compassion for agriculturists while in power at the center. Congress, communist parties, TMC and others have found a trump card in their hands in the form of proposed Land Acquisition Bill of the BJP-led government; they feel that the lost ground could be gained back by sympathizing and crying over farmers' alleged loss, causing severe blow to the economic lead India is on the verge to take. A march from Sansad Bhawan to the Rashtrapati Bhawan, where the largest opposition party collaborated with other groups was nothing more than a way to advertise false commitment towards Indian farmers who gained nothing apart from debts and suicides in decades of Congress reign.

The Ordinance of the BJP government that furthers the real interest of the farmers' community will lapse on the 4th of April and a candid leader, Narendra Modi, was left with no other choice than to re-promulgate the ordinance with the nine amendments passed by the Lok Sabha. And then, even if after efforts to form consensus over new ordinance with opposition parties, the conclusion is detrimental, a joint session of both the houses would do the needful, a notion which is in the Constitution as I believe that the makers of this binding supreme law knew about the communal divide of India which would give birth to unworthy political leaders, and hence dimness of ruling party in the upper house wouldn't let growth agendas prosper. A Bill that aims at consolidating separate labors of the government, Indian industry and general public by exempting five categories from requiring consent of land owners has to be accorded the right to become a binding legislation, in the interest of farmers, job-seekers, commerce and the nation at large. The Bill also carries upright provisions for guarantee of employment to one member of the affected family due to acquisition of land and power to the judiciary to take cognizance of officials committing mistakes.

To the sadness of Indian legislature, since more than two decades, the political party with majority in the Lok Sabha has always struggled for backing in the Rajya Sabha, a weird and unfavorable situation that has only accorded power to illicit politicians, and has made it practically unmanageable for governments to bring pro-growth legislations. In the past, we have seen ruling parties showering opposition leaders in Rajya Sabha with perks like immunity from CBI probe, bungalows in Delhi's elite localities and their inclusion in the cabinet. For PM Modi, it is time to rise above these tactics and pave way for prolific legislations by employing astute and honest deeds. For the members of the Rajya Sabha, it is a pure misconduct and misuse of their offices if works of government chosen by the public at large are hampered just for pity political paybacks.

Writers, and independent analysts and advisors do warn of imprudent decisions taken by governments, which ought to be paid heed to. I, in my article, 'New Land Acquisition Law-Merits and Concerns' dated 15th April 2014, pointed out flaws in the Right to Fair Compensation and Transparency in Land Acquisition, Rehabilitation and Resettlement Act, 2013. Hereunder is a brief transcript.

"The new government that will be looked upon as the driving force for infrastructural development will have to face the challenges brought in by this new piece of legislation. The real intention of urbanization and industrialization can thus remain unachieved.

The upcoming union government would be clueless to manage something that has promised too much for land owners who would now resist to any modifications, with hindrance to the much-needed infrastructural and economic growth."

(Posted on blog on 3 April, 2015)

□

Definition of 'Good Days'

In case we were anticipating that commodity prices would decline to the level prevailing in 1950s; or if we foresaw that basic necessities, along with a few add-ons would come in a 'free-of-cost package' post the formation of the Modi-led union government, the mistake is ours. 'Good days' as proposed by the BJP during pre-poll milieu no way predetermined any drop in the rates of sugar, diesel, or for that matter the rail fares. I believe that 'affordability' to every Indian with respect to shelter, food, clothing, education, and security was what that embraced the definition of 'good days'. Unluckily, the opponents are visionless to observe any revolution.

Tell me what shall your action plan be when your savings and earnings have continuously failed to match steps with your spending? Would you allow your family to still spend recklessly, or would you plan for ways that can enhance your inflows so as to stand tough as against the future outflows? Similar is the position of the new government at the center which has inherited a paralyzed economy, wherein resources were made available to corporates at throwaway rates, non-contributories were allowed to increase the demand of products by allowing them groundless subsidies, and nil management techniques were put in place.

The new government commenced operations by sending across a cordial as well as tough message to neighboring nations, realizing their vitality in the functioning of Indian economy.'Good days' did not promise that Pakistan would sign a Memorandum of Understanding with India with respect to Kashmir and terrorism; however Nawaz Sharif's visit to India can be viewed as the beginning of a better tomorrow. Unlike former Prime Ministers of India, Mr. Modi accorded supreme prominence to country like Bhutan and scheduled his first overseas tour to this nation. For sure, today neighbors are moreconcerned and welcoming than ever.

The PMO has been working devotedly since past more than a month and the executives have no opportunity to forsake the assigned tasks. Even the cabinet ministers are being observed with respect to timely completion of missions, and unsubstantiated foreign tours of MPs and ministers have been contained. When did you last hear about any training programme for newly elected MPs, except the one we witnessed when U.P. cabinet ministers attended unworkable session overseas at the time when the state was being harassed by lawbreakers? Today, armed forces, bureaucrats, ministries, and ISRO are all passionate for future endeavors.

Now those roaring over the hiked rail fares or onion and petrol prices shall study the underlying factors for the increase in rates. Only a structured and sturdy economy can substantiate the survival of 125 crore Indians, hence false perks like subsidy and unstructured fares can serve no purpose. Remember, a government is not just a price-changer; it is an administrative body that is accountable for resourceful functioning of the economy. Thus, 'good days' are not the ones wherein you can buy products at lesser price; rather 'power to all' with robust economic base is what that constitutes good days. Stop expecting like always, rather become participative.

(Posted on blog on 2 July, 2014)

□

Is AAP Heading Towards Devastation

The bottom line is that you assured people of utmost democracy, power in the hands of people and uncompromised transparency, venality to find no place. And the condition today is that those who backed the AAP ideology are feeling robbed. The protest that was against dynasty rule, corruption, lack of transparency, misuse of public wealth got a new shape when the faces of Anna's demonstration founded a political party, saying that there cannot be any other way than to be a part of this dirty cluster so as to clean Indian politics. In case names would have fulfilled the aspirations of voters, I am sure that Bahujan Samaj Party would have bettered the lives of Dalit and backward castes, may be reservation would no longer be desirable, and Samajwadi Party, Janata Dal United, Nationalist Congress Party and Jharkhand Vikas Morcha would have delivered a state of social democracy, public ownership, progression and of course, true secularism. The irony, however, is that names are just an indicative of your ideology, just as the 'Aam Aadmi Party' seeking authorities from the common man of India, and the battle between names and delivery is far than achieved in Indian politics.

Stings, counter-stings, allegations, counter-allegations are all now a part of the party that phenomenally won voters' mandate in the Delhi legislative polls of 2015. Power has become the only objective of members, the self-proclaimed volunteers, and the divide has come into the public domain, something that is taking away the fundamentals for which people voted in favor of the AAP. While in the last ruling, AAP leaders alleged that Congress and BJP aren't enabling them to bring the Jan Lokpal Bill, in the present run, Delhi CM sworn-in on the 14th of January 2015, and after two and a half months of ruling, we have seen no deliberations on this Bill, or any practical alterations to the long standing issues of the state. Now the situation has become worst, a group that claimed that all its members, be it Arvind Kejriwal, Kumar Vishwas, Yogendra Yadav or Prashant Bhushan are the pillars rendering forte to the sole aim of achieving people's rule in the country, has turned severely hostile, self-destructive and alienated. The ouster of two of the senior most members and drivers of AAP may appear as win to Kejriwal's camp, but let me remind you that your feat was allied with people's betterment, something that has been left utterly unheeded since you assumed rule in the state.

Mayawati, Nehru-Gandhi Parivar, Jayalalithaa and Lalu Prasad Yadav may differ in the Parliament over proposals for new Acts and amendments, but they all share something in common-minimum democracy in their respective political parties and concentration of authority in one person/family. I can remember two events in the Indian political setup that turned the normal trend and substantiated that autocracy and perpetuation cannot survive for long in a democracy-one was the rise of the Janata Dal and defeat of Indira Gandhi-led Congress, and the other was a clear mandate to Modi-led BJP in last Lok Sabha polls. While the latter is proving productive in all respects, the former saw abrupt rise of regional and vote-bank politics, split of power in hands of avaricious leaders and ensuing decline in development. The crucial question now is 'Will AAP land up as another BSP of Mayawati or will it reprise the crumbling of Janata Dal?' And if the answer is a 'Yes' to any of these two parts, I am afraid that the change anticipated by Delhi voters will end up in yet another five years of loot and devastation.

It is clear that the fraction which is losing in this AAP's internal rift is Delhi's public and the fraction winning is unproductive MLAs who are free from questions on development, and the corruption beneath. Along with on stake are the funds of people who donate to AAP thinking that money will be utilized in promoting good politics and governance. And finally is the hope of poor and backward castes that extended inclusive support to AAP but any of their sorrows doesn't seem to end, at least in the near future. Protesting the measures of the ruling government and running a government are two entirely different aspects, you were good when you protested, but the rush of winning over the political battleground has landed you in a deep crisis, and to the sadness, this has come when you are supposed to spend every single minute in re-framing the social, economic and administrative domain of Delhi. I can remember days when at the inception of the AAP, volunteers and supporters of Anna's movement against corruption were filled with high positivity, and to the contrary today, AAP has become a new entry in the long list of political parties of India that have so much to assure in their manifestos but in actuality they are the primary killers of growth, equality and secularism.

Dear CM of Delhi, be the change that you wanted to bring, be the flag-bearer in the race for all-inclusive prosperity and nation's much-needed supremacy. BSP, Congress and others may have learnt the lesson late; you cannot expect such favors, since the expectations and level of shrewdness of voters have changed drastically in past couple of years. It is high time that you focus more on the tasks associated with the office of the CM of Delhi, not with the office of AAP's convener.

(Posted on blog on 31 March, 2015)

□

Section 370 – A Gift by a PM to an Ambitious Ruler

Was the inclusion of article 370 in the Constitution of India backed by extreme gravity, or was it a way to accomplish the dreams of a striving ruler? It is said that Sheikh Abdullah, who shared close vibes with Mahatma Gandhi, approached the then PM Pandit Nehru with a view to outshining Maharaja Hari Singh for gaining absolute control and accomplishing the insertion of article 370, which however was opposed by the key driving force behind the Constitution, Dr. B.R. Ambedkar. Though deterred by many socialists and prudent personalities, the section helped the state own a distinct status and the residents therein now live under separate set of laws, which includes ownership of property, citizenship and fundamental rights. Above all is a separate Constitution. The defense, foreign affairs, finance, and communication domains, however, are under the administration of the union government.

What could have been the motive of our representatives to afford a state, which is a part of Indian soil, with such extraordinary rights? The Congress, which was challenged by the then Hindu backed associations, could have thought of winning the heart of minorities by extending privileges that comprehensively stand biased till date. Ever since, this article and the conflicts of Kashmir have been much-talked about, however, the political leaders have probably overlooked the solemnity of this subject. Leaders, quite often, disremember that the environment, which they desire to create, witnesses general public as key constituent. At large, the beneficiaries or the sufferers of the acts of our so-called secular leaders are the ones who often are unaware of cause of conflict.

Now let us consider a fact that has almost remained concealed from the general public since decades. In the month of May in 1954, the Pandit Nehru-led union government amended the article 35 of the Indian Constitution and added 35A, which extended to the state government of J&K the right to deny citizenship rights, and apply any restrictions with respect to employment under the state government, acquisition of immovable property and right to scholarship or other aids, no matter how unjust these measures are. The untenable article has helped the J&K government to enforce any and every limitation on the rights of Hindu migrants from West Pakistan who have been denied the citizenship. Was this never a concern for the Nehru-led government or the descendants of the so-called secular Congress that talks of prosperity of all?

Vital to note, section 6 of the J&K Constitution allows the state government to recognize Muslims, who migrated from the state to Pakistan, however re-migrated to the state thereafter, as citizens. Thus, the article 370, along with the article 35A is what has given the state government the power to do any favors or even injustice. Is country within a country an admissible equation? The temporary nature of article 370 can be comprehended by the fact that the President has the power to abrogate this post consulting the constituent assembly, which was disbanded in 1957. More the time lapses more will be the damage caused. The gift of Nehru to the ambitious ruler, Abdullah no longer finds space in the era of social and political justice.

The BJP that has almost out shined every other political group and is on the verge of forming the government at the center has advocated the annulment of article 370 ever since its inception. Though the measure would not be that easy to implement, let us know the backdrop of the viewpoint of BJP. Dr. Shyama Prasad Mukherjee, the person who devoted his life for securing equitable rights for all communities in the state of J&K, has left behind a goal for the descendants of the BJP. Plus, when we talk of the welfare and betterment of national minorities, why aren't we concerned about the minority community of J&K? Is minority at the national level the only community that seeks special kindness? You must agree with the fact that prosperity of any state cannot be thought of without bringing in economic viability.

It is a known fact of economics that large number of participants and contributories enhance the viability of any project. 'Economies of scale' is what every business enterprise wants to attain so as to reduce the costs and uplift the profitability. As a distinct state with abundant restrictions in place and with non-applicability of many vital Acts, the state of J&K can rarely achieve the goal of economies of scale. And, if the state could have, the rulers not would have been dependent on the Indian government for seeking assistance in terms of infrastructure, security, and food supply. Vital to note that the Constitution of J&K states that the state is an integral part of India-A clause that discloses the intention of the Constitution makers who knew that the state could not stand even for a day without the aid of the union government of India.

The 'Ultras' (extremists) of J&K many a times advocate comprehensive independence to the state, while a few among them even favor Kashmir's accession to Pakistan. Whom are they fighting for? The general public, anywhere in the world, would favor development and enhanced prospects to earn. Let us remember that in case the Indian armed forces are being blamed for the harassment of Kashmiri Muslims, the insurgents backed by the ISI are equitably responsible for the forced eviction of Kashmiri Pandits. 'Kashmiriyat', which fundamentally meant upholding the integrity of all Kashmiris, has been illicitly used to eradicate the minorities of Kashmir and establishing a Taliban-influenced milieu. Not much can be expected out of Pakistan, which has unlawfully occupied the portion of Indian soil.

Now, what can the solution be? Would the abrogation of article 370 and article 35A serve any purpose, or would it be better to let the state live on its own? In case the state would have the capability to prosper on its own, the residents would not have migrated to other states for want of education and earning prospects. Hence, a consensus must be achieved by our political groups, which represent the general public, with a view to putting an end to a scheme that is intolerable. The residents too in turn are supposed to liaise with the system that appears to be the best in view of uncountable bottlenecks. The political leaders, rather than engaging themselves in arguments, must strive to achieve the goal of real prosperity of the state as well of those who have been forced to vacate their homeland. The state, which has been the center of conflicts and mass killings since decades, now urges for prompt and real reforms.

(Posted on blog on 1 May, 2014)

□

The Dirty Politics of a Century-old Party–Not Again

When almost every opinion poll has predicted that the Congress would not even cross the 100 mark in the polls of 2014, the more than a century-old party is expected to maintain utmost sportsman spirit. However, considering itself as the sole body which can rule the nation, the party is likely to play another dirty game. Surely, the habit of being in power is tough to part with. The words of senior leaders of Congress have clarified that the party can go to any probable extent to stop Narendra Modi from being the administrator of the nation. Extending support to the so-called secular third front is clearly the agenda of the party, howsoever destructive this may be. Can we welcome such an absurd equation, yet again?

And the regional political parties, along with the Left front have been dreaming to witness a day when any one of their leaders can hold the office of Prime Minister. What national agenda does Samajwadi Party has, or for that matter the Left front has? Restricted to their respective states of operations, these groups have ambiguously projected their top leaders as the prime ministerial candidates. Ranging from Mayawati to Mulayam Singh and Mamta Banerjee to Jayalalitha, everyone can see hope on the basis that Congress would not be acceptable again and the BJP would fall short of numbers due to unfavorable attitude of particular communities.

The Congress is at the verge of its most appalling failure, which would even outshine the defeat in 1977 polls when Jayaprakash Narayan-influenced Janta Party restricted Congress to 153 seats. Vital to note, the Congress then was able to perform only in the south, which today looks to be floating in Modi's wave of development, along with north, east and west regions. The Congress, rather than locating the causes of such a cataclysm of the party and working on reinventing the organizational as well as the ethical structure, is ready to play the most unwanted game in the democracy. Alleging that the party would extend support to an anti-communal front, the key motive is to prevent BJP from governing the nation, and then pulling off the support.

Our crafty political groups can come up with any mathematical formula to give the resultant figure above 272. Surely, the Congress has the requisite know-how to perform such forbidden acts, time and again. Extending support to the H. D. Deve Gowda-led front and a subsequent pull off which resulted in the downfall of the government was a part of this episode. Other instances include the betrayal of the party to Charan Singh; extension of support to the 8th PM of India, Chandra Shekhar and subsequent pull off on the grounds that his government was spying on Rajiv Gandhi; and the rise and fall of Inder Kumar Gujral. Political volatility was created at every instance which can be regarded as a curse for the democracy.

Yet again, the Congress is heading towards the same path. And the hunger of becoming the topmost decision-maker of the nation runs within the leader of every political group. Shall the general public allow such dirty coalition knowing the urgency of reforms? Shouldn't the Congress, instead of coming up with such unsolicited propositions, conduct a self-assessment programme so as to undertake corrective measures within the party? The ultimate evaluator is the public. Tough and clear message has to be delivered to our so-called secular advocates so as to assure that they come up with real and moral goals at the subsequent occasion. The only way out to curb the Congress from creating a political chaos is 'the awakening of voters'.

(Posted on blog on 3 May, 2014)

□

Shouldn't Accountability Track Promises of the Manifesto?

How often do we see political leaders talk about or even remember the promises made in the election manifesto of their party? And, have we ever tried to question or evaluate the works undertaken by any Government with respect to the declarations made prior to forming the Government? To be honest, not many of us seem to care about the assurances given in the manifesto of the political groups. Definitely, we are bound to believe that the booklet with handsome promises is of no significance.

To discuss further, it is vital to understand what an election manifesto represents. The manifesto holds the intentions, views, and goals of the political group in a published format. Plus, it promotes new ideas and depicts the vision to bring in changes which the publishing party feels are necessary for the prosperity of general public. In other words, the manifesto must reflect the real intentions of the political party and the assurances made must be realistic and feasible. The picture here doesn't seem to be the same. Let us now evaluate the manifestos and the actual works undertaken by the political parties.

The state elections of Delhi witnessed the emergence of a political party that claimed to eradicate corruption and other social, economic and political curses once it comes to power. 'Jan Lokpal by December 29', '700 liters of free water', 'Commando force for women safety', and 'Better health and education' are some of the promises made in the party's election manifesto. Now, I feel they forgot to add 'Terms and Conditions apply'. While studying management, we are taught about planning for contingencies and surprises. However, the AAP did not make any strategy in case a coalition Government comes into the picture. So, we should understand why the party couldn't introduce the Jan Lokpal Bill by December 29. We should also not fall into the descriptive definition of what 'better health and education' stands for. As for AAP, such words and assurances were enough to lure voters and gather support.

The Manifesto of the Congress party for the upcoming polls again talks about strengthening and uplifting the backward classes, poor, and minority. Plus, it promises adequate health, accommodation, and pension services to 700 million people. Can anyone ask the party leaders how would they bring in such reforms? And, when the task of ruling the nation was undertaken by the Congress for almost 60 years, shouldn't these issues been sorted out much earlier than after 67 years of democracy?

It is easy to make promises and even easier for the political parties to overlook these. The instructions of the Supreme Court and the guidelines of the Election Commission in no way are able to restrict parties from luring voters with dishonest assurances. This calls for stringent measures and the setting up of a legislative body that must assess the performance of the Government in view of the promises made in the election manifesto. Political parties and their leaders must be accountable to deliver what was assured to the voters and any deviations must be penalized. Surely, the manifestos would reflect the real intents of the parties post such measures, which in turn would ensure adequate reforms and elevated prosperity.

(Posted on blog on 31 March, 2014)

□

Jail or Parliament – Where should Law-violators be?

The Constitution of India paved way for the Legislature to frame laws with a view to delivering a prosperous and peaceful state. The Union Governments acted fairly to enrich the country with distinctive laws that can safeguard the interests of public at large. The Code of Civil Procedure and the Code of Criminal Procedure are a part of this module. The supreme law-making body is expected to comprise of people with vision, aptitude, and above all integrity. The irony is that approximately 30 percent of the constituents of the 15th Lok Sabha were those accused of acute violations of law-forgery, theft, murder, and much more. Is the nation, which promises to be the most developed state 10 years down the line, anticipating reforms from such members of the Parliament? We have seen cash floating in the House with MPs accused of accepting bribe to withdraw support; severe cases of corruption; charges of rapes; and allegations of encouraging communal riots. What else are we waiting for? While three wings have been bearing on their shoulders the accountability to put across a state that treats all citizens alike and punishes the ones who hinder peace and sovereignty, not much has been delivered. The Judiciary has repeatedly made constructive attempts to uphold the dignity of the Parliament; however the Legislature and the Executive wings have been supportive to law-breakers.

With unanimous approach, the members of Parliament have trimmed down the principles laid down by the Judiciary; and the Executive wing on the other hand cannot be expected to do much as it is dependant on the Legislative body. Misuse of investigating agencies, elimination of charges against those involved in communal violence, and extended support to hardcore criminals have been the steps undertaken recently by the Union as well as distinctive State Governments. Misuse of power is easy and evasion is much easier. Let's talk about the solutions now. Voters have immense power to curb the influence and presence of law-breakers in the Parliament. Awareness and partition from self-centered perquisites would definitely bring in the much-awaited reforms. Why are we voting for those who have been charged with grave offences and can surely commit more with our support? Have we been tempted towards policies and packages for our particular community/caste? YES. Remember, the leaders who have been the key drawbacks in the development and growth of the nation, have been backed by the support of society. To welcome change, cast your vote, however restrain from voting for your caste in view of materialistic perks. Let simplicity and commitment win the race in the upcoming polls.

Extensive works shall be undertaken by the political parties, of which the most important is to nominate reliable candidates. Why despite distinct evidences, candidates are being nominated for elections? Shouldn't the Constitution of political parties be drafted in such a manner so as to shut every door for these leaders? What should then be the criteria of selection? Education teaches morality, if not completely, to some extent. Why shouldn't a questionnaire be prepared and responses gathered from prospective candidates? Educational background, social achievements, vision, and the goals after being selected should be asked. People with lesser academic knowledge can surely be given a chance by paying heed to past social works undertaken. The parties must make their selection criteria transparent, which will also assure that the chosen ones receive admirable response from the public during polls. Post winning, the Government must convince people with their hard work, and not through benefits showered on particular class/religion of voters. MPs that are charged with incidences of breaking the law of the state must be delivered with a Show Cause notice as to why their membership should not be terminated. Productive measures shall be resorted to with a view to upholding the dignity of the House.

(Posted on blog on 15 March, 2014)

□

Bottlenecks in the Efficiency of the UPA-led Union Government

The Constitution of India is principally federal with certain unitary features – Demanding unified endeavors from the Union and State Governments for collective prosperity of nation. Let us consider the performance of the past 10 years of the governance of United Progressive Alliance (UPA), a coalition of left political parties formed after the general elections of 2004. Absolute majority wasn't won by either of the political parties, which led the UPA rely on the external support from regional political parties for ensuring that the Government maintains the confidence of the Indian Parliament. The first prominent withdrawal was witnessed on the 8th of July 2008 when the Communist Party of India-Marxist (CPI-M) announced their discontinuance of support over the verdict of the Union Government to approve the Indo-U.S. Nuclear Deal (The question is wasn't this deal in the interest of nation?). On numerous other occasions, which include quitting of the BSP on the 21st of June 2008, move of MDMK on the 16th of March 2007, and move of the People's Democratic Party on 4th of January 2009, the nation witnessed the instability of the Government. Enumerated hereunder are the withdrawals that led to weakening the Union Government and slowing the pace of development.

1. TRS, Telangana Rashtra Samiti led by K. Chandrashekhar Rao was the foremost party to quit the alliance when party's president resigned from his Lok Sabha seat.
2. MDMK tied a knot with AIADMK in the state elections of Tamil Nadu and declared its withdrawal on the 16th of March 2007.
3. Pattali Makkal Katchi withdrew support in March 2009 and joined the AIADMK led front.

4. Accusing the Andhra Pradesh Government of communal conduct, the AIMIM's leader Asaduddin Owaisi quitted the alliance in 2012.
5. Mamta Banerjee after sequences of yes and no finally withdrew support on the 18th of September 2012 stating that TMC would not favor hike in prices of diesel, and FDI in retail.
6. Jharkhand Vikas Morcha withdrew support in October 2012 claiming the same basis as TMC.
7. Post the resignation of two MPs of DMK in 2012 due to severe charges of corruption, DMK moved from the UPA in March 2013.

Were all these moves for the benefit of the nation as a whole? The answer to this question isn't that complicated. Mayawati accused the Government of misusing the Investigating Agency and attempting to implicate her in the Taj Corridor instance. Mehbooba Mufti opposed the support of the Congress for the National Conference Government in J&K-led by Omar Abdullah. Where is the interest of the common man of India? At the initial stage let us also consider the diversity and communal richness of the country. Considering all the linguistic, communal, and ethnic multiplicities, management is a tough task. Plus, with a few Islamic fundamentalists who hold their own perception about the religion and with the emergence of a new class of revolutionaries 'the Maoists', the idea of a secular Constitution is at stake. Drafting and implementing of policies has become tougher as ever. When one set of people is looking forward to a policy that can control the ever-rising inflation and interest rates, another section of society hunts for reservation and subsidies – And above all is the reliance of the Union Government on the alliance partners. It is easy to conclude that the Union Government of a nation like India needs to be stringent and reasonable at the same time. Promoting the failures is effortless; however comprehending the underlying causes is hard. Post evaluating the deliveries of the UPA-led Union Government, we can spot the authentic bottlenecks.

One of these is the coalition of political parties with a motive to leading the state. Can anyone validate the instance when one of the coalition partners, Trinamool Congress led by Mamta Banerjee, prevented the Government from agreeing to share the water of the river Teesta with Bangladesh? The people of India are motivated to vote for pity interests while the bona fide interests of the nation are paid no heed to. The outcome is apparent. From the instances mentioned earlier, we can conclude that the Government at the centre has to rely on the support of regional political parties that employ illicit ways to extract funds and policies for a particular community/vicinity. To safeguard the Government, misuse of investigating agencies cannot also be overlooked. With the move of Trinamool Congress, the UPA had to rely extensively on the support of the Samajwadi Party led by Mulayam Singh Yadav and the Bahujan Samaj Party led by Mayawati. Compromises and delays in the implementation of valuable policies are clear outcomes of this affiliation.

Let's now talk about some visible solutions. In the interest of the nation as a whole, the structure and foundation of the Union Government has to be sturdy. To welcome constructive reforms, people have to acknowledge the fact that development follows stability. To allow the Government take swift decisions and implement measures that can bring in all-inclusive prosperity; we have to move away from our pity personal/communal interests. Regional parties that are backed by the support of a particular caste/religion should not be allowed to hamper the permanence of the Government at the centre. A voter must keep in mind that the Lok Sabha Polls take into consideration the entire of the diversity of nation – A stable Government can surely take quick and effective measures for the promotion of all castes and religions. Shouldn't we allow the UPA and its young leaders to prove their ability to lead the nation with our full-fledged support? The sooner we understand, the better we get.

(Posted on blog on 18 February, 2014)

□

Fostering Governance

RSS-BJP Meet – A Commendable Roadmap

Since coming into power in 2014, the BJP government has not only speeded up administrative tasks, the men in power have substantiated that they aren't a pack of hounds, rather are a commandingly motivated group that is assuredly heading towards the desired direction. Appraisals and assessments during the execution of plan not only reminds about any misses in the passage, these exercises also help steering clear of unwanted mistakes and to realize the expectations of people you are liable to. What is wrong if one of the world's most noteworthy voluntary charitable organization, the Rashtriya Swayamsevak Sangh (RSS), meets country's topmost decision-makers to consult and guide them towards a constructive roadmap for the future?

As alleged by some as unconstitutional, to be specific, by one from the pack of hounds in whose hands Delhi is scuffling at the moment, the RSS-BJP meet held on 2-4 September 2015, may have called for some criticisms, more so when the same is seen with the eyes of muddy Indian political arena, the truth is that this coming together is as much necessary and beneficial as are all other mid-term evaluations of government schemes and programmes. News reports do carry the facts of the meet, which embraces discussion over key social and political matters, including One Rank One Pension (OROP), border issue with Bangladesh and China, and talks over militancy concerns in Kashmir. When ministers along with persons of acumen from the RSS put across opinions and anticipations, the outcome wouldn't be futile like one of the Congress top shots attempting to score some political numbers through visits to OROP and FTII protest sites, indeed, the result will be practical answers to matters concerned with the society and economy.

Why is it Senseless to Term the Meet Illegitimate?

Many of us send proposals to the government when the law-makers plan a new law or an amendment to any existing legislation is proposed and the same is put on ministry's website for suggestions from the general public and other stakeholders. This is called participative and transparent governance, and sound ideas are considered to augment the overall productivity of the country. On similar lines, the RSS, an organization that through millions of its volunteers undertakes tasks of social betterment and is also the ideological mentor of the ruling government, when deliberates over prevailing issues with persons capable to devise and introduce new initiatives, problems and potentials are shared, legitimate answers are located and policy-makers are reminded of their indispensable duty of serving the citizens at the earliest and to the fullest.

A Comparison with the Past

The UPA rule witnessed a weak Prime Minister Office and concentration of power with a handful of people who imposed incompetent and biased policy initiatives on the nation. The committees and task forces formed during such time were a mere formality to refer key issues to specialized group of people, in fact, the decisions flowed from a single powerhouse. And alike is the milieu today with the AAP government, one or two men are in-charge of all possible tasks; this has led to people with dignity and sense of honesty to quit the party and expose one-man dictatorship within the group. In politics, it has been a routine to limit decision-making within a small cluster or family, more so because this doesn't let others to grow and hence demand any shift from ineffectual leaders. Isn't the same a valid reason why the Congress could not look beyond one family when it comes to electing party's President and Vice-President? Had there been an independent and shrewd group of evaluators and advisors, a sense of responsibility and delivery would have been a part of Congress' way of governance.

Why to Expect and not Lend Ears to False Allegations

Opposition parties and the so-called secular groups have repeatedly targeted RSS' right-wing belief denying the crucial role of the cadre in improving socio-economic and political scene of India. Voters who exceedingly backed the Modi-led BJP in 2014 and are satisfied enough today owing to government's deliveries in past more than one year shall also thank the RSS volunteers who communicated BJP's candidature to far-flung areas and helped the party secure a strong majority in the Lok Sabha, a pre-requisite for healthy governance. The RSS leaders as well as the bottom-most volunteers have chosen to stay away from active politics, which makes them eligible to represent the common man of India and ask the ruling government for quick corrections in the society. If at all the doubts are over the alleged pro-Hindu approach and article of faith of the RSS, people are to know that during the RSS-BJP meet, rehabilitation of Kashmir's civilians injured during militant and cross-border attacks is a significant topic of deliberation and the same calls for advancement of non-Hindus of the valley.

Since decades, opposition parties and their leaders have relied upon anti-government protests to regain public support. The OROP, FTII, land bill, amendment to labor laws and such other matters dominant today have also found illicit backing from opposition leaders. On the contrary, the RSS has assessed these subjects in view of all feasible possibilities and for the actual advantage of all and not just a particular class or cluster. When ministers discuss tasks and ideas with RSS leaders and debate what steps shall be taken to overcome barriers to success, the underlying bonuses accrue to the common people of India, not to political or corporate entities.

This is no Assessment, This is Coordination

No one has the constitutional right to call upon ruling ministers and assess or guide their working. This notion is duly honored during these deliberations and the attempt is to coordinate and harmonize rather than impose any special or unjustified expectations on the people in power. RSS does not have any extraordinary demands to be shared, what at all they are concerned with is how governance can be made more inclusive, participatory and just. From the people of Arunachal Pradesh and states sharing border with Bangladesh to the pain of army veterans and Kashmir residents, the points of discussion touch common spheres of our lives and the liability of the government to provide resolutions. In no sense, as purported by a former Jammu and Kashmir Chief Minister, this RSS-BJP meet can be termed as performance appraisal of the government. Indians shall be contented that a social organization is making sincere endeavors in discussing issues with leaders who carry the ideology of RSS, which shouldn't be a grievance so long as this ideology is unprejudiced, sensible and evenhanded, something we can be certain of owing to the past record of the organization.

Be assured that such form of inclusive governance, as is seen during such instances, will come as a shock to those political parties which are habitual to receiving dictates from a sole controller. For those who understand how periodic deliberations improve delivery mechanism and policy making, the RSS-BJP meet is a moment to cherish, not complain.

If someone claims that such meetings defy government's privacy to foreign relations and defence, they are to know that to make such meets possible there stands no need for the ministers and their staff to carry confidential papers for any sort of presentation. The motive of the RSS-BJP meet is clear and concrete-The government is chosen by the people to make their lives better and this task is to be accomplished in a limited period of five years. After regular intervals, the government shall be reminded of people's hopes, past policies weighed in light of their efficiency, and a roadmap for future laid to serve as a tentative guide for policy-makers. RSS is capably and diligently undertaking this work and deserves a pat on the back for the same.

(Posted on blog on 4 September, 2015)

□

Is the Narendra Modi Government a Suit-Boot ki Sarkar?

Barbs and Jibes

As soon as he returned after a two month-vacation at some undisclosed destination early this year, Congress Vice President Rahul Gandhi donned the war paint of a combative and invigorated politician and went for the jugular of the Prime Minister. No less. After all, he is the scion of the Nehru-Gandhi family, which seems to believe it is the only Indian family vested with the privileges to rule the nation.

Rahul had, in fact, chosen his adversary even before the fateful Lok Sabha polls of 2014 by scoffing at and heaping scorn on BJP's Prime Ministerial candidate Narendra Modi. How could a measly tea boy who had the 'dubious' distinction of hobnobbing with the RSS, become India's Prime Minister, he asked in a querulous voice.

Wasn't Narendra Modi a Hitler and a merchant of death? How could the good people of India repose faith in such a person who lacked the right pedigree and was eminently unsuitable for the job? He interposed such questions with regard to Modi's credentials and eligibility for the highest political office of the land. Rahul then decided to travel far and wide and tell people of the nation about the 'evil lurking around the corner' aspiring to become India's next Prime Minister.

Travel he did and told the people of the 'impending disaster' too. But what he failed to do was to tell the people who UPA was proposing to anoint as the next PM. According to him, people should simply vote for the UPA. Once UPA returned to power for the third time straight, the Congress parliamentary party would decide who is to become the PM. Simple and straight. As for himself, he would not mind shouldering any responsibility that his party deemed fit to offer him, which is how he presented it to the Indian voters.

What was left unsaid, but was clearly understood by the people was that the next PM would be decided by the Congress High Command, a euphemism for the mother-son duo of the ruling family, as had always been the practice in the past. In all probability, it would likely be a fall guy like Manmohan Singh who would be foisted by the Sonia-Rahul duo, who was happy calling the shots from behind the scene.

The electorate did not, however, fall for his gambit and preferred the more direct and forthcoming approach of the BJP, which had named its Prime Ministerial candidate. Modi had already arrived on the national scene in a big way, having captured the imagination of the people of the nation with his Gujarat model of development and pan-India vision vis-a-vis the other regional satraps who lacked a roadmap for the country's progress and a blueprint for the development of its economy.

All that the UPA had to offer against NDA's development-based program of action was a moth-eaten one-point agenda of their traditional 'Secularism' plank. The people saw through their game and accorded the UPA at the General Elections of 2014 the contemptuous cold shoulder that they richly deserved.

UPA versus NDA

A downright rejection by the people, first at the Centre and then in a series of state-level elections, did not, however, deter the Congress Party for far too long from making it difficult for the NDA to have a free rein at the Centre, despite the latter's humongous majority in the Lok Sabha. The UPA in general, and Rahul Gandhi in particular, focused on the NDA's Achilles Heel of inadequate numbers in the Rajya Sabha and started making it virtually impossible for healthy parliamentary debates to take place and some of the crucial legislations to be passed. The Congress Vice President led the shouting brigade from the front and did not flinch from leveling personal attacks on the Prime Minister.

Character Assassination

Rahul dubbed Narendra Modi's hallmark quality of self-confidence as vanity and narcissism. Instead of taking on the government on its policies upfront, he went for the soft option of character assassination of his favourite bugbear. He conveniently forgot that Modi had risen to dizzying heights of political power from less than a modest social background by sheer dint of hard work as a disciplined party worker and with determination that had lasted over four decades coupled with exemplary developmental work as the Chief Minister of a State which scored over several others in economic and social developmental indices.

Rahul criticized Modi of grabbing power by means of a publicity blitzkrieg, purportedly funded by corporate houses, which had allegedly sidled up to him in the hope that he would return them favours after coming to power at the Centre. Based on these flawed premises, Rahul's strategy was to take potshots at the Prime Minister, dent his pristine image, which was unmatched by any leader of the current crop. He thus tried his best to pull down Modi from the pedestal of high moral grounds, make him nervous and lose poise, which would have probably resulted in the latter making a faux pas, much to the glee of the Congress Party.

Rahul's Strategy

Instead of waiting for a major policy goof-up, Rahul unveiled a three-pronged strategy of provoke, shoot and scoot. So he just kept on looking for a chink in the armour. How could US President Barack Obama's second visit to India, which was directly attributed to a diplomatic coup by Modi, be allowed to be uneventful? So he decided to pick on Modi's suit, which looked distinct with his name embroidered all over and unleashed a tirade, including the following.

Rahul called it expensive in terms of cost, but cheap in terms of taste. What a vain person had the suit made the PM! Such narcissism! Such audacity on the part of the leader of a nation which had still not attained the stature of an equal participant at the high table of the world's economic power blocs! Such folly on the part of a man who dared to believe clothes made him and paraded around in cheap, vulgar clothes which reflected poor taste, like a proud peacock! How did he afford the expensive suit in the first place?

How could the people trust their money with such a man who shamelessly splurged money on symbols of vanity? If it had been presented to him, it must be by some industrialist or businessman with an axe to grind. Dig deep enough to find muck. In any case, let us not lose time in charging him of impropriety and lack of transparency before coming up with evidence or proof to make the charge stick.

Then Rahul creatively came up with a ballpark figure of ₹ 10 lakh as the cost of the suit and accused Modi of misusing public money on acquiring the symbol of his vanity, narcissism and megalomania. Till date, Rahul has neither come up with proof or evidence to substantiate his charge nor had the decency to own up to the baseless charges he made against the Prime Minister. That is so much for his intellectual honesty and credibility as a leader.

Sobriquet for the Government

Taking part in a debate on the agrarian crisis in Parliament in April this year, Rahul told the BJP representatives, "Yours is a government of big people, a suit-boot sarkar", in an obvious reference to Modi's suit that was the eye of a political storm during President Obama's visit in January this year. On protests from the BJP, he added, "The suit matter has ended, you have auctioned it, I will not talk about it. Happy? " So, Rahul officially declared his party position that the sordid suit matter had ended! Not because his charge made earlier that the Prime Minister had misused public money to the extent of ₹ 10 lakh could not be substantiated, but apparently because the suit had subsequently been auctioned off.

Rahul was solicitous enough to ask the BJP representatives if they were happy with the ending of the matter! How very gracious of this ignoramus and needler! If there indeed had been a misuse of public money on the part of the Prime Minister as he had charged, should Rahul have not pursued the matter to its logical conclusion with all the tenacity and resources at his command instead of magnanimously letting it 'end' with the suit's auction? Whether the BJP representatives were 'happy' or not about the closure of the matter, was Rahul not responsible for having caused a slur on Modi's name?

Was it all, at the end of the day, a simple matter of smoothening the ruffled feathers of the BJP with nary a thought about Modi's image and reputation? Did he not owe the people an explanation for announcing suo motu the 'end' of the matter which involved the 'stealing' of a large amount of public money? Was a quid pro quo involved here? Is this how the Prime Ministerial aspirant of Congress proposes to wind up his investigation into all the scams and scandals and make the Opposition ranks 'happy', in case he ever lands up in his dream job? That is a scary thought, indeed!

Accusations and Allegations by Rahul

Rahul accused the NDA government, which he derisively referred to as the 'acchhe din government', of failing the people and held it squarely responsible for pursuing an anti-farmers policy. And he made a series of other allegations and accusations including the following. The NDA government simply did not concern itself with the misery of the farmers in regions across the country, languishing under monumental debts owing to droughts, famines and hailstorms and driven to committing suicide. The Prime Minister was on a perpetual spree of foreign tours. Why was Modi not spending more time at home, to meet the farmers, hold their hands, commiserate with them and enact welfare schemes for their upliftment?

Rahul has been vehement about his party's determination not to allow the passage of the Land Acquisition Bill in the Rajya Sabha. In a bid to sound sympathetic with regard to the plight of poor farmers of the country, he falsely accused the government of first 'weakening' and then trying to smite by grabbing their land – all for the benefit of the influential industrialists, corrupt corporate houses and big businessmen and alleged that these are the very people who had funded Modi's pre-poll publicity campaign.

So according to him, India currently has a government that had come into being in the first place using the money power of the rich; a government of people who had sympathy and concern only for the rich; a government that worked for the rich and enacted laws to benefit them at the cost of the poor farmers of the country. Hence the sobriquet 'Suit-Boot ki Sarkar'!

Rahul has ever since been haranguing the government by castigating it with the sobriquet in his party meetings across the country to the amusement and titillation of the workers of his party and bemusement of the people at large – bemusement over such a bankrupt obsession with «Suit» by the Vice President of the oldest political party of the country while there were any number of crucial issues, ranging from terrorism at home to external threats, which begged urgent attention. Meanwhile, Rahul's sidekick Raj Babbar added «Loot» to his litany of charges and made the sobriquet «Suit-Boot-Loot ki Sarkar».

Failure of Congress

If in the eyes of Rahul, Narendra Modi and his political party were guilty of accepting financing from corporate houses and rich businessmen for their poll campaign in 2014, would he come forward and declare that he and his party were never beneficiaries of such a largesse from either the same or a different set of sources this time around or any other elections in the past? If both the NDA and the UPA had accepted funding from corporate houses, why should the latter pick on the former?

In any case, why had not the Congress Party which had been in power at the Centre for a total period of almost60 years not done anything with regard to prohibiting political parties fighting elections from accepting funding for their campaigns by corporate houses? Why is Rahul finding fault with the system of the functicning of political parties now, when his own party is playing the game by the same rules and is fully drenched in corruption, patronage, favouritism and abuse of power? Is it merely because of his party's loss of face in the elections?

Why not a Suit?

Now, at the face level of it, what is wrong or evil about a suit per se? Is it something which only rich people are supposed to wear and not meant for poor people? Is the Prime Minister of India expected to represent only the poor people and not industrialists and businessmen as well? Are those people who are clad in a suit, children of a lesser God? Is it wrong for a poor man to aspire for riches and be seen wearing a suit? Have the members of the Nehru-Gandhi family, starting with Jawaharlal Nehru down to Rahul and his brother-in-law, not been wearing suits?

Is it an unwritten law that the quintessential Indian politician should be only seen in a crumpled pajama-kurta and not in a crisp suit, whatever the occasion? In any case, when English has been adopted as an Indian language, why can't a suit be considered an Indian costume? Why the derisive urge on the part of Rahul to portray either the Prime Minister or the industrialists or businessmen as a butt of criticism for the mere act of wearing a suit?

Pro-farmers and Pro-poor Policies and Programs

Notwithstanding the merits of the Land Acquisition Bill and the benefits that will accrue to Indian farmers, what about the following pro-farmers and pro-poor policies and programs of the current NDA government, which Rahul has conveniently chosen to ignore?

- Enhanced Compensation for distressed Farmers due to crop damage
- Deen Dayal Upadhyaya Gram Jyoti Yojana
- Soil Health Card Scheme
- Pradhan Mantri Krishi Sinchai Yojana
- Jan Suraksha Schemes (PMJJBY, PMBSY, APY)
- Rashtriya Gokul Mission
- Pradhan Mantri Jan Dhan Yojana (World's largest Financial Inclusion Program)
- Pandit Deen Dayal Upadhyaya Shramev Jayate Karyakram
- Deen Dayal Upadhyaya Antyodaya Yojana
- Mission Housing for all
- Micro Units Development and Refinance Agency Bank (MUDRA Bank)

Time for Rahul to Reflect

Will it ever occur to Rahul Gandhi that the right thing to do would be for him to study these programs and policies with a critical eye for possible flaws, shortcomings or inadequacies and lack of dedication or commitment, if any, on the part of the NDA government in their implementation? Such a course of action that calls for extensive research, analysis and objective assessment on his part would fetch him the stature of a serious politician whose primary concern is for the development and progress of the nation and the welfare of the people.

Will Rahul Gandhi rise to the occasion and seize the opportunity to become richer in stature as a serious politician and thereby present the people a viable alternative to Narendra Modi as a people's leader or will he be merely contended with causing ripples in murky political waters with his provoke-shoot-and-scoot strategy? In any case, calling the government funny names for a strategy will only win him a few claps from his merry men and far from endearing him to the people make his stature not worth a picayune.

(Published in weekly magazine Uday India in Vol. VI, No. 35-36, 9-15 August, 2015 edition)

□

The Great Letdown of Delhi by the AAP

To understand how and why Arvind Kejriwal and his Aam Aadmi Party (AAP) government have let the people of Delhi down, one would do well to have as much of an understanding of the man himself and the dynamics of his brand of politics as possible.

The Man and the Party

An IIT-ian and a left-leaning political maverick, Arvind Kejriwal admittedly feels more comfortable holding dharnas and rallies than occupying a position of responsibility. He takes pride in calling himself a street fighter and a man of the masses. Yet he fought elections twice to become the Chief Minister of Delhi and once to become a Member of Parliament; if he had become an MP and his party garnered enough seats, he would not have fought shy of becoming the Prime Minister of our country.

He does not, however, truly believe in operating by the rules and norms of the system. He is a rabble rouser and a demagogue par excellence, given to dramatics. As a first-time Chief Minister, he had participated in dharnas and rallies organized by his Aam Aadmi Party (AAP). During the course of one such dharna just days before the Republic Day in 2014, he demonstrated that he had no compunction about holding up the traffic on a busy thoroughfare in the heart of the Capital city and slept on the roadside from where he signed files, much to the amusement and bewilderment of political observers and the common man alike.

Without any qualms, he proudly declared on camera that he was an anarchist. He openly hinted at a startling proposal to thwart the traditional Republic Day pageantry due shortly, where the US President was to be the special guest, by continuing to sit with his coterie and supporters on the road. He pooh-poohed the significance of the prestigious Republic Day celebrations and claimed that his theatrical display of power of the masses would make the occasion the best Republic Day celebration ever. He exhorted the policemen who were controlling the crowds to shed their uniform and join the demonstration. Nothing short of an open invitation to rebel!

The preposterous nature of the call made the people of the nation feel aghast with a sense of revulsion. That Kejriwal was not taken seriously came as a reflection of the people's sagacity and political maturity. It could not, however, be denied that he had brought matters to the precipice of anarchy on that momentous occasion.

No Ideology

A quick rundown on his brief track record as an active politician reveals beyond doubt that he lacks abiding faith in the democratic form of governance. His party lacks a clear-cut ideology. "Ideology is one for the pundits and the media to pontificate about, " says the party's website facetiously. He acts more like a fly-by-night politician whose concern is restricted at any given time to the burning issues of the day than like the responsible leader of a political party. He evidently lacks a vision, a game plan and a roadmap for the development and progress of our nation.

No Room for Dissent

His statements and activities smack of a remarkable degree of intolerance towards his political adversaries as well as his own party colleagues who have divergent views. He has used harsh, nay foul language, while talking about senior party colleagues like Prashant Bhushan, Yogendra Yadav and others who had protested against his autocratic style of functioning and had them unceremoniously thrown out of the party purportedly for indulging in anti-party activities. A classic case of equating a criticism of the party leader with an attack on the party itself, thus identifying the leader with the party and making the two synonymous – an egregious act of megalomania that did not exactly contribute to shoring up glory Kejriwal's way as a democratic leader!

Politics and Corruption

However, none of his inadequacies proved an impediment to Kejriwal's ability to bluster his way through and win the trust of the people of Delhi with the ease and élan of an experienced con artist or a mountebank. Exuding an air of moral superiority, he called every political party in the country corrupt and every politician a thief regardless of his political affiliation. These politicians and their parties were selfish and self-serving entities and beneficiaries of the largesse of rich industrialists, big business tycoons and unscrupulous hoarders of black money, he elaborated. Such people and parties would only serve their paymasters and never the common man, he sermonized.

Kejriwal pronounced them guilty of carrying on a sham democracy and held them squarely responsible for all the ills of the common man and the sorry state of affairs that prevailed in the country. He scoffed at the political system, which he said was incapable of producing good governance. He wanted a complete transformation of the system and transfusion of new blood into the body politic. He offered to revamp the system by becoming a part of it, rid it of corruption, give clean governance, improve the lot of the common man and make Delhi a model State.

A frontal assault against corruption was the main plank of his manifesto in 2014. He then promised to introduce the Jan Lokpal Bill within 15 days of assuming office, and spoke of bringing about Swaraj and reforms in key sectors like education and health. In actuality, however, he resigned after a brief 49-day period, complaining about non-cooperation from the Congress and the BJP in the passing of the Jan Lokpal Bill. Apparently, his strategy of governance was woven around the thumb rule that he would have everything or nothing. In short, being conscious of his inability to carry out his poll promises, he threw away the responsibility of governance giving the flimsiest of excuses and left the people of Delhi without a government.

Back to Delhi

Though he had been unable to discharge the duties of Delhi chief minister competently, he had started aspiring to become India's Prime Minister. So he shifted his focus to the 2014 Lok Sabha elections and filed his nomination in Varanasi to contest against Narendra Modi, who was the BJP's Prime Ministerial candidate. After suffering a humiliating defeat in the Varanasi challenge, he returned to Delhi and profusely apologized to the electorate in his campaign for the state polls in 2015, for abandoning the trust they had reposed in him.

He also categorically told them that he would not let them down again. He held a series of rallies and Jan Sabhas for this purpose. People believed he had a change of heart and was now a transformed man. Besides the people's readiness to believe that Kejriwal had changed and spoke from his heart, the combined support extended by India's Main Stream Media (MSM), NGOs as well as the Muslim and Christian communities, enabled him clinch a clear victory in the Delhi elections.

To dwell briefly on one of the tactical maneuvers of the anti-BJP forces, there were as many as five mysterious attacks on Churches by unidentified people in Delhi between November 2014 and February 2015, when Delhi went to polls. On every one of these occasions, there were protest rallies against the purported failure of the BJP-led NDA government to protect the religious rights of minority communities and the MSM merrily went to town with the story. These developments had their benign effect on the 'repentant' home comer's victory.

Promises and more Promises

While he was at the serious business of revamping the system and fighting corruption, he promised he would give the people of Delhi reasons to rejoice and a cause for celebration. The promises he made in his Party Manifesto included several people-oriented schemes like the setting up of 500 new schools and 20 new colleges, making the Capital city drug-free, filling up of 55, 000 immediate vacancies in government departments, special reservations for all senior citizens and youth, providing loans to young entrepreneurs at low interest rates, enforcing an education loan scheme, making Delhi safe for women and turning it into a manufacturing hub.

Over and above all this, he promised freebies ranging from a slash in the power tariffs to supply of free water and free Wi-Fi throughout Delhi. The most intriguing aspect of these promises was that he had no idea either before the polls or after getting elected as to where the required funds would come from for financing the populist schemes. He just went ahead and made reckless promises.

Second Chance

His apology and promises went down well with the people who thought that his 'repentance' was reflective of his humility and common man image and gave his party a landslide victory. Apparently, they thought that an overwhelming mandate would give Kejriwal and his fledgling party a much-needed breakthrough and facilitate them to focus on governance and make Delhi a model State as he promised, without having to depend on the support of other parties for survival.

The voters believed that with its massive electoral victory, AAP had got not only the opportunity but also a hassle-free political environment that was required for doing all the good work that the party had promised. Apparently, the people of Delhi had not bargained for Kejriwal's prodigious capability of making a series of reckless political moves and apologizing to the people for his 'mistakes'. How else could one explain the people's act of returning him to power a second time in less than a year?

Power and Water Woes

No sooner had his party returned to power then Kejriwal announced the catchiest populist scheme of his. He slashed electricity tariff by 50% for consumption of up to 400 units per month and announced free 20, 000 liters of water to every household per month. There is, however, no provision in the budget for the increase in subsidies. Furthermore, the government has a running feud with power discoms over optimum power procurement and distribution and the Delhi Electricity Regulatory Commission over the proposed increase in power tariffs.

A new power plant for Delhi has been promised. However, not much has been done about the allocation of funds. Nor has any action been taken towards land acquisition. The AAP manifesto also spoke about optimizing the Rajghat and Bawana plants for power generation with no indication as to how the government planned to do so. There is no sign of the proposal taking off anytime soon. Meanwhile, the people continue to suffer power outages.

AAP's election manifesto also promised every home in Delhi a water pipeline for supplying clean drinking water. In reality, however, few water pipelines have been laid. Large parts of Delhi are still waiting for water to be made available through tankers, etc. The government does not seem to be doing much more than quibbling over inner-party squabbles, scams and focusing on twiddling of thumbs. Meanwhile in June, his Law Minister Jitender Singh Tomar was arrested for faking two degree certificates and sent to Delhi's Tihar Jail.

Non-starter Schemes

Practically, all the other populist schemes enumerated in the AAP manifesto remain just that – promises, with little or no action underway. The government is clueless about ways and means of implementing the schemes including women's safety and reforms in education and health sectors. The reasons for inaction are many. To start with, Kejriwal does not seem to be reconciled to the idea of continuing as the Chief Minister of the glorified municipality of Delhi as a cynic of a political observer would be tempted to call the government of the Capital city.

He has been complaining of little or utter lack of powers vested in the Chief Minister. He feels hedged between an active and assertive Lieutenant Governor and the Municipal Corporations of Delhi, which are controlled by the BJP. Consequently, he is on a warpath with Lieutenant Governor Najeeb Jung as well as the Prime Minister Narendra Modi. While he holds Jung responsible for pulling him down all, he keeps blaming Modi for trying to put him out of the political scenario altogether. He is bitter about having to work with a cramped style. Non-availability of sufficient funds to finance his populist schemes, which are like a resource-draining bottomless pit, is staring him in the face.

He has been sulking over Delhi not having been granted full-fledged Statehood. If his current ambitions could be narrowed to a solitary one, it would in all probability be the securing of full-fledged Statehood for Delhi and his going down, in the process, the annals of history as the valiant hero who made it possible. His government is in the process of holding a referendum to ascertain the views of the people of Delhi over the grant of Statehood to the city. Whatever the outcome of the proposed referendum, he may quite likely take to the streets in the due course of time to seeking fulfillment of his dream.

Wilting under Pressure

Meanwhile, charges of monetary contributions from bogus companies and hawala operators for the funding of his party activities have caused a serious dent to his own image as well as that of his party.

Eviction of senior party colleagues and ideologues has left the party bereft of the cutting edge of ideology. The moral stature of the party as a self-avowed crusading force against black money and corruption is in shambles. Today the Aam Aadmi Party is perceived as a private outfit of an autocratic Kejriwal and a small band of supporters who are too much in awe of his authority to raise a voice in disagreement over any issue.

What has made Kejriwal's autocratic image truly horrid is his insatiable thirst for publicity. With a publicity budget of over 520 crore, he got a publicity blitzkrieg, singing his paeans on TV, radio and public hoardings, day in and day out, with nothing being subtle about it. The fly in the face projection of the image of a 'helpless' Chief Minister who is under constant attack by the Prime Minister, Lieutenant Governor and the Media, orchestrated at a humongous cost met with the taxpayers' money has already generated much revulsion among the public and a rebuke by the Judiciary.

The disclosure that the electricity bill for his official residence for one month was of a whopping ₹ 1.35 lakh has done no good to his image as an Aam Aadmi in the public perception. Pushed to a corner, Kejriwal is quite likely to take the easy way out and do what comes to him best – quit. Since people would not likely to condone another resignation under pressure, he is likely to force the hand of the Government at the Centre to make it feasible. Hence, his relentless criticism and massive showdowns with both the Lieutenant Governor and the Prime Minister!

The Big Letdown

Be that as it may, there is no escaping the public perception that Arvind Kejriwal and his Aam Aadmi Party are no more the vibrant political forces, which people had taken them for. They are more like the mere whiff of a flavour of the season gone by. The trust imposed by the people and the bonding with the common man are things of the past. The icing on the cake comes in the form of support by AAP to the corrupt and decrepit combine of Lalu Yadav and Nitish Kumar in the forthcoming Bihar elections!

This desperate move of Kejriwal instigated by sheer spite for Narendra Modi is the real whopper to drag his image all the way down in the eyes of the people of Delhi. To support, for political reasons, a leader indicted by the Court on charges of corruption and still claim to be a crusader of corruption is unimaginable! It is the bottom of the pits for Kejriwal who has let down everyone who supported him in good faith. That includes his own party men. The worst casualty of this letdown is going to be Kejriwal himself.

(Published in weekly magazine Uday India in Vol. VI, No. 38-39, 23-29 August, 2015 edition)

(Posted on Bharat Niti portal on 11 September, 2015)

□

Promises-based Politics vs. Delivery-based Politics

Now that the Aam Aadmi Party has won a clear mandate in Delhi, we must realize that the political setup of India has changed radically in past couple of years. Who could have ever imagined that the Congress would go completely out of picture and the BJP, a party that stands high in the name of India's present Prime Minister, would not make it to even two-digit figure in the verdict. I have been following AAP's groundwork since some time now and have realized that in a country like India promise-based politics and votes in the name of probable development of the poor and deprived can take you all the way to power. BJP, in the Delhi campaign, lacked promises and sheer groundwork, an area where the AAP scored full numbers. In a federal yet unitary polity system, now the AAP and BJP should come together for the development of Delhi, else we know that though after considerable time, voters do analyze their past valuations, something that has been substantiated with the downfall of Congress. Dear CM-to-be of Delhi, we wish you all the very best for the innings 2.0, this time you would have nil pressure from ally or the opposition, an equation that feels satisfactory at the day of verdict, but turns out highly cumbersome and demanding from the day of swearing-in. Though opposition, in my belief, was the most apt place for AAP for the time-being, attention-grabbing will it be to witness how the elected CM takes the state to new heights of success, something that you have been declaring and assuring for long; the days of tests have now arrived.

Delivery-based politics and subsequent triumph was the notion in 2014 when a 3-time successful CM of Gujarat was chosen for the topmost position based on his past actions and reforms. This could not be a case in Delhi as Arvind Kejriwal could run the state for mere 49 days, but in all upcoming polls, be it for any state or the nation as a whole, he should be ready to be evaluated based on deliveries. And you have the capability, this is sure; else no other man could have won the heart of Delhi with such extraordinary win. You have connected with the general public of Delhi, have reassured them of reforms in every domain, be it basic necessities like water and power or added perks like a Wi-Fi-enabled city. People have relied on your assertions, or I must say have extremely put their faith in your candidature, which of course is an undeniable and massive liability. In the 49-days governance, you proved that your intent to uplift the poor, by way of free water and cheaper power supply, was indeed honest, but management also asks for planning-based policies and not unforeseen decisions that bounce back to you as a horrible event to deal with. Now it is time that your administrative qualities, team-work, and pro-development thoughts would be tested hard; hence it is phase for apt planning rather than cheering the Delhi verdict or preparing hastily for polls in some other state.

For the BJP, this cannot be regarded as absolute loss for the party or for any of their leaders, be it Narendra Modi, Amit Shah or Kiran Bedi. This, in fact, is a result of shift of sentiments from delivery-based politics to promises-based politics, evident from vote share of BJP which has fell by mere 1 percent as compared to Delhi polls in 2013. This, however, is also the time when you would need to analyze some apparent mistakes like fielding candidates in the last-minute, bringing in outsiders and ignorance of dedicated BJP workers, arrogance, over-optimism and portrayal of leaders as rulers, not people's representatives, person-based and negative campaigning, and incapacity to connect with poor, minority and lower middle-class households even after delivering some pluses in the past 9 months. To be a popular political party in India one cannot ignore underprivileged and their ground issues. Wouldn't it be better if the BJP had appointed a couple of representatives who could connect with the public, raise their concerns and get them sorted? After all, you assured 'all-inclusive development', and mind you that a large chunk of voters aren't aware of rise and fall in GDP growth rate or thick influx of funds from overseas. India has been and will be a home to politics based on betterment of poor until their homes are filled with basic necessities. A rise in the vote share of the AAP is a clear outcome of move of poor and minority from the Congress to Arvind Kejriwal's guarantees; this is a mirror to what happened in general polls of 2014 when Hindus whole-heartedly backed BJP, especially in the north India. The irony is that there is no model code of conduct while appeasing minority, all rules apply when you talk for the Hindus.

Dear AAP chief, you have all those issues in your manifesto for the 2015 Delhi polls that are the nerves of the common man, and have been present for decades. Who doesn't need clean drinking water, cheaper electricity, safety of women, strong legal framework and protection from rising prices? It is, however, easier said than done. Now that power companies have congratulated for your win and have given a green nod to audit, it will be observed by every person of Delhi as to how you deal with the issue of electricity prices. Another tailback is providing ample water to every household, when you know that water level in the Haiderpur pond has started falling and Haryana isn't proving that co-operative, but these are realities, harsh realities that every government has to face, these cannot be termed as excuses for non-delivery; hence proper planning is the need of the hour. You will need to find answer to HOW, WHAT is already in your manifesto. It is no wrong if you take some amount of time to comprehend the basics, hurrying, as in the last session of your ruling, can be avoided. No one needs a free Wi-Fi or CCTVs all over Delhi on day of your swearing-in, step by step and a sustainable change is what that we are looking forward to. The foreign media has termed your victory as a 'political earthquake', this term is enough to understand how closely are you being observed and what is the impact of your coming in on even the stock and financial market, and these being the backbone of our economy, your carefulness and astute is much-needed.

Assigning different tasks to relevant departments and heads, inviting suggestions from the public and persons of acumen, informed decision-making, co-operation with other authorities viz. municipal council, other state governments and of course the central government, monitoring the works of departments, re-evaluating those candidates who might have won in the AAP wave but aren't deserving and capable, being accountable and promoting transparency are only a few aspects that we expect from the CM-to-be of Delhi. Also, a Jan Lokpal Bill isn't needed, by this I mean that an effective Jan Lokpal Bill is required, we have all witnessed the failures of women empowerment laws and anti-corruption act as well. 'Cheaper' doesn't mean free, rather means economical, that in turn would mean making people financially capable so as to deal with rising prices and economic ups and downs, notions that even developed economies are unable to get rid of completely. You have the responsibility to build not just a 'developed city', but also a 'sustainable city' that can remember for ages a person who could win the minds and hearts of the people of Delhi in such a manner that even sincere past deliveries of the Congress were totally faded out. Having won this contest with promises, I believe that the party and its chief, Arvind Kejriwal, would from now ask votes in the name of their deliveries and not the failures of other political men. You have the hefty and natural duty to prove that promises-based politics can aptly be turned into delivery-based politics, something that we expect from you in Delhi and Mr. Modi in the center.

This last appeal goes to the Modi-led central government. Look how well the people of Delhi connected with your 2014 call 'Congress Mukt Bharat', but why you failed to connect them with the BJP this time is the question that seeks answer. Dear PM, your policies in Gujarat were primarily focused on agriculture, self-employment in villages, adequate electricity to farmers before 24×7 supply in the entire state, betterment of girl child, education, suppression of corruption and such other basics. It is high time that the goods of your policy-making acumen flow down to the poor and lower middle class households, surge in the stock market and hiked FDI in sectors are secondary, though crucial. The youth, who were all in your support in 2014 and helped you secure a vote share of 46 percent in Delhi have now relied on AAP's promises, and why couldn't the discontented vote bank of the Congress shift to BJP rather having moved to AAP is a vital issue seeking your perusal; aren't delayed 'ACHHE DIN' and central government's lukewarm approach towards extending major benefits to the real needy a factor? Somewhat responsible is also the extremist Hindutva feelings with which though core BJP supporters could connect but the youth, Muslims, Christians and poor couldn't. Upcoming polls in Bihar and other states will yet again witness more or less same factors, identical voters, also competition from arch rivals as well as the newly loved-by-people AAP.

For the BJP there is no other option than to undertake measures that are honestly targeted at simplifying and enriching the lives of common man. You need to pay heed to the MSME sector that employs a large cluster of the total workforce of India yet is fighting everyday battles with government officials, policemen and IT inspectors. While framing the new Finance Bill direct taxation system needs to be made so friendly for businesses and individuals that tax rates of middle class households and businesses be lowered, though not affecting revenue, and harassment of businessmen curtailed. All in all, the democracy is witnessing a war between promises-based politics and delivery-based politics, and to fetch support on delivery lines in all the upcoming state elections, the BJP and its leaders need to focus high on ground-level concerns with a view to bettering living conditions for even the most underprivileged.

(Posted on blog on 13 February, 2015)

□

Stability - Key to Better Governance

Prosperity follows stability. Being a nation with diverse communal and ethnic richness, India is declared as a Sovereign, Socialist, Secular, and Democratic Republic by the Constitution. The Governments, Union as well as the States, are bestowed upon with a duty to treat all the communities alike and to frame policies that benefit all. Does today's newspaper have any news of such a policy that serves the need of the nation or the state as a whole? Rarely do we see the Government coming up with a model that suits every section of community. Though I would not stress upon the policies drafted for a particular community/caste in recent months, a slight glimpse is however necessary. The State Government of U.P. recently made amendments to the policy under which teenage girls are provided with monetary allowances to empower their educational base – A particular community was benefited post the amendments and this was looked upon as a step to lure the voters of this community.

Every one of us belongs to a particular religion/caste that makes India a nation with communal multiplicities. Now, when I think of measures that provide more opportunities to people of my community, it is apparent that the interests of the remaining communities are sacrificed. The current Union Government rests upon the support of distinctive regional parties that demand fund and plans that benefit either a particular state/caste. The motive is evident – These regional parties are backed by votes on basis of pity interests and offerings. Now arises the question that needs a definite and swift answer. Is India moving on a path that would lead to all-inclusive development? While we study the challenges of our nation in a textbook, unemployment, inflation, restriction to freedom, poverty, and infrastructure are the areas of concern. However, are the Union Governments from past many decades making any attempts to overcome these national bottlenecks? How can they? In 2004 Lok Sabha Polls, absolute majority was not gained by any of the political parties. The UPA formed the Government with external support from many regional parties. The conclusion – Ignorance of national bottlenecks and undue advantage to particular states/communities for ensuring the confidence of the Indian Parliament.

We have been talking about the consequences of corruption in a stricter manner since past few years. The rise of a newly emerged political party in the state of Delhi reflected the rage of society against corruption. Now, when top leaders of political parties talk about ending this anti-development issue, why do they forget about the recent closure of investigations against leaders of regional political groups? Investigating agencies are used as an illicit weapon to either protect such corrupts or to threaten them. Motive is clear – Support to maintain the requisite numbers. Let's talk about the solution now. Had there been a Union Government backed by extensive support from the voters, the nation would have witnessed better governance. The policy makers would have had the freedom to opt for plans that can bring in development for every community in case they did not have to rely upon the support from regional parties.

The nation has to rethink as to what it needs. Do we want pity benefits for our particular community/caste, or do we look forward to a nation that has ample employment opportunities for all? Do we want our caste to rely upon reservations, or do we want to welcome infrastructural developments that can promise prosperity beyond reservation? The voter has to decide whether he/she wants a nation that keeps in its secure fold all the communities/castes, or he/she wants a prosperous community that relies on reservations and sympathies. Remember, a Government that is stable will be proactive to draft plans that are unbiased and concrete. Let's hope for a better tomorrow that can promise success of all.

(Posted on blog on 19 February, 2014)

□

India needs Tough Political Leader with Vision

The nation has witnessed the descendents of influential political leaders been given immense and undue favor. The youth brigade representing the vibrant outlook is backed by the social capital that these leaders possess. Social Capital can be looked upon as the assets and resources gained with the help of links and proximity with dominant leaders. Politics of India seems to be providing superfluous advantage to those who come from a family of cabinet ministers, MPs, or Chief Ministers. The question is 'Whether or not these young leaders capable of delivering the much-awaited reforms?' The voters of the country will have to realize that candidature and political vision should to be paid heed to. Rebuilding the political community does not mean bestowing upon the responsibility of governance on those shoulders that are the representatives of dominant past leaders.

The Congress party is in a phase of rejuvenating and strengthening the roots. We can look at the recent visits and dialogues of Mr. Rahul Gandhi as an attempt to reinforcing new blood. It has been repeatedly spoken that the Youth Brigade of the Congress party has faces that hold extensive social capital backed by their ancestors. The BJP leaders, who constantly speak about the curse of family-driven politics, have recently agreed to tie up with a regional party run by leaders from the same family. The nation urgently calls for leaders who are visionary and can stand tough. The political environment of India, the largest democracy in the world, is significantly influenced by the diversity of cultures, religions, and castes. It is customary to witness occasions when the descendant of a Minister is showered upon with unreasonable favor. Accountability that comes into picture post responsibility seems nowhere. The consequences are predictable-Lack of national interest.

Regional parties, playing a vital role in driving the politics of the Center since past many years, are posing indefinite concerns. The Government lacks the decision-making power and thus has to depend upon those who favor prosperity of a particular community/region. The nation has been a spectator to incidents when the Central Government gave special and bulky packages to particular states for their betterment. Investigating agencies are used as a threat to fetch support from regional parties so as to ensure the stability of the Government. The voters of the nation need to learn from past incidents and have to take resourceful decisions in the upcoming polls. National parties shall be given the opportunity to form a stable Government and thus implement policies that are in the interest of the nation as a whole. The leaders of these national parties must strengthen their base and shall communicate their factual roadmap. Most significantly, commendable and visionary candidates shall be provided with a platform to become a part of the governance.

(Posted on blog on 3 March, 2014)

□

Can an Activist be a Capable Administrator?

It is now an established fact that the general public of India is more than rushed to eradicate the evils of social as well as the political domain. The participation of the youth, along with members from every sphere of the society in the movement of social activist, Anna Hazare, reflected the passion and willingness to overcome the deficiencies of our democracy. Any society would be blessed to have activists like Mahatma Gandhi, Medha Patkar, Kiran Bedi, Anna Hazare, and of course the mother of India, Mother Teresa.

Does the society gain with the presence of activists? What Mother Teresa delivered is even acknowledged at the global level, the impact of Anna Hazare's movement transformed the viewpoints of our rigid political leaders, and Kiran Bedi lives as an ideal to millions. Surely, activists are the voice of those who either are too busy, too restless, or often scared to come forward and demand social justice. Though our political representatives are the ones we choose for the betterment of our society, they often disremember this task.

Let us move forward now and analyze what good can the activists bring to the society in case bestowed upon with the task of administration. In recent times, the political sphere of India has been too busy accommodating new entrants who have moved a step ahead and have hopped over from being an activist to a politician. The extraordinary rise of the newly formed political group in the state elections of Delhi proved the zeal of the general public to bring in real reforms. Nothing much, however, was gained. The party has subsequently diverged from the route of bringing in reforms to a path that leads to conquering numbers without worrying about the principles sacrificed and dishonest measures adopted to accomplish the target. A question thus strikes, 'Can an activist be a capable administrator?'

The pages of history can be turned to locate the answer to this tough question. Mahatma Gandhi was the key force behind the eviction of the East India Company from India. This great personality united the dispersed thoughts and people of the nation, and created a milieu wherein the British were left with no other option than to vacate. Gandhi was a role model of communal unity and harmony. Until his last breadth, he advocated making India a nation wherein diverse castes and religions can be accommodated with peace. Post the day when India was declared to be a free state, the role of Gandhi transformed from an activist to a bureaucrat.

Be it the inclusion of the controversial Article 370 in the Constitution of India to which Dr. Ambedkar had never agreed to; monetary grants to Pakistan; the milieu and mass killing at the time of or after the partition; or the unproductive decision of appointing Nehru as the face of Congress, Gandhi's visionary capabilities can surely be challenged. Though he wanted India and Pakistan to be home to both Hindus and Muslims, he failed to foresee the eviction of Kashmiri Pandits from Kashmir and the merciless torture of Hindus in Pakistan.

A sneak peak at the contributions of those activists is necessary who, though influenced the nation with their works, stayed away from active politics. Two deserving names include Jai Prakash Narayan, the originator of J P Movement against the misdeeds of Bihar government and eventually the union government, and Ram Manohar Lohia, the leader whose ideology has been adopted by numerous political parties, however is rarely followed. Vital to note, Kiran Bedi was lured to become a part of the AAP on the grounds that post the outcomes of the polls she would be the one administrating the state of Delhi as CM, which, she never assented to.

Being concerned about the welfare of the society and being an administrator of a state are two distinctive equations. Alike incident was witnessed when the CM of Delhi resorted to walkout rather than resolving the basic concerns of water and power. To be a ruler, the courage to withstand tough circumstances and the vision to interpret future outcomes are the prime requisites. Administration demands sacrifices and diplomacy too. Remember, more the constituents and multiple the communities, more complicated it is to uphold the unity at all times. Shall we then not conclude to the fact that activists who do not have anything to lose become vulnerable to sacrifice morals so as to get hold of power once they aspire to become politicians. The general public, too, realizes this fact, which in turn lessens the faith.

(Posted on blog on 2 May, 2014)

□

Incompetent Sports Bodies Ruining Players' Zeal

Now that all of us know the mishap at the Incheon Asian Games, let me tell you a few more depressing facts. L Sarita Devi, the Indian boxer people are talking about these days, had to scuffle hard, or shall I say, beg (I am sorry, brave heart), for the USD 500, the fee for lodging a protest for mala fide judging. Further, the appellate board told that the judges' decision cannot be reversed, while the USD 500 fee wasn't returned. Then, we hear that the medal has been awarded back to the boxer post she filed an apology in writing, which was something that Indian officials coerced her to do. Busy celebrating the gold won by another Indian iconic boxer, the same officials were nowhere when the judges bluntly awarded a dishonest decision against Sarita Devi. What more to expect. Let me also tell you that the IOA (Indian Olympics Association) is currently headed by former BCCI president, N. Srinivasan's brother. While he was being elected, he was the only contender for the position; hence you can imagine the 'fair voting system'.

Known to us all is the appalling fact that the IOC (International Olympic Committee) suspended IOA on 4 December 2012 due to corruption in the process of election within the Association and non-adherence of IOC rules. The ban was revoked on 11 February 2014 only when the IOA conducted fresh polls. This can never be a normal happening. A body responsible for selecting athletes to represent the nation at Olympics and other international athletic meets lost recognition for 14 long months. And then we say that China and USA are the nations our athletes shall aim to compete with. Leave aside the scarcity of quality sites and tools for players, even the talented players, capable to fetch respect for India at global platforms, are left to destiny by the officials. The lady who brought India first medal at the 2014 Asian Games, Shweta Chaudhary, had to manage with a bronze as the serial number of her regular pistol was conveyed incorrect to the Korean custom by Indian officials. Nonetheless, she had no regrets and blamed no one.

All this isn't new. The laid back approach of Indian sports bodies is widely acknowledged but rarely anyone dares to challenge the setup. We talk of corruption in ministries and government offices, but these autonomously working bodies, which are not answerable to any statutory authority, are never paid heed to. The sports ministry has been asking for details of expenses on IOA and NSFs (National Sports Federations) officials during the Glasgow Commonwealth Games. Moreover, the ministry also questioned the IOA for sponsoring sports federations' officials to the Asian Games basis that the amount spent on sending these unwanted people could be better expended on good governance. The Cycling Federation of India recommended a Congress MP and his wife for a 'paid trip' to Incheon; while on the other hand, India was charged with USD 10, 000 for withdrawing from seven sports at the last minute. Where is the IOA focusing? Same is the case with the BCCI or the Indian Hockey Federation, bodies that many a times make headlines for corrupt behavior by officials and coerced process of polls.

And let me also tell you that these so-called autonomous bodies are not free from the clutches of politics. With many politicians heading state councils of BCCI and NSFs, it is expected that the sports ministry must have a control over the operations of these rich federations. But the irony is that the most affluent cricket board of the world, the BCCI, works as per self-designed laws, which do not allow transparency in operations. Beyond understanding are the instances when we hear the addition of cricketers in the Indian cricket team backed by close nexus with the members of the selection committee. Contracts awarded to Nimbus and Sony by the BCCI, though are under suspicion, but the probe cannot be initiated. The Supreme Court of India in 2012 commented 'Cricket should be kept free from politics and the game should not become a ball for politicians'. This was in reaction to the row where some officials parted ways with Bihar Cricket Association (headed by Lalu Prasad Yadav) to form Cricket Association of Bihar.

While SAI (Sports Authority of India), a nodal agency of the Sports Ministry of India funds training programmes for many sports, the ministry does not have an exclusive control over the functioning of sports agencies. Almost every of the sports federations, though at liberty from the supervision of the government, have politicians as members/ heads. Let me also tell you that the Table Tennis Federation of India has MP Dushyant Chautala, son of Ajay Chautala as the VP. Likewise, the All India Football Federation has Praful Patel as Chairman. Vijay Kumar Malhotra heads the Archery Association of India, Akhilesh Das Gupta heads the Badminton Association of India, Raninder Singh heads the National Rifle Association of India, Abhishek Matoria is the President of Indian Amateur Boxing Federation, Vidya Stokes is the lifetime patron of Hockey India, and Birendra Prasad Baishya heads the Indian Weightlifting Federation. It is apparent that with political men competing for positions in sports bodies, veteran sportsmen stand no chance of playing an apt role for the betterment of relative game.

When the Indian sportsmen represent the country worldwide, the union government is supposed to be the decisive controller. 'India' is the state they play for, not for any of the federations. To avoid distressing instances and malpractices, as have happened in the recent past, the ministry will have to knock down uncontrolled sports federations, which have become a home to politics and uselessness. Sooner than later, the GOI will have to curtail such quasi-political setup. Herein, the federations and boards should be made a statutory wing of the SAI. Plus, political intervention, of any manner, should be stopped. Headed by capable bureaucrats with former expert sportsmen as members of respective advisory boards, indeed, these bodies will function more proactively and unbiasedly. Only then we can expect timely allocation of funds, unbiased selection, and India's domination in the arena of sports. For speedy advancement of sportsmen and to elevate the sports milieu of India, curbing the present state of affairs is much-needed. Else, we can continue cheering mere one or two gold medals in Olympics. But then, stop expecting much from Indian sportsmen.

(Posted on blog on 7 October, 2014)

□

Abolish Planning Commission or Make it More Proactive and Realistic

Ever since the all-powerful Planning Commission was set up in 1950 by a cabinet resolution to assess, coordinate and allocate government's resources efficiently for social and economic growth, this non-statutory body has often been criticized as a bunch of "arm-chair advisors and ivory-tower experts" who have failed to capture the pulse of ground realities.

With 30 divisions manned by 109 senior officers and staff strength of over 800, the Planning Commission, though lacking any Constitutional and legal authority, has been distributing and monitoring plan funds to the state governments and central government departments right since its inception. The panel had been central to the process of projects getting clearance, timely funding and also coordinating with ministries, sectors and states.

However, state governments, mainly those run by regional parties opposed to the political party at the Centre, have rarely been satisfied by the funds allocated to them by the federal government on the recommendation of the planning body, which is not accountable to Parliament.

While many policy-makers and economists have called for revamping the plan panel, mandarins of the erstwhile UPA regime have also advocated a change in the role of the planning commission. Furthermore, recent media reports say that the new government views the Planning Commission as only adding to red tape and as a creature of the old 'Licence Raj' serving no useful purpose in the current liberalized economic scene.

Even former Prime Minister Manmohan Singh himself, in his farewell speech, called for a review of the Commission's role in an increasingly open economy. India's former Finance Minister P. Chidambaram has also favoured downsizing of the Planning Commission and said that the plan panel should be a much more limited body tasked with drawing up prospective plans. At the moment it is too big, flabby and unwieldy, he emphasized.

The extreme opinion currently floating around is about abolishing the planning body, as many believe under the new dispensation of Narendra Modi there is hardly any space for planners devoid of grassroots connects and exposure, as the focus is now more on realistic execution and result-oriented implementation.

While abolishment of the Planning Commission may be a huge blow to the ivory-tower expert community, it is unlikely to happen soon. However, reliable sources say Prime Minister Narendra Modi, who is the commission's new chairman, would review the planning body's functioning and opt to restructure it.

The election manifesto of the BJP had also talked about revamping the Commission since it is seen as a legacy of our country's socialist past. It had said that the Centre should only be an enabler and facilitator for state governments.

For the first time since its inception in 1950, this year the Planning Commission was not involved in the decision-making process while finalizing the gross budgetary support for the Indian Railways. Furthermore, the recent decision to give the Finance Ministry charge of allocations for state and central level ministries shows the Commission will not function in its present form any longer.

The fact that Yojana Bhavan has been divested of its financial powers seems to hint at the end of the important role the Commission used to play so far. It also indicates the beginning of the biggest change that the Indian fiscal space has witnessed in decades. Recently, Rao Inderjit Singh, Minister of State for Planning (Independent Charge) made the nature of the likely change clear by indicating that his government was undecided about appointing a new Deputy Chairman for the Planning Commission.

Till May 2014, the key post of the Deputy Chairman was held by Montek Singh Ahluwalia. He and former members of the Commission resigned, vacated their offices and stepped out of Yojana Bhavan on May 27. Most of what were on the Members' tables have since been transferred to Secretary-level officers posted as principal advisers at the Commission.

As such, currently everything related to the Planning Commission is in a state of flux. The Prime Minister has yet to decide whether he wants to appoint a Deputy Chairman. So far, this has always been a Cabinet-level post in every government.

In view of the aforementioned developments, it is recommended that the Narendra Modi-led NDA government should mull over the following three options while deciding on the future of the Planning Commission: (i) Restructure the Planning Commission or recast its role; (ii) Merge it with the Prime Minister's Economic Advisory Council; or (iii) Totally scrap the Commission forthwith.

Here, let me elaborate on the scope of each of the above recommendations:

(i) **Recasting the role of the Planning Commission:** If the Central government believes that the Commission should be rejigged with a different structure and role from its conventional mandate of allocating funds to states and schemes, then the government should first take away the extensive powers vested in the plan panel.

Since, Rao Inderjit Singh has been made the Minister of State for Planning with Independent Charge (MOSPI) under the new dispensation, he happens to wield more powers than the previous ministers. As such, the Commission can be made a part of MOSPI, and the current overlaps between MOSPI and the Commission can be eliminated.

Once that is done, the panel's traditional role of doing budgetary and Plan allocations can be totally scrapped. The plan panel can then be assigned the task of monitoring implementation of projects. This would mean checking the progress of projects cleared by the state and central governments and also keeping a tab on how much of the allocated money has been spent. It can also review steps required to avert cost overruns with regard to each project.

The government can also do away with Five Year Plans and in lieu have annual plans for quick decision and fast implementation, which can be monitored by the Planning Commission working under MOSPI. The 12th Five Year Plan that started from April 1, 2012 has not made any concrete progress so far.

So scrapping the current Five Year Plan also does not pose any kind of problem. This move will perfectly align with Modi's mantra, which says India needs implementation and not just planning and vision. Moreover, Modi has always been publicly critical of centralized planning and of one-size-fits-all approach.

(ii) **Merging the plan panel with PM's Economic Advisory Council:** In 2012, a committee, which was headed by Dr C Rangarajan, had recommended eliminating the distinction between Plan and non-Plan allocations. The forthcoming Financial Budget that will be presented by Arun Jaitley on July 10, 2014 is expected to implement this recommendation for the first time.

As the interim Budget has already transferred most centrally-sponsored schemes to state governments, this time the Planning Commission has no major role to play in the allocation of funds to states. And each state government has made it very clear that they want the new arrangements to be continued and further expanded.

In the above context where the traditional role of the Planning Commission has been scrapped, its importance is on a declining curve. Furthermore, since Modi is against centralised planning he does not want Delhi-driven policies or resource allocations for states, but state-specific solutions.

As such, the Central government can consider merging the Commission with the Prime Minister's Economic Advisory Council (PMEAC), which was set up in a bid to provide a sounding board for inculcating awareness in government on different points of view on key economic issues. PMEAC has been reconstituted time and again with different organizational structures headed by various economists of recognized international eminence.

The Planning Commission has been the Nodal Agency for the PMEAC for administrative, logistic, planning and budgeting purposes. As the work of these two organizations are closely connected and even seem to overlap in certain areas, their integration will definitely lead to optimization of resource allocation.

(iii) Abolishing the Commission: Lately, because of the growing pitch for federalism, and better Centre-state relations, in certain cases the Planning Commission has been left out of the loop completely where states are concerned. The Finance Ministry has started dealing with the states directly for seeking their demands and for distribution of funds.

The Commission has also been left out from discussions to fix the size of the gross budgetary support as many Central ministries and state governments believe they are much better off without the Planning Commission sitting on top of their heads. Earlier, the figure was generally arrived at after discussions between the plan panel and the finance ministry, with the prime minister taking the final call.

Claiming that the Planning Commission is largely a Soviet-era relic and has outlived its utility in the era of a market-driven economy, some say that the plans drafted in the air-conditioned chambers of Yojana Bhawan are more in the air and less on the ground. As such the planning body has become a 'good for nothing' commission and this country cannot any more put up with such lavish nonperforming commissions, they argue.

In view of the above, there have been vociferous demands from some quarters for the outright scrapping of this outdated entity. For instance, emphasizing that there is a need to rethink on the need for institutions such as the Planning Commission, economist Arvind Panagariya, who is also a professor of economics at Columbia University in the US, says the Commission should be abolished.

Elaborating further, Panagariya says planning has become a habit in India and this habit needs to be broken. "We are in a market economy. It has to be planned, but not by the Planning Commissions, but by the ministries. It is time for a rethink on such institutions, " he emphasizes.

(Posted on blog on 9 July, 2014)

□

Weighing the Evolution of 11th Five-year Plan

The think tank of India, Planning Commission, is viewed as the body of intellectuals that can apprehend the needs of the society and economy, and devise policies and measures accordingly. The progress of the nation and the allocation of funds are dependent on the strategies formulated in the five-year plans. It is expected that the government, the ministers, the regulatory agencies, and the bureaucrats would contribute in the best possible manner for the success of the plan. Considering India as an economy, the five-year plans can be looked upon as the most prominent set of fiscal and economic budgeting. Let us briefly evaluate the delivery of the 11th plan and conclude as to whether the think-tank and administrators succeeded in their tasks of planning and administration.

Vital to note that at the mid-term review of the plan, the Planning Commission lowered the targeted growth rate of 9 percent per annum to 8 percent. Let us also consider some credentials. The agriculture growth rate from 10 percent in 2003-04 declined to 3.8 percent in 2006-07, which was the last FY for the 10th plan. As per the mid-term assessment of the 11th plan, the average growth rate (2007-10) was just 2.2 percent. For the industry sector, the 11th plan targeted facilitation of FDI, PPP initiatives, world-class infrastructure, and foreign technology collaborations. The plan foresaw manufacturing and general industrial sector growing at an average rate of 10-11 percent, which however in real terms slipped to even 2.6 percent in 2008-09 and 3.5 percent in 2011-12.

As always, the 11th plan too focused on elementary, secondary, and higher education. Plus, improving the quality of education was also the target. The literacy rate, which as per the census of 2001 stood at 64.8 percent with a gap of 21.6 percentage points between males and females at national level, grew to just 74.04 percent in 2011 indicating a decadal growth of mere 9 percent in the decade. Reducing malnutrition to half its present level, Infant Mortality Rate to 28 per live births and Total Fertility rate to 2.1 percent, and access of clean drinking water to all was the goal of the 11th plan in the health domain. It is appalling that the World Bank has estimated India as one of the highest ranking countries in the world in terms of children suffering from malnutrition. Access to clean water was also far than achievable.

In terms of employment generation, the plan aimed at generating 58 million work prospects during 2007 to 2012. The rate of unemployment, on the contrary, reached an all-time high of 9.4 percent in December 2010. MGNREGA scheme was introduced, which has been creating artificial work prospects for the rural population, and in turn is broadening the economic gap. Other areas of focus for the 11th plan were social justice, rural development, infrastructure, energy, transport, science and technology, environment and forest, water resources, urban development, and women's agency and child rights. The planners though were smart enough to project healthy figures in terms of development, most of the domains witnessed decline even from the previous figures.

It is shocking to note that the government assesses the mid-term achievements/drawbacks of the five year plans, however overall appraisal post five years can nowhere be found. Either, the planners and those responsible for the execution of the plans are assured enough that the goals envisaged would be attained, or they realize the ambiguity of their vision and expertise at the very beginning of the plan. Else, aims like infrastructure, rural, and urban development would not have been threatening for the so-called intellectuals to handle. Good governance advocates not just planning and implementation, but also the appraisal and control of the devised plan so as to curb any deviations from the projected outcomes. Plus, in case the planning squad could not deliver feasible and effectual plans, surely the change of personnel should be looked for.

(Posted on blog on 16 May, 2014)

□

A Brave Move of the New Indian Administrator

The arrival of the new Indian leader has been sensed across the globe. For the very first time, Indian politics was at the center of discussion in every probable nation. It was overwhelming to notice overseas newspapers and news headlines flooded with the win of BJP, and more precisely, Mr. Narendra Modi. Plus, the formation of a stable government at the center has boosted the confidence of the global market; hence stakeholders are much more relaxed and aspirant. Though the Modi-led union government will have to prove what was promised during campaigning, the beginning has done a lot.

What would you say when you hear an Indian leader calling the head of the government of Pakistan in the swearing-in? The move could have been doubted in case the leader was someone who advocated support on religious lines. However, the story here is distinct. A leader, who warned the neighboring nation for forbidden acts within the borders of India, is now looking forward to an entirely unlike equation. This has proven a fact that a capable leader can never be predicted. A competent administrator realizes the need of the hour and takes appropriate actions accordingly.

When the past union government comprehended only one way to maintain relations with a not so participative neighboring nation, the new Indian leader has demonstrated that ways shall be devised as per the circumstances. And this is what he meant when he invited the leaders of the governments of all South Asian states to attend his swearing-in. The foreign secretary has confirmed that the nations have accepted the invitation; however their turnout is not sure. The PM of Pakistan seems to have been dominated by the extremists; however he favors cordial relations with India. Whether or not the leaders visit, India has a win-win situation.

Considerable to note in this context is the fact that despite numerous official invitations from Pakistan, the former PM, Dr. Manmohan Singh did not even once dared to cross the border. Neither was the former government ready to take a stringent route, nor were the leaders capable of sorting things with dialogues. And the same leaders are today viewing the measure of the upcoming PM as forbidden. The CM of J&K, however, has favored the call and viewed this as a way to building warm relations with a neighboring country which shares closest vibes when talked in terms of culture and history.

The game cannot be always played with same old rules. And the new leader has made an endeavor to revise the principles which shall be in the favor of all South Asian nations. Not just Pakistan, cordial relations with all other neighbors are being looked forward to for mutual betterment. Though funds to Indian corporates flow from European nations, neighbor countries play a key role in sharing of agricultural produce and manufactured goods, which demands healthy associations. The beginning may have appealed many; it would be remarkable to witness what shall be the policy of the new government and the vibrant leader.

(Posted on blog on 24 May, 2014)

□

PM Modi's 'Preventive' Measures Rather than 'Active'

It is true that with rise in responsibilities, productivity may decline. But, when we are concerned about a country, wherein people are anxiously waiting for real transformations, productivity can never be compromised. Mr. Modi has undoubtedly proven his administrative capabilities while ruling the state of Gujarat, wherein even the massive earthquake and the communal riots could not hold the pace of development. And then was the verdict of the nation in the favor of a person who promised for good days for all. While no one for sure can challenge the caliber of the PM of India; I feel a bit worried with a few roll-back measures.

Roll-back of hiked rail fares for local commuters, three months push for food security, and deferred gas price increase are not the propositions for which Mr. Modi has been known for in the past. Remember the rise in the power tariffs in the state of Gujarat in the initial months of Modi's governance, which though was a detested move; however had paid unexpectedly well in the subsequent years. Or for that matter recall the near-ban on liquor in Gujarat, which now is being acclaimed by all. This was the real-Modi, fearless and progressive, unmoved by any pressure or adverse circumstances-Moves that turned 'Gujarat' to 'Vibrant Gujarat'.

With clear majority in the center and with Mr. Modi as the strategic ruler, the BJP-led union government is expected to overlook what the rivals or even the NDA-constituents criticize, and to go for hard decisions, which may appear unpopular in the short-run, however, can add to the country's GDP in the long-run. For instance, the Fertilizer Minister, Mr. Ananth Kumar has recently ruled out any hike in the price of urea, even though the subsidy on fertilizers has been adding to the burden of the government. Vital to note, the Fertilizer Association of India has estimated that subsidy burden with respect to fertilizers is likely to cross INR 100000 crore.

Another noticeable event is the deferred enactment of the Food Security Law by a quarter. The announcement came just a day after the government decided to postpone the hike in gas prices by three months. In the same context, it should also be considered by the union government that the food subsidy bill is likely to touch INR 115000 crore in the prevailing fiscal year as compared to INR 92000 crore in 2013-14. Next is the partial rollback of rail fares probably due to the intervention of the Shiv Sena. The union government overlooked the fact that of 25 million passengers every day, more than 50 percent are suburban commuters.

Mr. Modi's words, on the completion of a month for his government, may have armored many of his unlike-Modi moves, but India looks forward to much more. And knowing that this person has all the capacity to deliver, responsibilities have doubled. Mr. Modi has confessed that his government had no 'honeymoon period' and hence it appears that he comprehensively appreciates his accountability. The PM will too have to realize that even a trivial roll-back of vital decisions reveal either wrong strategy-formulation at the foremost stage, or the push of external factors on the working of the government. For sure, decisions once taken with utmost will and on valid grounds shall not be reverted unless warranted.

Mr. Modi's vision and temperament, which prepared every common man to witness just the reduction in prices and upsurge in prosperity, now needs quick expansion and application. Conditions are however more tough and harsh, and the Modi-led government in the initial days has to scuffle with bad monsoon, the Iraq crisis, farmers' expectations, and the inherited paralyzed economy. And no one appears to swallow the bitter pill of enhanced prices. The best way out will be to disremember the criticism and take hard economic decisions that can pay off in the long-run. 'Preventive' governance will have to be overruled by 'active' governance.

(Posted on blog on 28 June, 2014)

□

Let Party-line Bureaucracy be the Mantra of Our New Government

How powerful are the bureaucrats and how important are their administrative capabilities for running the government effectively in a democratic country like India? Experts and analysts say bureaucrats are the real government – the ones working behind the scenes, influencing policies, making decisions and achieving results – when the politicians are enjoying the spotlight. Hence, to a large extent the bureaucracy does run the politicians and thus runs the country.

As such, the importance of bureaucracy with regard to taking the real decisions and getting things done can never be overestimated. Therefore, a motivated, well-organized, efficient and rational bureaucracy with the right vision is the secret behind the successful operation of most modern governments. Furthermore, officialdom is a fundamental part of any democracy, rendering solidity and consistency to the administrative setup, even while welcoming new rulers after every electoral process.

In other words, leaders come and leaders go, but bureaucrats stay, thereby ensuring administrative perpetuity. Political groups compete hard to grab power-packed positions claiming that they are doing it for the country's prosperity and citizens' pride. However, bureaucrats are not elected nor selected on the basis of the results they have delivered in the past or based on the performance of the government they have backed to date in the administrative process.

In the Indian governmental scenario, numerous civil servants have consistently held offices during the reign of political groups with completely dissimilar approaches towards development, governance and policy making. The allotment of secretaries to distinct ministries, after our new government took charge in the last week of May 2014, also reveals that many past office-bearers of the UPA regime have been wholeheartedly accommodated, which substantiates the organizational eternity theory.

Here, one may say that since the elected representatives are the policy framers, they are the ones who weld supreme power. However, the fact that every endeavor of theirs needs endorsement and support of the concerned bureaucrats to ensure targeted results cannot be overlooked. In such a scenario, why should accountability also not flow to these office-bearers, and why should they not be held liable for the non-performance or letdowns of the government in power?

In the currently prevailing system, the administrators have found it very easy to escape liability by pinning the blame on their political masters and claiming that they were just following orders. This is just an excuse. Moreover, if what these officials claim is true, why should they even hold an important position in the governmental hierarchy? In fact, every bureaucrat should be loyal not just to their superiors, but also to the law and democratic principles of their nation. They must also stay steadfast to their own conscience, ideals and expertise in both economic policy and political thinking.

Since bureaucrats were never intended to be the lapdogs or whipping boys of politicians, blindly obeying political superiors in a bid to escape personal responsibility or official accountability is not a bureaucratic virtue. If a public official is doing that, then he is simply following a mistaken model of administration since blind obedience cannot be termed as a democratic value. In no way can any country afford the burden of those who are given so much authority, weld so much power and are paid so well without having to bear a proportionate responsibility and accountability.

Undoubtedly, bureaucrats are not the only ones at fault. So, accusing the bureaucracy alone is not fair. However, liability for the wrong conduct has to be invariably fixed where it is due. So, let us here look at the big picture and seek the right solution. What can the civil servants do if they are dominated by political masters who are guided by absolutely different economic policy, political ideology and a distinct style of functioning?

This mismatch in political thinking and style of functioning can retard the pace of delivery and adversely affect the overall performance of the respective ministries and the concerned government departments.

As such, bureaucrats who do not appreciate or agree with the policies and ideology of the political party in power should voluntarily move out from very important positions to obscure roles or they should be compelled to opt out from holding powerful positions in the government because by staying in such important positions they may end up acting as obstacles in the decision-making process or on the path of achieving the targeted goals.

Since the perpetuation of these officials will not bring in the desired outcomes, only those bureaucrats who are supportive and favourably inclined to the ideology of the political party that holds the reins of power should be drafted to all the important and powerful positions. In this context, 'party-line bureaucracy' may be a workable solution while deciding on the appointments as well as transfers and postings of senior officers.

Party-line bureaucracy envisages appointing civil servants not only on the basis of their competence, but also by taking into account their affinity, enthusiasm and ideological orientation for the economic policies and political principles of the ruling party. This measure will not only ensure that right persons are posted at the right place at the right time, but will also guarantee total commitment of those bureaucrats and enhance their efficiency and productivity.

It is equally important to set up an effective whistle blowing mechanism so that all kinds of wrongs, frauds and scams, if any, get detected and eliminated promptly. In view of whatever has been delineated above, it is my sincere suggestion that the NDA government should prefer the candidature of adept bureaucrats, who agree with as well as appreciate and admire the policies, ideology and political thinking of the BJP, while finalizing the appointments, transfers and postings of senior officials in powerful executive positions in various government departments and ministries.

Once this aspect of party-line bureaucracy is taken care of, the next goal for the current NDA government is to create a framework that will motivate the officialdom to deliver outstanding results in all the work assigned to them, and also in all other activities and responsibilities they undertake. For that to happen, all bureaucrats should be made to think, plan, function and execute like the private sector CEOs. Furthermore, their performance should be measured like CEOs and each one of them who delivers outstanding results should be rewarded generously.

Currently, the performance of bureaucrats is measured by the Performance Management Division of the Cabinet Secretariat using Result Framework Documents (RFD), which gives over 80% weightage to process goals and less than 20% importance to outcome goals. Because of this, there is hardly any pressure on our civil servants to become outcome or goal-oriented as their performance is not being judged on the basis of the results they generate. As such, there is no way to differentiate between deadwood and high performers.

To boost the performance of all our government officials and to make them more accountable, there is an urgent need to design and use appropriate RFDs having some Measurable Time-bound Real Outcomes (Metros), which will make them more result and performance-oriented and less process and procedure-oriented. They should also be empowered enough to enable them to accomplish the desired goals. Finally, the performers should be generously rewarded, while appropriate action should be initiated against non-performers and deadwood.

(Posted on blog on 18 August, 2014)

□

PM Modi's First Year Amid Record-high Expectations

₹12 p.a. as premium for ₹ 2 Lakh accidental death and disability cover under the PMSBY, ₹ 330 p.a. as premium for life insurance cover for death due to any reason under the PMJJBY, Atal Pension Yojana for the 88 per cent of total workforce engaged in unorganized sector qualifying them for a pension after 60 years of age, and financial inclusion of millions of unbanked households under the PMJDY. I will call these the most prominent achievements of the Modi Sarkar, since we have been a spectator to policies in the past that just endorsed opulent and middle-class families to relish our national resources. Times when monarchs overlooked the impoverished class, when only smooth roads, buildings and highways were the King's aim, when correction in fiscal deficit and stock markets was any government's only line of action, we are seeing a paradigm shift with the arriving of a newfangled government. Most fruitful Budget session in a decade with record number of legislations passed is an anonymous feat.

Other notable big bang reforms embrace infusing a sense of buoyancy in the defence domain by clearing around 40 defence acquisition proposals, apart from revitalizing the ones that couldn't see implementation during UPA's rule; beating the government's own target of containing fiscal and revenue deficit; transparent auction of coal mines; ease in doing business (one form replacing the bulky set to commence a new business); self-certification of documents and its endorsement in all states; and above all, the fact that these are all sustainable, not like those so-called appeasing actions that end up in ruins, eating up the economy and boiling down to devastating the pace of growth.

Why I call it PM Modi's first year, and not BJP's year, is for the reason that the landslide victory in 2014 general polls rode on the back of Narendra Modi, the individual who was not only projected as the forthcoming administrator but was also conceived by voters in exactly the same way. And this person has toured as many as 17 foreign nations since being voted to power, has headed almost all the meetings and deliberations, be it with the RBI, Niti Ayog or the Cabinet Committee on Security, Economic and Political Affairs. Though running a democracy, as large and vivid as India, is no one-man show/onus, it, more or less, has become one due to universal acceptance of our PM as symbolic of our society, economy and corporate circle. Now that the PM not just relishes a commanding office in New Delhi, but also faces the heat, criticism, applaud and also pats on the back from people he is liable to, it becomes indispensable to assess his deliveries in the past one year, and know whether or not he could validate the faith of his voters.

At time when forecast by commanding market observers are indicating splendid days in the near future for the economy, accusations of being biased towards one community and rarely paying heed to attacks on minorities and their places of worship have made the aura somewhat faded. Land Acquisition Bill that is said to boost infrastructure and industry is acclaimed by businesses; however farmers' resentment and opposition's fury remain a setback. On one hand, crores of poor households managed a bank account in their kitty; on the other, lakhs of aspiring job-seekers are still staring for 'good days'. In the past, not many cared about the functioning of the central government, this time the settings are different and the internet-savvy and politically-literal public is reading and evaluating every work of the government against their self-set parameters, which are exorbitant, but this is what that placed Modi at the topmost echelon of Indian politics. Now call it burden or driving force, you ought to deliver.

It is not whether you like the phenomenon, 'Modi', or dislike it, it is either he is striving towards a progressive and sustainable tomorrow or he is not. Then counting measures that are to make long-term corrections in our lives is not only adjudging if we chose the most apt ruler but is also informing ourselves about existing facilities that we can make use of to augment our way of living. For say, the Union Budget 2015 gave us few social security schemes, which if enrolled would pave the way for hassle-free living. The Soil Health Card Scheme for enhanced productivity of farms, the Beti Bachao, Beti Padhao Scheme, the Clean India initiative, the Sansad Adarsh Gram Yojana, the PM Jan Dhan Yojana and similar other measures of the central government have assuredly hit the bull's eye, and have assimilated social furtherance with economic dexterity. On upsurge is denunciation of the PM for his being more receptive towards corporates; however the mentioned arrangements verify his concern for the poor.

Coming to his vision for developed India, which isn't conceivable without placing at par our urban infrastructure with that of other advanced economies like Japan and US, was it not insightful to think of smart cities and bullet trains, and launching the Digital India and Integrated Power Development Scheme? In this context, transparency in working of every government department and a corruption-free state are also to be considered as pre-requisite to match global standards set by these developed states, and post one year of ruling, which is rigorously backed by people's frustration from scams during the UPA rule, these still remain a painful area. The biometric attendance system has though improved working hours of officials of the central government and CPSEs, actual work is done by will and not just by being present in the office. The State Bank of India lately was included in the list of most outstanding establishments world-over and was ranked second to India's RIL; if you ask a savings account holder about his experience with the bank, grievances are, even today, way higher than the interest paid on deposit.

One area, where the incoming of Modi-led government marked notable adjustments, is the Indian economy. The GDP growth rate that was plunging steadily roughly during consecutive 12 quarters prior to the BJP assuming office observed a reversing trend and institutions like IMF and World Bank have placed India at the uppermost position, and it is expected to the core that we would surpass China in 2015 to become fastest growing major economy and this gap will soar further in 2016. This projection may not become headline in our agriculture-dominated society but the corporate circle, employer of most of urban population and rural migrants knows the underlying pluses. FDI inflows, which were excessively wary of Indian taxation regime's retrospective nature, are considering India as the most viable investment destination and poured in over USD 42 billion in the calendar year 2014. The flip side, however, is heavy selling by overseas investors in the past few days owing to uncertainty over minimum alternate tax; the same has resulted in freefall of the Sensex to over 6-month low and also in decline of the Indian currency.

No country can survive in vacuum; self-sufficiency is easy said than attained equation. In his one year of ruling, PM Modi, who realizes that integration of Indian economy with other economies of the world is more than necessary to attain inclusive growth, started the execution of this from Bhutan where he discussed insurgency in northeast India and the hydro-electric deal. New Development Bank to compete with west-dominated IMF and World Bank was an outcome of the Brazil visit; US-2 aircrafts for Indian Navy came from the Japan visit; in the US, PM asked for permanent membership for India in the UN Security Council and endorsed India as one of the flag-bearers of peace on earth; defense and civil nuclear power was on the top of the agenda in France; in Germany, businesses were wooed to Make in India; and stalled deal for procurement of Uranium kicked off from his Canada visit. Much more was fetched from Seychelles, Sri Lanka, Fiji and Australia.

In our country, the irony is that short-term perks supersede improvements intended for the long-run. And for the present government, our anticipations were sky-high; hence some discontent and condemnation is obvious. Voters assume instant overhauls in flaws and when this remains undelivered, anger mounts. We tend to forget that employment is dependent on employability of people and for the same skills are obligatory. We also overlook a fact that employment generation is not a one-day game; it takes ample time to boost investment, amplify industrial efficiency and ease process of starting business, areas that are being perused by the ministers; hence waiting rather than moaning is a better notion. Single-window clearance for businesses, skill development initiatives by over 20 ministries of GOI, probable enactment of GST, long-awaited reforms in labor laws, groundbreaking initiatives in the field of education by MHRD and promising Make in India drive are to add to our competence and produce plentiful job prospects for the youth workforce.

Along with, the government must also think of integrating skill development, education system and Indian industry, three dissimilar-appearing domains, which more or less are aimed at competent workforce for Indian corporates and MSMEs. One of the most vital areas of alarm for the PM is his projection as pro-rich and pro-Hindu by the opposition, and subsequent shift of BJP supporters to rival parties. Delhi debacle revealed much but disorders are yet to be remedied. Ravaging of churches may not be openly attributable to BJP and Hindu groups; the heat, however, is scorching Modi's magic. Also is farmers' bitterness over the land acquisition bill at a time when this vulnerable cluster is gravely affected by rain and bad produce. You may seek support claiming that opposition is just playing politics over the issue, but seeking favor from already-depressed man is like losing his trust forever. When BJP or RSS are referred to as pro-Hindu, yes, you are not to suppress Muslims or Christians; however standing unshaken for Hindus' well-being is expected, so is your authentic assurance to minorities.

That recent selfie of PM Modi with Chinese Premier Li Keqiang at Beijing's Temple of Heaven has been termed as the 'mightiest selfie ever' by the international media. When you criticize a PM's overseas tours saying that domestic obligations are snubbed in view of macro-economic reforms, remember that we cannot stay off the global radar, which was a case during 10 years of UPA ruling and a feeble PMO. And there exists a micro as well as macro aspect in all the endeavors, for say, the Make in India cannot generate employment for youth unless businesses across the globe view India as manufacturing hub. In the same context, challenges for PM Modi are wide as with shaky infrastructure, unskilled labor force with wide gap between school education and actual work and lack of bipartisan consensus even much-promising Make in India drive is vulnerable to die a mourning death like some of the robust initiatives of the previous NDA government.

For the people of India, it is a phase of change, something that we have always known, is fended off by stakeholders. Remember, change is the originator of furtherance and it may look deterrent, but is not always so. For PM Modi, use of apt change management techniques will help a lot to let people identify with government's endeavors, and this is what that will make him an acceptable leader, like India's former PM, Sh. Atal Vajpayee, applauded by all, even by sheer opponents. For better connect, monthly report of tasks done, along with evaluation by a group of judicious and unbiased appraisers, is desired. All in all, yes, there exists no mutually acceptable and foolproof methodology to judge whether the government of world's largest democracy delivered as per expectations or not, for expectations themselves are vague. Sure, however, is that India's standing in this one year has unquestionably upgraded, so have pluses flown to the common man. But, interminable expectations still await you, dear PM, and these can be a driving force during the remaining four years.

(Posted on blog on 27 May, 2015)

□

Momentous to Economy

Prime Minister Narendra Modi's Economic Diplomacy

Engaging the Neighbours

India's foreign policy was inherited by Prime Minister Narendra Modi from his predecessors. However, its contours were redefined by him with his 'Neighbourhood First', 'Extended Neighbourhood' and 'Act East' doctrines, as well as the 'Make in India' program. He scored his first diplomatic coup when he invited to his swearing-in ceremony in May 2014, the Heads of Government of all SAARC countries, including Pakistan and China, with which India has had full-fledged wars and any number of border skirmishes as well as military stand-offs.

Modi's gesture of sagacity and good neighbourliness was followed by a State Visit to India by the Chinese President Xi Jinping, which our Prime Minister reciprocated by visiting Beijing. All these moves sent a message to both the belligerent neighbours of India as well as to the rest of the world. These neighbouring countries were expecting, with some degree of trepidation, a major shift in India's so-far-benign Foreign Policy, after the leader of the India's leading Hindu nationalist Bharatiya Janata Party (BJP) was voted to power with a massive mandate in the national elections in 2014.

Modi scored again when he proposed Foreign Secretary-level talks with Pakistan, which were subsequently scuppered by the latter. Similarly, even as there was an incident of border incursion by the Chinese troops on the eastern front, he was busy discussing the strengthening of bilateral relations between India and China with the visiting Chinese President Xi Jinping at Ahmedabad. During Xi Jinping's visit, 12 Agreements were signed between the two countries. China committed to investing US$20 billion in India over the next five years and establish, among other things, an Industrial Park in Gujarat and another in Maharashtra.

During Prime Minister Modi's visit to China, 24 bilateral Agreements were signed. It came as a remarkably refreshing gesture on the part of the Indian Prime Minister when he demonstrated his willingness to sit down at the negotiating table with a country that had seized sizable stretches of Indian territory and was a staunch ally of Pakistan, with which India has been having border problems. The common denominator of the talks was the desire to keep bilateral relations in the economic sector moving for the mutual benefit of the two sides. It was unfortunate that Pakistan was not willing to see reason and share Modi's wish for the improvement of India's common destiny with that country.

Apart from inviting Heads of Government of SAARC countries, Modi exhibited his concern for the collective welfare of the South Asian neighbours when he exhorted the DRDO scientists at an ISRO launch event to work for the development of a dedicated SAARC satellite. This satellite, he said, should share the fruits of technology like telemedicine, e-learning, etc with the people across South Asia, with the aim of complementing the currently operating Indian Technical and Economic Cooperation Program in the region. Another occasion soon presented itself for Modi to demonstrate India's solidarity with its neighbours especially during the latter's hour of need.

When Nepal suffered a series of devastating earthquakes in April this year, India rushed its first plane containing relief material, medical assistance and medical teams within six hours of the first quake. This was followed by relief operations code-named 'Operation Maitri', the largest of its kind launched by India outside of its borders. India committed an aid of US$1 billion for the rehabilitation efforts of Nepal. Modi announced, "We will wipe the tears of every person in Nepal."

Visit to Neighbouring Countries

Furthermore, as part of his 'Neighbourhood First' doctrine, Modi undertook a series of whistle-stop tours to South Asian countries, starting with Bhutan and Nepal. The other countries on his itinerary were Sri Lanka, Myanmar, Fiji, Seychelles, Mauritius and Bangladesh. During his landmark visit to Bangladesh, the Instruments of Ratification of the Land Boundary Agreement were exchanged between the two sides and as many as 22 bilateral Agreements signed. Modi also announced a US$2 billion Line of Credit (LOC), which would be used in infrastructure, power, health and education projects.

This LOC will also create 50,000 jobs in India and provide a major boost to project exports from India and help numerous Indian companies. It would also accelerate the 'Make in India' program. Besides, Indian ships have been allowed access by one of the Agreements to the Chittagong and Mongla ports for the first time. The Chittagong port had been built and maintained by the Chinese and access to that port was, in particular, of strategic importance to India in addition to trade purposes. In short, Modi's historical visit brought the two countries closer to each other than ever before in the past.

All the proactive gestures and moves of Modi for the collective welfare of India's South Asian neighbours were reciprocated with a left-handed compliment by a peevish Pakistan, which accused India of trying to throw about its weight as if it were a regional super power! Pakistan demonstrated its recalcitrant nature once again when at the November 2014 SAARC summit in Nepal, India supported three pacts to enhance connectivity and energy cooperation in the region, and the agreements fell through when Pakistan dissented. With the recent cancellation of NSA-level talks between India and Pakistan by the latter albeit for a reason which could not be sustained, and frequent shelling across the border by the Pakistani troops, it remains to be seen if Prime Minister Modi would be visiting Pakistan to attend the SAARC Summit to be held in that country next year.

'Make in India' Initiative

The flagship program of Modi, namely 'Make in India', is an aggressive economic push designed in a bid to give a fillip to the country's manufacturing industry by encouraging global companies to set up their manufacturing facilities in India. During all his foreign visits and meetings with visiting foreign dignitaries, Modi has always highlighted the program and assured global investors how India's demographic dividend, competitive cost of production of goods, special investment facilities such as tax exemptions, infrastructural facilities, etc makes it a lucrative and ideal manufacturing hub.

The program is aimed at job creation and skill enhancement as well as achieving high- quality standards in the industrial sector and minimizing the negative impact on the environment. The initiative hopes to attract capital and technological investment in India and boost GDP growth and tax revenue. Modi has reached out to the regional powers such as China, Japan and Australia with proposals for investments under 'Make in India' program and has been promised over US$55 billion in foreign investment over the next five years.

FDI Inflows

According to the World Investment Report 2015 by UNCTAD, FDI inflows in India rose by 22% to US$34 billion in 2014, and the upward trend is expected to persist against the backdrop of a boost to manufacturing sector as part of the 'Make In India' initiative. FDI inflows to South Asia rose to US$41 billion in 2014, primarily owing to a good performance by India. FDI inflows to India are expected to maintain an upward trend during 2015 as economic recovery gains ground. Meanwhile, in terms of the sectoral composition of FDI inflows, the manufacturing segment is likely to gain strength, as policy initiatives to revitalize the industrial sector are sustained, including, for example, the 'Make in India' initiative launched in mid-2014, the report elaborated.

India ranked 6th among the most promising investor economies and 3rd among top ten prospective home economies. The report further said that in the manufacturing sector in South Asia, FDI success stories had come up, with the Indian automotive industry showing how large-scale inflows could reshape the trajectory of industrial progress in low-income countries. Meanwhile, External Affairs Minister Sushma Swaraj stated in the Parliament that FDI inflows increased in 2014-15 from three out of four major investing nations visited by Prime Minister Narendra Modi, last fiscal. All the 26 countries visited by Modi from June 2014 to July 2015 had a substantial economic component.

Emphasizing that the Prime Minister's efforts have helped in creating a positive image of India, Swaraj said, "As a result, FDI equity inflows increased from US$24.3 billion in the financial year 2013-14 to US$30.9 billion in 2014-15, a growth 27.3%."

Liberalization of FDI Regime

During the last few months, India government has, on its part, liberalized the FDI regime in various sectors including medical devices, defence, railways, construction and insurance. In May 2015, the Cabinet allowed non-repatriable investments by non-resident Indians to be considered at par with domestic funding, in a bid to encourage capital inflows in manufacturing and infrastructure.

Improved Relations with the US

After Modi took over as India's Prime Minister, there has been a marked shift in our country's bilateral relations with the US as he has put the US at the heart of India's international strategy. During President Obama's visit in January 2015, India and the US broke the seven-year-old logjam in operationalizing their landmark civilian nuclear deal. The two countries also decided to jointly produce military hardware including the next generation Raven mini Unmanned Aerial Vehicles (UAVs) and specialized kits for C-130 military transport aircraft. They also renewed an enhanced Defence Framework Agreement for the next ten years. They further agreed on a Working Group to explore aircraft carrier technology, besides the designing and development of jet engine technology.

During his forthcoming visit to the US to address the UN General Assembly session, Modi will meet Apple CEO Tim Cook. This has led to speculations that Apple is exploring opportunities to invest in manufacturing capacities in India. Furthermore, Foxconn, the contract electronics manufacturer and a key supplier to Apple, has meanwhile signed a pact with Maharashtra under the 'Make in India' program to invest US$5 billion over five years on a new electronics manufacturing facility. Also on his schedule is a meeting with Facebook founder Mark Zuckerberg on September 27 at the company's headquarters in Palo Alto, California for a Q&A session that will be hosted live on Facebook.

The other business heads Modi will be meeting are Google CEO Sundar Pichai and Tesla Motor's Elon Musk. Also, according to a press report, JP Morgan will organize an exclusive meet for 15 CEOs from the financial sector. Time Inc will be hosting a dinner with 100 CEOs specializing in infrastructure and manufacturing sectors. Besides 'Make in India' and 'Digital India', Modi will also focus on renewable energy. He will hold a roundtable on the subject at Stanford University. This will be one of the key topics of discussion in his conversation with President Barack Obama in New York on September 28.

Engaging Japan

Of special significance has been Modi's visit to Japan last year during which Japan announced a US$35 billion package over a five-year period on India's developmental programs. The two countries signed five pacts covering defence exchanges, cooperation in clean energy, roads and highways, building of smart cities, cleaning up of Ganga river, healthcare and women. Japan also agreed to help India in providing financial, technical and operational support to introduce Bullet trains. Furthermore, the Prime Ministers of the two countries reaffirmed the importance of defence relations between India and Japan in their strategic partnership and agreed to upgrade and strengthen them. Alive to the possibility of a threat from a rising China, the two leaders agreed to accelerate talks on the sale of an amphibious aircraft to India. They also agreed to speed up talks on a so-far elusive nuclear energy cooperation deal.

Deals in Canada

On his three-day visit to Canada in April this year, Modi had succeeded in securing a landmark nuclear energy deal, which will see the North American country supplying India with 3.2 million kilos of uranium over a five-year period. This deal brings to an end a long-standing moratorium on Canadian exports of nuclear materials to India. In the 1970s, India had used Canadian technology in its nuclear program. According to Canadian producer Cameco Corporation, which will supply the uranium, India is the second fastest growing market for nuclear fuel.

Indian Diaspora

During all his visits abroad, Modi has been engaging the Indian diaspora, which has become an important input to Modi's foreign policy initiatives in several countries. By virtue of the political clout they wield in their country of residence and because of their access to centres of power in those countries, members of the Indian community in countries like the US, Australia, France, Germany, Canada, etc are useful contacts with the overseas companies and establishments for selling the 'Make in India' program.

He has succeeded in convincing the overseas Indians that India has the strength, and now what is needed is the opportunity to expand its economy and that Indian diaspora has a crucial role to play in this area. The Indian diaspora is very conscious of the fact that no other Indian Prime Minister had cultivated them in the past as a useful link in their foreign policy endeavours. As such, they are all very eager and ready to take up this call in right earnest. Meanwhile, Modi has already made a mark for himself in hardselling Indian economy under the 'Make in India' program.

Homework

While the endeavour to hardsell Indian economy will continue during Narendra Modi's future visits abroad, some more homework needs to be done by the NDA government. These would include the passing of the Land Acquisition Bill and the Goods and Services Tax Bill without further delay to make the prospective global investors venture into the untested business waters of India with hope and confidence. In the meanwhile, there are already many reasons for us to rejoice over Prime Minister Narendra Modi's Economic Diplomacy.

(Posted on blog on 24 September, 2015)

☐

How to Combat the Menace of Black Money

There is no standard definition of 'black money'. As such, black money can be defined differently from different perspectives. From a legal perspective, any unaccounted earnings that remain undeclared to the fiscal authorities and on which requisite taxes have not been paid, may be termed as black money.

Origin of Black Money

There are two ways black money originates in our country. In the first case, black money is generated through perfectly lawful activity, but it is accumulated dubiously by failing to declare income and by evading taxes due on that amount. This kind of black money is found in abundance in sectors such as real estate and construction as well as bullion and gold jewellery, where there are large scale movements of unaccounted funds.

The second and more probable source of black money involves earning money through activities not permitted under the law. Such activities are considered illegitimate in India and may include smuggling, bootlegging, blackmailing, operating prostitution and pornography rackets, indulging in rampant corruption, terrorism, drug trade and other such criminal activities.

A classic case of how rampant corruption in the ministries and government departments leads to generation of black money was witnessed when the Congress-led UPA government, which was in power between 2004 and 2014, distributed scarce natural resources – such as coal blocks and 2G spectrum – to select cronies at the expense of the our country's national interest. It obviously led to accumulation of black money in the hands of a few.

It is known that banks and financial institutions seek an appropriate debt-equity ratio prior to sanctioning a corporate loan. Many business houses approach banks with a loan application that reflects an inflated cost of project, with overstated cost allocated for capital goods to be procured from foreign/domestic suppliers and exaggerated cost of construction. By doing so, corporates deceitfully lessen their burden of equity and many a times even steer clear of bringing in any equity in the project. Otherwise, the difference is kept in a concealed foreign bank account and post laundering of the black money component; funds are diverted to an altogether different project.

The modus operandi of such corporate houses, in case of capital goods procured from foreign, is to strike a deal with their own front company (though not a 'related party'), located in a tax haven nation, which in turn negotiates with the manufacturer/supplier. Upon receipt of goods in India, the billing is done by the front company by substantially inflating the price. The practice is also resorted to in purchase of indigenous capital goods and construction of building/ plant by availing credit of an amount higher than the actual cost.

In a few other instances, proprietorship firms and even a few corporations falsify the disbursement of salary to employees by showing dummy employees in the books of accounts to enhance the incurred expenses, thus leading to creation of black money.

One of the major poll planks of the new BJP-led NDA government was it would track down and bring back Indian black money stashed in foreign banks and offshore accounts and also curb the avenues for generation of domestic black money. The quantum of domestic black money is currently pegged at 7% of India's GDP (around US$1.9 trillion in 2013) and it exists mainly due to corruption in high places in the government and the prevalence of large-scale cash transactions as opposed to the use of proper banking channels.

Parking Spots for Black Money

Domestic black money is presumably invested in real estate, construction and the service sector as well as bullion and gold jewellery, which constitute two-thirds of the economy. Meanwhile, a huge proportion of black money also goes out of our country in the form of illicit financial flows across international borders through hawala operators. Thereafter, they end up in foreign tax havens or are held as illicit wealth or deposits in Swiss bank accounts.

Till the early 1980s, the marginal rate of taxation in India being very high – the highest taxation slab was as high as 90% – the tendency of the rich and wealthy was to keep their money abroad, particularly by trade mispricing. A study by Global Financial Integrity says between 2002 and 2011, nearly US$344 billion of illicit money moved from India to various tax havens. Meanwhile, the Associated Chamber of Commerce and Industry of India (Assocham) has pegged the Indian black money stashed abroad at around ₹ 120 lakh crore or US$2 trillion.

Surprisingly, a huge amount of black money that goes out of India through the hawala operators are re-routed back into India in the form of foreign money via the Foreign Direct Investment (FDI) route. According to a White Paper on black money published in 2012 by the Union Finance Ministry, the main inflow of FDI in India was caused by the return of black money. FDI statistics perhaps point to this fact.

As per data released by the Department of Industrial Policy and Promotion (DIPP), from April 2000 to March 2011, FDI from Mauritius was 41.80% of the entire FDI received by India, whereas Singapore contributed about 9.17%. So, more than half of the FDI received by India during that period probably was black money subject to 'round tripping' and was not real FDI but black money that got laundered into white money and re-entered the country of origin.

Though all of the money from Mauritius and Singapore may not be black money, it would be presumptuous to assume that the rest of the FDI flowing in from countries like the UK, the US, Japan, Germany, Switzerland, the Netherlands, France and Korea is all money, as white as snow.

Our government's White Paper further observes, "Mauritius and Singapore with their small economies cannot be the sources of such huge investments and it is apparent that the investments are routed through these jurisdictions for avoidance of taxes and/or for concealing the identities from the revenue authorities of the ultimate investors, many of whom could actually be Indian residents, who have invested in their own companies through a process known as round tripping."

If secret bank accounts and the tax haven system had been transparent, this money may not have left the shores in the first place. Round tripping and huge amounts of black money movement happens because the compliance costs of round tripping is lower than that of paying taxes, unless the money is illegally earned in the first place.

For illegally-earned money, secrecy and concealment is essential and round-tripping is one of the most obvious options for legitimizing the income. The tax havens exist to act as conduits and parking spots for black money.

Another instrument that enables unscrupulous people to generate and launder ill-gotten money anonymously is Participatory Notes. PNs are leveraged instruments involving Indian equity, debt or derivatives issued by Foreign Institutional Investors (FIIs) to individuals and institutions who wish to invest in Indian stock markets without registering themselves with the market regulator, the Securities Exchange Board of India (SEBI).

What worries the SEBI is the source of huge amount of foreign money that flows into the country through this route. More often than not, black money generated in the country is sent out by hawala operators and re-routed by Participatory Notes targeting the Indian capital market in a bid to rig share prices or to manipulate stock market operations.

Strategies to Combat the Menace of Black Money

As a first step towards combating the menace of black money, our government has already constituted a Special Investigation Team (SIT) comprising top bosses of the country's premier investigation, enforcement and intelligence agencies. The officers who form part of the SIT include Secretary of the Department of Revenue, a Deputy Governor of the Reserve Bank of India, Intelligence Bureau Director, Director of Enforcement Directorate, Director of the Central Bureau of Investigation, Chairman of the Central Board of Direct Taxes and the Director of the General Narcotics Control Bureau. Director General of the Directorate of Revenue Intelligence, Director of the Financial Intelligence Unit, Secretary of the Research and Analysis Wing and a Joint Secretary (Foreign Tax and Tax Research) in the Finance Ministry are its other members.

The Terms of Reference for the SIT, issued by the Department of Revenue under the Finance Ministry, states that the elite team will investigate all matters "with respect to unaccounted monies being stashed in foreign banks by Indians or other entities operating in India that may arise in the course of such investigations and proceedings."

The SIT submitted a report to the court in August 2014 with some details related to over-invoicing of power equipment imports and how this leads to generation of black money. The report has suggested that all bulky imports should be comprehensively scrutinized for over-invoicing and that Double Taxation Avoidance Agreement (DTAA) was not the apt route for fetching requisite data from foreign banks. In such cases, the scrutiny work should be assigned to the squads already working in the field of taxation and revenue intelligence.

The task of managing taxation matters, arising from cross-border deals and transfer pricing, currently lies with the Director of Income Tax (International Taxation), which in turn stands accountable for curbing the cases of black money with more than 50, 000 employees. Doubtful financial transactions come under the purview of the Financial Intelligence Unit. Similar other roles are assigned to the Central Board of Excise and Customs, Directorate of Revenue Intelligence and the Central Economic Intelligence Bureau, which are staffed with well-qualified and competent people. However, since India still ranks high when illegal money deposits in foreign banks are taken into consideration, what needs to be done is the overall restructuring of all these departments.

Next, the NDA government needs to take note of the report submitted by the MC Joshi Committee, which advocates rigorous imprisonment under the Prevention of Corruption Act, setting up of the National Tax Tribunal and reporting of bulky financial transactions (global) to the law enforcement agencies (similar to the USA Patriot Act). Our government should also announce a suitable Amnesty Scheme or a Voluntary Disclosure Scheme for those who are ready to reveal their black money records, pay tax and transfer their black money lying abroad into our country.

The RBI's measure of calling back the pre-2005 currency notes will also help the authorities to get rid of unaccounted money lying with a section of unscrupulous elements. Furthermore, the Whistle Blower laws, which can play a key role in reporting and tax recovery, will have to be reinforced, along with more liability on corporate auditors.

An area, which most of the time goes unnoticed, is the route used by offenders for moving their black money from India to foreign banks. It is not just the hawala; rather many such ways still remain uncovered. In this context, as recommended by the SIT recently, India should revisit all the Double Taxation Avoidance Agreements (DTAAs), redraft them so as to add new covenants that can allow Indian authorities to pierce the veil and introduce penal provisions to attach the Indian assets of offenders. This is important, because agreements need to be in place with Switzerland under the Automatic Exchange of Information provisions for the Organization for Economic Cooperation and Development (OECD) countries.

A much better option is to pass a domestic law like the FATCA (Foreign Account Tax Compliance Act) introduced by the US. Indian citizens living outside India, who still retain Indian citizenship, should report their financial accounts held outside India to the Indian Revenue Service, and foreign financial institutions should be required to report to Indian authorities about their Indian clients. This will of course need to be moderated in the Indian context, but the principles can remain the same.

Another major recommendation of the SIT is to amend the Prevention of Money Laundering Act so that the Enforcement Directorate (ED) would be able to attach properties of defaulters who do not bring back black money. These are very effective suggestions, but many things will have to be weighed well before any particular option is selected and implemented.

For repatriation of black money stashed in foreign banks, the Union government can also consider promulgating an ordinance to nationalize black money held by our citizens in tax havens abroad and bring the money back into the Indian financial system. The proposed ordinance will be in consonance with the Swiss Federal Act on the Restitution of Illicit Assets Act of October 1, 2010.

Simultaneously, the government should take steps to minimize generation of black money. To begin with, it could put an end to Participatory Notes, the main attraction of which is the anonymity it provides. Because of this, even terrorists are known to park their funds in PN as it enables them to generate and launder their ill-gotten wealth anonymously.

Another source of black money generation that needs to be plugged is the Indo-Mauritius Double Taxation Avoidance Treaty (DTAT). Under this treaty, no resident of Mauritius would be taxed in India on capital gains arising out of sale of securities in India, whereas capital gains arising out of sale of shares or securities for an Indian would be subject to capital gains tax. Currently, as there are no taxes on Mauritius-based FIIs investing in India, the tiny Indian Ocean island nation has emerged as the largest investor in India, accounting for almost half of the country's FDI. The tax losses to India as a result of the DTAT are estimated at thousands of crores of rupees.

Furthermore, all vulnerable sectors of the Indian economy, for instance bullion trading and real estate, need immediate attention. Under-reporting of transactions, forged paperwork, and parking of illicit money are very common practices in bullion trade as well as in the real estate sector. Similarly, to mitigate corruption, India needs more of economic liberalization with respect to permits, licenses and approvals from government departments.

Finally, some more measures that can be considered for repatriating as well as curbing generation of black money are briefly enumerated below:

1. Checking and redrafting the existing Double Taxation Avoidance Agreements (DTTAs) in a bid to make them better and with a view to remove confidentiality clauses (wherever possible).
2. Creating Agreements for Information Exchange where DTAAs are not possible.
3. Setting up Income Tax cells in key tax havens to work in real time with local authorities.
4. Making taxes low and penalties high.
5. Simplifying tax provisions and creating greater incentives to pay tax.
6. Reducing multiplicity of taxes and eliminating accounting and compliance barriers.
7. Using all international platforms available to India to fight businesses trying to evade taxes.
8. Designing Gold Deposit Scheme with complete tax immunity.
9. Creating agreements of revenue sharing with governments in tax havens like the one that exists between the UK and Switzerland.
10. Putting in place a consolidated code for dealing with black money and tax evasion, instead of using different provisions spread across multiple obscure statutes and treaties.

11. Creating domestic and international automatic information exchange with banks and payment gateways.
12. Creating, strengthening and integrating databases that make it easier for monitoring agencies to do their job.
13. Offering amnesty for repatriating black money.
14. Pursuing greater economic liberalization, implementing aggressive reforms and reducing license raj.
15. In order to curtail the instances of overstating of the project cost while applying for a corporate loan, a statutory agency under the supervision of the RBI should be formed that must work together with the banks to examine and authenticate the pricing of imported capital goods over and above a specified amount. A policy similar to the 'Transfer Pricing' between related parties can also be devised. Along with, in all cases of corporate loans, banks must be directed to validate whether or not the loan applicants have brought in the equity amount upfront and the same has been expended prior to disbursement of the loan amount.

(Posted on blog on 12 September, 2014)

□

Gold VDIS for Better CAD and Fiscal Deficit

Indians' love for gold is in the open. From festivities to investments, almost every other Indian hinges on gold. Even if we leave apart those hefty gold investors, even the Tier-II and Tier-III towns play a key role in driving the demand for gold in India. Shares and stock market are unknown in such provinces, and beyond a savings bank account or a savings scheme under the Post Office, rest is the holdings in gold. No bills, no accounts, and hence most of our gold purchases remain disguised. This adds to the already-high unaccounted money which easily beats the taxing authorities. We talk about dealings in real estate transactions that contravene with the legislation by bringing only the 60-70 per cent of transaction value under the tax bracket. Here, shall the authorities not pay heed to a crucial fact that gold has always been a relaxed way to conceal black money?

Records reveal that Indians own over 25, 000 tonnes of gold. On a yearly basis, almost 900 tonnes is added to this holding. If measured in terms of currency, the value of this gold is USD 1.2 trillion. Being the world's top bullion consumer, and sometimes second to China, import of this precious metal remains always at its high, accounting for our trade deficit. The upsurge in the inbound shipments has many a times been followed by a hike in tax on import. In order to maintain the current account deficit to a sustainable level, gold imports have always been a target. Now all that consumption of gold in our country is not just confined to jewelry purchases; a substantial portion of this can be attributed to investments in gold. And all such purchases are rarely backed by invoices, thus rendering the transactions go unaccounted for. USD 1.2 trillion or even more, that we have in the form of gold, is something that has a dirty nexus with black money.

Vital to note, the study, that was presented a couple of months ago to the new SIT on black money and to the Finance Ministry, reveals that the extent of unaccounted money in India may be as high as 71 per cent of the GDP. This means that this dirty parallel economy could be up to USD 1.4 trillion. The report lays special emphasis on the role of gold with respect to laundering of the unaccounted money. The Indian gold market is as non-transparent as the real estate market, as per the report, which tells how easy it is for anyone to park black money in gold. The CBDT too reported a couple of years ago that procurement of gold bullion and jewelry is the second largest parking lot for the unlawful money next to the real estate sector. A 1-percent tax on purchase of gold by any manufacturer/retail customer was the way to collect tax on cash acquisitions owing to the outlook that such cash may have come from an unaccounted source.

In the search and seizure operations of the Income Tax Department, cases have shown that enormous sum of black money converted to gold and jewelry is stockpiled safely in bank lockers. World Gold Council counts India's annual gold imports at a breathtaking above-900 tonnes, which means that almost USD 50 billion flows in India in the form of gold and is then acquired without any audit trail. Real estate dealings can be made less vulnerable to black money laundering by ensuring declaration of true value and entire receipt flowing into the economy; however in case of gold, upsurges in import duty or levying of tax on cash purchases cannot be an ample measure. Directorate of Income Tax, in an investigation conducted in 2009-10, found that the real estate, and the gold jewelry and bullion sectors, along with the manufacturing sector account for the leading chunk of unaccounted money. The government, hence, needs to pay heed to gold.

Herein, the government must urgently consider coming up with a scheme for voluntary declaration of any hidden holdings in gold. The declared gold can be taxed at 30 per cent and then be allowed to flow freely, thus helping lessen our gold imports and trimming down CAD. Tax evaders would pay taxes, and interest and penalty (at lesser rates), along with the promise to keep their identity unrevealed. Plus, source of income should not be asked. The measure can conclude to unearthing of at least 40 per cent of black money laundered via investments in gold. This would roughly sum up to USD 400 billion. Tax of 30 per cent would mean addition of USD 120 billion to the government's treasury.

This, on one hand would bring down the fiscal deficit, add to the economic dexterity by pumping up education, healthcare, agriculture, and industrial sectors by way of dedicated allocation of funds, and by adding almost 12000 tonnes to our gold, this would render zero import of gold for next 12 years, thus trimming down the CAD.

(Posted on blog on 20 September, 2014)

□

Financial Inclusion is Lacking Without Retail Equity Participation

While most of the Indians know about the Reserve Bank of India, only a trivial fraction is aware of Securities and Exchange Board of India (SEBI), a statutory body regulating the functioning of the stock market. Bullish trend in the NSE or BSE is cheered by many, but of us how many have actually held shares/debentures, or for that matter have earned any dividend/interest? Of course, almost every economist and all books on fiscal matters regard banking and stock market as the backbones of any economy. India has so far been successful (though greater heights have only been attained after the Pradhan Mantri Jan Dhan Yojana) in widening the services and the customer base of banking sector; however the percentage of Indians holding a demat account is still below 2.

Leave futures and options, the irony is that a common man is unfamiliar with NSE, BSE, NSDL, or a Depository Participant. Let me consider this with respect to requirement of funds by any corporate house that, in case zero or low commitment funds are absent, needs to approach banks, financial institutions, and foreign investors. Yes, the scenario will sound more apt if we talk just about the listed companies on recognized SEs; still it cannot be denied that with requisite push to the number of transactions in the SEs, more and more companies would look forward to entering the sphere. Herein, it is vital to note that the Bombay Stock Exchange (BSE), the oldest exchange in Asia, has just over 5000 companies listed, of which more than 1200 are in the suspended category.

Shares, of course, is one of the most relaxed ways for corporate houses to raise money for taking up a new project or for restructuring as they carry nil commitments (dividend is payable only on profits).

Bank loans, on the contrary, carry debt servicing charges and hence are to be taken care of even when the business does not prove viable. With respect to shareholders, shares means contributing in the corporate house's evolution, earning some extra bit which is not possible with fixed rate of interest in banks, and tax benefits. The economy, on the whole, with an upsurge in transactions on share market, profits from controlled foreign liabilities, and much greater savings. Banks and FIs are also to gain with decreased NPAs and reduced burden of handling cumbersome records.

Money vs. Capital market is a gone discussion. Today, every economy knows the crucial role of capital market, without which sustainable development is unmanageable. Herein, the Indian economy embraces just over 20 million demat accounts, of which more than 30 per cent are zero-balance with nil transactions. Another 5-8 per cent is held purely by commodity traders who do not have any equity exposure. The months of February and March this year witnessed record closure of demat accounts (over 52000 closed in January), despite the anticipated bullish trend in the stock market. It was only in 2008, that a push was seen in the number of demat accounts when Coal India came up with India's largest equity public issue. The Rajiv Gandhi Equity Scheme (RGESS), which was launched with the aim of enhancing equity participation, has not yielded any outcomes.

Enhanced sharing of retail investors is indispensable if the new government is targeting better milieu for corporates and financial inclusion of common man. The RGESS allowed investments by retail investors of up to INR 50, 000 in the domestic capital market with 50 per cent tax savings. However, the then-rulers failed to comprehend the fact that even the literate and working section of our society is unaware of the basics of share trading. Those lured towards the bullish trend have lost their money owing to high risks and low data. Experts have many a time revealed how market makers build up market for a particular stock without any fundamentals, owing to which an unknown investor participates with a view to making quick profits, however, ends up losing the hard-earned money when the market abruptly falls. The capital market, in the current state, has made it dreadful for the corporate houses to plan timely expansions and strategic restructurings. Cited hereunder are some proposals to the vibrant new PM.

Prior to launching any scheme such as the RGESS, the concepts of capital market, share trading, risks and gains, and IEPF are to be made acknowledged. Along with, banks and other DPs will have to be encouraged to open no-frills demat accounts, since most of the closures are backed by obligatory annual maintenance charges and nil transactions. The PMJDY model can be replicated. SEBI and the MCA must realign their rules related to IPOs and FPOs. NDSL and CSDL have though provided an apt platform for trading, the quandaries in understanding the milieu, that changes every other second, are to be curbed. Entering into four agreements and 20 signatures for opening a demat account is the primary hurdle. Investor education, both at pre-account opening stage and post-account opening stage, is necessary. Hindrances while investing in overseas stocks, for instances, problems faced by Indians in buying the recently launched Alibaba IPO due to Indian brokers not attracted towards overseas trading accounts, need to be curbed.

It is now a known fact that the intermediaries follow their prospective clients only until they get a demat account opened; however no aids like newsletters or seminars are arranged for making the client aware of the prevailing trends. This renders most of the accounts dormant or losses incurred due to false market trends sponsored by market makers. With limited know-how of the capital market, employees of the PSU banks fail to encourage the prospective customers for demat account opening. In tier-II and tier-III cities, trade fairs, literatures and briefings on capital market can change the current trend. Along with, depositories and stock exchanges are to be stimulated to spend a part of their earnings in organizing investor education programmes. DPs should also be directed to send regular updates to customers with future projections on current stocks so that investments are not based just on the trend set by market makers. Though the list of suggestions is not exhaustive, if the push is accorded to Indian capital market similar to the lately launched PMJDY, viability along with stability can be expected.

(Posted on blog on 22 September, 2014)

□

Concrete Proposals to Reduce India's Current Account Deficit

A country's current account is said to be in deficit when the sum total of its imports, payments to foreigners on investments they hold in the country and cash outflows to other countries is greater than the sum total of its exports, factor income and inflows of cash from abroad. Thus, the current account deficit (CAD) also reflects the difference between outflow and inflow of foreign currency.

India's current account deficit became something to worry about when it touched an all-time high of 4.8% of the GDP (Gross Domestic Product) and the country's economic growth rate hit a low of 4.5% in 2012-13. This was primarily due to the hefty crude oil imports coupled with high gold imports and a simultaneous fall in exports because of the global slowdown.

Fortunately, due to the dramatic improvement in the external economic situation, India's CAD declined to manageable levels in 2013-14 and the year ended with a CAD of 1.7% of GDP as against 4.8% recorded in 2012-13. Since then, this improvement in CAD has augured well for the macroeconomic stabilization in our country. And as per the latest figures, India's CAD in Q1 of 2014-15 narrowed sharply to 1.7% of GDP (US$7.8 billion) from 4.8% of GDP (US$21.8 billion) in the corresponding quarter of 2013.14. The lower CAD is primarily on account of a rise in exports and a simultaneous decline in imports.

According to a Citi group research report, India's CAD for 2014-15 would be contained at 1.9% of the GDP or US$39.3 billion, majorly helped by continued restrictions on gold imports as well as strong exports growth amid a recovery in the world economy. Though the current year's projected CAD at 1.9% of GDP is lower than 4.2%

recorded in 2011-12, it is still marginally higher than the 1.7% CAD posted in 2013-14.

To eliminate Indian economy's vulnerability to oil price, capital account shocks and other such factors, former RBI governor Y.V. Reddy recently suggested that our country should aim at a zero CAD in the medium term. Though the idea of targeting a zero CAD may find little support, all efforts should be made to bring down India's CAD as much as possible – ideally to the zero level over the next 3-5 years.

While striving to lower CAD, it should be remembered that a research conducted at the Indira Gandhi Institute of Development Research indicated that India's current account deficit is countercyclical – that is, CAD rises when output declines and not when demand rises. For instance, during 2007-08, which was a period of high consumption as well as soaring investment and output growth, the CAD was contained at 1.3% of the GDP. Thus, this counter-cyclical tendency needs to be paid heed to, wherein, unlike the pro-cyclical tendency (that is linked with overconsumption), CAD is linked with output.

Boost Exports

To bring down CAD, undoubtedly the major focus of our government has to be on boosting the country's exports. It is in this context, our Prime Minister Narendra Modi in his maiden Independence Day speech on August 15, appealed to companies around the world to 'Come, make in India'. This call has the potential to turn India into a global manufacturing hub. By openly inviting the world to come and manufacture in India, Mr Modi was trying to fix the problem of sluggish growth of our manufacturing sector, which has so far put India at the mercy of imports.

To support our Prime Minister's Independence Day clarion call to foreign companies to 'come and make in India', the Union government needs to take a slew of initiatives aimed at boosting exports. First and foremost is to develop our country's overall export potential by providing cheap export fund to the manufacturing sector in a bid to reduce input cost as well as to promote R&D and innovation aimed at enabling production of qualitative and competitive products. Our government should also provide sufficient export financing to put Indian manufacturers on an even footing with their foreign competitors and provide expanded support for small business exporters in the labour-intensive sectors.

To enhance exports from the Micro, Small and Medium Enterprise (MSME) sector, the Union government should expeditiously implement the short and medium term measures recommended by the six-member inter-ministerial committee headed by then Finance Secretary R.S. Gujral, which had submitted its report in August 2013.

Furthermore, the Narendra Modi government may also consider setting a goal of doubling India's exports over the next five years and announce all the requisite steps to enable Indian businesses achieve this goal. The relevant steps could include expanding the role and responsibilities of the Export-Import Bank of India as well as the Export Promotion Councils (EPCs), exploring the scope for opening up more and more markets for Indian goods in different countries, hiring experts who can offer guidance and consultancy services to Indian companies to foray into new markets, while also facilitating exports of their products to various countries around the world.

Reduce Imports

Our import bill is principally driven by crude oil as nearly 85% of the oil we use is imported. As such, when India's total import bill in 2013-14 stood at US$450 billion, crude oil import at US$95 billion accounted for 21% of the total imports. In a bid to reduce its dependence on imported oil, our country has already initiated the process of exploration of shale gas through the ONGC, which is expected to dig 30 shale gas exploratory wells across the country by the end of the current fiscal. Shale gas is natural gas trapped within layers of shale rock and can be utilized as cooking gas and for other commercial purposes.

ONGC estimates India's shale gas reserve to be in the range of 500 to 2, 000 trillion cubic meters. However, much more endeavors in this direction need to be completed before we can exploit this resource optimally. Though, there is not much scope to reduce the crude oil imports bill in the near future, the solution to this problem lies in creating new energy sources that can replace petroleum cost-effectively as well as in reducing the total subsidies for LPG, kerosene and diesel that currently amount to about US$25 billion a year. Besides, wherever possible the government should strive to bring down our country's petroleum consumption by relying on public relations campaigns aimed at encouraging alternatives to petrol and diesel, lower fuel usage, tapping solar energy, promoting carpooling and use of public transport, bio-diesel, bio-ethanol, etc.

Secondly, India is currently facing acute coal shortages. State-owned Coal India Ltd (CIL), which accounts for over 80% of the domestic coal production, has been missing annual production targets during the last few years. Furthermore, CIL is awaiting environment and forestry clearances pertaining to its 241 projects. As such the production of coal has been constrained. As against a total consumption of 739.42 million tonnes (MT) of coal during 2013-14, the supply was only 571 MT. To bridge this demand-supply gap, India had to import 168.42 MT of the dry fuel during 2013-14, which has added significantly to the import bill.

Hence, to reduce coal imports, the coal ministry will have to fast-track coal extraction from the mines from the explored and environmentally cleared blocks held by CIL. Moreover, environment and forestry clearances pertaining to its 241 projects should be expedited and coal mining work should be started immediately.

The next major item on our country's import bill is gold. India had spent US$28.9 billion in 2013-14 on import of gold. As Indians are enamored of gold, there is an innate desire in most of them to accumulate maximum quantity of gold. Even the intellectuals find it impossible to convince their families not to buy gold, as investment in gold is perceived to be a great idea. India government has several times attempted to trim our craze for gold by increasing taxes on its import. However, so far such attempts have only pushed up gold smuggling.

To stem India's burgeoning current account deficit, cutting down the huge annual imports of gold is one of the best options as this commodity can be termed as the mother of all non-essential imports. For curbing fresh imports of gold on a sustainable basis, banks and NBFCs should be banned from selling gold coins and from providing loans against gold. Our government should also come up with some innovative and radical ideas comprising massive and sustained persuasion beginning from schools to public campaigns.

Many Indians prefer to purchase physical gold as it is perceived to be a very effective hedge against inflation in the long run. Keeping this fact in mind, our government should design attractive gold bonds offering 'super incentives', which can act as a substitute to investing in physical gold. And our government may also have to launch some aggressive super campaigns to promote the acceptance of these gold bonds. The 'super incentives' can be gradually withdrawn once the concept of paper instruments as substitutes to physical gold gets accepted.

Focus on Import Substitution Industrialization

To reduce its current account deficit, India also needs to focus on Import Substitution Industrialization (ISI) that advocates replacing foreign imports with domestic production. Depending on imported goods that can be produced in India is an unhealthy trend as it drains our foreign exchange reserves and also increases pressure on our country's current account. ISI as a trade and economic policy has the twin advantages of reducing current account deficit while improving domestic companies' global competitiveness.

Currently, many Indian traders deal in Diwali products such as fireworks, fancy lights and statues of Indian gods and even household items imported from China. They just import them on a large scale and stack such products in their godowns and display them in their showrooms. Even consumer products like cigarette lighters, batteries, locks, car stereos, toys, fans and energy saving lamps, among others, are flooding the Indian market.

The Narendra Modi government needs to take a note of this trend. Without further delay, it should come up with an effective and viable Import Substitution Policy (ISP) that will provide stimulus to the domestic industry and also fight the evil of joblessness. Industry analysts believe the Indian manufacturing sector has the competence to attain a growth rate of more than 12% provided the door for inviting funds, talent, and innovation is wide open both at the small scale as well as the large scale.

Refining and upgrading existing Export Processing Zones, assisting our small and medium enterprises to interact with global players, widening of incremental exports incentivisation scheme and streamlining the process of clearances from government departments are some other pressing needs. This measure will also prove constructive in terms of large-scale employment.

Lure Foreign Direct Investment

India can also focus on attracting long term overseas capital flows by way of foreign direct investments, to lower its current account deficit. With the industrialized world growing at a relatively slow pace, capital always keeps looking for profitable opportunities abroad to earn a high rate of return. Currently, India provides that opportunity as it recorded a GDP growth of 5.7% in the April-June 2014 quarter and expects to cross the 6% mark for the full financial year 2014-15.

Going forward, the quick and pro-active policies of the NDA government would act as a growth propeller for the Indian economy, which will further strengthen business confidence and provide added stimulus to growth. And our government is expected to continue on its path of implementing the reforms agenda in a bid to restart the investment cycle and revive the overall demand in the economy.

Latest media reports say India can attract billions of dollars in FDI from Japan as Narendra Modi during his first official visit as Prime Minister has promised speedy clearances for fresh investments from Japan. The areas that can attract such investments include railways, smart city projects, biotechnology, clean energy, electronics, defence equipment and technology, and overall infrastructure space.

Since Modi has also promised to improve ease of doing business as well as fast-track the government clearances, provide clarity in policy regime and more business-friendly environment, there is huge potential to significantly increase the FDI flows from many other industrialized countries across the globe.

Develop India as a Preferred Educational Destination

India, which offers good academic standards, globally recognized degrees and diplomas, low cost education as well as safe and violence-free environment, has everything going for it to enable it to emerge as a dream educational destination. For students desiring to pursue higher education in the engineering field we have IITs, NITs and other renowned technical centers of learning. If design is their calling, they can head for National Institute of Design (NID), Centre for Environmental Planning and Technology (CEPT) or School of Planning and Architecture (SPA). If management is their thing, they can choose from IIMs, Indian School of Business (ISB), SP Jain Narsee Monjee and many other B-schools. Film-making? Well, there's a choice there as well: Asian Academy of Film and Television (AAFT), Film and Television Institute of India (FTII) or the National School of Drama (NSD).

Despite this, every year over 6 lakh Indian students head for foreign shores for higher education after completing their graduation in the country. If the latest developments are any indication, Indian students have started eyeing foreign universities even for pursuing a wide range of undergraduate courses in computer science, product designing, journalism and mass communication, fashion designing, fashion photography, bespoke tailoring, business management, visual merchandizing and branding, petroleum engineering, drilling technology, beauty and spa management, among others.

The major reason for this migration of students is because they do not get admission in quality institutions within the country. For instance, Delhi University announced a 100% cut-off last year. With such high cut-off marks, majority of students are unable to secure a seat in good Indian colleges and universities. Thus, India currently faces a huge capacity constraint in the field of quality higher education. In view of this, our government in collaboration with the private sector should aggressively scale up the number of high standard quality institutes, colleges and universities that offer world-class education. For India, it is a viable proposition since we already have the technical know-how, expertise and experience to go ahead and implement it under the public-private partnership (PPP) model. What is required is political will and slightly tweaking our priorities.

One of the major advantages that will accrue to India from the above proposition is it will avert foreign exchange outflow of over ₹ 95, 000 crore in the field of higher education, which can contribute in a big way to ease the pressure on our country's current account.

Encourage Tourist Inflow

Our government should aggressively seek out ways to encourage tourist inflow, particularly from the West by easing the visa regime and encouraging foreigners to choose India for holidaying. Though India has everything, including beaches, backwaters, snow, desert and different weathers, to attract foreign tourists in large numbers, our strict tourist visa regime acts as a major impediment. This in turn, results in lesser foreign exchange earnings.

India's visa regime has reportedly been deflecting foreign tourists from the US, Canada and Europe to Sri Lanka, Bhutan and Nepal. The NDA government should, therefore, consider restoring India's foreign missions' flexibility for granting tourist visas as it would definitely help in attracting more visitors. Currently, India has agreement with different countries, including Japan, Finland, Luxembourg, New Zealand, Cambodia, Vietnam, Philippines, Laos and Myanmar, under the visa on arrival system. To give a boost to the tourism sector, it would be advisable if the tourist visa on arrival regime is implemented with other countries also.

Motivate Outbound Indian Travelers to Opt for Domestic Tourism

Lately, our country has emerged as the fastest-growing outbound tourist market in the world and in absolute numbers India is second only to China. The number of Indians travelling overseas is set to rise from 15 million currently to around 50 million by 2020. This will mean a significant surge in spending overseas. In 2011, Indians travelling to Asia-Pacific spent US$13.3 billion, which is set to rise to US$91 billion by 2030.

This makes Indians the second-biggest spenders in the world on overseas travel, after China. So, while encouraging foreign tourist inflow to India, our government should also strive to motivate Indians, who normally vacation abroad, to choose domestic tourism destinations over overseas destinations for their future holidaying.

India's rich history, cultural heritage, beauty, diversity of religion and medicine fascinate the diverse segment of budget and luxury tourists as well as leisure and business travelers alike. In fact, India is probably the only country that offers various categories of tourism with its geographical diversity and rich cultural heritage. However, due to various constraints, India's domestic tourism potential has not been tapped fully, till date.

The World Travel and Tourism Council (WTTC) has ranked our country among the leaders for long-term (10-year) growth prospects. Moreover, Conde Nast Traveler magazine has ranked India among the top 10 tourist destinations of the world. To encourage more and more

Indian tourists to opt for holidays within the country rather than going abroad, our Tourism Ministry should aggressively tap the unexploited tourism possibilities in the rural belts of the North-East, Jammu and Kashmir, the Andamans, Kerala, Karnataka, Goa, Rajasthan and the temple circuit of Tamil Nadu by setting up proper facilities there and by providing air, water and surface-transport linkages and connectivity.

If the airports nearest to these tourist destinations are connected with direct flights to Mumbai, Delhi, Bangalore, Ahmedabad, Hyderabad, Chennai and other metro cities, then many of the outbound Indian tourists can be easily lured to spend their extended weekends in these rural belts.

To promote domestic tourism among outbound Indian travelers, our government should also offer tempting incentives to tour operators, travel agencies and portals, hotel chains, service providers and other stake holders for promoting the diverse range of tourism packages comprising adventure tourism, heritage tourism, medical tourism, honeymoon tourism, eco-tourism, rural tourism, pilgrimage tourism, wellness tourism, wildlife tourism and MICE (Meetings, Incentives, Conferences and Exhibition) tourism at several tourist destinations and circuits spread across the length and breadth of the country.

Given the distance between various destinations and tourist circuits, the government should also ensure that ease of travelling – right from hotel booking, airlines booking and transfers from and to hotels – are all available at the click of a button and all the requisite facilities comprising hotel stay, food, transport, shopping, etc are all within very affordable and budgeted rates.

This point needs to be specially taken care of because there have been complaints from outbound Indian tourists that some of the overseas destinations like Dubai, Thailand, Singapore and Malaysia are currently working out cheaper than domestic tourism destinations like Kerala for Delhiites, tempting the latter and their families to go abroad for holidays.

If all the measures delineated above can be implemented efficiently and effectively, our country can avert significant amount of foreign exchange outflow in the tourism sector, which in turn can be diverted into our domestic tourism industry. This will not only help in containing India's current account deficit, but it also has the potential to generate large scale employment opportunities and thus give a major boost to India's GDP growth.

Attract More Overseas Remittances

Since a substantial portion of the NRI remittances get invested in fixed deposits, real estate, stocks and bonds, they can be termed as permanent foreign currency inflows that can help finance India's current account, unlike the NRI deposits that are repatriable.

There are some countries around the globe where they have shortage of skilled and unskilled manpower. On the other hand, some of our Indian states have acute unemployment problem. With the help of the India's foreign ministry and overseas missions, our government can try to coordinate with concerned authorities in such countries with a view to tap the prevailing job opportunities there for the benefit of its unemployed citizens. In fact, our government can contemplate setting up a separate ministry to facilitate this process. Once these Indians land up good jobs abroad, the money they send home to their families and relatives would definitely boost the total NRI remittances that our country receives.

It is also observed that many Indians working overseas tend to use illegal and parallel transactions to send money home. RBI should study the reasons for their resorting to illegal means and provide them the required incentives so that they are motivated to use the official channel for such remittances. Furthermore, the Reserve Bank of India (RBI) should try to boost the total remittances received from abroad by resident Indians by scrapping the existing limit of 30 remittances allowed per annum from NRIs. Earlier this limit used to be 12 remittances a year. After scrapping the limit, the change should also be publicized sufficiently so that NRIs desiring to take advantage of this move are able to send remittances more frequently.

Bring Back Indian Black Money Stashed Abroad

A recent Assocham study has pegged the Indian black money stashed abroad at around ₹ 120 lakh crore or US$2 trillion. The Narendra Modi-led government has already constituted a Special Investigation Team (SIT) to unearth and bring back this black money to India. Assocham has said it will submit its proposals to this newly constituted SIT.

Our government should come out with some tempting incentives or concrete proposals in the form of either an amnesty scheme or a voluntary disclosure program to facilitate transfer of all the Indian black money lying abroad into our country. If our government succeeds in its efforts at bringing in the said black money stashed abroad, it will instantly enable India to have a significant surplus in its current account.

(Posted on blog on 4 September, 2014)

□

Economic Agenda on the Top Priority of the New Government

Over 66 percent of the voting population in the world's largest democracy cast its ballot in 2014, reflecting palpable electoral dissatisfaction with India's administrative and economic milieu. The exuberance at the expected change in government was so high that the Bombay Stock Exchange (BSE) surged 15 percent and the rupee gained four percent between March and May 16, 2014, when Narendra Modi was declared victorious in the national elections. The excitement notwithstanding, the fact of the matter is that the new government inherits a beleaguered economy which is rife with poverty, unemployment, unmanageable inflation, fading investment, decelerated growth and lack of adequate infrastructure. Before we get into reviewing what the Modi government can or will do to jump-start India's economic growth, it is important to understand where the fault lies.

Planting New Trees and Felling the Burnt Ones

A couple of years back, normally referred to as the boom period, inept macroeconomic policy paved the ground for the current economic mess. The erroneous fiscal outlook and faulty monetary policy manufactured India's largest-ever credit rush. This conspicuous failure of India's economy is rooted in utopianism, which cannot be corrected by a one-size-fit-all solution. Grandiose measures will have to be replaced by complex and involved management of macroeconomic factors such that the current long view of the economy is transformed into a more meaningful short view. Macroeconomic policy in India lacks a deep institutional foundation, resulting in the country bopping from one crisis to another. The return of international markets to normalcy any time soon is a far cry. India will have to deepen its liquid markets to absorb the shock of a stagnating world economy. For this to happen, the country needs to replace its existing regulatory framework with large-scale reforms in the financial sector because without these reforms macroeconomic and financial uncertainty will remain. Reformation of the regulatory framework is essential also to prevent the misgivings raised by the knee-jerk economic interventions that administrators in India tend to make when there is a financial crisis, fiscal crisis and price instability. But these reforms can only be meaningful and effective if there is sustained economic growth; however, with less than five percent growth of the gross domestic product (GDP), the new government faces the uphill task of reviving India's crippled economy, which has grown at its slowest pace in a decade.

Despite the clear need for economic reforms, the government does not have the fiscal space for far-reaching reforms as the tax-to-GDP ratio has slipped to 10.2 per cent from a peak of 12.5 per cent in 2007-08 and tax revenues are unlikely to recover immediately. The new government plans to tackle supply side constraints, a major cause for galloping inflation. As indicated in the book titled, 'Getting India Back on Track' (Bibek Debroy et al., London, 2014) fiscal consolidation, financial sector reform, capital account convertibility, and countercyclical monetary policy are the four components of the reforms that macroeconomic stability and reduction of business cycle volatility beckon. To forestall financial ailments like banking distress, world economic meltdown, bankrupt pension systems, and securities scandals that have plagued India in the recent past, a sound framework for financial regulation is required. In India today, stressed loans aggregate $100 billion, or 10 per cent of all loans. A recently released report of the RBI-appointed P.J. Nayak Committee suggested that banks could raise equity if government stake in them was reduced. The report also recommended that some weaker banks could be merged with strong ones. While addressing a joint parliament session on June 9, 2014, H.E. Pranab Mukherjee, the President of India, said, *"We will work together to usher our economy into a high growth path, rein in inflation, reignite the investment cycle, accelerate job creation and restore the confidence of the domestic as well as international community in our economy."* The to-do roster is long, but the vital actions that top the new government's economic agenda are narrowing the fiscal deficit, making the business climate congenial, introducing anti-inflation measures, and perking up efforts to reduce the current account deficit. All the measures that the government undertakes will have to be linked with its revenues as it does not have enough leeway to make grand plans which require substantial expenditure.

High Inflation and the Bottomless Pit of India's Fiscal and Current Account Deficit

India's fiscal deficit may have narrowed over the last two years, but, as of March 2014, it still lingers at 4.6 percent of GDP. When put in context, this figure is alarmingly high, especially if we consider China, which recorded a fiscal deficit of only 2.1 percent last year. Moreover, there is a high chance that the fiscal deficit may actually be higher than the quoted figure, given the probability of statistical jugglery by previous state head honchos. India's fiscal deficit touched 45.6 percent of the full-year target within two months of 2014-15. While the deficit target slippage is a worry, the underlying source-below par revenue (collection from taxes and duties) – poses a huge concern. The government would have to take cognizance of the fact that stagnant revenues and messy expenditures will pose great difficulties in meeting the 4.1 percent-of-GDP fiscal deficit target set in the Interim Budget.

Foreign Direct Investment (FDI) is likely to be considered a major avenue for raising capital. Additionally, in the upcoming budget the government might consider introducing an aggressive disinvestment plan to reduce the fiscal deficit. This would partly compensate the shortfall in the country's revenue collections and rein in its deficit proportionately. A larger effect of this will be visible in case these funds are used for funding capital expenditures that would help kick-start investment activity and growth. However, for a healthy investment cycle to be initiated, it is important for the government to harmonize with the central bank's efforts to restrain inflation. Controlled inflation, which can be achieved by containing high levels of food inflation, is an essential precursor to ensure buoyancy in investments. During his joint parliamentary address, Mukherjee added, *"Containing food inflation will be the topmost priority for my government. There would be an emphasis on improving the supply side of various agro and agro-based products by reforming the Public Distribution System. My government will take effective steps to prevent hoarding and black marketing."*

Another expected measure for reducing the fiscal deficit and eliminating, not just alleviating poverty, is rationalisation of central subsidies. Subsidies can be divided into productive and transfers. The latter has averaged around three percent of GDP, almost double the levels of the past decade. Such subsidies have become unviable as economic growth has stagnated over the period. Welfare policies impact inflation and growth, thus it is imperative that India's archaic policies are revised to reduce inflation and accelerate economic growth. Since agriculture is the means of livelihood for over 67 percent people in India, far-reaching changes in that area are expected. The government is expected to increase both public and private investment in agriculture. The government could consider allowing private sector to build storage and stock-gain, and shift from physical transfer of grains to consolidated cash transfers. Agri-infrastructure will be one of the major avenues of investment in agriculture. Farming can be made profitable through scientific practices and agro-technology. One of Modi's biggest achievements in Gujarat was the revival of agriculture, and he is likely to mirror that across the nation. The agricultural value added in Gujarat grew at double the rate of that in India, and was among the fastest rates recorded anywhere in the world. Thus, at the national level a market stabilisation fund for farmers to get the optimum price for their produce is very much in the offing. Modi is likely to give attention to every state and see how agriculture can be boosted there. For example, he is expected to recharge the sugarcane industry in Uttar Pradesh by giving sugar mills incentives to clear their arrears of over INR 7, 500 crore. Bad subsidies do not augment the output, but good subsidies do. If the non-merit subsidies on fuel and fertilisers are phased out over a period of time and direct cash transfers are introduced, then the genuinely poor and vulnerable households stand a chance of directly receiving the much needed financial relief. Decontrol of oil is expected to continue in the new regime, and oil subsidies, which total INR 1 lakh crore, could be restructured. However, scrapping or revising a subsidy is a politically contentious decision and might take more time and effort than expected.

In the past, the current account deficit (CAD) was reduced through artificial means as all the expenditure in the fiscal deficit had not been accounted for. The CAD was reined in by almost halving gold imports, thus reviving gold smuggling. The new government is likely to review gold import duties within three months of coming to power. Another way to keep the CAD under control is to boost manufacturing exports. Modi, who has turned around the manufacturing base in Gujarat, is expected to appoint a commission to advance manufacturing in the rest of the country.

To re-ignite growth, the government would need to up the capital expenditure, which has reduced from four per cent of GDP in 2003 to 1.7 per cent today. Despite it being a tough task, high volumes of expenditure would be needed to start rebuilding infrastructure. In order to step up its revenue collection, the government is expected to rationalise and simplify its tax regime to make it conducive to investment, enterprise and growth. Tax evasion is also an area which is likely to be addressed through tax reforms. The July budget is likely to set a deadline for the implementation of two key tax reforms – the Goods and Sales Tax (GST) and Direct Taxes Code (DTC) – which till now did not get consensus from all the states. It is estimated that with GST in place, India's GDP will shoot up by a minimum of 1.5 to two percentage points, and the DTC will positively impact compliance.

Growth Steered Forward by a Congenial Business Environment

It is important to address the environment that characterizes investment in India. Improving the business climate should be the anchor of the new government's agenda. The reforms that the new government pushes would pivot around making infrastructure available and giving precedence to resource-based industries. The share of the manufacturing sector in India's GDP is around 16 percent, which is abysmally low when compared to other Asian countries. The foremost thing that has plagued the manufacturing sector is government policy which leads to a difficult business environment, rigidities in deployment of labour, insufficiency in infrastructure, regulatory delays and absence of transparency, high cost and unavailability of bank credit. While keeping land costs at acceptable levels and reforming labour laws such that employers can hire and fire are important policy level changes, the most critical is addressing issues related to the business environment. The business environment stands to improve if India replaces the multitude of forms with a combined application form for getting the mandatory clearances. Currently, in India, businesses need to file over 100 returns; doing business in India would become much easier if a system of one common return was instituted. The business environment would perk-up if the time taken to start and exit a business is reduced significantly. Reducing the compliance burden would help remove the clutter from India's business environment. Uniformity across the country in terms of registrations would ease the business environment in the country. Modi's government has introduced a deadline on every process of regulatory clearance. This would help remove red-tape and bring about more transparency. Cost of commercial credit could be reduced by introducing more competition in the banking sector by issuing fresh licenses on a regular basis. Modi has already mobilized efforts in the direction of making the business climate congenial in India. For example, with respect to the mining industry, he is keen on a model similar to Ultra Mega Power Projects, by which mining rights would be awarded as a package, with all clearances in place. This is directed towards reducing the time spent on obtaining permissions.

And the verdict is...

It has been nearly three decades since Indian voters delivered such a momentous verdict. Whether Modi and his team will be able to stand up to their promises and agenda of hope is yet to be seen. Among the first indications will be the soon-to-be announced Union Budget of 2014 in which Modi might have to take some tough decisions to jack up the process of India's economic recovery.

(Posted on blog on 8 July, 2014)

□

Clash of Political Groups and the Decline of Economy

Known to all Indians is the fact that every political group has a distinct vote bank and the subsequent coming in of such groups varies the economic policies followed by the preceding governing party. The clash between the DMK and AIADMK in Tamil Nadu brings in new perks and measures, which are in favor of one or the other set of people. Subsidies flow emptying the reserves of the government and thus adding to the letdown of the economic structure. When viewed in a broader sense, we can observe new governments coming up with all new sets of economic proposals as a way to recover the paralyzed economy; however no gains are secured.

Many experts talk of delinking the economic wing and the political arena, which would ensure that any change in the administrative squad would not allow the economy to writhe. On the contrary, the Constitution accords supreme power to the government so as to devise workable policies for the betterment of the economy. Hence, economic and political wing are somewhere or the other in each other's pocket. Indeed, India has witnessed numerous Finance Ministers with distinctive approach towards the economic arrangement, along with governments with altogether different perspective with respect to extending monetary favors or curtailing them.

In the year 2011, the arrival of the new government in the state of U.P. also welcomed drastic changes in the government expenditure structure. Subsidies too changed their recipients in the direction of the prevailing wind. Same is the scenario when new union governments steer clear of the strategies of the former government, leaving many vital projects in the midway, thus adding to the depletion of valuable and ever-scarce resources. We have even seen cases where funds are allocated by ministers in the areas of their concern despite the fact that real assets rarely augment. Funds distribution and policy making have become more of person-oriented.

Economic momentum that is much-necessary is broken up with limited tenures of governments and the subsequent coming in of all new set of decision makers. Plus, the bureaucracy too modifies the manner of working in view of the new ministers. At last, the outgoing government leaves a burden of massive public debts, which rarely bothers the new government, rather eats up the fortune of the nation. Also, with restricted term of five years, none of the groups of administrators bothers about long-term goals that demand consistency and nil wastage of resources. 'Mutual good' is thus replaced by economic opulence of just a few clusters.

Ranging from the foreign policy and guidelines for the corporate sector to the reservation system and defense outlays, every new government comes up with unalike game plans that set aside the preceding measures. Certainly, the economic environment demands persistence, along with deep-rooted consistency. For instance, when a newly formed government announces a sudden decline in the tax slabs or custom tariffs, the revenues are sure to suffer unless balanced. For quite long, we have been witnessing every Finance Minister with altogether dissimilar principles that may prove to be a blessing in the short-run; however fail when uniformity lacks.

Either the political groups will have to come up with a clear consensus on the economic wing, or a structure outlining precise powers and limitations of the newly formed government will have to be adopted. Else, post every five years, resources would be moved from one scheme to the other, leaving nothing in the end. Having promised a prosperous tomorrow to all Indians, the new Modi-led government will have to fairly assess the former allocation of funds and policies in place with respect to subsidies, taxation, corporate sector, and government spending. Those necessary and constructive shall not be allowed to die owing to likings of new ministers.

(Posted on blog on 7 July, 2014)

□

Yet Another Bottleneck for the New Government – Ambiguous Subsidy Regime

The UPA 2 government might have concealed the failures of many years by coming up with a Bill that assures food to all. The actual picture, however, is quite distinct. In case this had been such an easy and advantageous scheme, the administrators would not have delayed this for decades. Plus, what else could a human expect? Food is now almost guaranteed. However, producing, procuring, distributing, and managing foodgrains call in for labors and outlays. Thus, the scheme might look too lucrative; execution of this would demand sweats. Remember, procuring food for two third population of India at excessively cheap rates, and that too when the upcoming monsoon does not promise proper yields would be one of the most threatening tasks for the new government at the center. Though, the implementation of the scheme would call in for elevated pains, the new government now cannot even back out.

This isn't all. Ever since the democracy witnessed government elected by the people, products and industries have been subsidized. Ranging from fuel to food and education to health, subsidies are a part of every other domain. The motive is to ensure that the general public can procure basic necessities at manageable rates. On the contrary, the World Bank criticized the subsidy culture of India and commented that this has enhanced the incompetence of the Indian economy. The union government of India funds almost USD 60 billion from the revenue generated to the subsidy programmes. Realizing the adverse impact of subsidies, the chairman of PM's Advisory Council advocated trimming down of fuel and fertilizers subsidies so as to maintain fiscal deficit within the budgeted level. The new government post the 16th

will have to consider all the pros and cons of the ever-high and vague subsidy system.

Considerable to note, subsidies on non-merit goods are five times more than subsidies on merit goods, which depicts the wrong measures and directions of the subsidy regime. Amongst the merit goods are the construction of bridges and roads, followed by scientific research and education. Agriculture is the main constituent of the non-merit subsidy rule. The element to note is that in case of electricity, the per capita subsidy in richer states is substantially higher as compared to poorer states. Let us now notice what is eating up the state's money. The most vital explicit subsidies that form a part of union government's budget are the food and fertilizers subsidies. During 1974-75 subsidies on food accounted for almost 70 percent of the total expenditure on subsidies, which fell to 20 percent during 1990-91; however elevated to 40 percent during 1995-96. Export subsidies too are another key component.

Next, let us also take a sneak peak at the much highlighted programme, MGNREGA, with more than USD 25 billion spent as wage payments until now. Promising earning prospects for the residents of the rural areas, the scheme was devised with a view to promoting labor work. While the world is talking about technological advancements, this scheme is a reverse model. Above all, the projects are charged with severe misappropriation of funds. Plus, the outlays on this scheme have contributed towards the hike in the labor cost for private and agricultural projects. Inflation, too has mounted owing to the fact that the spending capacity has multiplied. Rather than improving the productivity, the scheme feeds people with ready food. The new government will have to rethink this project and come up with some control measures to curb deviations from the anticipated outcomes. Comprehensive streamlining of MGNREGA is much-needed for the real betterment of economy.

Are the state welfare schemes and subsidy programmes beneficial in real terms? A clear distinction is necessary between subsidies that are unsoundly eating up the government's money (for instance excessive food subsidy) and those which are assisting the economy (for instance export subsidy). Plus, it must to be comprehended that state welfare programmes move money into the hands of those who are unproductive, rather than encouraging the entrepreneurs. This creates a gap between production that lessens due to unavailability of funds and consumption that upsurges due to grants. The gap becomes wider when the unemployed are assured of supply of necessities, which in turn demotivates them to work. Also, what can be expected out of direct money transfer? Rather than utilizing, the beneficiaries are vulnerable to spend the cash received on immoral activities. Restructuring of the subsidy regime is therefore the urgent need of the hour. Surely, the anticipated disaster of the UPA is backed by extensive mismanagement that resulted in unjustifiable rise of prices and wages.

(Posted on blog on 11 May, 2014)

□

The Masters of Planning – Were They Truly Effective?

The change of administration at the center is much likely to bring in healthier changes in the organizational structure as well as the working culture of the think tank of the nation, the planning commission. It is for sure that the veteran administrator, Narendra Modi, who has exceptionally been advocating a comprehensive overhaul of the commission, would favor quick amendments. Vital to note, even the UPA reign PM, Dr. Manmohan Singh acknowledged that the commission had been working unproductively, and to match steps with the dynamic economic circumstances changes are necessary. Dr. Singh emphasized that the new world is distinctive hence the traditional sets of rules and regulations of the commission are futile.

Let us analyze the role of the commission in nation building since its inception. With a view to providing requisite pace to the economy and uplifting the rate of development, the GOI in the year 1950 came up with a proposal of setting up a body of intellectuals that could device plans recognizing the available resources and allocating these in the best possible manner to extract maximum utility. Inflationary pressures, scarcity of resources, deficiency in the supply of foodgrains, move of people inside the borders of India in search of home and shelter, and balance of payments disparities were the concerns that led to the formation of Planning Commission. The body was bestowed upon with the task of framing feasible and effective plans, without worrying about the day-to-day administration tasks.

The directive principles of the state policy as enumerated under the Constitution of India sets guidelines and mission for the government, and demands for adequate means of livelihood for men and women, proficient use of material resources of the country, and justifiable distribution of wealth and means of production. To uplift the standard of living of the Indians and to provide satisfactory earning prospects, the planning commission was to play a key and intelligible role. Ever since then, the commission has been equipped with workforce that has a proven track record so as to analyze the bottlenecks, recognize the opportunities, and formulate policies that could ensure prosperity and utmost utilization of country's resources.

Let us briefly know what is expected out of the commission. The foremost task remains assessing the capital, material and human resources of the nation, and augmenting these with respect to country's needs. The intellectuals are expected to devise plans and define step-by-step implementation process so as to help achieve best outcomes. The commission is also looked for ascertaining factors that restrict the economic development and for determining the nature of machinery that is necessary for successful execution of the devised plan. Thereafter, the commission must appraise the progress of the plan and suggest measures to ensure that the anticipated and achieved results are the more or less the same.

Now let us review the economic development of the nation which was expected to boom post the constitution of the planning commission. The limited resources of the nation were allocated under the licensed framework. Prices were administered, distribution was controlled, and production and imports were licensed, which resulted in economic as well as social unrest. The ones who were able to secure licenses and means of production flourished, leaving aside the rest to struggle. Nor was the objective of eliminating the curse of poverty and unemployment paid heed to. Rather than building durable assets, the government created artificial earning prospects that though were able to create prompt difference, however were a curse for long-run.

Until now, the ever-prevailing concerns of lack of drinking water and health facilities, mounting infant mortality rate, restricted literacy level, regional disparities, and rising unemployment are waiting to be dealt with. The urban infrastructure is not matching steps with the rise in the rate of urbanization. The mismanagement of natural resources viz. land, water, and minerals is known to all. Unequal distribution of national income remains a primary distress. Furthermore, the ever-high fiscal deficit, rise in prices, mounting public debt, and critical balance of payments circumstances have not just made the life of a common man miserable, they have also lessened the scope of procuring funds for the Indian concerns.

What can the solution be? Urban infrastructure has to match steps with the rate of urbanization. Development institutions in the backward regions of the country and their delivery system have to be strengthened. Economic diversification is the need of the hour. Special needs of capital, processing, and marketing for small land holdings have to be paid heed to. Wastelands have to be recovered and green cover to be extended with incentives to promote efficiency in the use of natural resources. The interests of the poor and underprivileged have to be protected. Above all, top to bottom restructuring of the economic management is necessary with a view to providing requisite pace to development rate. Deficit financing in terms of government's borrowings from the RBI has to be checked.

The planning commission that works as the body to formulate plans needs to think more than just allocation of resources. Efficient utilization of the allocated resources too has be paid attention to. The commission will have to play an integrative role and will have to coordinate the working of the central and state governments to bring in cost efficiency and productivity. Social infrastructure and human development are the areas of urgent attention too. Schools, hospitals, and scientific research institutions have to be encouraged, along with establishing a sound system of education and knowledge enhancement. While on one hand, market mechanism can serve as the tool for economic dexterity, planning in terms of scarce resources and social goals can assure development of all.

Considerable to note, the work of planning commission has been criticized by multiple committees. In the month of August 2011, the report tabled in Lok Sabha by a panel headed by Yashwant Sinha portrayed the failure of the commission ranging from delay in preparing the approach paper for 12th five year plan to wide imbalance in development across and within states. The futuristic vision, which shall be the core of planning, was absolutely missing. The panel realized that there was broad disconnect between planning, budgeting, and adequate monitoring and control functions. Can the nation expect timely economic and social reforms owing to the fact that the 12th five year plan, which was due to be commenced from April 2012, was approved by the apex policy making body, NDC in December 2012?

The UPA reign PM, Dr. Manmohan Singh realized the urgency of restructuring the working and accountability of the commission, though he was quite late. The failures of the government in almost every sector made the PM comprehend the fact that the think tank was employing same old techniques of planning in the era of changed social and economic circumstances. Worried about the future, Mr. Singh had asked four questions to the commission so as to undertake the work of streamlining. Ranging from the approach of the commission and new functions added to additional roles in light of the new economic world, the questions though have been answered by the commission's members, nothing could be attained. The puzzled and sterile members could not deliver anything more than mere plans.

The nation and the economy can expect much from the tested brain of the new administrator, Mr. Modi. His visionary capabilities and quick decision-making attribute are what that can bring in requisite modifications in the working ability of the commission. Planning Commission too will have to realize the strengths and opportunities presented by the internal as well as the global environment, along with paying requisite heed to threats and weaknesses of the economic system. Since decades, five year plans have been embracing the same goals, however nothing much has been achieved. Time has come to think out of the box and come up with groundbreaking concepts. Surely, the members of the new commission formed post the polls would realize their actual task of nation building and will deliver the anticipated outcomes.

(Posted on blog on 15 May, 2014)

□

Economic Restructuring – How Should the New Government Act

Post the 16th of this month, development and earning prospects will be the areas of concern for all. It can be interpreted that the nation is on the verge of electing a stable government at the center, which can take tough, wiser, and above all, quick decisions. The ruin of the economy is what everyone has talked about; however past cannot be altered. The future has to be rendered pace, stability, and robustness. The new government is probably to be led by a personality who has delivered more than the expected outcomes in Gujarat and is looked forward to for equivalent consequences across the nation. It is however vital to note that only with the consolidated endeavors of distinct departments of the government, expected outcomes can be accomplished. I will discuss prominent areas of concerns and probable measures that can add to the prosperity.

SWOT analysis will be a pre-requisite for the new government; post the ministers hold their respective departments. Every ministry must spend reasonable time in evaluating the strengths and weaknesses of the national economy and their respective areas of concern; and in comprehending the opportunities and threats posed by the external environment. Planning is the base of project implementation, hence sturdy plans and feasible goals should be set. We know that none of the ministries in past years has justified its role in the strengthening of the economic, social, and technological spheres of the nation. Remember, the new ministers would be inheriting burning chairs with limitless bottlenecks and past failures. Top to bottom restructuring will be the sole solution for the departments to bring in the much-needed synergy.

When economy is talked about, Finance Ministry is the department of the government that is looked upon for bringing in viability. Ranging from the expansion of banking services and financial inclusion of all to controlling the inflating prices and interest rates, the finance department has multiple targets to accomplish. A way has to be located with a view to minimizing the NPA level that has emerged as the most prominent threat for the financial system. Apart from the declared figures, probable NPAs are to be uncovered, which otherwise can add to the trouble. While past NPAs are the areas of concern, the government along with the financial intermediaries will have to come up with measures that can check likely NPAs. Incapable borrowers have to be recognized prior to their turning into bad debts so that appropriate recovery mechanism can be resorted to.

Financial inclusion is the need of the hour with expansion in terms of number of bank account holders and participants in the savings sector. After all, savings of the households and retail investors is what that provides the requisite pace to the investment domain. Inclusion will not only ensure basic banking facilities to all, it would also serve as a way for mobilizing savings and allocating credit. Entrepreneurial credit products have to be rationalized so as to help enterprises secure credit on easy terms, which in turn will bring in technological advancements. Financial inclusion as a target would remain unachievable until the strict KYC norms are addressed to. The general public while approaching the branch for a bank account has to deal with concerns of extensive documentation and unfavorable attitude. Also, to pave way for new entrepreneurs and fresh talent the lending mechanism has to be simplified and rejuvenated.

Ranging from betterment of the agricultural sector to the advancement of manufacturing units, challenges are many. The topmost necessity is to bring in technological encroachments sooner than later. Lack of proper infrastructure and technology is the prime hindrance of many sectors. Expansion of railway network and advanced tools for procuring coal are the only solutions to enrich the power sector. This in turn would automatically pave way for the success of business entities as well as the agricultural sector. Undoubtedly, technological advancement will be an effective answer to distinct bottlenecks. It has to be recognized that multiple state-backed and private projects are awaiting implementation, which has increased the overall cost of resources. Plus, the capital and the money markets that have extended money to these projects are on the verge of losing their stake. Quick decisions and workable strategy will be the key drivers.

We talk about revolutionizing education, literacy, agriculture and SMEs, and providing access to clean water in every of our five-year plans. The planning commission has been including the same targets since past many decades, however real outcomes have remained unachieved. The working of the commission in the last ten years projects that the department comprehensively failed to recognize the distinct needs of the states and carried out its operations with the same old laidback attitude. The most vital part 'Planning' was for sure missing. Preparation of vision documents for the coming future and devising effective policies is the core of the working of the commission. However, this body of so-called thinkers and planners failed to realize the goals. The commission rarely has any control mechanism to evaluate deviations from the anticipated outcomes. Inclusion of competent strategic planners and visionaries can be an answer.

To be precise, every discrete department of the government will have to focus on respective strengths and weaknesses, and will have to devise appropriate plans accordingly. Else, as seen in the reign of the UPA, departments would blame each other for the letdowns rather than recognizing their role in the nation building. For sure, the country would be led by a person with requisite know-how of dealing with worst situations; however, sole leader would not be able to deliver conclusions that are being anticipated. The team too will have to accept the accountability and work dedicatedly. The declining GDP and the inflating prices are not the only concerns. Basic necessities and the overall restructuring of the social as well the economic sphere are being looked for. Surely, tough time would commence once the outcomes of the polls are declared, where from the representatives will have to deliver what they have promised.

(Posted on blog on 9 May, 2014)

□

Economic Restructuring – Is that all?

Is boom in the economic prosperity of the nation the only factor that can overcome the concerns of millions? Try walking into a police station to get a complaint registered, approaching your local representative to get the road repaired, or asking for swift justice in the court and you would know what else we need. Surely, the general elections of 2014 are unlike the previous ones; however the political parties just have two prominent subject-matters to talk about-Secularism, and Economic Inefficiency.

Post the industrial reforms of 1991, liberalization and globalization delivered pace to the economy, which in turn paid incentives to private entities, employees, and the government. Sad to note, neither the educational facilities improve nor the poverty figure declined with the same pace. The consumer electronics, telecommunication, retail clothing, and automobile market are uninterruptedly fetching revenues, and we still are just focusing on economic dexterity. Though, the GDP growth rate needs to be worked upon sooner than later; judicial, legislative, and political reforms too are much-needed.

In June last year, the Central Information Commission declared to embrace political parties under the purview of the RTI. Without delay, the political groups united and the roll back was announced. Considerable to note, more than INR 35, 000 crore are being expended in the polls of 2014, the figure that has made the general election most costly than ever. Untraceable cash contributions to the funds of the national parties account for more than 75 percent.

Fielding of candidates with severe charges of corruption by almost every political party remains unchanged. The government, with a view to extend a helping hand to law-violators, made legislative amendments to the ruling of the Apex Court that would have restricted politicians convicted of crimes to hold their offices. The Election Commission despite noticing numerous violations of the model code of conduct has not even debarred a single candidate. Shouldn't the state be delivered with much stringent laws that can restrict the involvement of law-breakers in politics? Plus, model code and Constitution for every political party must be in place that can promise undeviating and strict conformity.

The mounting figure in respect to the number of pending suits, which is currently 32 million, is expected to rise as new courts are rarely coming into the picture. The judiciary, which was looked upon as the most honored wing, has also been charged with incidences of dishonest conduct. The Judicial Standards and Accountability Bill, proposed by the government, encountered protest from the constituents of the judicial wing. The Bill aimed at assuring transparency in the functioning and independent investigation of charges related to judicial corruption.

First-time voters, who stand at 230 million in number, shall bring in change that can restrict politicians from luring public in view of caste and communal differences. Until when, would we select our representative on basis of religion and caste favoring attitude? More than economic reforms, the nation calls for deeper and sturdy restructuring of the political, judicial, administrative, and legislative pillars. Upcoming MPs must too consider this willingly.

(Posted on blog on 7 April, 2014)

□

Pushing the Industry

Proposals for Conquering PM's Dream 'MAKE IN INDIA'

In the 'Doing Business Index' of the World Bank, India's rank lately slipped two slots, a setback that has presented a tough challenge for the new PM as well as the investors. The tailbacks range from obstructive business environment and scarcity of capital to the challenges involved in procuring land, labor, and licenses. Let it be very clear, if the PM is aspiring for enhanced work prospects for the unemployed and India's dominance in the global manufacturing arena, our industrial sector needs to grow at 12-15 per cent annually and its share in the GDP will have to recover. In the past few days, overseas investors have ameliorated their views towards India, but much seems to be focused on the services sector. Hereunder, we have endeavored to segregate distinct aspects of doing business in India, and along with are some proposals that can change the milieu.

Human Resource

This can be termed as the most fundamental. Citizens prosper with better opportunities and so do businesses. The government has amended the Apprenticeship Act 1961, the Factories Act 1948 and the Labor Laws Act 1988. Mentioned below are some issues that the government should consider urgently.

1. Multiplicity of labor authorities puts ambiguous picture. For states as well as the center, all aspects related to labors should be dealt with by a sole authority that shall take care of industrial disputes, enforcement of labor laws, maintenance of industrial peace and such other functions.
2. Industrial corridors, investment zones, and such other infrastructure development projects must embrace a scheme

dedicated to Workers' Housing plans. Be it even a smart city, low-budgets homes must be a basic part.

3. Skill development for active workforce demand partaking of industries in designing the curriculum and certification of academic courses.
4. E-learning, R&D, train the trainer, and job-oriented skill expansion programs are the areas of focus that can promise comprehensively competent workforce.
5. Similar to 100 smart cities initiative, 100 universities be identified and developed in the coming years to match steps with global leading players.

Funding

From over-dependence on foreign institutional investors to lack of long-term lending financial institutions for stable and promising corporate investments, bottlenecks are many; however solutions stated as under can bring in the break through.

1. Long-term lending by financial institutions be promoted and a couple of FIs must be recognized to undertake this function.
2. Government can think of diluting stake held in PSU undertakings and banks through capital market, thus raising fresh equity.
3. Retail investors in capital markets to be fortified via information sharing programs and deepening of capital market.
4. Amalgamation of a few public sector banks to match global trends with respect to magnitude of operations.
5. Implementation of guidelines for year-on-year growth of MSME credit, along with zero-tolerance in terms of payment defaults to MSMEs and use of commercial bills.
6. Fill equity gap of MSMEs by allowing sources of capital such as private equity, venture capital and angel funds. Listing on BSE and NSE without need of floating an IPO.

Infrastructure

It all starts with resources. From railways to ports and from export oriented zones to land acquisition, every sector demands constructive measures. Hereunder are some key solutions.

1. PPP model be thought over and executed for development of railways substructure, right from procuring of railway stocks

for ease of mobility to commercialization of excessive land available with Indian Railways.

2. Privatization or franchise arrangement of public sector ports.
3. To promote hefty PPP infrastructure development projects, clearances prior to even bidding.
4. Connectivity of ports, airports and railway corridors with industrial centers, especially connectivity of coal extraction plants and places of consumption.
5. Smart cities with assured and reliable access to water, power, sewerage, and such other basics, along with inclusion of homes for low-income earners and affordable dormitories for MSME workforce.
6. For all industrial zones and corridors, skill expansion centers to be made obligatory with a view to upgrading the quality of personnel as well as production.
7. Inevitability and fairness to be accorded to the Right to Fair Compensation and Transparency in Land Acquisition, Rehabilitation and Resettlement Act with a view to ease land acquisition both for land owners and industrialists.
8. Change in Land use to be notified in a time-bound manner for impartial deals.
9. Any idle industrial space shall be allocated for time-bound period to avoid wastage of crucial resource.
10. Coal sector demands revamping of CMN Act and MMDR Act, along with developing such a facility that transportation of extracted coal becomes swift and resourceful.
11. Private investment in exploration and carriage of coal, along with setting up of coal dealing mechanism for transparent and quick sale and purchase.
12. To rejuvenate E&P industry and fund-providers, gas pricing concerns be addressed.
13. To attract flow of capital into the country, minimum area development norms can be reworked, and better inter-linkage of agencies involved in real estate development.

Road for Creativity and Global Competitiveness

1. 'Zero Defect-Zero Effect' production be encouraged and e-commerce players be made to follow norms of the industry.

2. MSMEs and other industries will spread wings only when the produced goods are in demand locally. Procurement by government, essentially from indigenous players is the need of the hour.
3. As done in the defence, excessive dependence on imports in terms of capital goods, coal, electronics, food grains, and such other commodities that can be made in India to be dispensed with.
4. Businesses to be encouraged to undertake valuation of quality of production and efficiency of labor so that global competition be met and beaten.
5. MSMEs to be promoted by way of compulsory procurement by state departments, at least 25 per cent of their needs, from this sector.
6. Multi-tier support system for MSMEs by collaborating with industry clusters and R&D institutions for inducing technology-based effectiveness.
7. Liberal policies and assistance programs for MSMEs to nurture innovation.
8. Rationalization and merging of programs run to help MSME producers in marketing their output through participation in trade fairs and events.

This is a glimpse of the roadmap towards successful execution of 'Make in India' dream of the government. It cannot be denied that the fiscal and legislative environment too needs a shift to a conductive phase, where GST and subsidy rationalization are pressing demands. For the same, the government can consider proposals of various committees, introduction of third party certification mechanism to replace the inspection system, and single-window clearance backed by supporting legislation. It is evident, that the above proposals are not exhaustive, but are capable to fetch promising outcomes if executed with authentic and dedicated labors.

(Posted on blog on 4 November, 2014)

□

Recommendations to Ensure Rapid Growth of MSMEs

Prime Minister Narendra Modi cherishes a commendable vision to take India to new heights on the socio-economic front. For this to happen, first our country has to catch up with the developed world in the manufacturing and industrial sector. Unfortunately, even after more than two decades of economic liberalization, India has barely managed to scratch its existing potential. The Micro, Small and Medium Enterprises (MSME) sector contributes significantly to manufacturing output and exports of our country. It also provides maximum opportunities for both self-employment and jobs, outside the agriculture sector. The inclusiveness of this sector is underlined by the fact that nearly 50% of the MSMEs are owned by disadvantaged groups of society. As such, if India is to develop faster and achieve new heights, then our government needs to aggressively promote the growth and development of this particular sector.

Overview of the MSME Sector

Currently, the MSME sector contributes 8% of the national GDP and accounts for around 40% of the total exports and around 45% of the manufacturing output. According to the Fourth All India Census of MSMEs, the total number of enterprises in the sector is 36, 176, 000 of which 1, 564, 000 are registered enterprises. An overwhelming 72% of India's 36.17 million MSMEs are engaged in the services sector, whereas the balance 28% are in the manufacturing segment.

MSMEs are complementary to large industries as ancillary units and this sector contributes enormously to the socio-economic progress of our country by providing employment to over 80, 524, 000 persons. In a country like India where millions of people are unemployed or underemployed, the MSME sector has thus emerged as a major provider of jobs by creating more employment opportunities per unit of capital. Furthermore, MSMEs are the nurseries for entrepreneurship and innovation. They are widely dispersed across the country and produce a diverse range of products to meet the needs of the local markets, the global market and the national and international value chains.

During 2011, the total production of MSMEs amounted to ₹ 10, 957.6 billion (at 2001-02 prices) and the sector manufactured more than 6, 000 products ranging from traditional to high-tech items. Meanwhile, the MSME sector has also played a vital role in fulfilling other socio-economic objectives. It has emerged as a powerful tool for dispersal of economic wealth and power. This sector has also contributed handsomely towards removal of regional disparities and economic backwardness in the rural and less developed segments. As a result, it occupies a strategic position of unique importance in the Indian economy, and also has the potential to lift the country to the bracket of developed nations.

Recognizing the importance of the sector and with the aim of making it a significant player in the global marketplace, our central government has passed the MSME Development Act 2006. The objective of this Act, which came into effect on October 2, 2006, is to facilitate the promotion and development of the sector and also to enhance the competitiveness of the MSMEs as well as to redress all the matters connected therewith and incidental thereto. Meanwhile, under the Public Procurement Bill 2012 approved by the Cabinet on April 1, 2012, all public sector undertakings (PSUs), central government ministries and departments will have to procure at least 20% of products and services required by them from the micro and small enterprises (MSEs). Though the public procurement policy for MSEs has become effective from 1 April 2012, the provision of 20% procurement of products and services will become mandatory only from April 1, 2015.

Challenges faced by the MSME Sector

Despite the Union government passing the Public Procurement Bill 2012 mandating that 20% of all government procurement of goods and services should be from MSEs with effect from April 1, 2015, several PSUs and agencies are yet to initiate the process of measuring how they will procure from the sector. Moreover, the transaction costs that the MSEs would have to bear for registration, earnest money deposits, etc are considerably higher than what most small enterprises can bear. Financially, for most of the firms in this sector, cash management and working capital cycles are very tight. So, additional transaction costs will impose a fairly large burden on them. For small firms with limited management capacity, the concerned registration process also tends to be very complex. That is a huge stumbling block. Qualification criteria are set so high as to be intimidating; the perception that MSEs cannot meet quality standards is reinforced when such hard-to-meet criteria are imposed.

Furthermore, PSUs and government agencies have to climb a steep learning curve before implementing the procurement rules from April 1, 2015. To start with, there is no comprehensive database on MSEs. Moreover, there is very little information about the capacity and ability of the MSEs that can be drawn from the available data from registration. Besides this, a massive challenge for MSMEs is finance, and when a significant proportion of all MSMEs are proprietary firms rather than corporate structures, even small changes in cash management and working capital cycles can create unanticipated problems.

Though there are large numbers of startups coming up all over the country, at the field level there is a high death rate or sickness rate of new enterprises. This is specifically because of a lack of healthy entrepreneurship ecosystem in many states across the country. This can be attributed to the failure of the concerned state governments to provide the required policy thrust for startups and also to the absence of backward linkages where large corporates source from local SMEs.

Over and above all these, the MSME sector has also been reeling under various other disadvantages that have been historically affecting small enterprises in India—such as lack of capital and credit facilities, infrastructure deficit, higher fixed costs compared to the large-scale sector and lack of access to global markets.

Boosting the Growth of MSME Sector

History shows that MSMEs of countries like Japan, Korea, etc managed to emerge as global players only because of the persistent and effective support they received from their respective governments. Though the Union and state governments in our country have been striving to support the MSME entrepreneurs by making things simpler for them, still there are certain issues related to policy and government support that need immediate attention. Moreover, facilitation from government is required to minimize transaction costs for technology upgradation, market penetration, modernization of infrastructure, etc. Taking into account the diverse issues and challenges currently inhibiting the growth of the MSME sector, given below are some recommendations categorized under six different focus areas, which if implemented properly will facilitate the rapid growth and development of the Indian MSME sector.

(1) Finance, Including Credit

Credit is a crucial input for promoting growth of the MSMEs, particularly the MSE sector, in view of its limited access to alternative sources of finance. Currently, entrepreneurs have to face lot of trouble when they try to get loans from banks. So, first and foremost, granting of loans to entrepreneurs in the MSME sector should be simplified and made hassle-free with the aim of increasing required fund flow to the sector and for ensuring that every entrepreneur gets timely loans without having to go through avoidable, time-consuming and complicated procedures and formalities.

The complex terms and conditions for availing of loans also pose a stumbling block. A survey of 540 MSME units reveals that 71% of the entrepreneurs were not even aware of the credit guarantee schemes launched by the central and state governments. Those who were aware could not take advantage as banks, which administer such schemes, are themselves not equipped to guide the customers—either the staff are not trained or they lack information.

Collecting account receivables is also an area of major concern. When PSUs delay settlement of outstanding dues to corporates, the latter in turn delay the same to SME firms and a never-ending loop comes into play. Zero tolerance in case of defaults and use of commercial bills with minimum proportion of dues under the bill system and fixed date of payments can be a corrective measure to resolve this issue. Next, while on one hand MSME firms face the scarcity of collateral during early stages, unnecessary borrowing for capital needs is a worry too as interest is to be borne all throughout; on the other, bank credit on inventory has to be assured as this would also eradicate the issue of collateral. A hidden aspect of MSME borrowing is a move towards non-bank sources such as commercial paper, which increases the burden of interest rates, thus taking away the competitive edge of the borrowing firm. Hence, our government should formulate strict rules and legislations to resolve these issues.

Furthermore, our government and the Reserve Bank of India (RBI) should strictly implement guidelines for year-on-year growth of MSE credit. Moreover, the reach of the MSEs to the banking network has to be substantially enhanced through setting up of branches near clusters. In fact, a cluster-centric approach is the best bet for addressing the credit needs of the MSME sector, because of reasons of operational convenience and trust building. To address the risk perception of banks, particularly for lending to MSEs, the credit guarantee schemes need to be further strengthened with enhanced budgetary support.

Lack of equity support for the MSME sector inhibits their growth. In order to fill equity gap, access to finance needs to be enlarged through alternative sources of capital such as private equity, venture capital and angel funds. The Securities and Exchange Board of India (SEBI) should also come up with specific measures to encourage SMEs to raise funds on the already existing dedicated platforms for SMEs and start-ups on BSE and NSE, which allows small companies to get listed without an IPO.

(2) Technology

The low technology generally used by the MSME sector has been a major cause for poor competitiveness of the sector. So the Union and state governments should set up a multi-tier support system by collaborating with industry associations, industry clusters and private R&D institutions for inducing technology-based competitiveness in the sector. This support system should be given the required encouragement to enable it to develop appropriate technologies for various manufacturing processes, which in turn will lead to substantial reduction in cost of manufacturing by improving labour productivity, reducing material wastage and minimizing energy consumption.

Steps should also be taken to support innovative ideas in a bid to develop them into marketable products, facilitate linkages of MSME clusters/Mini Clusters to public and private R&D institutions, and finally subsidize the cost of technology available in the international market. Government should formulate liberal policies and assistance programs to nurture innovative ideas of academic institutions and techno-preneurs.

Government assistance may vary depending upon the level of technology and the transaction cost involved and may be kept at an attractive level. To facilitate absorption of globally competitive manufacturing technologies that are available in the international market for various industries, government may subsidize the industry. Meanwhile, the extent of support may be decided based on the type of industry and the level of technology being adopted.

(3) Infrastructure Development

For MSMEs, land and infrastructure constraints are major problem areas, especially in bigger cities and metros. As production processes of majority of MSEs can be accomplished in flattened factories, such complexes may be encouraged by providing financial support under the Integrated Infrastructure Development Scheme of the central government. Likewise, accommodation problem of industrial workers may be addressed by establishing dormitories on a sustainable basis.

Maintenance of industrial estates (mainly maintenance of roads, drainage, sewage, power distribution and captive power generation, water supply, dormitories for workers, common effluent treatment plants, common facilities, securities, etc) are very important for the successful functioning of enterprises in industrial areas. Industrial estates are generally developed by the state industrial development bodies (for example, GIDC in Gujarat, HSIDC in Haryana, and RIICO in Rajasthan). It may be appropriate to handover maintenance of industrial estates to industry associations, local bodies, state government agencies or Special Purpose Vehicles (SPVs) on self-sustaining basis.

In advanced countries, hi-tech and innovative enterprises start in modular industrial estates. To encourage such ventures, Modular Industrial Estates having Raw Material Bank, Technology Resource Centre, Design Centre, Business Centre, Tool Room, Testing Centre, Incubation Centre, Training Centre, Mini Trade Fair Centre, etc should be set up near Centres of Excellence like IITs. Furthermore, our country currently has no specialized testing facilities for certain high-end products, such as leather items. Therefore, the exporting MSME units have to avail these facilities from overseas testing labs. As such, there is a need for creation of such testing facilities at suitable locations adjacent to clusters of such industrial units.

(4) Marketing Support

Marketing is the most important tool in business development that leads a product from creation to customer through different channels. Marketing is a dynamic activity that calls for constant updating of marketing intelligence and new tools of marketing. It includes a whole gamut of activities such as packaging, labeling, trade mark, bar coding, brand building, advertising, domestic and international exhibitions, buyer-seller meet, e-marketing and customer service to name a few. Generally, MSMEs don't have the financial muscle or wherewithal to make their presence felt in the market. It is here that our government can pitch in and help them.

While marketing of products of MSMEs mostly depend upon the market forces and individual efforts of the concerned enterprises, government and its various departments and organizations can play the role of a facilitator to help the MSME sector in these endeavours. Ministry of MSME and its attached organizations have been assisting the sector through certain schemes and programs. However, emerging marketing-related challenges call for scaling up of these programs and introduction of certain innovative policies for the sector.

There are multiplicity of market development assistance programs to support MSMEs for participation in domestic and international trade fairs, bar coding, packaging and standardization within the Ministry. There is an urgent need for rationalization and consolidation of such programs under various broad heads. There is also a need for up-scaling of such programs with higher financial allocations.

Lately, Indian MSMEs have acquired global competitiveness in sectors like auto components, leather goods, garments, engineering items, gems and jewellery, etc. In the services sector, education, healthcare, grooming and beauty therapies have enormous export potential. Direct export from enterprises in these segments should be accelerated by enabling services like B2B meetings, events, seminars, dissemination of information about new markets and products, offshore warehousing, product promotion, etc. As individual enterprises do not have sufficient resources to take up such initiatives, our government should set up Business and Facilitation Centers with the aim of providing necessary help through cluster and consortia-based initiatives through the PPP model.

(5) Skill Development and Training

Lack of skilled manpower and information as well as lack of reach to modern technology are key issues affecting the growth of the MSME sector. Compared to many other countries, India enjoys an advantage because it has a huge population in the productive age group. If this comparative advantage can be augmented with adequate skill development, India can become a global supplier of quality manpower. In this context, it is very encouraging to know that the Narendra Modi-government is planning to launch a new Skill Development Program by March 2015, which will bridge the gap between educational institutions and the labour market. The proposed scheme is expected to move beyond the target of skilling 500 million youth by 2020 that was set under the National Policy on Skill Development 2009 formulated by the UPA government.

To coordinate the entire process of conducting skill development programs, the central government should set up a virtual SME University, which will standardize the training curricula as well as certify the trainers and the trainees on completion of the program. Eventually, the university can also become a repository of the details of the persons who have been trained under various programs of the Ministry as well as other Ministries and discharge the function of a virtual Employment Exchange. To enhance workers' skills and proficiency, our government should also set up 100 Tool Rooms or Technology Development Centers (TDCs), including Central Footwear Technology Institutes (CFTIs), which will provide specialized training to the existing and prospective workers in the manufacturing sector. Such institutes should be set up in industrial clusters and districts, with state-of-the-art machines in a bid to impart training to make the participants readily employable in high growth sectors like auto components, engineering, readymade garments, leather products, etc. To make such programs self-sustainable, they should be taken to the self-financing levels, which will also make them qualitative. To ensure high success rate of such programs, they should be made practice-oriented by involving industry associations in the training, which will also help in identification of the skill gap, development of appropriate training curricula as well as handholding of trainees via internship and apprenticeship arrangements.

Our government, in collaboration with specialized agencies, should arrange to impart regular training to MSME entrepreneurs on risk management strategies, delivery channels, product development related issues, financial management and such other key business parameters so that they are well-equipped to profitably manage their ventures and make them successful.

(6) Institutional Structure

The institutional and legal framework for promotion and development of the MSME sector in our country is spread both at the national and state level. While the state governments have the primary responsibility for the development of MSMEs, the central government supplements their efforts through a range of initiatives. Here it is worth noting that the employment-intensive MSME sector has suffered tremendously due to a plethora of laws, rules and regulations that kept on accumulating during the control regime of the licence-permit raj. Ensuring compliance with so many rules and regulations of that era has considerably stifled the growth of the MSME sector. To unshackle the growth of the sector, our government should immediately address the following issues that obstruct the growth of the MSME sector.

(i) Environmental issues
(ii) Labour issues
(iii) Amendment of MSMED Act
(iv) Exit policy
(v) Restructuring of the DICs and MSME-DIs

To elaborate further on the environmental issues, the relevant policies should be made uniform all over India, while extending appropriate relaxation of controls for MSMEs. On labour issues, the immediate need is to consolidate the plethora of labour laws into one industry-friendly law. The MSMED Act 2006 was enacted to promote the growth of the MSME sector. However, there is an urgent need to strengthen various provisions of the Act along with the enactment of appropriate rules under various sections, which will help redress diverse issues and challenges such as inadequate physical infrastructure, complex regulatory environment and inadequate availability of skilled manpower that have constrained the growth of the MSME sector.

Furthermore, while amending the MSMED Act, an appropriate provision enabling easy rehabilitation or exit of nonviable SMEs should also be incorporated. In fact, it would be better if our government brings in a single comprehensive MSME law (to replace the MSMED Act 2006) that would include the Labour Law, Factories Act, Land Acquisition Act, 25% land allocation in all industrial corridors, and an Exit Policy (on the lines of Chapter 11 in the US). This new MSME policy should also enable simplified procedures for clearances such as online applications and easy procurement procedures. Raising competitiveness and productivity in the MSME sector should also be a critical focus area of the new MSME law. To achieve the same, funds as well as technology may have to be brought in from abroad for the MSME units, for which relevant provisions should be appropriately incorporated.

It has been noted that banks while extending loans to MSMEs struggle with limited data on the credit history of the borrowing firms. To resolve this issue, our government should set up a Credit Bureau at the all-India level with its regional offices in all the states. Currently, the District Industries Centers (DICs) under the state government and the MSME Development Institutes (MSME-DIs) under the Ministry of MSME, provide the requisite facilitation to new and existing entrepreneurs for developing their enterprises. The state and central governments should formulate an appropriate restructuring plan for them in order to attune them to the contemporary entrepreneurship scene and likely future developments so that they can play a more helpful role and also discharge their functions more effectively.

If all the above recommendations are implemented in right earnest, then over the next few years the MSME sector will certainly emerge as a highly vibrant and dynamic sector of the Indian economy. This in turn, will open up huge employment opportunities at comparatively lower capital cost and also help in the industrialization of rural and backward areas, thereby reducing regional imbalances as well as assuring more equitable distribution of national income and wealth.

(Posted on blog on 20 October, 2014)

□

Consensus Between Judiciary and Legislature to Boost Investors' Trust

It was not just the cancellation of 122 odd licenses awarded by a dishonest telecom minister, but was much more than that. In 2012, when the honorable Supreme Court announced revocation of 2G spectrum almost 80 million customers; banks who lent INR 30, 000 crore to five firms; companies who shared infrastructure; and foreign investors including Norway's Telenor and Russia's Sistema went into a state of anarchy. This is not a single incident that led to an environment wherein stakeholders lost trust in the Indian market. Now criticizing the same does not mean that the same should not have happened. Justice, for sure, is above anyone's interest or loss. But am I wrong in saying that 'economy' is a synonym of 'country'? And for a stable economy, surety of business is indispensable. The mistake, of course, was committed by the legislatures, but what about the sufferers who followed the prescribed regulations and extended money and labor? I can remember what Justice AK Ganguly, added to his verdict, 'I am only doing my job', knowing the ruin that the judgment would do to the Indian corporate sector.

Recent is the Apex Court's judgment in the Coalgate scam where the honorable judges scrapped 214 coal blocks and ordered auction of the same post 6 months of judgment. Prior to coming to the consequences, let us notice that the court also asked companies to pay INR 295 per tonne of coal they extract and that too with retrospective effect. In case you had prepared the budgets and forecasts for the year, please rework. We are all aware of the scarcity of coal with power plants and the subsequent impact on Indian industrial sector. Also, households are paying hefty charges for electricity. Banks, which extended loans to companies, will suffer from steeply rising bad debt liability (Indian banking sector has an exposure of more than INR 5 lakh crore to the power sector). Of all the banks, the public sector bank, PNB has a peak exposure at 2.6 per cent of total advances to the mining sector. Others are the NBFCs ranging from REC and IDFC to the Power Finance Corporation. Something vital to note from the judgment are the words of the honorable judge, 'There was no proper application of mind in distribution of coal blocks'. Plus, the court commented on lack of transparency and paramount irregularity.

We all agree that the honorable court accorded supreme place to justice. And integrity, indeed, must prevail. Nevertheless, the pain of those who without any fault fall into the grip of helplessness is something that in case not taken care of can fade away even the tough labors of the new Indian PM. 'Make in India' can succeed, but business security is the foremost essential. Even the susceptible stock market has a safety device, Investor Protection Fund to defend investors. Then how can the fund-seeking corporate sector of India prove detrimental to investors who extend substantial capital? But the democratic arrangement places judiciary above all, which in fact is lawful too. Who then is at fault? Yes we all know. They, however, are at fault since decades. Something relaxing, if has happened in the recent past, is the verdict of courts against high-profile politicians, put behind the bars. The rest, however, will learn, is not assured. Another depressing fact is the statement given by S&P's credit analyst that Supreme Court's ruling in the Coalgate can hurt significantly improved investor sentiments towards Indian corporate sector.

World Bank has lately predicted India's economic growth at 6.4 per cent in the FY 2015-16 and has also said that the country is benefitting from 'Modi dividend'. Share market is bullish and so are the entrepreneurs, but the recent conclusion by the Apex Court in the Coalgate scam has probed many in-house weaknesses. Remember, overseas fund-providers will not just rely on the pluses of the new government at the center. Rather, while finalizing strategic restructuring and investment visions, the due diligence report focuses on all-around factors that can upset the venture in the long-run. The new Act for the corporate sector, as known to all, is packed with gaps and holdbacks. Then we have lack of consensus between the union and state governments. Scarcity of adequate infrastructure is apparent. Then can we also bear the burden of revocation of concluded business deals? INR 2.87 lakh crore, as submitted by private companies, is the amount that they invested in coal extraction projects. Now, the GOI is seeking legal opinion in the matter of annulment of title deeds and forfeiting of bank guarantees. Mess, all over.

Anything we say, the judiciary will do its job, rightful and intact, and this is what we all expect from our honorable wing of democracy. A workable resolution can be agreement between the judiciary and the legislative wing. What about setting a threshold limit for business transactions that involve government and private players as parties, and then placing a supervisory judicial board to assure arm's length dealing? From the beginning till the conclusion of such business deals, a judicial personality should have the power to administer, and upon completion, such deals should become unalterable. Along with, the government can set up a board, with legislative and judicial members, to prepare a due diligence report of hefty dealings. Once approved, corporate players must have the immunity from being harassed or penalized later. An Investor Education and Protection Fund can be created which shall be funded from the compulsory CSR aid. The Fund will advise domestic and overseas investors beyond resolving grievances and making good any authentic loss to the corporate houses. Let us hope that the new government and the new CJI will think over the prevailing pulls in the Indian market and will curb them.

Lastly, can I request India's honorable and worthy judges to also notice the pain of the corporate houses, their shareholders, and employees prior to declaring a deal void ab initio? There is no harm in assessing the overall impact of a decision, though we respect the fact that the judiciary bears the burden of uprightness. But righteousness cannot be at the cost of guiltless. Invalidation of deals is untenable. International and indigenous investors, who extended money, labors and time in the 2G and Coal allocation ventures, now stand crumbled. Wouldn't the milieu be much auspicious in case the honorable court had also awarded compensation, by nationalizing the developed substructure, to make good the loss incurred by investors who followed the prescribed laws? Or at least, an option to pay the amount as per the prevailing market prices so as to carry on operations. Penalize dishonest officials and ministers rather. It is high time that the suffering of business houses be paid apt heed to. A commission, with ministers, fiscal and judicial experts, and veteran judges as members, must develop such a setup that decisions once taken by the GOI, and involving weighty allotments/sanctions and grant of licenses be made irrevocable guaranteeing stable business atmosphere to investors.

(Posted on blog on 13 October, 2014)

□

Legitimize Lobbying and Regulate it with Legislations

Lobbying can be defined as an act or process initiated by organized individuals or advocacy groups with the aim of influencing legislators, politicians, bureaucrats or public officials so that the policy decisions made by them are usually for or against a specific cause or in favour of an individual, group or business entity who have hired them. Individuals or groups who undertake the work of lobbying are called lobbyists and they are typically employed by corporates or interest groups that want specific public policies or policy decisions to favour them or their causes.

However, the term corporate lobbying has come to acquire a negative connotation and in the normal course it is perceived as a euphemism for bribery. This is because in many cases, businessmen and corporate houses employ lobbyists to influence government decisions and public policies in a bid to extract illegitimate gains through corrupt means. However, it is worth noting that every process of getting work done may have its own merits and demerits. To understand exactly how the process works, let us discuss this in more detail.

If a human rights activist tries to influence lawmakers and administrators to get endorsement for a universal convention, or in case a business house hires a consultant to present a proposal to the bureaucrats or financial institutions or to liaison with government authorities, lobbying can be treated as legitimate and acceptable. On the other hand, if a business house resorts to some unethical or illegal means to induce a law-making body to take a decision or amend an existing rule in its favour with a view to extract undue benefits at the cost of others, then it is clearly an illicit application of this process.

Lobbying with the aim of gaining unconstitutional access to the law-making process should be absolutely forbidden, except in cases wherein services of experts are hired to speed up the process of obtaining licenses and commercial loans. But then, how would you rate the process of obtaining commercial licenses from the concerned authorities by building close rapport and bribing them? This has been the case in the past wherein large corporate houses extracted many undue favors from government officials. Here the 2G scam immediately comes to our mind.

Lately, lobbying as an exercise aimed at creating social and corporate awareness has been gaining momentum. Activists, who are the voice of those who cannot retaliate against the wrongdoings of the law-making body, approach and influence such officials with a view to bring in social reforms. Something on these lines happened a couple of years ago when a movement called India Against Corruption (IAC) gained enormous support and the then Union Government was left with no other option than to approve the recommendations put forth by the activists. In light of the above, it is obvious that the pros and cons of lobbying have to be considered and evaluated with due diligence.

In another context, let us take the case of a group of local corporate houses approaching policy-makers to highlight the bottlenecks and threats imposed by global intervention and demanding easy and supportive measures for domestic producers. Until and unless the intention of influencing the legislators is detrimental to the interests of local small scale businesses or the general public, lobbying can be regarded as a welcome measure. Furthermore, representing a client's proposal in a bid to highlight the latter's core professional competence with a view to obtaining speedy approvals shouldn't be viewed as a dubious or negative practice.

Although it is not yet recognized in a statutory or non-statutory form in India, lobbying by various interest and advocacy groups is widespread across the country. So bringing more clarity to the difference between legitimate and illegitimate lobbying as well as designing a proper framework where lobbying can be legally used as a business tool by corporates desiring to have a bigger say in a participative democratic process is currently a key concern in India.

Presently, lobbying in India is done through Public Relations Firms and some well-connected individuals who share close vibes with ministers, government officials and legislators. Since lobbying can provide our government with useful policy-related information and expertise, India needs to determine a regulatory model that suits its socio-economic and political milieu. Some countries like the United States, Australia, Canada, Germany, Israel, Hungary, Taiwan, Poland, Slovenia and Lithuania treat lobbying as a legitimate right of their citizens and regulate the activity with suitable legislations.

For instance, the United States passed the US Lobbying Disclosure Act (LDA) in 1995 and further strengthened it in 2009. Under the law, lobbyists are required to register within a prescribed time frame and also file their financial activity reports regularly. However, in India we have no such laws, and the cases of lobbying are only governed by Section 7 of the Prevention of Corruption Act, 1988, under which it is illegal for a government official to accept gratification other than the legal remuneration in respect of an official Act.

Even the Supreme Court of India has commented about the adverse influence of some of the powerful corporate houses over the government and policy-making bodies. Though lobbying is supposed to be at a nascent stage in India and the country does not regulate it, the new government at the centre needs to move towards that direction and draft an appropriate law outlining a concrete action plan and specific measures that can curb all the demerits of lobbying, while simultaneously retaining all its merits. For instance, the law should make it mandatory for all players and stake holders involved in the lobbying process to sign a Code of Ethics and to submit their financial activity reports regularly.

When the government drafts the proposed law, it should also remember that in the present scenario clearances and approvals cannot be obtained unless bribe is paid to expedite the process. So, the new law to regulate lobbying should make it mandatory for bureaucrats, ministries and public financial institutions (PFIs) to respond to applications received by them within a stipulated time period. It should also strive to pave the way for the much-needed transparency and accountability in the policymaking process so as to totally eliminate the scope of influencing government policies with money, bribes or through other illegitimate means.

(Posted on blog on 30 July, 2014)

□

Some Urgent and Bold Reforms Needed in the Indian Banking Sector

The increasing level of non-performing assets (NPAs) has become one of the major concerns for the banking industry in India – more so for the public sector banks (PSBs). For instance, in the nine months ending December 2013, gross NPAs of United Bank of India (UBI) nearly tripled and grew at an appalling rate of 297% on an annualized basis and touched a staggering 10.82% of the total advances.

During the same period, NPAs in all PSBs grew at an average rate of 75%. The gross NPA levels in India's largest bank, the State Bank of India, stood at 5.73% as on December 31, 2013. Other major public sector banks such as the Punjab National Bank and the Central Bank of India also have high levels of gross NPAs at 5.40% and 6.48% respectively. Amongst the big state-run banks, only Canara Bank has gross NPA level of less than 3%. Bank of Baroda is on the borderline with gross NPA ratio of 3.3%.

Clearly, the SBI group and the PSBs have made some poor lending decisions and probably have ineffective monitoring mechanisms. In this context, it is worth mentioning that the new private sector banks have managed their balance sheets very effectively over the same period and their average gross NPAs are at 1.96%. At 0.3%, the net NPA ratio of HDFC Bank is the lowest among all large banks.

NPAs directly mirror the performance of banks. A high level of NPAs reflects high probability of a large number of credit defaults that adversely affect the profits and net-worth of banks and also erodes the value of their assets. NPA growth involves the necessity of provisions, which reduces the overall profitability and shareholder value.

As the NPA-related problem not only affects the banks, but also the overall health of the Indian economy, there is an urgent need to redress this issue on a fast-track as well as a top-priority basis. And it would be prudent, if this issue of NPAs can be tackled at the level of prevention rather than cure. To be able to do that, we have to first understand that the causes for an account becoming an NPA are of three types: (i) Causes attributable to the borrower; (ii) Causes attributable to the economy and environment in which the borrower and bank operates; and (iii) Causes attributable to banks.

The first set of causes that are attributable to the borrower may encompass lack of expertise, mismanagement, willful default, fraud, disputes, diversion of funds, lack of proper planning, dependence on single customer, imbalance of inventories, poor quality management and lack of quality control. Similarly, the second set of causes may comprise government policies, taxation laws, civil commotion, industrial recession, political hostility, sluggish legal system, changes in consumer preference, lack of infrastructure, etc. As the banking sector has very little influence on these factors, we shall not elaborate them here.

However, the third set of causes are attributable to banks and may include wrong selection of borrower, poor credit appraisal, tough stand on issues by banks, inflexible attitude of banks, non-inspection of units, delay in sanction, lack of trained staff and technical expertise, inadequate commitment for recovery of loans, lack of accountability, etc.

To be able to monitor, curb or eliminate some of the above causes that tend to increase the NPAs in the banking sector and lead to further erosion of values of a number of state-run banks, the Indian government should expeditiously muster the will to push through some of the bold reforms enumerated below.

(1) First and foremost, there is an urgent need to implement the governance reform roadmap articulated in the PJ Nayak Committee report submitted to the Reserve Bank of India (RBI) in May 2014. The said committee has suggested reduction of government capital in PSBs and proportionate increase of private capital, merger of nationalized banks, transfer of ownership of PSBs to investment companies, repeal of the bank nationalization act and coverage of banks under the Companies Act. The report also wants the government to refrain from issuing any regulatory instructions to banks.

The governance reforms agenda outlined in the said report should be implemented by the Government of India in right earnest as it already aligns well with the BJP's economic policy of smaller role for government in running businesses as well as maximum governance and minimum government.

The advantage of this policy is that PSBs will get more autonomy and they will learn to function like private business houses in a competitive environment. Once that happens, no politician or minister or powerful business tycoon will pressurize banks to roll over credit lines to troubled, but well-connected big firms, that most private banks steer clear of. This in turn will ensure that PSBs don't allow cronyism to creep in while making lending decisions. This will enhance the quality of loans and definitely bring down the levels of NPAs in public sector banks and make them more profitable. This in turn, will create much higher value for the government's equity holdings in state-owned banks, which can eventually be sold off or diluted for better value.

In view of what is stated above, the P.J. Nayak Committee recommendations seem to align perfectly well with the BJP-led NDA government's reforms policy aimed at repairing public finances and putting the economy on a higher growth trajectory by providing managerial autonomy to PSUs to compete globally.

(2) In the present scenario, a major factor that is instrumental for high NPAs in PSBs is absolute lack of accountability among officials who have the power to take decisions, grant loans and effect recoveries. Currently, no one is held accountable for the increasing levels of NPAs in state-run banks, nor is the responsibility for the deteriorating asset quality fixed on any specific person or position. Because of this, no one in particular bothers to take the right decision in a timely manner or to avert delays in sanctioning or releasing the loans, or for ensuring that efforts to recover the outstanding loans are initiated at the right time and in an appropriate manner.

In view of this, a culture of accountability has to be introduced, responsibility has to be fixed on the concerned officials, time-limit for all important decision and functions should be preset and punitive action should be initiated against officials responsible for red tapism and bureaucratic delays as well as for arrogance, non-cooperative attitude, shirking of responsibility and corrupt practices. This measure will bring in the much-needed attitudinal change among the staff and management, which in turn will drastically improve the work culture in PSBs.

(3) Currently, PSB customers don't have access to a proper and effective grievance redressal mechanism for expeditious resolution of complaints. There is also no tangible structure to ensure that senior bankers don't shirk their responsibility. Moreover, there is an absolute lack of transparency in the functioning of PSBs and also an absence of fixed or predetermined time-frame for project appraisal, disposal of loan applications and release of loans. Since all these tend to adversely affect the performance of the banking sector and also contribute to increasing NPAs, the Union government needs to create a suitable grievance redressal mechanism with the required structure and efficacy and an appropriate timeframe for prompt disposal of complaints, including the last escalation point within that timeframe.

(4) The Union government should also separate the post of chairman and managing director/CEOs in state-run banks and give them a fixed term of three or five years so as to bring in more accountability. Furthermore, their selection should be made in a timely, transparent and professional manner, and the prevailing practice where ministers or politicians can influence such decisions has to be scrapped. To improve corporate governance, government should also specify eligibility criteria such as professional qualifications and experience for independent directors appointed to bank boards. Also, the remuneration offered to top-level executives of state-run banks should be revised to narrow down the huge difference between the compensation levels of executives holding the same ranks in public sector and private sector banks.

(5) To curb corruption and keep the state-run banks sound, stable and profitable, the scope of receiving bribery for approving loans to undeserving business entities by violating prudential norms, needs to be totally abolished. A robust and transparent decision-making process, which is effectively monitored by the bank's Board of Directors, should be put in place. This will tremendously reduce the discretionary powers and corresponding opportunities for arbitrary action and corrupt practices, which are currently enjoyed by senior bank officials.

(6) An RBI-appointed working group under the then executive director, Anand Sinha, had in 2007 ruled out Islamic banking in the country, saying current regulations don't permit the model. Moreover, immediate past Governor of RBI, D. Subbarao, had explicitly stated in May 2013 that implementing Islamic banking model in India would

be impossible because it is inconsistent with our country's banking regulatory set-up where interest is charged and given.

It is really surprising that despite the assertions of two top RBI officials (Anand Sinha retired as RBI Deputy Governor and Subbarao as Governor) that implementing Islamic banking would be impossible in India, the then UPA government gave a go-ahead in August 2013 to a Kerala government's proposal to launch a financial institution named Cheraman Financial Services Ltd (CFSL) based on the principles of Islamic banking.

CFSL is a Kochi-based Islamic NBFC and is the latest incarnation of Al Baraka Financial Services. It clearly shows this was a political decision by the Congress-led UPA government to appease a particular community in Kerala with an eye on the fast-approaching 2014 Lok Sabha elections. And if the Kerala election results were any indication, this move seems to have paid rich dividends to the Congress party and its ally, the Indian Union Muslim League (IUML).

Furthermore, recent media reports say that RBI has lately become favorably inclined towards Islamic banking and has begun the process of reviewing its regulations and has set up an internal committee to examine how Islamic banking can be introduced in India. The Union government should immediately instruct the RBI to disband this committee as Islamic banking is not suitable for India for reasons enumerated below.

First and foremost, Islamic banking is bound by Islamic laws and the basic purpose of establishing an Islamic bank is to cater to the diverse economic and banking needs of the Muslim community while encouraging Islamic principles laid down by Shariah (religious laws based on the teachings of Koran). India being a secular country, communal and religious laws like Sharia should not be allowed to regulate our banking system.

Secondly, in the prevailing statutory and regulatory framework it would not be possible for banks in India to undertake Islamic banking activities because before allowing banks to do Islamic banking, drastic and appropriate amendments will have to be introduced in the Banking Regulations Act, 1949. Alternatively, a new law envisioning creation of a parallel banking system and a separate regulatory set-up will have to be formulated.

However, as India is a secular country there can't be separate laws for its citizens based on religion. Our Constitution allows freedom to practice one's faith, which is a personal matter. However, if religious laws and beliefs start intruding into areas like banking and other important aspects of our economy, it will go against the very concept and foundation of secularism, and India will no more be perceived as better than any Islamic country.

Furthermore, permitting Islamic banking in India has the potential to open up avenues for the inflow of terror funding and money laundering. So it would always be prudent and advisable to keep India outside this religious financial network by disallowing Islamic banking in our country.

While the above six recommendations are the most crucial and should be vigorously pursued and promptly implemented to safeguard the Indian banking sector as well as to boost its performance and profitability, at the individual level all the PSBs invariably need to focus on the following aspects in a bid to build the required capabilities to cope up with the emerging challenges of the dynamic banking environment, nationally and internationally.

(7) Without adversely affecting the quality of their services, every state-run bank should design and pursue innovative strategies in a bid to cut down and control their costs, optimize resources, increase their presence across the value chain, renew focus on R&D and innovation and create a dynamic and performance-oriented work culture. For instance, one of the future strategies of all PSBs should be to earn more of other income and reduce their dependence on interest income.

(8) To render better customer service and to fulfill customer demands more effectively as well as to improve the profitability, efficiency and productivity of the banking sector, all ourstate-owned banks should adopt the latest and the most cost-effective technologies and information systems. The best hope for PSBs is to embrace and promote low-cost mobile and internet banking with proper safeguards, including legal aspects and measures to enhance customer protection.

(9) Another area that needs urgent attention of PSBs is improving the staff productivity. Most PSBs are saddled with a large number of inadequately trained or demotivated personnel. Such banks need to downsize staff and cut their costs. They also need to redistribute and train staff to strengthen the neglected areas of marketing and innovation, which are needed to retain and win over more customers.

(10) Finally, the Union government and the RBI should put in place a Citizens' Charter to ensure speedy, efficient, fair and courteous customer service in the banking industry. This step will not only check areas of deficiencies in customer service, but also make it easier to introduce measures for improvement of work culture, inculcate greater customer orientation among bank employees as well as identify and eliminate structural and operational rigidities and inadequacies that tend to adversely affect the working of public sector banks.

(Posted on blog on 4 August, 2014)

□

Business Ethics and Profitability

Most business owners and entrepreneurs would totally disagree with any positive relationship between ethical conduct and paybacks. Quite often, management books lay emphasis on best business practices, which theoretically establish an affiliation with output as well as viability. In the real world; throat cut competition, ever-high customers' demands, employees' aspirations, and personal voracity rarely allow the entrepreneur to add in best ethical values in policy development and decision-making. For instance, when good governance expects the business to fairly publicize the flaws of a product, consumers are often deceived by fabricated depictions.

Tough job it is to honestly make the workforce aware of the upcoming slump in the business; however annual appraisals are the periods when promotions and salary hikes are constricted alleging that the company could not fetch adequate profits in the last FY. The flowing money in form of hefty pay packages in the IT business extracts every bit of hard work from the employees. Not every letter of employment reveals real job responsibilities, which lessens the passion of the employee while at work. Business ethics seem to be confined to just management lectures, in real, however, only a few employers accord value to the hopes of the workforce.

Contractual obligations are taken care of by the law of the land. Any contract with a supplier or a trade customer demands ethical business conduct so as to ensure that none of the parties makes unjustifiable profits. Indeed, the bulky number of suits in corporate courts and tribunals substantiate the tricky covenants added in the contracts, which leave one of the parties at unanticipated loss. With abundant suppliers and customers, businesses rarely pay heed to the damaged relations, and disremember the lesson of good corporate governance.

Eventually, the loss is shared by the whole corporate world since everyone works within the same group.

The accountability of businesses towards the society at large, or for that matter towards the government, which takes care of the social betterment, is unquestionable and crucial. Corporate taxes and corporate social responsibility (CSR) norms necessitate unavoidable contribution to the advancement of the society. Be it a large corporate house or a small proprietorship concern, every business craves to escape liabilities to the maximum possible extent. Tax evasions with the help of dummy employees, unscrupulous accounting devices, corruption, and dodgy selling techniques have superseded all the ethical business values prescribed by corporate theorists.

It is tough to comprehend why businesses overlook a basic fact that they all earn while being a part of the society. The stakeholders, be it the consumers, suppliers, creditors, employees, or the government, are the vital pillars in the triumph of any business concern, hence ethical values and good corporate governance deserve devoted attention. Rather than escaping the fusion of business practices and business ethics, the top to bottom hierarchy of workforce needs to be acquainted with explicit corporate guidelines, and any deviation shall be recorded and curbed. The boost in the contentment of all stakeholders is sure to advance profitability of businesses.

(Posted on blog on 23 July, 2014)

□

CSR-Brave Initiative, However Scope of Enhancement

Every business operates within the society and earns revenues from the social sphere. End-users of every product/service are the constituents of the society and hence this sphere deserves to be awarded. With a view to delivering defined and compulsory measures for corporate houses with respect to paying back the community, the Companies Act 2013 embraces Corporate Social Responsibility norms.

Definitely, this must be viewed as an opportunity by the business houses to create a better nation and hence add value to their market standing. I disagree with those who look at this as an unwanted compulsion. Remember, in case direct and indirect taxes did not have statutory validity, revenue of the government would have been lesser, which subsequently would have not delivered the prosperous economy we live in.

Section 135 that comprehensively covers the subject-matter of Corporate Social Responsibility should be briefly looked into prior to any appreciation or criticism. Whether private or public, every company with either a net worth of INR 500 Crore or turnover of INR 1000 Crore or net profit of INR 5 Crore is mandatorily required to spend at least 2 percent of its average net profits for the immediately preceding three FYs on corporate social responsibility activities mentioned in the Schedule VII of the Act.

The rules embrace holding, subsidiary, and foreign companies which have branch or project office in India. It is considerable to note that while computing profit, profits from any overseas branch of the company, including those operating as separate entity and dividends received from any other company in India which separately complies with CSR obligations are to be excluded. Eradication of hunger and malnutrition, promoting education and gender equality, and setting up homes for women and orphans are few of the CSR activities mentioned in the Schedule VII.

An express mention of exclusion of contributions to political parties from CSR activity definitely deserves applauds. Compulsory composition of CSR Committee with inclusion of at least one Independent Director too adds to the strength of this Section. However, some loopholes too are to be paid attention to. The task of undertaking CSR activities can be entrusted to a registered trust or society, or even a company established by the entity's holding, subsidiary, or associate company for this purpose.

Corporate corruption is unhidden. Misappropriation of funds cannot be overlooked. The Board or the management though proficient in their relevant business, however holding deficient expertise of social welfare may be lured to extend CSR funds to trusts/societies working under their illicit supervision. Plus, ultimate profit to the company/shareholders and programmes only in Board's preferred area can be the objective rather than the motive to bring in unbiased social prosperity. Though an express mention of the fact that companies are restricted to use CSR fund for any business related activity, indirect appropriation of fund that will eventually lead to the affluence of shareholders is probable.

Public sector/government companies run under the administration of state/central government too are under the obligations of CSR rules; however ministers, who directly and indirectly influence the Board, are vulnerable to employ CSR funds exclusively in their constituencies. This can result in overflow of funds in one area; however the most deprived areas can stay unnoticed. Inequality in income distribution will thus be accompanied with inequality in social welfare. Yes, there are ways to trim down such instances comprehensively.

To ensure that the funds, which would go as high as thousands of crores with fair participation both from the private as well as the public sector companies, are pooled and then utilized for actual social welfare, the MCA can look forward to establishing a statutory body with independent members holding requisite expertise of running welfare programmes as constituents. The body shall be entrusted with the task of applying funds to the activities that call for immediate attention. This way, the government would also be able to extend welfare programmes beyond the revenues generated from collection of taxes and grants. Surely, the capacity of the government would be enhanced and real reforms would come sooner than later. The underlying target of all-inclusive prosperity can thus be achieved uncomplicatedly and assuredly.

(Posted on blog on 21 April, 2014)

□

How Fair is it to Condemn Corporate Houses?

New politicians, new ideas, and all new campaigning tactics. Definitely, transparency and equivalent favor to all should be an inseparable part of any democracy, however, is it fair to comment on reputed business houses without proper evidences? The election season is at its peak and the phase of pointing out flaws in other political groups has traversed every limitation. Though our ancestors too viewed the criticism of competitive forces, however, altogether new techniques have taken over. Political parties, and specifically newly emerged groups have found a safe route to grab publicity.

Targeting corporate houses for their relationships with politicians has become customary. With a view to fetching attention and converting the same to votes, new political leaders when left with no other evidences of corruption or mala fide governance come up with 'exclusive photographs' and 'hot conversations' of other politicians with industrial entrepreneurs. Surely, the voters pay heeds to such instances; however, shall our support rely on such factors?

While almost every other voter aspires for safe and prosperous job prospects, where are these opportunities created? Can a nation, howsoever rich in terms of social aspects, survive without a stable economy? And, can we think of an economy without corporate houses? Not just the job-seekers, the shareholders, investors, financial institutions, creditors, and consumers are affected even with a slight detriment to the standing of any company. Then why it has become a trend of today's politics to convict companies and their entrepreneurs in a courtroom of its own?

Media, electronic as well as print, has provided an effective platform to political leaders to share views with the mass. And, what we have been witnessing since past few months are 'Breaking News', wherein new leaders come up with some papers and declare the illicit relationship between a government and a corporate house. That too, alleging that a common man's money is being mismanaged and unjust favors are being extended with a view to extract monetary favors from corporates. Then what? The press conference comes to an end and the whistle blowers disremember to rely on our judicial system. Easy, isn't it?

In the past recent days, we have seen a political group alleging extension of unjustifiable courtesies to Reliance Industries. Let me make you aware that as on March 31st, 2013 the company engaged 23519 employees for its operations, along with providing earning opportunities to 29462 temporary employees. As per the survey of Brand Finance, Reliance is the second most valuable brand in India, hence has abundant shareholders and plays a vital role in representing the nation's economy in the global arena. Those attacking Adani Group must realize that this conglomerate in energy, logistics, and resources sector extends jobs to 10400 (2012-13) employees and has more than 45000 non-institutional individual shareholders. Any decadent endeavor to damage company's repute will result in a collective loss.

The role of industries and corporates is indispensible in any economy. While a government is expected to introduce measures so as to enhance domestic and global investment, political groups on the contrary are on the verge of declaring every corporate house corrupt. Can we ever think of a state leader who maintains an arm's length relationship with corporate entrepreneurs to bring in the prosperity we aspire of? Definitely, the government and corporate houses are bound to interact, share grievances, and come up with united measures to uplift the economy. Bona fide allegations are what can help overcome corporate corruption; however, the ongoing scenario will worsen the economic catastrophe.

(Posted on blog on 18 April, 2014)

□

Widened Role of Independent Directors – Real vs. Deemed Independence

To facilitate enhanced transparency in the functioning of the Board and Committees, the Companies Act 2013 has brought in the much-awaited reforms. The Act broadly describes the selection criteria, roles and responsibilities, manner of appointment, and vacation of office by an Independent Director (ID). Prior to moving forward, let's understand the term 'Independent Director'. A person, not having any pecuniary relationship with the Company, or its promoters and directors, and is appointed by the Board as Independent Director, falls under this category. It is expected that with the enhanced recognition and capabilities of the ID, the company would handle its operations much prudently and the stakeholders are sure to benefit.

Further, the appointment of an Independent Director shall be approved in the General Meeting and it is now mandatory for every public limited company to have at least one-third of the total number of directors as Independent Directors. The Board of any company can search for suitable ID from the database maintained by various authorities, one of which is http://www.primedirectors.com/, a corporate governance initiative by NSE and BSE, and launched by the Chairman of SEBI. Professionals seeking directorships can visit the platform so as to add their candidature to the database.

The Companies Act 2013 has enumerated distinctive headings that define the roles and responsibilities of IDs. Few prominent responsibilities include (1) assisting in bringing an independent judgment to bear on the Board's deliberations especially on issues of strategy, performance, risk management, resources, key appointments, and standards of conduct, (2) satisfying themselves on the integrity of financial information, and that financial controls and systems of risk management are robust and defensible, (3) safeguarding the interests of all stakeholders, particularly the minority shareholders, and (4) determining appropriate levels of remuneration of executive directors, KMPs and senior management, and playing a prime role in appointing and where necessary recommending removal of executive directors, KMPs and senior management.

The IDs of a company shall hold at least one meeting in a year, wherein all IDs must strive to be present, without the attendance of non-IDs and other members of the management. Herein, the IDs shall review the performance of the Chairperson, non-IDs and the Board as a whole, and shall assess the quality and timeliness of flow of information between the management and the Board. The Act also mandates constituting CSR Committee consisting of at least one ID, Audit Committee with IDs in majority, and Nomination and Remuneration Committee with not less than one-half of the members as IDs.

To bring in effectiveness in the functioning, the Act also mandates that no ID shall hold office for more than two consecutive terms of 5 years;however such ID shall be eligible for re-appointment after the expiration of three years. Also, an ID shall not be entitled to any stock option, and may receive remuneration by way of fee, reimbursement of expenses for participation in Board and other meetings, and profit related commission as approved by the members. Further, every ID shall, at the first meeting of the Board in which he participates as a director and thereafter at the first meeting of the Board in every FY or whenever there is any change in the circumstances which may affect his status as an ID, give a declaration regarding compliance with the criteria of independence.

Surely, the enhanced role of Independent Directors would enable the stakeholders trust the functioning of the management as well as the Board. The Board, on the other hand, would become more vigilant while undertaking the tasks of policy making and use of funds. However, it is too early to say that every of the deficiency in the working of the company and in the utilization of stakeholders' funds can be regulated with these measures. Incidences of selecting known professionals by the Board for the role of ID can also not be overlooked. Though the Act bestows upon the shoulders of IDs the responsibility of ensuring fair management, the target can remain unachieved as the management can come up with planned and pre-compromised professionals as IDs. Such presence would not define transparency and vigilance in real terms.

To transform the deemed independence to real one, the MCA along with regulatory bodies (SEBI and RBI) has to play a vital role in the appointment of IDs. I would suggest that the Ministry and SEBI must actively participate in such appointments in listed companies, wherein the Board is vulnerable to play with provisions. The compulsion of assent of shareholders can rarely serve any purpose. The discussion of MCA with the Institute of Directors, UK with a view to utilizing their expertise for training Indian professionals willing to become IDs is truly welcomed; however a well-staffed Committee must be set up by the SEBI that shall ensure core legitimacy and transparency, similar to the selection of Statutory Central Auditors (SCAs) undertaken by Selection Committee of GOI on basis of list forwarded by the RBI.

(Posted on blog on 30 April, 2014)

□

Need of Proficient Process of Selection of Independent Directors in PSU's

Independent director is a silent monitor on a company board-works as a watch-dog--and when it comes for public sector enterprises his role becomes more important for a healthy corporate governance. Independent director's increased presence in the boardroom has been hailed as an effective deterrent to fraud and mismanagement, inefficient use of resources, inequality and unaccountability of decisions.

Moreover, the independent director plays a complementary role in providing professional and managerial advice to the Board. They are drawn from the public men, technocrats, management experts and consultants, and professional managers in industry and trade with a high degree of proven ability.

However, unless the selection of independent directors (IDs) is transparent and free from the administrative ministry concerned, the powers given to them can have a negative impact on PSU autonomy. In many cases, the practice of administrative ministry final say in selection of independent director has delayed some of the important decisions for the company.

For example, Coal India had to put on hold plans to raise coal prices, sign fuel supply agreement with power companies and initiate a price pooling mechanism as ID posts were vacant. The public offer of other companies such as NHPC, Power Grid has also been delayed due to non-appointment of independent directors.

Therefore, the need of the hour is to change the process of appointment of IDs. The responsibility for selection of IDs should be given to a sovereign, independent and impartial committee and removing the role of administrative ministry in their selection. At present selection committee under Department of Public Enterprises

(DPE) selects candidates out of the panel recommended by the concerned ministry. However a panel of eligible persons to be IDs is being maintained by DPE but this appears to be mere formality as this panel is never being used by DPE for nomination of IDs in PSUs. It could be considered by Government to give powers to DPE to nominate IDs in PSUs, from a panel being maintained by DPE, without the interface of concerned ministry.

Moreover these appointments be done proactively much in advance so that seats on the boards of PSUs do not remain vacant and true purpose of IDs being on board is fulfilled.

Further, only a conducive and legally binding atmosphere would enable the IDs to play the following key roles expected of them:

- Help in bringing an independent judgment to bear on the Board's. Being totally independent of the company or its management, provide a candid view of the faults or shortcomings of the company's plans and suggest measures for improvement.
- Bring an objective view in the evaluation of the performance of board and management
- Scrutinize the performance of management in meeting agreed goals and objectives and monitor the reporting of performance
- Add value to the decision-making process of the Board of Directors by giving positive inputs and constructive criticism, wherever required
- Safeguard the interests of all stakeholders, particularly the minority shareholders
- Moderate and arbitrate in the interest of the company as a whole, in situations of conflict between management and shareholder's interest.
- Facilitate sustainable development of the company.

Moreover, the enhanced role of IDs would enable the stakeholders trust the functioning of the management as well as the Board. The board, on the other hand, would become more vigilant while undertaking the tasks of policy making and use of funds. However, it is too early to say that every of the deficiency in the working of the company and in the utilization of stakeholders' funds can be regulated with these measures

It is also widely accepted that a process of continuous improvement of this institution is essential to address the challenges facing the ID system, so that the gap between what is expected of the IDs and what they actually deliver is reduced. While international experience could provide a useful guide, all legal and regulatory reforms necessary to make the institution truly independent and effective in India need to reflect the realities of (a) concentrated ownership and (b) paucity of competent IDs.

It is however recognized that raising corporate governance standards would require going beyond legal and regulatory reforms. Management, institutional investors and media have to play a complementary and facilitating role.

(Posted on blog on 8 May, 2014)

□

Real Development

Why GST Should be Expeditiously Implemented?

Despite the extensive reforms that India's indirect tax system has undergone since 1991, our country still has a highly fragmented, inefficient and distortionary tax structure characterized by multiple tax rates, barriers to inter-state trade and cascading of taxes. The numerous amendments over the years have also made it one of the most complicated legislations in the country. As a result, considerable time and large amounts of money are spent by both the taxpayers as well as the government in long-drawn tax disputes, which in turn locks up billions of rupees in taxes. All these tend to hike up the cost of our products and services.

Besides this, the firms that desire to sell across states face a border tax, local sales tax, central service tax, federal excise, central sales tax and other duties that often vary from state to state and from product to product. This multiple tax system has increased incentives for corruption. Moreover, over the past few years, India has witnessed long-drawn litigations with regard to cross-border transactions and transfer pricing issues involving big multinationals such as the Vodafone Group, IBM, Royal Dutch Shell and Nokia, which have made headlines internationally and also dampened foreign investor sentiment in India.

In this fast-globalizing world when developed nations are striving to bring down tariff barriers, our Union government has also been trying to introduce a simple, stable and predictable indirect tax regime comprising a national sales tax known as the Goods and Services Tax (GST). It aims to streamline the tax administration and creating a single, unified market, while also bringing in higher revenue for the Central government and the states. Unfortunately, as GST requires a Constitutional Amendment and ratification by half the state governments, its implementation has been pushed back several times since it was first announced in the Union Budget of 2007-08.

Furthermore, the 115th Constitution Amendment Bill was introduced in Parliament in March 2011, but consensus on the modalities of the GST has remained elusive. However, according to latest media reports, Prime Minister Narendra Modi has given directions for GST to be rolled out by April 2016. On September 15, 2014 Mr Modi met Finance Minister Arun Jaitley to find out how far the GST preparations have progressed.

The Finance Ministry has already set up a GST cell headed by a joint secretary-level officer. This cell, which also has officers from the Central Board of Excise and Customs, will be the secretariat for the empowered committee of state finance ministers and it will pilot the key bills through Parliament and monitor their subsequent progress through state legislatures. The setting up of the cell shows the ministry has now begun to rush the timetable for the GST roll out.

The only way to untie the GST knot is to treat it as a federal (i.e., centre-state) issue and not just an economic efficiency issue – which is well known. This means Prime Minister Narendra Modi must wear his old hat as Gujarat CM to sort out the issue from the point of view of the states. Mr. Modi has reportedly advised the Finance Ministry to ensure that all the elements are in place, before making the announcement for a nationwide roll-out of the tax. When implemented, GST will replace all the domestic taxes on production and sale of goods and services. While the Finance Ministry is in favor of a single rate of tax in the bill, it has conceded to the demand by the states for a band within which their levies would flourish. Currently, a rate of 12-20% is suggested as tax band, and this is reasonable for growth.

GST thus has two clear beneficiaries – business and central government – and one possible loser, the states. I say 'possible loser', because some states will gain from GST and others lose. States as a whole may not lose, but as long as there are some losers, one can hardly blame states for fearing a post-GST world. The Confederation of All India Traders, which has most retailers under its umbrella, has argued for a single rate. Meanwhile, representatives of major industrial houses have stepped up their lobbying with the Centre in a bid to make GST a reality. States are demanding different rates of GST. Now irrespective of such diverse demands of stakeholders, the actual roll-out of the GST will be the single most economic reform in our country.

Likely challenges in implementation of GST

Implementation of GST may not be easy in view of the many glitches and diverse challenges that are likely to crop up right from the beginning. Some of the expected challenges are as follows:

1. The federal character of the Constitution of India gives autonomy to states to raise their own revenues. Accordingly, our Constitution gives powers to the Union and the states to levy and collect taxes as per Union, State and Concurrent List. So, one of the major challenges to the introduction of GST is the apprehension of states that the federal system would get diluted. As such, implementing the proposed GST legislation across the country will require a Constitutional Amendment via voting in both houses of Parliament, plus the support of 15 of the 29 state governments.
2. GST has to be implemented simultaneously by the central and state governments. While doing so, the central government would only be able to offer the proverbial carrot, but cannot weld the stick as it doesn't have the Constitutional authority to impose such ideas on the states. In this scenario, some states may express stiff opposition to GST fearing loss of autonomy. So the Centre would be at the mercy of the state governments with regard to this decision. And striving to arrive at a consensus among all the 29 states having different political parties with their own ideologies and agendas won't be an easy task.
3. Under GST, taxes would be levied on the basis of the Destination Principle, which means goods and services would be taxed where they are finally sold or rendered. As such, many state governments have a fear that they may lose revenue or may have to forgo some portion of the tax they may otherwise be entitled to. Though the central government has put forward a tax revenue sharing program, some States are yet not fully convinced of its feasibility.
4. In the initial stages of its implementation, the Indian economy is likely to witness high inflation rates, and product prices may go up. The central and state governments may also have

to incur unanticipated administrative costs thereby pushing up tax collection costs. There are also concerns that the tax burden on the low income group may go up. Furthermore, the industries would also need some handholding to understand GST mechanism and to be able to follow them faithfully.

5. Finally, implementation of GST may not be easy to begin with, given the migration to a new and untested information technology (IT) system. Even more difficult would be tackling the complex taxes and integrating them into the new model. For example, CENVAT conversion to an input tax credit mechanism could be complicated and excise duties, exemptions, conversion of specific tariffs into ad valorem duties, etc would add further layers to the task. So, one of the biggest challenges in the run up to the GST is setting up of a national IT framework that can act as a clearing house for the taxation of inter-state movement of goods.

Why GST should now Top India's Agenda

Currently, the GST system is the most important taxation reform that is being contemplated in our country. Any tax-related reform is difficult to implement, and in a federal republic like India where states weld immense powers, the related problems tend to get compounded. So despite all the likely glitches and challenges, the Union government should go ahead and expeditiously implement the GST framework as it will bring in the following advantages and benefits for the stakeholders.

1. The GST framework will usher in a simple, stable and predictable indirect tax regime. It would also be a comprehensive and all-encompassing tax on both goods and services as they pass through the value chain. It would replace most of the complex multiple taxes that are currently being imposed at various levels by the central and state governments as well as the local bodies and thereby make India a single market. Thus, GST aims to economically unify our country by removing all kinds of barriers to trade among states. As such, the supply chain would become faster, seamless and more efficient.
2. The introduction of the GST system will ensure a transparent, unambiguous and easy-to-comply-with tax law that will ease the pressure on industry and help growth. Hence, as soon as

GST is implemented, our country's GDP is expected to receive a big boost because of a major drop in transaction costs. Economists and industry analysts believe GST will add as much as 1.5-2 percentage points to the growth rates. At a time when the Indian economy is sub-performing, this measure has the potential to kickstart a new investment cycle. The manufacturing sector in particular will be a big beneficiary of GST as the economic system becomes more competitive.

3. The benefits of GST are obvious. It is a self-policing tax with little scope for avoidance because whenever anyone sells a good or service he adds the fixed rate of GST to it. However, since he will get a rebate on GST already paid on goods and services bought from his suppliers, he will demand proof of GST payment by his suppliers. Thus all GST taxpayers ensure that GST is paid by their suppliers to get the rebate.
4. As GST is aligned with a corresponding information technology platform, the tax payment system will get streamlined. With manufacturing growth, the objective of employment generation on a large scale will also be promoted. Simultaneously, in the long run, GST would also help moderate inflation by the lowering of transaction costs. Timely credit refund, where applicable, will incentivize firms in compliance, which in turn will bring in more revenues for both the central and state governments. Eventually, India will have a better tax system that is rational, standardized and stable and also simple, fair and neutral.
5. The GST system will immensely benefit the Indian economy as it will simplify India's tax structure, broaden the tax base, and create a common market across states. It will also ensure a transparent, unambiguous and easy-to-comply-with tax law that will ease the pressure on industry and help growth, which in turn will lead to increased compliance and push up India's tax-to-gross domestic product ratio. According to a study conducted by the National Council of Applied Economic Research (NCAER), GST is expected to increase economic growth by between 0.9% and 1.7%. Exports are expected to increase by between 3.2% and 6.3%, while imports will rise between 2.4% and 4.7%.

6. India's business and corporate sector will also benefit as the average tax burden on business enterprises and companies will decline. This will bring down production costs thereby making our country's exports more competitive in the international market. The highest rate of taxation under GST is expected to be around 15% in the first year, and it will come down to 12% in the second year. By comparison, the rate of various indirect taxes currently being levied in India amounts to roughly 20% or even more. Goods deemed necessary or of basic importance will be taxed at a lower rate. In view of these benefits, the business sector has already indicated that it will more than welcome the GST.
7. As GST is an all-inclusive tax at the national level on the manufacturing, sale and consumption of goods, it will ensure that Indian consumers are not taxed multiple times like it happens now. This means that taxes like octroi, CENVAT, central sales tax, state sales tax, entry tax, license fees, turnover tax, etc will no longer be present as all of them will be subsumed into GST. This will lead to a more willing and increased compliance, thus increasing the total amount of tax collected and that too at a lower cost of collection. Of greater importance will be the end result – lower costs of goods and services. This will immensely benefit the consumers, leading to more consumption, which in turn will give a major boost to India's economic growth.
8. GST will not only simplify the taxation structure, but it will also broaden the tax base by bringing more taxable goods and services under its purview. As the proposed GST framework will have two components – a central GST and a state GST, with the central GST going to the centre, and the state GST going to states, none of the states will lose control on their revenues after its implementation. Once the total GST rate is decided, the Central GST and the States GST will be agreed upon. The modalities of sharing of tax revenues with the states and the reimbursement of any shortfall in their tax kitty will also be worked out and a consensus reached on that. The central government has agreed to give states compensation for revenue losses arising out of GST for three years, after its implementation.

9. Furthermore, GST is not simply VAT plus service tax, but a major improvement over the previous system of VAT and disjointed services tax, which is a justified step forward. Moreover, with the collection of both the central and state taxes proposed to be made at the point of sale, there won't be any confusion about when this has to be paid. Currently, different taxes are collected at different stages of the process so there is a tax on manufacturing, one at the time of sale and even another one when goods move from one place to another. Under the GST all of these will be eliminated making it easier to implement and follow.
10. Finally, as India currently has a complicated tax structure, complying with all the provisions therein tends to make it very burdensome, tedious and time-consuming. Since most businesses also face commercial and legal hassles in this regard, our taxation structure is also corruption prone. The end result is that goods cost more, and customers naturally seek cheaper alternatives. Since India already faces competition from China and other countries, if we continue with the current taxation structure, we will effectively price ourselves out. To avert such an unwelcome scenario, India should invariably implement the GST system as early as possible.

(Posted on blog on 25 September, 2014)

□

Endeavors to Turn Developing India to Developed India

Many years ago, India was anticipated to supersede almost every developed country. 'The upcoming superpower-India' was the phrase that presented a dream of prosperity and dignity to all Indians. Should we blame the past governments, our political leaders, the corporate world, India's judicial system, or ourselves for the uninterrupted downfall of our economy, our security, and above all, the standard of our living? Passing over the blame to the government, to opposition, to bureaucrats, and to the common man has just not served any purpose. Then, what is the answer that we have been unable to locate? Definitely, 'renovation' is the key.

We have been debating over the hiked petrol rates, dropping currency valuation, elevating current account and fiscal account deficit, and the uncontrollable interest rates. Did any of these so called essentials of our economy exist when we started off our voyage towards an organized economic setup? Hence, when we think of renovating our fiscal and economic structure, shall we not locate the underlying causes of disaster, which once taken care of will automatically boost the overall setup? Mentioned hereunder are some endeavors, which in case paid proper heed to by the new government, can surely prove to be a blessing in disguise.

An Unbiased Subsidy Structure

The foremost area of concern shall be equivalent flow of paybacks. Be it the perks extended by the governments to the reserved classes, or the funds allocated by the central government to the states, every single penny should be assigned to the most justifiable part. Herein, a complete restructuring of our vote-motivated subsidy regime will prove an effective weapon. When we all know that most of the recipients of our subsidy regime are those who can afford these benefits on their own, why should government's limited resources be misused? Detecting states that need urgent funds to enhance the living standards of residents is the need of the hour.

Education at Any Cost

Would the declined interest rates prove to be of any help in case the youth of the country remains uneducated and unemployed? Education shall begin with the commencement of life so as to let the person match steps with the society. 8 million children of our country are spending their crucial childhood days working at fireworks factories, local eateries, or as pity house maids. Is the Right to Education Act serving any purpose? Street children beg for their living and even the ministers pass by disregarding the fact that the upcoming shoulders of India are weakening to the core. Not just compulsory, but vigorous efforts to bring kids to schools are looked for. Street children do not dream for cut down diesel prices, they just hunt for books.

Cooperative Legislation for Businesses

Can the economy survive for even a single day without the business sector? Be it a sole proprietorship concern, or an MSME, or an MNC, the corporate sector prospers only when the laws of the land are supportive and unambiguous. While many sectors scuffle with limited supply of resources, the others are punished with retrospective taxation, delayed clearances, never-ending corruption, and vicious rules of ministries. Easy finance, clear-cut taxation laws, fast clearances, and quick supply of essentials such as power, coal, and other natural resources should be the main concern of the new government.

Intact Security to All

Prosperity cannot stand for long in case the security wing of the country is vulnerable. Ranging from cyber to terrorist and naxal to communal, riots and attacks have been shattering the mankind as well as the economy of India. Be it the police administration, cyber security, or the trial structure, the country expects workable reforms that can assure every Indian a secured livelihood. Herein, enhancement of our technology and tools is much-needed, along with allocation of funds towards the security wing. The new Prime Minister has displayed his urge towards bettering the security structure of India; however backing from states is much-needed.

Basic Amenities for Sure

When a report reveals the fact that 80 percent of sewage is drained into our rivers untreated, you can understand what we all are drinking. Slums in every metro city depict the unequal distribution of wealth which has been prevailing since ages; however none of the governments could come up with any workable strategy. Further, every other child in India suffers from malnutrition, which can never be a position in a developed or even a developing economy. Funds of the government have to be wisely routed towards enhancing the living standard of the underprivileged. Else, we will continue to be listed among the array of poor nations.

Affordable and Speedy Justice

The ever-escalating count with respect to number of undecided suits in our courts stands at more than 32 million, which is sure to elevate as the way for new courts is rarely being paved. Our judicial system, which was once looked upon as the most esteemed wing, has on number of occasions been blamed for unethical conduct. The Judicial Standards and Accountability Bill as proposed by the government encountered unjustifiable protest from the components of our judicial structure. Transparency in the working of the judiciary and uninterrupted enquiry into charges of judicial corruption was the aim of this revolutionary bill.

We can understand that the new government needs adequate time to repair the very roots of our economic, political, fiscal, and social wings. The PM, Mr. Narendra Modi, has been voted for in the hope of a recovered India. Unwanted criticism will be like hampering the pace of the ministries, which are the sole groups that can vary the complete picture. The areas as mentioned above are not just the only spheres of responsibility; however with enhancement of these vital areas, the roots of our overall structure can be expected to strengthen. Not just the government, the states, the opposition parties, and above all, every Indian will have to put in the hard work.

(Posted on blog on 21 July, 2014)

□

Expect Nothing Without a Systematic Road Transportation System

If I begin with the fact that most of our literate Indians do not even know the precise meaning of road transport signals, rest of the paragraphs can be dispensed with. The milieu, however, has deteriorated to such an extent that mentioning some crucial facts is essential. The fatality risk (road traffic accidents) is above 10 per 100, 000 people, which even crosses 11 when metropolitan cities are talked about. And when the new government favors easy living for the common man, they will have to realize that our bicyclists, pedestrians, and other non-motorized commuters are the most vulnerable to these fatal risks, which is contrary to other developed nations where commuting by car or public transport vehicles is more risky. Doesn't the fact reveal that though we have those red and green indicators, rarely does anyone cares to follow the laid down rules. And if someone disobeys that red signal, it is easy to escape by bribing the traffic policeman.

Pervasive corruption in Regional Transport Offices is known even to the law-protectors. Isn't it surprising that prior to the introduction of biometric data recording system in the process of issuance/renewal of driving licenses, any person could easily get a license without visiting the RTO even once. Yes, the problem lies within us and if the intentions of the new PM, as he delivered on the 68th Independence Day, come true many of our road transportation concerns will eradicate. But prior to awakening the common man with respect to following the traffic rules, or for that matter along with such awakening, the government and other officials will have to play a vital role. When we know that the economic viability of a country and residents therein is linked with mobility of people and goods, the domain, indeed, cannot be left in vain.

Another fact that uncovers this grave concern is that India ranks top in the world in terms of cases of road accidents with more than 14 deaths and above 50 injuries every hour. Next, let me come to the issue of pollution which comes into play when our worn-out vehicles move freely on Indian roads. Herein, Suspended Particulate Matters (SPMs), which is the most hazardous to human health, need a special mention as its emission exceeds the limit set by the World Health Organization in most of our metro cities. In this context, if one would check as to how many of the vehicles running on our roads have a legitimate PUC (Pollution under Control Certificate), the alertness of our transport system and law protectors will be exposed. And do the travelers in India even know that if a vehicle is found visibly polluting, even a valid PUC stands void.

The failure owes to modal split (percentage of travelers using a particular transportation mode/number of trips per such mode), scarcity of road safety policies, unawareness of general public, laidback approach of transport officials, and poor infrastructure. Adding to the curse are those freely moving hawkers, unlawfully parked vehicles, and recklessly driving two-wheelers. Rules pertaining to use of helmets, seat belts, number of commuters, and pollution are rarely followed in rural as well as urban parts of India. Also, it is beyond understanding how distinct streams of transport viz. pedestrians, cyclists, motorcyclists, cars, buses, rickshaws and auto rickshaws can move on same busy road. And when you visit the states of U.P., Bihar, or Punjab, you can find buses and autos parked in the center of roads for engaging passengers, thus leading to anarchy.

Time has arrived to discuss some workable solutions. Foremost, the most viable answer to the concern of transportation chaos is developing regional economies. By this I mean that a specific region must embrace the entire requisite infrastructure ranging from services, shopping, work prospects, and leisure facilities. Though this target is more than challenging to achieve; however the outcomes will be lesser fatal accidents and better standard of living. Next, the new leaders will need to restructure the public transport domain particularly buses. In this context, it is to be noted that most of Indian commuters rely on personal means rather than on metros, rails, and buses. Publicly owned bus systems need special heed. Herein, it becomes vital to know that the Calcutta State Transport Corporation relies heavily on subsidies as the revenues are capable of covering only three-fourth of cost of operations. Fares, if needed, shall be hiked just like rails.

In view of economic dexterity, every government promotes the sale and use of privately-owned vehicles viz. two-wheelers and cars and hence the fact that the roads of our country aren't apt enough to carry such high pressure goes overlooked. Many western countries promote use of bicycles and other green channels that not only take care of the environment but also ensures safety and public health. Also, the price differential in terms of petrol and diesel should only be allowed to promote farmers and public transport operators, and not to privately-owned diesel cars. The Motor Vehicle Act demands urgent amendments with respect to hardening of vehicle emission standards in India which are way sloppier than Euro standards. More than half of the Indian vehicles are above 5 years old, many among which are decades old, hence not complying with the standards set for environmental prevention, thus demanding for apt dumping laws.

It is evident that not all in this direction can be attained by only the Ministry of Road Transport and Highways of India, currently headed by Mr. Nitin Gadkari. Unified efforts are the need of the hour and all officials, government departments, automobile companies, and the common man have to be the contributories. Car-pooling and such other constructive means are to be promoted. Along with, public awareness programmes for promoting better conformity to laws should be frequently organized. It is expected that the new law-makers will recognize the issues of road congestion, fatal accidents, and ever-rising air pollution. Works in this direction seem to have begun when the new Minister announced scrapping of RTOs, studying of traffic laws of six different countries for firming our law, and proposal of cancellation of driving license of someone who jumps the red light thrice. To end corruption, however, the most spirited role has to be played by us who look for easy and deceitful ways to escape laws and punishments.

(Posted on blog on 12 September, 2014)

□

How to Arrest Rural-Urban Migration

India's latest census and its 15th since 1872, states our country's urban population has been surging at a higher pace as compared to the rural population. This development is being attributed to the rising migration from rural hinterland to urban centers, which in turn leads to further growth and expansion of cities and towns as well as addition of newer urban areas.

In India, people from villages migrate to cities for various reasons. These reasons can be economic, social or environmental. If people move to urban areas in a bid to earn their livelihood or boost their income or enhance their career opportunities, those reasons can be classified as economic. Similarly, if people migrate to escape the aftermath of natural calamities like famine, flood, earthquake, etc, such migration can be attributed to environmental reasons. Migration can also happen because of some other reasons or due to a range of push and pull factors. So, let us here discuss the causes for rural-urban migration in much more detail.

Specific Causes for Migration

To reiterate, migration from rural to urban areas occurs for several reasons. Growth of industries and their concentration in urban areas is one of the major causes of rural-urban migration. As a result of skewed up industrialization, people from the rural areas move towards industrialized centers in search of income and employment. This in turn results in unplanned and haphazard growth of cities and towns.

Another reason that contributes to migration is poverty. One yardstick for measuring of poverty can be income levels. Due to dearth of employment opportunities, a large number of villagers in India tend to be unemployed or underemployed. As such, they don't have a source of steady income, which tends to make them relatively poor.

Thus, poverty has become a chronic problem in rural areas because of which many villagers are unable to afford even the basic amenities of life. Such people migrate from villages to cities to escape poverty.

Even those who are financially better off may prefer to move to cities for other reasons such as in search of greater educational opportunities for their children, better healthcare facilities for their aged parents and higher standards of living and improved quality of life for themselves.

Then there is the ambitious and dynamic segment of the rural population, especially those who belong to the younger generation. They may relocate to cities solely because they aspire to boost their professional exposure and work experience. Their craving for a greater variety of opportunities, people, culture, art, food and entertainment can find fulfillment only in big cities. Hence, they also migrate seeking greener pastures for professional growth and exposure.

War, famine, earthquake as well as other natural calamities can also be reasons for rural-urban migration. Large sections of rural populations may migrate to urban centers to escape the sufferings inflicted by such natural calamities and in search of protection, food and medical aid during such periods of disasters and hardships.

Living in cities permits individuals and families to take advantage of the many opportunities of proximity, diversity and marketplace competition. This in turn, improves their quality of life as well as exposure to career advancement opportunities. Cities also offer them better access to a range of business and employment opportunities as compared to what were available to them in their villages. So, once they migrate from the rural hinterland to urban areas, majority of them prefer to permanently settle down at the new locations.

Problems Created by Migration

First and foremost, rural-urban migration has detrimental effects on the village economy. Some segments of micro, small and medium enterprises (MSMEs) may cease to exist over a period of time as there is no one left to run such businesses or work in local firms or demand products from such enterprises because a good number of people have migrated to cities. Secondly, the scope for setting up new business enterprises and making them successful also becomes bleak because of the same reasons.

Secondly, massive rural-urban migration can increase chances of spread of diseases from urban to rural areas. Because, when people who have migrated to big cities and are working there return to their home village to visit their families, relatives and friends, they may also carry infectious illnesses and diseases contracted by them in the cities. This can lead to spread of such diseases in rural areas.

Another major problem caused by migration is unwanted and unhealthy urbanization. In simple terms, urbanization can be defined as a process of concentration of population in a particular territory. Since most of the migrations that happen are the result of unplanned movement of people from rural areas to urban centers, they cause economic, social and environmental problems for the cities, and also for those residing in them.

Some other problems emanating from large-scale migration are unemployment and underemployment as well as shortage of basic amenities like water supply, sanitation, sewerage and electricity. Another challenge is a dearth of housing facilities, which in turn tends to create large slum populations in cities. For instance, Mumbai has almost 50% of its population living in slums, despite their per capita income being quite high. Similarly, Kolkata has 32% of its population living in slums. Overall, 15% of India's urban population is estimated to be living in slums.

As cities develop, other adverse effects can include a dramatic increase in costs, often pricing the poor people out of the market. For example, escalating housing costs and rents may make it difficult for the lower income groups to get affordable accommodation close to their workplace. This may compel them to move away to far-flung places in search of affordable accommodation, which may hike their commuting time and commuting cost.

Furthermore, extensive urbanization or indiscriminate growth of cities can lead to many other adverse effects. Some of them are enumerated below:

- **(i) Disintegration of joint family**: High cost of living is a major problem in all big cities. In megalopolises such as Mumbai, Delhi, Chennai and Bangalore, it becomes very difficult for lower income groups to maintain a decent standard of living. Even joint families can't be maintained in cities on account of high cost of living. So people prefer to live in nuclear families.

(ii) **Impersonal relationships**: The concept of good-neighbourliness and community life is almost non-existent in urban centers. So, people often become self-centered and they show little concern for fellow human beings. Hence, urban life tends to become monotonous and get characterized by highly secondary relationships. This may have an adverse psychological impact on individuals.

(iii) **Problem of pollution**: In industrialized cities, pollution is a major problem. Air pollution may be caused by smoke-emitting industrial units or by excessive movement of vehicles. Similarly, water bodies in cities also tend to get polluted due to discharge of effluents by chemical factories, dyeing units, textile mills, etc.

(iv) **Stress**: Urban life is characterized by stress that can even strain family relationships. In cities, female members in the family are also compelled to take up jobs in a bid to meet the increased cost of living. Changing role of women tend to create stress in the family, which may result in strained relations or even lead to painful divorces.

(v) **Increase in crime rates**: Urban centers are known for higher crime rates. Theft, dacoity, murder, cheating, pick-pocketing and rapes become quite common in such places due to over-crowding, scarcity of resources, unemployment, poverty, stress, etc.

(vi) **Environmental hazards**: A major consequence of migration is the environmental problems caused, which may destroy the physical appearance of cities. Some portions of cities or their structural environment may get damaged due to over-crowding, as migrants encroach public places or they put up illegal houses or create unhealthy slums in and around the city because they have to shelter themselves and live within their limited incomes.

How to Arrest Rural-urban Migration

Since, one of the major causes for the rising migration from rural to urban areas is lack of productive employment, creating earning opportunities by generating sufficient number of jobs and business opportunities in rural areas would be the best way to stop people from migrating. This can happen through promoting agriculture in various ways like creating awareness, printing agricultural literature and reaching them to farmers, distributing good quality seeds, constructing cold storages and warehouses and encouraging farmers to put in their best in a bid to improve yield and output and then encouraging farmers by facilitating them for their good performance.

Secondly, a good number of Indian villages are in a state of utter neglect and under-development with a large number of impoverished people as a result of past legacies and defects in our planning process and investment pattern. To correct this situation, every village in our country should be provided with basic amenities like clean drinking water, uninterrupted power supply, sound healthcare, quality educational institutes, good public transport, modern communication network and internet access as well as other facilities. These steps will open up ample avenues for gainful employment and steady source of income for villagers.

Lack of irrigation facilities and water scarcity are also major issues facing the countryside. As such, Indian agriculture is mostly dependent on monsoon rainfall. Unless there is an increased thrust on enhancing irrigation coverage across the country, the agriculture potential of India's rural hinterland cannot be fully realized. Moreover, new social and engineering solutions are needed to deal with water scarcity. Simultaneously, new water reservoirs are also required to deal with floods and droughts.

To enhance income and livelihood security of the rural poor, our country should give a major impetus to various activities related to rural development. The government should ensure that the benefits of economic reforms percolate to all the villagers across the length and breadth of our country. To ensure that the corporate sector also pitches in and contributes to the cause of the rural poor, special incentives and tax rebates should be given to companies in a bid to motivate them to invest in promotion of agricultural and rural development related activities. Rural and agricultural development should also be made an important part of various corporate social responsibility (CSR) initiatives.

Currently, most jobs in rural areas are agriculture related or dependent on agriculture. They often tend to be seasonal and therefore unreliable. For the rural masses to overcome poverty, villages should be able to provide economic opportunities throughout the year. A large percentage of the rural populace should also be able to earn a decent living through non-agricultural occupations. Our government strategies and investments should be directed towards this goal.

Small scale industries that can be linked with agricultural operations spread over rural areas and smaller towns nearby may be the answer. Villagers should find it easy to make a decent living without migrating to big cities. The false lure of the cities as an attractive place for better living should be totally abolished by making village life economically attractive. For this to happen, our government should promote economic prospects and focus on infrastructure development in rural areas. It should also create ready markets for supporting agricultural and economic activities and also development of sustainable agricultural practices in the rural sector.

The Central and state governments should formulate appropriate policies and programs for the development of rural areas with the fundamental objective of ensuring their sustainable development by ensuring adequate working and living conditions and the preservation of natural and cultural heritage. Measures for the development of rural areas should encompass aid for investment into farms, processing of agricultural products, environmental protection measures in agricultural and forestry areas, land improvement measures as well as reconstruction and development of the countryside.

The Reserve Bank of India and the National Bank for Agriculture and Rural Development (Nabard), in close coordination with regional rural banks and district cooperative banks, should come up with short-term and long-term projects, programs and policies aimed at providing credit and micro-lending facilities to small and marginal farmers as well as to village artisans. This step will not only ensure that villagers have easy accessibility to finance, but it will also strengthen rural banking so that it can serve as the backbone of development in rural and remote areas on a sustainable basis.

Finally, any rural development program can be successful only if the unfettered population growth is curbed. Indian population is burgeoning at a feverish pace. Whatever little economic progress is made possible by the governments get eroded by the faster increase in number of mouths to feed. The scanty health services, the negligible primary education facilities and sparse housing are further strained, thereby keeping the poor always in poverty.

As such, India's economic growth would be seriously hampered if the country's population growth is not checked. The available resources are spread thin leaving the poor unhappy. The poor think children are a means to augment earnings, while the truth is that increase in population would never lift them out of poverty. Therefore, population control is the immediate imperative, with two-child norm and sterilization through incentives and gentle persuasion. Rural poverty and high fertility are closely linked. One cannot be solved without tackling the other.

As the potential in rural India is immense, the above corrective measures will boost the purchasing power of the rural population, thereby creating enormous demand for goods and services. When this happens, the possibility of reverse migration of people from the urban slums back to the villages will become a strong possibility.

Before concluding this article, it needs to be mentioned that the Saansad Adarsh Gram Yojana (SAGY) recently announced by Prime Minister Narendra Modi is an excellent program that can help in arresting rural-urban migration. The scheme encourages Members of Parliament from both Houses to identify and develop one village from their constituency as a model village by 2016, and two more by 2019, covering over 2, 500 villages of the 600, 000 villages country-wide.

Since there are 800 parliamentarians in our country, around 2, 500-odd villages can get covered within a span of three years. Similarly, if all Indian states initiate similar schemes with their MLAs, 6, 000 to 7, 000 villages could get covered. One good village can inspire the entire area because of which a positive viral effect could gradually begin.

(Posted on blog on 26 November, 2014)

□

Net Neutrality 'must' for Inclusive Development

Just at a time when I was struggling hard to comprehend my son's friend's idea of linking the ambulance service in the capital city with various hospitals via GPS tracking technology and an easy-to-use mobile application, this talk of the town, 'net neutrality', erupted, and all my plans to back his project with some initial funds came to hold. After learning that if service providers are given unasked jurisdiction over determining what services (websites and web applications) can be made freely/cheaply accessible to the users, it is self-understood that innovators and thinkers would indeed breathe the last of their skills. For say, had my service provider given me an option 10 years back to use Orkut, a Google-backed social networking application free-of-cost, which means all my surfing would have cost me nothing except minimal fixed charges, I would have never explored Facebook, and you would agree that Mark Zuckerberg would not have become one of the world's richest and most influential entrepreneurs. So now my due diligence exercise for the ambulance project remains suspended until TRAI decides on this crucial matter.

Net Neutrality-This may look complex since it takes account of technical equations like protocol, bandwidth, ISP, bundling and deep packet inspection; however, as a layman and a regular user today of internet services like YouTube, Google, Gmail and Flipkart, this can be construed as against discriminating between services available over the net by internet service providers, by way of reaching a deal with specific web applications, of course in exchange of money, to allow users surf these applications at comparatively higher speed and cheap data charges. This boils down to the state that when we would have an option to just pay throw-away prices to access particular prominent websites, we would refrain from trying anything that exists outside this sphere, thus putting the groundbreaking works of new aspirants at menace. The most recent of such endeavors was the Airtel Zero, that aimed at partnering with few players and tempting consumers to go for attractive packs and restrict their net usage to just these notable services. The outcome is 'Preference over Others', this time not on caste, color or power, but on how willing are they ready to compensate the service provider/s on behalf of the consumer.

And if at all this comes true, I am sorry for my young friend who dreamed of lessening the pain of panic-struck individuals for whom calling an ambulance at odd hours is like a miracle come true. Had you been able to come up with this a few years back, this may have helped Nirbhaya, and you could have been quite established now to pay service providers for adding your application to 'premium' list. Clear winners, if net neutrality is not attained in India, will be the telecoms and handful of application makers, and losers would include all the remaining ones. While for new entrepreneurs, roads to success will be blocked, for the users, competition would be slayed; hence ultimately, we would end up paying more for time-worn facilities having relished the initial discounts, mouth-watering offers. Do not also forget the 'pro-rural and pro-poor' service, internet.org, as announced by Mark Zuckerberg, which will do nothing except promoting just Facebook and few others, real accessibility to knowledge will remain unattained.

I was imagining, had this concept of 'fast' and 'slow' lanes and severely cheap internet surfing have evolved 10 or 15 years back, Wikipedia, our trusted source for all-around information, which runs as a not-for-profit service, would never have managed to reach the existing stage. And until this ease of access is equitable, how can the government of India even envisage success of the much-promising Digital India drive? For inclusive growth, open internet is much-desirable, is indeed a pre-requisite. Identify this-now when the ones batting for non-neutral internet say that despite being world's no. 3 with respect to number of internet users, our penetration (users from within the country's overall population) is merely 20 per cent (that of the United States is 85 per cent), they wickedly overshadow the very basic verity that access to limited platforms like Facebook and Gmail will be of no use to farmers who need reliable information and forecasts on weather and agriculture, and their children who need lessons on Chemistry and Math, not just social networking.

Net neutrality, in true sense, not just favors indiscrimination towards web applications, but it also is the guiding principle for free speech, right to communicate and of course, social justice. Today, when the political party leading the nation used social networking as a way to reach the otherwise unreachable, when you and I are very much enabled to interact with our friends/relatives outside the border of India via Skype and WhatsApp, when a click gets us a taxi and when hidden talent in far-flung areas becomes 'viral', concepts like paid prioritization and discrimination against the content flowing in the network find no legal place. Don't forget, nothing in this world comes for free or cheap, applications that will run on our mobile phones without consuming much data will bear the cost of this data and ultimately the same will be borne by us.

For real and sustainable development and power in the hands of people, internet is to remain open and indiscriminative. I stand for 'Net Neutrality', so do I except from you.

(Posted on blog on 26 April, 2015)

□

FDI – How to Reap the Real Benefit

Foreign Direct Investment has proved out as one the most vibrant contributors towards procurement of funds by Indian entrepreneurs and as a measure for trimming down the Current Account Deficit. Foreign investors have been considering India as a secure and sound investment place. As per the United Nations report, the FDI inflows grew 17 percent in 2013 touching USD 28 billion, which proves that the investors are assured of the competency of Indian enterprises. In the recent past, doors have been opened for the foreign investors in sectors ranging from telecom and stock exchanges to PSU oil refineries and defense with a view to provide the requisite push to the economy.

What FDI aims is resolving multiple concerns at a time. Funds are the pre-requisites for running any business concern, however, domestic funds are unable to meet the demands of the economy, and hence foreign investors are encouraged so as to provide the much-needed stimulus to the industry. Plus, rather than burdening the Indian concerns with the obligations of servicing debt, FDI is a much convenient option, wherein the loss incurred, if any, would not result in severe implications. It is vital to note that India has brought in USD 306.88 billion as foreign investment since 2000. The participants are nations ranging from Singapore, Mauritius and Netherlands to U.K. and Canada.

At the same time, it has to be comprehended that the paybacks from foreign investment do not accrue automatically and uniformly across nations, sectors, and communities. The DIPP and FIPB, along with RBI have been playing a significant role in attracting foreign funds; the need for broad, transparent, and enabling policy environment for investment as well as to build institutional and human capacities for proper implementation is being sensed until today. It has to be realized that the UNCTAD survey projected India as the second most favorable destination for investment after China; however our policy and IP Rights regime have not been able to reap the complete benefit of transnational flow of funds.

Caps imposed on the equity holding of overseas investors in distinct sectors including aviation have to be reconsidered. On the contrary, the mounting participation of foreign players in some sectors too has to be analyzed keeping in view the limitations and potential of our domestic system of flow of funds from financial intermediaries to businesses. A competent and stricter Intellectual Property Rights regime is the need of the hour. This would encourage groundbreaking companies to handover new know-how and business devices to their counter-parts in India, which in turn would boost the overall FDI structure as well as the productivity, development, and employment.

FDI in retail sector has been the most talked about subject matter of foreign inflow of funds. The new government must analyze the pros and cons keeping in view the interests of the consumers and retail traders at large. The potential gainers post the implementation of this module will be the consumers who will profit from competitive prices and superior quality products. The real estate sector too will benefit as vacant spaces in shopping malls would be utilized, which in way will also boost the banking sector. The losers, on the contrary, can be the small scale retailers and manufacturers, along with unqualified workforce. Special privileges to domestic retailers and manufacturers, and training sessions for existing workforce can be of massive help.

The recent variations to the route for foreign funds viz. automatic and approval, have added to the dexterity of the FDI regime; however the delay in clearances from FIPB and other government departments has been an area of concern. Under automatic route, Indian concerns have the expediency to file returns of the funds routed and shares allocated post the completion of activities to RBI; however prior approval from FIPB, sectoral caps, and cumbersome documentation create hassles under the approval route. The Board and the government have been recurrently enhancing the sectoral caps, and adding more and more sectors under the automatic route; real paybacks will be unattainable until proper restructuring is done.

(Posted on blog on 17 May, 2014)

□

A Few Workable Proposals for Mr. Modi

Boosting the paralyzed economy is no easy task. Laid down rules and proven measures can surely direct the future actions; however cannot assure success until the present drawbacks and threats are addressed to. Yet another year of sub-5 percent growth rate in 2013-14 has added to the curse. The sufferers are not just the corporate houses and the affluent section of the society, the paralyzed economy augmented the gap between the present workforce and work prospects, beyond widening the difference between earning capacity and inflated prices of products/services. Problems have been discussed a lot; let us now look upon some workable solutions.

What shall be the foremost area of attention? I am sure that the visionary capability of Mr. Modi would look for measures to enhance the productivity. It is known to all that vital projects, embracing power and technology, are waiting commencement of operations owing to the lack of executive decision-making of the past government and ministers. The outcome is the incremental capital-output ratio that has halved over the span of five years. The delay has added to the cost of these projects and the factors of production are now extremely demanding. The new ministers will have to accelerate the pace of clearances and decision-making.

I am sure that curbing the ever-high inflation would remain a topmost priority for the Modi-led union government. Herein, the subsidy regime will also have to be considered, which is almost 4 percent of the GDP and hence accounts for more than USD 80 billion of funds being extended to programmes that are incapable to yield equivalent output. The basic law of economics states that this cash results in excessive demand, which in turn creates supply-demand disequilibrium and augments the rate of inflation. The public distribution system demands prompt attention, along with curbing of subsidy on diesel, and better supervision of food stocks.

The private sector has suffered high debt-servicing conditions owing to the prevailing inflation and the laidback attitude of the past government. Something that can prove a blessing is the positive real rates. The positive real rates will be capable of shifting the domestic savings to financial assets rather than physical assets. Also, the recapitalization of public sector banks would enhance the deposit ratio of banks, which in turn would assist the banks to step into a much better and growth-oriented milieu. Plus, the real rates would appeal the investors to move towards the capital market, hence adding to the borrowing power of the corporates.

The economists believe that the country would need to grow at more than 8 percent every year so as to sustain the global reputation and influx of foreign funds. Growth is the only factor than can assure dignity of work to the workforce that upsurges by 10 million new entrants per year. The support extended by the general public to the Modi-led BJP in the general elections of 2014 depicts the outlook of the residents. For sure, the households are expecting realistic prices for goods of basic necessity, and the youth is anticipating better and secured work prospects. I am quite sure that the Modi-led union government would get matters sorted out, sooner than later.

(Posted on blog on 2 June, 2014)

□

Union Budget – Progressive, Pro-poor and Youth-oriented

FM Lays Out Blueprint for Economic Revival, Fiscal Prudence, Infrastructure Growth, FDI Push and a Stable Tax Regime

The maiden Union Budget of the Narendra Modi-led NDA government presented by Finance Minister Arun Jaitley in Parliament on July 10 has been prepared from a long-term perspective. Laying out a blueprint to revive India's sluggish economy, it has outlined a slew of measures to achieve fiscal prudence, job creation, FDI push and a stable tax regime as well as to give a major fillip to the infrastructure and manufacturing sector.

Delivering the budget speech, the Finance Minister said his budget aims at a 7-8% growth over the next three-four years, less fiscal deficit and a manageable current account deficit. Towards achieving them, he has chosen fiscal prudence over grand schemes in a bid to nurse public finances, tame inflation and simplify tax laws as he believes that by doing so, growth, investment and jobs will follow.

Emphasizing that the prevailing economic situation presents a tough challenge and there was a need to introduce 'fiscal prudence' that will lead to fiscal consolidation and discipline, Jaitley said his government will aim to retain the fiscal deficit target for 2014-15 at 4.1% of GDP and reduce it further to 3.6% in 2015-16 and to 3% by 2016-17. The budget will prefer to lower the fiscal deficit by boosting revenues rather than cutting down on expenditure, he elaborated.

While reviving growth and reining in the fiscal deficit, the budget also nurtures a vision to improve investor sentiment and business climate, boost agriculture and manufacturing sector, generate employment opportunities and meet all the expectations that began to build up since May 16, after it became amply clear that the BJP-led National Democratic Alliance would form the next government with a clear majority. In that sense, the budget can also be termed as youth-oriented, farmer-friendly and pro-poor.

To promote skilling and vocational training among youth and to make them job-ready, the budget has made several announcements. To encourage rural youth to start their own ventures, Jaitley has announced a spending of ₹ 100 crore to start village entrepreneurship training schemes. Recognizing the importance of stepping up vocational trainings and bringing it at par with the higher education system, he has announced the 'Skill India' programme and allocated an amount of ₹ 14, 389 crore for job creation, a huge part of which will hopefully be spent in training the youth.

The Finance Minister has also proposed setting up of five new Indian Institutes of Technology (IITs) and five Indian Institutes of Management (IIMs) across the country at a cost of ₹ 500 crore.

For the farmers, the budget has announced a slew of much-awaited measures. Focus on increasing irrigation facilities, farm markets, financial help to landless farmers and Kisan TV to provide real time information to farmers would help in increasing productivity of the farm sector. Moreover, Haryana has been gifted a horticulture research institute and Jharkhand an agriculture research institute, while Maharashtra will get agri-biotech clusters.

The budget is not only progressive, but it is also pro-poor. It has tried to address the aspirations of almost all sections of the Indian masses, including the downtrodden. Landless farmers will be given cheaper credit, the rural poor have been promised broadband, cheaper TVs and better roads, Dalit-focused schemes have been allocated more money, the middle class have been given tax breaks, the youth got the Skill India and Digital India programs and India's holiest river will get funds for a clean-up.

Not surprisingly, Narendra Modi has endorsed the budget through a tweet that stated: 'Finance Minister presented a Budget that is a ray of hope for the poor and downtrodden. It converts people's hopes and aspirations into trust.'

To give a fillip to the infrastructure and manufacturing sector, a 10-year tax holiday for undertakings that generate and transmit power has been unveiled. Focus on industrial infrastructure such as a plan to establish seven industrial cities in India would enhance industrialization and create employment opportunities in the economy.

The allocation for urban infrastructure earmarked at ₹ 50, 000 crore is really appreciable and this would expedite the pace and urbanization in the country and give a massive boost to growth and expand the national economy much faster.

The boost to Real Estate Investment Trusts (REITS) and Infrastructure Investment Trusts is very encouraging news for the real estate and infrastructure markets as it offers innovative and modern tools of investment to Indians. These are all important signals.

Investment allowance of 15% to the manufacturing companies investing ₹ 25 crore in plant and machinery would accelerate capital investments and propel manufacturing growth. Steps undertaken to revive SEZs would help to rejuvenate the investment cycle. Similarly, facilitation to manufacturing units to sell their products through retail and e-commerce would reduce the selling cost and benefit both manufacturers and consumers.

Furthermore, it is also a taxpayer-friendly budget as the income-tax exemption limit has been raised by ₹ 50,000 to ₹ 2,50,000, the PPF ceiling to ₹ 1,50,000, housing loan rebate to ₹ 2,00,000, investments under 80C to ₹ 1,50,00. In view of this, through appropriate tax planning those drawing a salary up to ₹ 6,00,000 can bring down their tax liability to nil.

The Finance Minister has also assured investors that retrospective amendments to tax laws will be undertaken with extreme caution. Promising to set up a high-level CBDT committee to deal with retrospective taxation, Jaitley said all fresh cases arising out of the 2012 Retrospective Amendment to the Income Tax Act, 1961 will be looked into by the committee. However, the existing tax disputes, arising out of the said amendment, and are pending in Courts, will be allowed to reach their logical conclusions, he said.

Speaking about his government's plan to introduce the Goods and Services Taxes (GST) this year, Jaitley said the GST aims to replace a series of existing taxes such as excise duty, service tax and value added tax (VAT). Revealing that discussions with state governments with regard to GST implementation have been encouraging, he said GST will streamline the tax administration, avoid harassment to businesspersons and also result in higher revenue collection both for the Centre and the States.

The budget also highlights the Union Government's intention to overhaul the subsidy regime in a bid to ensure that subsidies reach the targeted beneficiaries. While food subsidy for FY15 has been increased to ₹ 72,970 crore, the oil subsidy has been retained at ₹ 63,427 crore. Furthermore, there are plans to link the National Rural Employment Guarantee Programme to genuine asset creation and can't be used to dig and fill up holes and pits as it were.

Taking into account the fact that our Finance Minister got only 45 days' time to prioritize his priorities and for drawing up the budget for 2014-15, he has done an excellent job because this budget is undoubtedly very progressive, astute and realistic.

(Posted on blog on 11 July, 2014)

□

What Next for Mr. Modi – Tailbacks and Solutions

Post-poll surveys have given a picture of the formation of a stable government at the center led by the National Democratic Alliance. It is almost sure that the nation would be administered by a leader with proven track record in the state of Gujarat. Covering lakhs of kilometers for campaigning and connecting with people is a past proposition. What await Mr. Narendra Modi are the aspirations of the unemployed, lack of prospects for entrepreneurs, high price-victim households, and paralyzed economy. Though tough circumstances have in the past as well tested the brain of this proficient leader; tacking the ambitions of millions of Indians would call in for elevated hard work and visionary capabilities. The new government must not forget that post five years of governance; it shall too be evaluated by the then voters.

Ranging from bringing in transparency with respect to auctioning of resources like coal and spectrum to advancing the legislative and technological domains, the nation expects enormous reforms from the new government. Vital to note, UPA inherited an exceptional GDP, which will not be the case with the NDA. The crying GDP of below 5 percent, ever-high fiscal deficit and balance of payments, and restricted earning prospects for the youth will be the key areas of consideration. Mr. Modi has demonstrated in Gujarat that out of box measures deliver expected outcomes if planned and executed in a well-defined manner. Thus, rearrangement of the complete fiscal and economic domain with a view to exploit the opportunities and curb the limitations will be the need of the hour.

Overseas Direct Investment and Foreign Direct Investment can be encouraged, leaving aside the areas wherein such investments can cause troubles. It is to be noted that FDI can bring in the much-awaited prospects of enhanced production means as well as employment. The new government can rethink the duties payable by importers with a view to infusing healthy competition in the domestic market and helping Indian consumers attaining superior-grade goods and services at comparatively low prices. Unorganized employment too is an area of concern. Though such employment trims down the count of unemployed residents; standard of living never boosts up. For instance, youth unable to fetch a salaried job, opts to earn via labor work, which can never uplift the status of living of the Indians.

Another area of concern is the elevating share of the service sector in our GDP. Though India has been the most preferred outsourcing partner of multinational companies since past many years, the more than tolerable share of this sector can mutilate the pillars of the economy. A lesson here has to be learnt from China which has been a hub of manufacturing and is now competing developed nations with hostile outlook. The solution is not to curb the service sector, rather workable and quick reforms have to be instigated for the furtherance of the manufacturing sector. Import of technical know-how, machines, and new techniques of producing must be encouraged with a view to extending competitive edge to domestic producers. Herein, rethinking of the FDI policy can play a vital role.

The pros and cons of the globalization aspect have to be reworked. The new government shall allow extensive bringing in of technology, however imports in sectors like garments can be limited to help domestic producers reap the advantage of available resources. Import of distinctive goods and services has to be reevaluated in light of the detriment caused to domestic producers and workforce. A preferred model can be an assessment in terms of loss of earning prospects for the domestic workforce, and advances in the cost and manner of production. Rather than baselessly following the regulations forced by the WTO, India will have to open new doors and shut those which are prejudicial to the economy. Surely, Mr. Modi and his men will prove talented enough, and will comprehend state of affairs prudently.

(Posted on blog on 14 May, 2014)

□

Hindutva, or Development – What is Mission Modi and What should be a Voter's View?

Besides 'Economic Revival', 'Open Government and Accountable Administration', 'Rural and Urban Development', 'PPPP Model', and 'Corruption', the BJP Manifesto-2014 also talks about the construction of Ram Temple in Ayodhya within the framework of the Constitution and Uniform Civil Code. As expected, the Congress has appealed to the Election Commission with a charge that the inclusion of the Ram Temple construction is a violation of the model code as it is an attempt to fetch votes on religious lines.

Is the BJP so guilty to have said that they would facilitate the construction of the Temple, however Constitutional and other statutory implications would be adhered to? What was the Congress attempting while appealing to the Shahi Imam that the Muslim votes should not split? Wasn't that the infringement of the model code of conduct as laid down by the EC? What is the AAP attempting by favoring swift judicial settlements in cases against the Muslims? Surely, every political party is looking forward to fetching support in view of communal and regional disparity. What matters the most is the use of illicit ways to lure particular communities to vote in favor.

The RSS, which has been trying to convince the citizens with the development model of Narendra Modi, doesn't absolutely deny the fact that the integrity of the Hindus is in danger and the Modi-led government can only be the revival force. The RSS workers in Muzzafarnagar are talking to the general public to educate them with the datum that the central and the state government have dishonestly favored special communities to fetch support. The fact is that these governments have relied upon the votes of these particular communities, however, have betrayed them as well as the justice.

Some of the RSS workers who have been assigned the task to promote the development model of Modi agree that Hindutva too is a vital parameter. While they are not provoking the Hindus to resort to unlawful measures, they are attempting to make it possible for every voter to exploit the right to choose a deserving candidate. Why then the honest attempts of the RSS and BJP workers to educate the Hindu voters being considered as communal? It is an established trend now, that the party that talks about the betterment of the minorities is secular in real sense, however the political group/leader favoring the prosperity of the majority and the entire nation is communal.

Definitely, the voters need to comprehend the real intentions and motives of the political entities. Inclusion of matters like the swift justice to a particular community and advancement of special religions in the Manifesto are easy ways to attract votes. Rather, the vision and capability of the candidate must be assessed in view of past deliveries. The focus of the voter, to any religion he/she belongs to, should be aimed at strengthening the roots of the economy and all-inclusive prosperity for all religions, regions, and castes.

(Posted on blog on 8 April, 2014)

□

Base of India: Agriculture

Rescue Farmer – Our Anndaata from Misery

Isn't it a shame that a very basic issue that repeatedly was a part of Hindi literature and films has always remained an incomprehensible subject for our elected rulers? I can reminisce the work of Munshi Premchand, Godaan, a Hindi novel, which revolves around a poor peasant, Hori and rural society, and depicts clearly the pain of borrowing from private moneylenders who never allow a farmer to prosper. Alike was the case with the family portrayed in Hindi film, Mother India, that though gained worldwide recognition but could not invoke a sense of duty in our lawmakers. Having lived a major part of my life in rural India and as a son of a farmer, I know the day-to-day hurdles and stigma, how a poor farmer borrows a mere 10 thousand rupees from Sahukaar to purchase a cow or to dig a water bore and the monthly interest rate of 10 per cent never lets this 10 thousand to be really paid off. We talk about APMC and government meddling with respect to selling off produce at least at minimum guarantee price, but do we know that a farmer cannot afford to wait for those cheques to be released, and the only way to get instant money to finance basic needs of daughter's marriage and children's fee is to part with the produce at rates much lower than the market price offered by local baniyas.

The national capital, many a time, becomes the initiator of prime time news, protests, and this paves way for discussions, remorse and blame games. Won't you agree, if the Nirbhaya case had not happened in Delhi, the after effects wouldn't be same? Now the capital is again in the news, a mix of social disgrace, economic inequalities and political drama, for a happening that reproduced the tragedy of Indian farmers, who account for more than half of our working populace, yet are deprived of basic needs. Farmers' pain, their suicides has for the very first time now become news headlines; the dialogues and interpretations, however, by so-called intellects and our chosen representatives revolve just around accusing other political parties for what happened during AAP's protest, the cheques too have been handed over to the deceased farmer's family, few aspirants of the parliament/state legislatures have even shed tears, some have apologized for not behaving appropriately while being present at the cursed place. Now shall I not ask my politicians, who are so very moved, shaken and grief-struck after this suicide, to assure that no farmer of India would choose suicide as the most easily available escape route from bad weather and debt?

Some are saying that AAP volunteers and leaders incited the deceased, others say that it was a gimmick that went wrong, some are saying that the suicide note wasn't his, and most of us are indifferent, why because a farmer committing suicide is nothing new in our country, rainfall playing the villainous character. A place, where the producer of grains is such grimly depressed, can never become world's superpower, even if we predict that the endeavors of the current PM would boost the economy markedly. While the Delhi suicide took away a son, a father and a husband, and almost every one of us has a feeling of sorrow running inside, let me remind you all that the National Crime Records Bureau of India reveals that 46 farmers intentionally end their lives every day in India. Records also tell that since 1995 more than 3 lakh farmers have opted for this unsolicited path; hence just noticing the incident of Delhi or the Parliament's debate on the land acquisition bill would serve no purpose, of course until we find a constructive and non-politically driven solution, something that isn't possible unless we diagnose the entire situation prudently.

It isn't only the weather that adds to the sorrow of agriculturists, in realism, it is the debt, more specifically, the money borrowed from private and unauthorized lenders that threatens the borrowers of social and financial humiliation. Then are the factors ranging from low produce value and pitiable irrigation facilities to high cost of inputs and indeed the deficiency of social infrastructure like toilets and schools. Studies have added to this endless list of causes reasons like no opportunities to earn alternative income, troubles in farming semi-arid sections, lenders' priority to businesses over agrarians and also the curse of alcohol and other addictions. It is common that the interest on money extended by private lenders to already-bleeding farmers is exorbitant and collection of dues at the time of harvest leads to selling off the produce hastily at throwaway prices.

The till-date measures by the central and state governments have proven ineffective in managing this issue and in infusing prosperity in the lives of farmers. Having focused only on credit and debt, political men have overlooked fundamentals like generation of income and productivity. What about the insult and even physical abuse of vulnerable farmers at the hands of Sahukaars, what about middlemen who take away all the profit, what about dropping water level, lack of private investment and India's backwardness in terms of agricultural research? Now that a stressed farmer has brought the matter into high-level discussions having displayed the melancholy of grain producers in Delhi, it is expected that the law makers probe not only the death of one from lakhs, but also lay foundation for better lives of Indian farmers. Also at this point in time, mention of the land acquisition bill placed in the ongoing session of parliament is evident, and the need is to assess the proposed changes diligently, not politically. This suicide also tells how our political leaders use a subject, which is so critical that a human doesn't think twice prior to taking away self's life, just to gain political mileage.

Suicide by farmers is worldwide occurrence, but we cannot use this equation to cover up the flaws of our social, economic, environmental and political domains. The caretakers of GDP and inflation have to realize that agriculture's share in GDP has constantly declined since 1951, and more than half of our workforce that is directly or indirectly dependent on this sector is scuffling to live a judicious life. Films in the past covered the despair of farmers, but this too has now become an outdated subject. The bottom line is that none of us relishing our lives at the stake of poor and vulnerable sections wants to feel the pain. The Delhi incident could have gathered attention, but it is yet to see whether it could invoke our sense of duty. Role of media, volunteers and political party/leaders during the Delhi suicide incident can be deliberated by investigating agencies, but for law makers, it is time to assess ground concerns of our food providers in the parliament and boil down to concrete measures.

No one who blames the Congress reign during past many decades for the misery of peasants is entirely off beam. Why isn't a farmer able to borrow from legitimate sources at the time of harvest, their daughter's marriage or when a cow is to be purchased? The actual picture of loans from government institutions is wicked where a farmer has to part with least 20 per cent of the sanctioned amount as illicit commission to broker and the bank official. Do not forget that the global warming and massive urbanization we worry about is an outcome of the members of farmers' families shifting to cities for livelihood. To feel the pain, plant a tree outside your homes, give it water and care for it until it grows high, and one day when it would dry up, you would know why a farmer ends his life so easily when the crop is damaged and the borrowed money still runs high on interest and principal. Remember, sympathies find no answer when the issue is such grave and lives of the pillars of humanity, our farmers, are at risk.

(Posted on blog on 27 April, 2015)

□

Let the Agriculture Sector be the Economy Booster

When we know that every second Indian earns livelihood from agriculture and allied activities, that agricultural growth rate determines the prices of basic commodities and even the banks' interest rates, and that India ranks first in the world in terms of production of many fruits and vegetables, then how can we allow this crucial sector to account for only 16-17 percent of the GDP? Inflation, unemployment, unequal income distribution, and below average productivity are a few concerns that can undoubtedly be taken care of if workable measures are undertaken to uplift the agriculture sector. On the verge of losing exclusivity, the area demands attention.

And when we talk of boosting agriculture, replicating Gujarat's way of administration appears to be most promising. Everyone knows that when the rest of India was struggling hard to attain 4 percent growth rate in agriculture, Gujarat emerged as a state that delivered almost 10 percent growth rate for 10 long years from 2001 to 2011 owing to good governance and real reforms. In the same context, it is vital to note that Mr. Modi-led state government, which inherited 10 thousand check dams, has elevated the number to 15 thousand, thus assuring that 60 percent of cotton farming area is irrigated. The measure has helped the state to upsurge cotton production by 800 percent in the past decade and also attain 300 percent hike in food grain production.

The World Bank in 2008 pointed out how poor roads, unwarranted regulations, and unhelping market structure prevent Indian farmers to freely access the market, which along with outdated irrigation arrangement is accountable for decline in the agricultural output. In the year 2011, the World Bank appreciated economic progress of India; however revealed how unproductive and incompetent agriculture sector is resulting in gap in income as well as human development. The World Bank laid special emphasis on facilitating rural non-farm entrepreneurship, and policies that could encourage competition in agricultural marketing so that farmers receive best prices.

Horticulture revolution in Gujarat is an example that can be followed by many other states like Maharashtra and Bihar. How the APMC, which has been a subject-matter of just discussions, was managed in Gujarat is too a learning bit. Plus, how the state has been responding positively to those who wish to set up private mandis is something others need to pick up. In many of the articles of newspapers, you can read how and why the farmers of Bihar have no other option than to sell off their paddy produce even below the minimum support price. The farmers also part with their staples rice and wheat produce at 20 percent less than the MSP. And why isn't anyone seem to be cared about the much-needed 'organic farming'? Remember, helping these farmers in production and marketing of their produce will assure lessened poison in our food.

Indian governments, since long, have been trying hard to push the growth rate of the industrial sector, hence numerous industrial corridors viz. DMIC, CBIC, and ADKIC are projected, which aim at united cooperation from multiple states. The 'Pak-China Economic Corridor' is an attempt by two nations, Pakistan and China to exchange technology pertaining to fertilizers, pesticides, agro-chemicals, and seeds so as to boost their agricultural sectors. On similar lines, agricultural corridors embracing feasible states shall be set up in India, which should aim at developing robust system for this sector, along with extending help within the group. Elevation of our agricultural sphere, wherein its share in GDP should match shoulders with other sectors, will proudly bring back the saying 'Krishi Pradhan Desh-Bharat' for the nation.

What Mr. Arun Jaitley recently spoke about regarding delisting fruits and vegetables from the states APMC Acts can be a constructive step towards bringing down the food inflation. For now, almost everyone knows what market area, market committee, and wholesale marketing norms under the APMC have delivered with respect to shielding farmers from exploitation. Along with, the government will have to focus on water rich provinces of the east, which will in turn add to productivity, food security, and commercial viability. Lastly, when many reports reveal that our production is not the prime factor for high prices and unavailability of food grains, it becomes easy to comprehend where the holdback subsists-Carriage of produce.

If we look at the global picture with respect to agriculture and farmers, no farmer would ever want his successors to carry the same profession. Despite setting aside USD 956 billion in the 2014 U.S. Farm Bill, the government of the U.S. hasn't been able to convince farmers to pursue the same job. Alike is the case in the entire Europe where every one farmer quits work in every one minute. At some places, farmers' sorrow is connected with unfair land acquisition; while at others, the subsidies aimed at their advantage are relished by agro-based companies. Nations with flourishing GDPs (backed by contribution from the industrial or the services sector) have though earmarked funds for the betterment of farmers, farmers have rarely benefitted.

When we talk of financial inclusion, equality in income distribution and such other pluses, can we overlook the fact that almost 3 lakh Indian farmers have committed suicide since 1995 owing to minimal surviving aspects? China has demonstrated to the world how an economy can boom even with more of industrial share in GDP as compared to share of the services sector. The rule that with escalating economy the share of agricultural sector dips has to be smashed by India. This is the time when we can set an example and can emerge as a nation with sturdy economy backed by the agricultural sector. Common man-turned-PM, Mr. Modi, is expected to pay heed to the concerns of those who are the backbone of mankind. Indeed, ones who help the rest of the Indians to overcome hunger can never be left in vain.

(Posted on blog on 28 August, 2014)

□

Storage of Procured Foodgrains – The Ever-Prevailing Concern

We can easily witness the deficiency of food in distinct zones of the country; however, it is shocking that procured foodgrains are lying haphazardly in the open areas, with no sincere attempts to distribute grains to those who are in need. The Food Corporation of India (FCI) alleges to have 1820 godowns nationwide with a storage capacity of 30.52 million tonnes. Though the government with a view to minimizing the storage and transit losses approved the policy of integrated bulk handling and transportation facilities in the year 2000, nothing much has been achieved.

The candidates of the general elections of 2014 though appeared to be concerned about malnutrition and the dipping prosperity of farmers, none of the political leaders came up with any suggestion or agenda to develop an infrastructure wherein the procured foodgrains can be stored hygienically and can then be dispersed in the areas of consumption. Though newspapers and electronic media consciously captured the storage of foodgrains in the open and subsequent loss, political groups are least worried. The gap of understanding between the need to export surplus and subsequent import during deficit is wide. Plus, corruption too makes the circumstances worst.

The reports last year presented the fact that tonnes of wheat is being damaged owing to the lack of storage capacity, on the contrary millions of Indians writhed to get hold of food for a time. The parliament witnessed some tough sessions, however real solution to this concern has not yet been achieved. Of almost 63 million tonnes of grains procured by the government, 28 million is stored in the open with ever-high vulnerability to damage and losses. The estimated loss in rupee terms due to such storage shortages is INR 60000 crores. It has been claimed that 194502 metric tonnes of grains were damaged between 2005 and 2013.

Besides Punjab and Haryana, Madhya Pradesh has emerged as one of the bulk producers of grains in India. It is estimated that the storage capacity in the state of Punjab is 14.3 million tonnes. Of this, 12.1 million tonnes space is already occupied by the produce of last year. For the current year, the state is expected to generate 14 million tonnes of produce, of which more than 70 percent will again be stored absurdly in the open. Plastic covers are being used to cover the foodgrains stored around the platforms, which renders the produce unhygienic even for consumption by animals. Who stands accountable for such disasters?

Swift measures are the need of the hour. While on one hand the government and FCI will have to come up with a sturdy plan of action for enhancing the storage infrastructure; transportation of foodgrains to the areas of consumption has to be taken care on the other hand. FCI has to recover from the laidback attitude so as to ensure that the presence of this corporation is beneficial for the public at large. Else, a PPP model has to be introduced with the restructuring of the organizational structure of FCI, which would stimulate the working as well the decision-making and planning modules of the corporation. Decentralized storage, with creation of storage units at the block level can be an effective solution if undertaken appropriately.

It is considerable to note in the same context that the Food Minister, K V Thomas advocated extensive reorganization of the FCI claiming that the corporation is turning out to be a 'white elephant'. In the year 2012, top to bottom revamping of the FCI was looked for by the Food Ministry; however no sincere attempts were made. Corruption in the corporation is known to all and the staff at numerous times has been charged with allegations of mismanagement. The Apex Court too had to take cognizance of the wastage of grains lying with the FCI and it was advised to take measures for rapid distribution of foodgrains to the needy.

Another way out until the above mentioned measures are carried out is the use of 'Silo Bags'. These special bags are three-layered polythene bags, wherein two layers help prevent the stored produce from UV rays and damage from water, while the third black layer prevents the grains from sunlight. For 18-24 months, this measure prevents the stored grains from vermin as well as other damages. Madhya Pradesh government has started the use of these bags; however other states are still to re-think their storage parameters. Surely, quick decisions and extensive reorganization are the measures that can help prevent the foodgrains from damage.

(Posted on blog on 7 May, 2014)

□

Food and Employment Security – Can Our Economy Allow This?

For how long do we feed our children? Post a certain age, they are expected to earn their livelihood and feed the family. In the same context, surely, helpless and deprived members of the society deserve extraordinary treatment owing to the fact that our moral values advocate this. Child welfare programmes, schemes for differently abled members, and arrangements for the families of soldiers, are as justifiable as earning prospects for an educated youth. On the contrary, assuring basic facilities for all the members of the society despite their non-participation in the process of nation building cannot be justified. This may sound cold-hearted in a country wherein the residents struggle to earn funds and to procure meal for a time.

Let us view this comprehensively. The UPA-led union government came up with two schemes that might look socially viable at first glance; however when comprehended prudently, the food and employment security schemes are neither socially nor economically sustainable. In case they were, the Indians would not have to wait for so long. Or for that matter, every nation in the world would have implemented such a scheme and could have afforded to be listed among the array of developed nations. The foremost concern that strikes is the fiscal deficit of the GOI that nobody could now even remember as to when this was in a positive figure. Means, the caretaker of the family has been spending more than the earnings since past many decades.

Let us take a bird's view at the scheme that assures food. Approximately two-third of the Indian population would be provided with rice at INR 3/Kg, wheat at INR 2/Kg, and coarse grains at INR 1/Kg. Some categories are even eligible for daily free of cost meals. The outlays to back this project are estimated to be INR 1.25 trillion annually. Further, the Technical Advisory Committee on Monetary Policy has commented that the scheme will inflate the food prices unexpectedly. The execution of the Bill will bring in acute rise in the already-high fiscal deficit that in turn would result in macro level inflationary pressures. Competition would be trimmed, money will be shifted from investments in agriculture to subsidies, and the rising demand of proteins, fruits and vegetable will be least taken care of.

Secondly, the MGNREGA scheme that was executed with a view to guarantying earning prospects to the residents of the rural part is no way distinct from the Food Guarantee scheme. With the government turning into a creator of employment, the results are hyperinflation, deficiency of investment, overpriced labor, and elevated cost of living. Better wage and simpler work under the MGNREGA scheme have lured laborers, which has created shortage of workforce in agriculture and manufacturing concerns. Vital to note, agriculture labor cost has augmented by 300 percent owing to the fact that laborers in the rural parts prefer easier tasks under the scheme and are contended with what they are earning. A will to work extra and think beyond boundaries has perished.

Think what MGNREGA is doing in real terms? Uneducated rural inhabitants are being motivated to earn their livelihood under the shelter of artificial earning prospects created by the government. Can the so-called beneficiaries of this scheme ever rise in terms of education and living standards? The economy on the other hand is crying too. INR 2.3 trillion have been expended by the government with no additions to durable assets that could promise sustainable development of the rural areas. With high wages demanded by the rural inhabitants, the producers are forced to elevate the process of the goods. Supply constraints have reached their supreme high. And known to all, is the corruption and misappropriation of funds by the contractors and officers-in-charge of the scheme.

Social benefit schemes are unquestionably the pillar of success for the society at large. Western countries have even more of such schemes as compared to India; however those nations are developed and can afford such measures. Plus, in no way are they declining the will of the members of the society to work hard for earning livelihood. The bureaucrats of India have been short of visionary capabilities when such measures are talked about. Above all, is the illicit gain that the political parties look for while considering such schemes. Votes are what that motivates our law-makers to come up with such absurd propositions. It is almost sure that a new set of administrators would come to power post the 16th of May and the nation urges for real works with top to bottom restructuring of such obnoxious and socially evil schemes.

(Posted on blog on 10 May, 2014)

□

New Land Acquisition Law – Merits and Concerns

With a view to inject much-needed transparency and to address the concerns of land holders, the Right to Fair Compensation and Transparency in Land Acquisition, Rehabilitation and Resettlement Act, 2013 has replaced the more than a century old Land Acquisition Act, 1894. The prime motive is to facilitate land acquisition for industrialization, infrastructure, and urbanization on one hand and to address the concerns of dependent livelihoods on the other.

Surely, the wellbeing of the land owners has been taken care of extensively, the chief objective of acquiring land is somewhat deserted. The acquirers and end-buyers of the infrastructural projects would appreciate the transparency; however more than justified and lucrative benefits to the land owners are tend to slower the pace of infrastructural development. Discussed hereunder are some of the highlights of this new revolutionary-termed Act.

Let's focus on the special provisions of the Act for the benefits of the farmers. The Collector is bestowed upon with the responsibility to ensure that no other unutilized land is available prior to considering any land acquisition. Farmers will be entitled to up to 4 times the highest sale price (though this would add to the cost for the end-buyers). For ensuring fair acquisition, a clause has been added that demands prior-consent of at least 70 percent land losers in case the government looks to acquire land for public-private partnership projects and 80 percent in case of private companies.

Above all, the share from increased land value when acquired land is sold off to another party has been set to 40 percent which shall be distributed amongst the farmers. Land that is acquired if used for urbanization purposes would result in offering of 20 percent of the developed land to the farmers in proportion to the area of their land acquired at a price equivalent to cost of acquisition and development. Amounts accrued are exempted from Income Tax as well as Stamp Duty.

Other prominent factors include payment of compensation within a period of three months from the date of the award, plus monetary and infrastructure R&R entitlements within six months and eighteen months respectively from the date of the award. Considerable to note, mandatory employment for one member per family, or INR 5 lakh per family, or INR 2000/month as annuity for 20 years are the options that can be availed by the affected families.

Surely, the concerns of the land owners have been addressed to maximum possible extent; however the coin has the other side too. Benefits that have been showered upon the land owners would add to the cost of acquisition which subsequently would be extracted from the purchasers of the projects. Another bottleneck for the acquirers will be the time duration for receiving consents from the authorities, Gram Sabhas, and the requisite percentage of the land owners. The move of the Government has been much appreciated by the land owners and experts.

In a country wherein approvals from the authorities are the chief bottlenecks towards effective project implementation, the new law seems to enhance such disturbances. To assure that the infrastructural development moves with an accelerated pace, the authorities will have to realign their procedures and guidelines. Time-driven approvals and sanctions are much-required. The new government that will be looked upon as the driving force for infrastructural development will have to face the challenges brought in by this new piece of legislation. The real intention of urbanization and industrialization can thus remain unachieved.

The incapability of developers to acquire land for such high consideration is rare to serve any purpose. Not just the developers, the Infrastructure Finance Companies (IFCs) and lending institutions would suffer from the unjustifiable increase in the compensation and other perquisites. The servicing of debt by the developers can become problematic in case the end-buyers find it uneconomic to invest/buy.

The law-makers' progressive thinking and strategic management skills are somewhat missing. The upcoming union government would be clueless to manage something that has promised too much for land owners who would now resist to any modifications, with hindrance to the much-needed infrastructural and economic growth.

(Posted on blog on 15 April, 2014)

□

Nourishing Health and Education

Swachh Bharat Abhiyan: Implementation and Impediments

Choking were the streets and sidewalks with piling up mounds of rotten garbage and belching were the gutters and sewers, with no signs of being cleared any time soon. This could be the description of any Indian city or town, small or big. The situation in rural areas was no better. Defecation in the open was too common a sight with the poor and the needy of the society's soft underbelly having no recourse to toilets at home. In fact, a dedicated toilet was not an intrinsic part of a typical home in an Indian village or a small town. Lack of hygiene and consequent outbreak of diseases was, therefore, an inevitable consequence of such a sad state of affairs.

Women having to go out into the open at odd hours to attend the nature's call became easy prey to human predators. Tourists were aghast at the unseemly sights and revolted over the highly deplorable sanitary and hygienic conditions. A country of exquisite beauty, rich cultural heritage and inestimable spiritual treasure, unmatched practically elsewhere in the world, had started slipping down the popularity charts of international tourists for the sheer lack of an efficient waste management system and sound infrastructure in the area of sanitation and public hygiene.

All this resulted in a woeful lack of self-esteem on the part of the Indian society, which had been making strides in practically all sectors of economic development and took pride in laying claim to the title of a fast-emerging economic powerhouse in the South Asian region in close contest with China. The most ironical feature of the situation of helplessness that Indians suffered was despite their being finicky in their personal hygiene and keeping their houses spotlessly clean as a mandatory requirement in their regime of offering daily prayers, they were dismayed over the lack of a waste management system on the part of civic authorities. Consequently, both a state of mass inertia and hopelessness gripped the Indian society, compounded by a forlorn feeling of low self-esteem.

Prime Minister Launches Program

Well, in the above paragraphs we talked in the past tense, as the idea was not to indulge in an exercise of self-flagellation about the conditions prevailing in India. The intention, on the contrary, was to capture in a nutshell the woeful state of affairs as it existed before a fresh breeze of change started sweeping across the landscape of the country last year and thereby ushered in a new government at the national level that dared to think differently both at the macro and micro levels to address the monumental challenge of sanitation and hygiene.

.While the situation today is not much different from what it was before Prime Minister Narendra Modi unveiled his Swachh Bharat Abhiyan or Clean India Mission, from the ramparts of the Red Fort on the occasion of India's Independence Day on 15 August 2014, there is a marked difference in the country's determination to tackle the problem of filth and squalor. For the first time in the history of modern India, a prime minister had thought it fit to talk about one of the most pressing needs of the people, namely toilets and that too on an occasion which used to be kept exclusively reserved by his predecessors for making lofty speeches on the government's achievements in areas like economy, education, industry, defence, poverty eradication, etc. Modi made a passionate appeal for uplifting the country from the depths of ignominy to which it had sunk in the matter of cleanliness, with particular focus on construction of toilets in each and every household in rural areas and separate toilets for girls in schools to ensure privacy and security. He unfurled a grand scheme for cleaning government offices and public places and presenting a clean Bharat in dedication to Mahatma Gandhi on his 150th birth anniversary on October 2, 2019.

Swachh Bharat Abhiyan

The scheme called 'Swachh Bharat Abhiyan' is no less daunting in sheer magnitude and scale than the Herculean task of cleaning the Aegean stables. The fact that no other leader of the country before him had retrospected on one of the most basic needs of the people, and presented a time-bound master plan for implementation of the scheme, in which political representatives of the people, and local authorities were involved with the active support and cooperation of the people themselves, resulted in a special resonance of the scheme for the people.

Film stars, sports persons, captains of industry and other celebrities were enlisted not only for popularizing the scheme, but also to set personal examples and act as role models to motivate people to help themselves in the mammoth scheme on a scale never witnessed in the country ever before. Brand ambassadors were appointed and several organizations and commercial establishments roped in for implementing the scheme. More than three million government employees and school and college students are to participate in the drive. The total cost of the program is expected to be a whopping ₹ 62, 000 crore (US $9.8 billion), to be shared by the central government and state governments.

Challenges and Impediments

The challenges to the program are many and the impediments in its implementation are no few in number.

- The greatest of the challenges lies in the sheer magnitude and scale of the program. The program is an ambitious, nationwide campaign aimed at making India completely clean and 'open defecation free' by October 2019. It plans to construct 12 crore toilets in rural India by October 2019, at a projected cost of ` 1.96 lakh crore (US$31 billion). The government is conducting the program in concurrence with the Indira Awaas Yojana, a rural housing scheme. Although the Swachh Bharat Mission began on October 2, 2014, the government had begun constructing toilets prior to that date. Under that scheme, the Modi government was left with an allocation of ` 32435 crore (US$5.1 billion). The program has also received funding and technical support from the World Bank and from corporations as part of their corporate social responsibility initiatives as well as from the state governments under the Sarva Shiksha Abhiyan and Rashtriya Madhyamik Shiksha Abhiyan schemes.

  As of May 2015, as many as 14 companies including Tata Consultancy Services (TCS), Mahindra Group and Rotary International had pledged to construct 3, 195 new toilets. As of the same month, 71 Public Sector Undertakings (PSUs) in India had extended their support for the construction of 86, 781 new toilets. Between April 2014 and January 2015, 31.83 lakh toilets were built. This indicates the scale of the program. However, there is quite a long way to go towards completing implementation of the scheme.

- The question is how long could the interest of the people be sustained in the necessity and viability of the program before their spirits start sagging and they go back to their old ways. People's attention has to be kept riveted on the scheme. They have to be constantly reminded about the soundness of the scheme and why it must succeed. People have to be convinced that the government is quite serious about this program and that it is beyond politics and is essentially an exercise in self help.
- Another big challenge is to change the mindset of millions of people. People need to be educated about sanitation and hygiene. Although Indians do have a proclivity for cleanliness at home, they seem to behave differently in public places, which are not kept clean by the civic authorities in the first place. It would appear that «If you can't beat them, join them» kind of syndrome is in operation. Urinating on the roadside, spitting and littering are some of the unseemly acts commonly indulged in by a person who feels utterly hopeless about the dismal state of affairs. The same people who indulge in such activities while in India conduct themselves responsibly while abroad, mindful of stringent local laws, civic sense and norms of behaviour. Although their duplicitous behaviour at home and abroad is not entirely explicable, it is apparent they seem to be driven by a desire to blend with the milieu. Call it an act in trying to look nonchalant, if you will. Such people have to be convinced that public places in India also can be transformed into clean and well-maintained places as in developed countries, if not more. To start with, enough numbers of garbage bins and skips should be kept at public places to encourage people to make use of them instead of littering around.
- Once garbage bins and skips are placed at strategic places for use by the public, strict legislation should be enacted to make littering, spitting, urinating or indulging in such unhygienic

and unseemly practices legally punishable. Use of non-admissible grades of plastics and other non-bio-degradable material inimical to the maintenance of healthy environment and ecology should be banned by legislation.

- The workforce for cleaning has to be optimal in strength. There are any number of cities and towns in the country that are understaffed on account of shortage of funds for purposes of cleaning of streets and removal of garbage. This lacuna should be rectified by appointment of adequate number of cleaning staff to work in several shifts depending upon the severity or acuteness of the problem. Appointment of cleaning staff will per se not solve the problem. They have to be paid decent wages. Their working conditions should also be improved such as by issuing of liveries, surgical masks, disposable gloves and sturdy equipment and cleaning materials to enable them to clean and collect garbage with least exposure to health hazards. Unless they are paid reasonable wages and their working conditions ameliorated, they cannot be expected to have any degree of pride in their job or carry out the work without giving cause to complaint or dissatisfaction.
- Garbage has to be collected regularly and transported to designated places located away from residential areas and water bodies before it is segregated into biodegradable and non-biodegradable categories. Wherever possible, solid waste should be converted into natural manure for farms or recycled for the benefit of the communities generating the waste matter. This is an area where great care has to be taken to ensure that no possible use, which could be made of the solid waste in the process of its disposal, is allowed to go unexplored. Disposal of hospital waste and industrial waste is yet another matter that deserves serious consideration. With Narendra Modi's 'Make in India' program coming into force in a big way with the setting up of more and more industrial establishments and manufacturing hubs, disposal of waste output has to be reckoned. The authorities need to have a master plan for disposal of all kinds of garbage, for the preparation of which expertise, technical acumen and eco-friendly approach have to be judiciously applied in a bid to get optimal benefits.

- A mandatory system of voluntary cleaning of government offices by the personnel working in those offices on certain designated days in a year should be introduced. This would help establish a sense of appreciation of the need to keep the premises clean by the people working there themselves and instilling in them dignity of labour. This practice is already being followed in quite a few countries like the former Soviet Republics.
- There should be a cordial tie up between welfare associations of residential complexes and those in charge of commercial and industrial establishments on the one hand and the civic authorities on the other so as to ensure optimal cooperation in collection of waste material at regular intervals.
- Civic authorities have to find ways and means of generating revenues, which could be allocated for cleaning operations. One simple way would be to sell stickers of different denominations to households, industrial and commercial establishments which generate garbage, to be affixed on garbage bags for collection.

When people are educated and motivated about the program, its necessity and winnability, and the implementation is in full flow, more impediments would perhaps come to the fore. Those could be successfully addressed with all the experience and hindsight gained during the implementation of the program.

(Published in weekly magazine Uday India in Vol. VI. No. 45-46, 18-24 October, 2015 edition)

(Posted on Bharat Niti portal on 21 August, 2015)

(Posted on blog on 29 June, 2015)

□

Integrate Skill Development, Education System and Indian Industry

It is quite apparent. Skill Development, Education System, and Industry can never stand separate, and in case they are made to, none of the domains would produce optimum, or even satisfactory outcomes. The country has separate ministries with capable heads for all the three areas, but unless one compliments the remaining two, success would remain far than accomplished. Economy and society both are a combination of diverse factors that move the wheels, and if any one of the wheel isn't in sync, the movement stops. Let this be very basic-What good can we fetch by producing engineers for the electronics industry, if the need of this industry is handful when compared with the number of pass-outs? Wouldn't then it be better to pave way for more IT engineers at a time when India is an IT hub for the entire world? Similarly, when studies and surveys have depicted that the Indian industry would need millions of skilled workers in the upcoming years, should the same old and worn-out system of imparting education be allowed to continue? To realize the promises made to the general public with respect to employment and economy, and to make true the dream, 'Make in India' of the PM, it is high time that we consider basics ranging from streamlined vocational educational training to involving business units in the process of skill development of labor force.

We shall assess this in a systematic manner, foremost being the need to recognize the flaws in the present setup. There can be thumbs up for the government's initiatives in the recent past, the National Skill Development Agency (NSDA), an autonomous body to coordinate and harmonize skill development efforts of the government and the private sector, been formed in 2013. National Skill Development Corporation (NSDC) is an institutional structure to motivate the private sector for skill development and has so far set up more than 1700 centers. Polytechnics and Industrial Training Institutes (ITIs) are in place, but their limitations with respect to providing diploma courses in conventional disciplines i.e. engineering, electronics and computers is a severe stumbling block when it comes to courses for the youth in new and emerging areas of work. The University Grants Commission (UGC) has been promoting B.Voc. Programs, which shall run parallel to programs like B.A. and B.Com.; however degree colleges did not show interest due to absence of faculty, industry experts and infrastructure. A few efforts are being done by the National Institute of Open School (NIOS) that offers vocational education to general and prioritized groups through study-cum-training centers, and Janshikshan Sansthan (JSS) that aims at enhancing vocational skills and quality of life of wage workers and their families. Then we have many present and projected institutions that run/will run under their respective ministries, but the issues of lack of awareness of the general public, coordination, and incapacity in capturing modern industry trends stand.

Streamlining of skill development programs and education wing of India has to be paid heed to in light of global best practices in education and vocational training. Countries around the world have recognized the very roots of education and skill development, which rest in changing the norms as per the industry's demands and trend of economic development. For instance, imparting basic computer knowledge through polytechnics will serve no purpose for an overextended time since the phase of economic evolution has changed immensely in the past few years. Limited contribution of employers, be it in the organized sector or the unorganized one, is troublesome too. Korea interpreted the issue of lack of skill development arrangement in as early as 1970s and hence they imposed in-plant training obligations for large firms; under the Job Skill Development Program run in the country, employers provide training to insured employees assisted by funds from the government. Germany has in place an apt dual system of vocational education that integrates school-based and work-based learning; trainees spend a day or two in vocational school and three to four days at the employer's place, progress of trainees evaluated by way of final analysis where they show theoretical as well practical knowledge gained, thus making Germany a place with employers and vocational schools having a joint educational and training responsibility.

Many a time, the school as well as the university learning structure in India, and the way we carry out skill expansion for such a large workforce and even large prospective labor force are criticized. Indeed, the government is answerable to both the concerns along with rewarding Indian business houses with skilled personnel through industry's partaking in the process of skill development. 12 million people are expected to join the workforce every year and by all means such large talent pool has to be sheer capable. Then we know that agricultural growth rate would not cross 4-5 percent hence main part in the economic growth of the country would be played by secondary and tertiary sectors, which in turn need aptly qualified skilled labor. With the 'Make in India' dream and acceptance of skill development as a national priority for next one decade, reforms will come only when the government integrates skill development, education system and the Indian industry. Quality of training, trainers, standardization of training process and effective assessment should be paid attention to. Trainers for the skill development mission are to be wisely procured, based on laid down criterions, and the existing ones must be considered with respect to basic instructional skills and know-how of present trends. Along with, training content should pay heed to rapidly changing industrial needs and technology. Should we then not crave for an active partnership between schools, universities, business houses and the government? Indian universities will have to think of Work Integrated Training Programmes (WITP), hence providing learners the opportunity to engage in on-the-job training at the works area of business houses.

Theoretical knowledge alone will hardly serve any purpose. WIPT structure will ensure that students earn while they learn and are motivated towards adopting real challenges and expectations at workplaces. Universities should largely endorse B.Voc programmes and the students must get credits for theoretical classes as well as practical workshops at the industry level, thus fortifying the foundation from the very start. Enhancement of skills of already employed workforce demands such short term courses that cater to the need of specific skill sets required for specific industry. In this scenario, people with nil or partial academic qualification should be targeted by way of giving them credit for the duration of their past employment. Next, specific skill development should be promoted in contrast to general skill training, for say, not all learning basic computers at the polytechnic level can be absorbed; rather skills should be planned for every industry, even for the unorganized sector, for say, plumbing, construction and sewing jobs. Skill development must be disseminated with minimal education criterion for the training-seekers so that education reaches maximum. The partners in skill development should be business houses who should be eligible for CSR benefits for the money spent on training students in-house. It cannot be denied that on-the-job training system would add to the throughput of businesses as well.

All in all, the existing curriculum at the school and university level has to be aligned with existing and upcoming needs of the Indian industry. Certification should be sensible in a way that global universities and employers consider the same, thus opening extensive prospects for students around the world. 'Make in India' dream of the Prime Minister not just demands inflow of funds and outflow of products/services, it asks for quality work delivered in an efficient manner, which is possible when right people owning right job skills are placed at the right places. Lessons alone can serve limited purpose; we all know that half of the degree holders in India remain unemployed. Skill development has to be made broader than the present system of basic accounting and computer lessons; every industry, be it from the manufacturing or services sector, can deliver optimum results when specifically skilled manpower for undertaking tasks is available without problems. Two pre-requisites when ability enhancement is talked about are 'continuous skill development' and 'centralized certification' of trainings. To summarize, three pillars to a better Indian economy are meaningful education system, robust skill development setup and active involvement of businesses in mentoring the workforce. Existing curses of unemployment, poverty, illiteracy, technical know-how disability and incompetence of our products/services in global market will then find no place in India.

The present minister of state for skill development and entrepreneurship can be seen urging corporate players to partake in the skilling initiatives of the ministry. A tripartite agreement between NSDF, NSDC and Power Grid Corporation of India (PGCI) that will see PGCI contributing CSR funds to national skill qualification framework is the first and foremost of such partnership between government and corporate house. The ministry is also to take care of the implementation of national skill qualification framework in a way that states utilize the funds apportioned for this task resourcefully with nil leakages at even the most basic level. Distinct ministries would undertake skill development in their respective sectors; hereafter coordination and apt supervision would be the sole key to success. Skill development centers cannot be allowed to become a mode of corruptly procuring funds from the government, rather they are to be made the birthplace of able workforce in India. We have seen how data and reports on such activities are forged by supervisors; hence need is to build a transparent and competent reporting mechanism, where details of such centers, trainers, trainees, training modules and work assigned post the completion of training be accessible with ease. Perpetual work prospects i.e. employability of Indian labor force and constant supply of skilled personnel to the businesses is the paramount aim; hence 'continuous skill development' is the buzzword. Be it the school/ university education, NSDC, NSDA, NSDF, NSQF, ITIs, polytechnics or the multi-faceted industrial setup of India, all have to come at one place with a single goal of extending quality education and skill development to every Indian citizen and their deployment at suitable place of work.

(Posted on blog on 30 January, 2015)

□

For Effective 'Clean India' Project, Apt Waste Management is Obligatory

When I waited for a wastebasket for long to dispose of a wrapper of wafers, it became evident that without the ancillaries, the Clean India project cannot serve the purpose. Why was that man throwing away the paper plate on the railway track and not in the bin was the question that the same person rebutted with saying that the railway station does not host wastebaskets in proportion to the stretch. Ok, the government or other local bodies would pay heed to the concern and let us hope that public places will have adequate measures enabling people to get rid of unwanted things. Once we are off, the management/disposal of this waste comes into the picture, which unless taken care of, will make a fuss of the dream mission of the Indian PM. It is true that news channels cover the tip of the iceberg, while beneath is the massive anxiety, proper management of the accumulated waste. Tell me, have you not seen overflowing garbage containers? And the waste collected is then dumped in abandoned stretches of land, recognized as landfills. Just forget separation of biodegradable waste from the non-biodegradable one or any other measures for treatment of the collected solid waste by the municipality.

The Report of the Committee for Solid Waste Management, in 1999, recommended that the composting of food wastes is the most effective process that has to be followed in view of Indian soil which needs organic measures to do away with loss of fertility and for lesser reliance on chemical fertilizers. As per a study of the Central Pollution Control Board, Indian urban parts generate almost 1.3 lakh tons of solid waste every day, figure that is massive and not something that can be allowed to be just put away in landfills. The honorable Supreme of India constituted the committee mentioned above and urged the authorities to comply with the suggestions, which aimed at reducing the unplanned open dumping of waste by advancement of landfill sites, arranging for waste processing and adequate disposal facilities, and restricting dumping in landfills to only the waste that does not allow its composting. Let me also tell you that the MSW Rules prohibit any littering and throwing of garbage on roads, and bestow upon the shoulders of Indians the responsibility to deliver amassed waste as per the collection and segregation system of the city. On the contrary, open burning of solid waste and landfill fires are prevalent.

Along with all other venues of pollution, this burning adds Carbon Monoxide, Particulate Matter, Sulfur Dioxide, and Hydrocarbons to air, which is far more harmful than unclean roads and other public places. Countries such as Africa, Thailand and Netherland have depicted how nations, though not that commercially robust, can handle management of solid waste. Not just have they managed the waste well, but have also created wealth and jobs, along with reducing carbon footprints and climate disruption issues. India, the country that is now being looked upon as a preferred investment location, will certainly become an industrially rich nation, but the content of solid waste will upsurge too. Then if the PM will look at the 'Make in India' and the 'Clean India' campaign collectively, not only does he need to better the corporate milieu, but also needs to push reforms in the waste management domain. Limited budget for waste treatment, ill-equipped municipal bodies, and lack of efficiency in amassing waste are some visible bottlenecks apart from the approach of garbage collectors and even the common man who disposes the same in any and every possible manner. Yamuna in Delhi is in actuality not flowing owing to the toxic waste that reacts with water and white deposits accumulated at the surface.

While boiling down to the solutions, putting into practice the recommendations of the MSW Committee seems workable enough. The same suggests that at least 80 per cent of waste-clearance vehicles should be on-road, with double shifts in case of scarcity. It recommends that waste management infrastructure should be an indispensable part in new development areas, something that can be linked with the '100 smart cities' plan of the government. Waste treatment and such other ancillary charges are to be linked with the cost of living index, along with levy of administrative charges for chronic littering. In terms of work for the municipal bodies, biodegradable and non-biodegradable waste is to be separated, where the former can be subjected to composting, while the latter can be recycled, with plastic, paper and metal then serving as bent resource. Regularizing use of compost product, derived from waste, in agriculture and combustion of rest in a waste-to-energy (WTE) facility so as to recover energy has to be thought over.

The waste-to-energy models need thorough analysis and the same can be executed by considering a strategic PPP model. In Okhla region of Delhi, a private concessionaire manages a large scale waste to energy project, wherein 1500 metric tonnes of waste is processed every day to produce power. Similar other projects are being run in the states of Maharashtra and Gujarat. Japan is the largest user in the world in the thermal treatment of MSW with 40 million tonnes; numerous thermal treatment plants therein are using the process 'Direct Smelting'. How can the PPP model in the WTE setup help India can be viewed in a way that the solid waste, which currently is gathered by the municipal bodies can be allowed to be processed by private companies for generating energy by utilizing the lands of municipalities. Municipal bodies can share the revenues and MSW can act a revenue-generating asset, thus relieving them from the burden of disposing. All in all, not just 'Clean India', the apt ruler of India will have to extend the same to a sustainable solid waste management structure for escaping environmental pollution, improving the lives in urban India and trimming down diseases.

(Posted on blog on 18 November, 2014)

□

The Clean India – Is it that Tough?

Cleanliness doesn't need labors, rather it needs will. Why would anyone be pained to put things in place, unless someone else disorders them? Though the country we live in has a global impact in terms of cultural heritage, moral values, production capacity, and brainy natives; why don't our roads, towns, railway stations, and markets match the global standards with respect to cleanliness? From Mahatma Gandhi to Mr. Narendra Modi, every capable leader has advocated the vitality of a clean nation, wherein the natives shall realize their fundamental duties and every single Indian should be a contributory towards nation-building.

Is that so tough so keep a place clean? Yes, it can be when not all inhabitants participate in maintaining the purity, rather create a messed up state for others too. And then we expect the authorities to be the sole caretaker of this concern. Remember, chaos is sure where one passes the responsibility to other and continues the same trend. And when we are so concerned about the cleanliness and hygiene of our homes, why aren't we even a bit alarmed about the purity of our nation's roads and marketplaces? That's not all. Many of us are least bothered to know the location of dumping waste while walking through the street.

The customs of India are tough to comprehend. While on one hand we regard our rivers as goddesses and cows as our spiritual mother, we stand with eyes closed when the rivers are jam-packed with waste and the cows tussle with polythene packets, thrown by households, in search of food. Most of us possess utmost faith in God; however belongingness is nil towards the world that he has created for us to live. 'Why should I?' The words help Indians to part with their basic obligation of upholding the purity of India. It is sad to notice that the Indians disremembered this vital concern until the PM intervened and expressed distress.

So, where from can this begin? Self–realization would be the key determining factor. Else, covering up for the wrongs of others would never counterpart with the extent of damage caused. Refrain from throwing even the tiniest waste item anywhere apart the designated place of dumping. Also, talk to others and educate them on the gravity of this issue and how every individual can be a shareholder. The viewpoint of preserving cleanliness in and outside own home and passing away the waste will no way serve any purpose. Dependency on authorities will have to end and personal pains be taken to recover the mess.

Authorities can too play a dynamic role. Public awareness shall be created with the help of workable communication channels. Also, the law-breakers will have to be penalized with nil escapes so as to ensure utmost adherence to the concrete rules. The municipal corporations will have to part with their laidback approach and no work policy. Remember, the cleaner India would call in for additional opportunities and dignity to life. Our rivers, roads, and public places are craving for speedy rescue and zero tolerance in the future. And when we say that India is the center of world's legacy, let us demonstrate this in real terms too.

(Posted on blog on 13 June, 2014)

□

Indian Rivers-Rescuers or Eradicators

Were you familiar with the fact that eighty percent of the sewage remains untreated and flows directly into the rivers? Out of 40000 million liters of sewage produced every day, only 20 percent is treated as per the report of Centre for Science and Environment. Subsequently, this untreated waste seeps into the groundwater, thereby adding to the susceptibility of public health towards disorder. Shockingly, only 160 towns out of 8000 have both sewerage system as well as a sewage treatment plant, the report reveals. Tests conducted by laboratories expose the fact that in almost whole of India the nitrate level is way higher than the recommended level.

Why the sacred rivers of India are on the verge of becoming eradicator rather than rescuer of the mankind is not a tough question to answer. Factors liable for the disastrous conditions are unjustifiably growing population of India, industrialization, urbanization, wrong agricultural practices, and to some extent, our religious and social norms. Having augmented five-fold in the twentieth century, our population has multiplied the content of waste which is disposed-off in our rivers. It is a disgraceful fact that the UNO has categorized India as one of the nations with poor water quality. 85 percent of diseases are associated with unfortunate water standards.

The rate of urbanization augmented from 10.8 percent in 1991 to as high as 28.5 percent in 2001. This unplanned move has added to the content of waste water, sewage, and solid/domestic waste that is passed into the rivers, which further boosts the ever-high burden. Though we feel proud of being a resident of the posh areas we live in, have we ever cared about the waste that we produce not just naturally, but also artificially (use of polythene bags, and improper dumping of discarded items)? Indeed, municipal corporations of cities located at the banks of rivers allow usage of rivers as dumping yards for sewage as well as trade effluent.

Be it the chemical, pharmaceutical, and leather industry or metal plating and dye industry, the untreated effluent is passed into rivers, which has resulted in a milieu wherein the report of 1994 revealed that owing to high bacteriological and metallic contamination water of almost every industrialized zone is unfit for drinking purposes. The fact that the water of river Damodar has been acknowledged as unhealthy even for consumption by non-human creatures exposes the extent up to which our rivers have been damaged. Inapt agricultural methods, too, add to this concern by disseminating animal wastes, pesticides, and crop wastes in rivers.

Though our centuries-old religious norms back our actuality, pollution of our sacred rivers as an outcome of our social practices is not unknown. Cremation of dead bodies on river bank, dipping of idols in rivers and lakes, bathing by the mass on distinct ceremonial events, and disposal of domestic wastes and carcasses of animals are everyday events that are fairly responsible for the prevailing level of river pollution. Indians may be recognized as people who consider rivers as Goddess; however the unjustifiable rituals followed by us are not just harming the rivers, they in fact are creating a severe concern for the upcoming days.

The new government at the center with Mr. Modi as the head seems to be alert and thoughtful enough about the alarming condition. Having promised cleaner and recovered Ganga, the Prime Minister has certainly diverted our much-needed attention towards this misfortune. The Budget as announced by the FM, Mr. Arun Jaitely sets aside INR 2037 crore to clean the river Ganga. Along with such allocations, the government will also need to pay proper heed to the underlying factors responsible for river pollution as discussed above so as to make sure that the revenues of the government are not persistently wasted on river cleaning programmes.

(Posted on blog on 15 July, 2014)

□

Roots: Women and Children

Empowering Our Women 'Truly'

Why at all did the need to recognize one day in a year as 'Women's Day' arise? If the society had been 'equal' enough, 'just' enough and 'compassionate' enough for our women, there wasn't a reason to allocate a special day to celebrate the abilities of women, and to make the world remember that our rules are to be amended to realize their true potential and to make this society a better place for them. The BBC documentary on Nirbhaya has not been accepted readily, rather banned, the reason behind is not any flaw in the film, but a defect in the attitude of men, if not all, many of us, which takes women for granted and considers men superior to them. The convict in the Nirbhaya case openly mocked justice alleging that the victim was at fault for such disastrous and inhuman incident, and if today we would wish each other 'Happy Women's Day' without seeking a remedy to such thoughts of men, the work will not be even half done. Accept it, be it the house of the poor or of the rich, in the rural part or in the urban, men and women are rarely considered equal, given similar opportunities.

When I analyze the Indian setup, I find we are, in many cases, living at either of the one side of two extremities. Sometimes we turn liberal enough and expect from the censor board of films to allow us relish movies which embrace bold and sensual scenes, while at other times, we don't think twice prior to terming a woman 'slut' if she has a few male friends and she does not form consensus with our long-prevailing conservative thoughts. Men on the other hand have all the permits in this world to relish life the way they want, be it in a night club, or even with a paid sex worker. A man indulged in adultery is 'cheering his life', while a woman working as a bartender is 'easy to get hold of'. These are harsh realities of our society, prevalent since ages now, talked about, discussed, condemned, but real betterment still far than achieved. I have a lot many things to refer to, there are numbers to reveal how every other woman in our society is a victim to violence, molestation, verbal abuse, and many other wicked happenings, a lot of which do not even come in open due to lack of public support and our mentality to blame a woman for the misconduct of men.

Isn't it true that boy and girl child in Indian households are seldom treated alike? While for boys, who we think will be our future guardians, we look for quality education, for the girls, we are ready to compromise. Boys may stay out for long hours, but girls doing so break the so-called household ethical values. To some extent, I agree that women need a bit extra protection owing to the shaky law and order situation we have in India, but suppressing our girls and women in the name of preventing them from any mishaps is indeed a torture. To fight evils, one has to come out and face the risk, then why hold our females, who have all the acumen and daring to turn down ills, from expanding their wings and attaining goals that we men have been so far unable to. Mother Teresa, Sarojini Naidu, Margaret Thatcher are not just examples of great women, they tell us that women have an inherent capability to bring revolutions; we men, when we try to prove how much concerned we are for women by raising voices and asking for women empowerment, tend to forget that real betterment lies in making women capable to react to such ills themselves rather than making them dependent for their rights.

There is a bit for everyone to do, be it men, women, government, NGOs or others. Men have to pay heed to a fact that women are equipped with all the forte and will to make society a just place for them; hence what we men have to do is to just pave way for them rather than demonstrating ourselves as advocates of women empowerment. For women, I may have no suggestions, except that you must recognize your potential and shed the approach of being dependent, it is all within you, you can run companies, can innovate products, can lead governments, and be a social and economic transformer. NGOs and governments are to realize that they exist because the society needs them for few changes. Then to implement schemes and prevent any humiliation of women is their indispensable duty, they ought to perform, deliver results. In a world that should see no difference between men and women, there exists a wide divide, and this divide is the cause of destruction of some and superfluous powers to some. The aim is not to pave way for another Mother Teresa or Kalpana Chawla, but to develop a society that sees no shocks when a woman conquers the space, sets up a business venture, originates new rules of science or becomes the head of a government.

Today, the extremities we live in, where at one end even short skirts and Valentine's Day are readily acceptable, while at the other we are still scuffling for toilets for women in rural parts of India, work to be done is immense, and all have to play a part. Accept it, India is still developing, unless we match our education, employment, social security and other standards with developed countries, we cannot fully endorse westernization of our thoughts. Hence, Indian women are to respect this and never forget that we carry moral values from our ancestors, which help us stand a step ahead than other parts of the world. Men are to realize that women in ancient India were far more respected and cheered as compared to present times; the fault of course is ours. In case my daughter isn't getting the same privileges as my son, I am on the losing side. If my wife cannot do what I am permitted to, the failure is mine not hers. Let not differences become so wide that we would need other 'days' to realize our failures; for me such days are no more than a mirror which shows that we are shameful to not have been able to achieve what was meant to be achieved.

(Posted on blog on 8 March, 2015)

□

For Better Economy and Society, Make Every Child above 14 Employable

They can never be an inspiration, but they challenge our will and acumen in dealing with skill development of the younger generation. I am talking about those operating centers where future extremists are brain-washed, trained and are made a full-fledged terror to humanity. Extremist groups do not have a sanction from any authority, they run operations in secret areas exploiting all unauthorized ways to procure trainers, trainees and machinery for teaching. Yet they have been able to produce millions who join the brigade and pose a serious threat to economies and societies around the world. On the contrary, I can see young blood in my country, dipped in depression, drugs, begging and such other forbidden tasks that never add a bit to the economy or social growth. For radicals, this cluster is their probable workforce, while for the government that we choose for betterment of our lives; they are either non-existent or a burden. How can the candidates during election campaigning even promise to eradicate poverty and unemployment when they do not have even a single fool-proof plan to deal with the issue of unskilled and prone-to-evils young generation?

The idea here is quite simple. The present government wants to improve infrastructure, the basic road to development; these are those capital assets that serve the function of conveying people, goods, energy and range from railways, roads and highways to water management and energy infrastructure. Also add solid waste management and present-day need, communications structure to this. Developing infrastructure is fundamental to inviting growth of society and economy, and all-inclusive betterment. But with limited workforce, though we have more youth than rest of the world (UN World Population Report), I say limited as Indian youth is one of the most unskilled, with only a trivial fraction having access to skill development centers, universities and vocation trainings. Of all the young ones, we see every day on roads, in trains and buses performing pity jobs, how many do even know that something like National Skill Development Agency or Industrial Training Institutes (ITIs) exist in India? One of the key reasons being nil elementary education certificates due to which children aged above 14 years cannot access platforms (ITIs and vocational training institutes) where abilities compulsory for industrial employment are imparted. UNFPA Executive Director, Dr. Osotimehim has said "Young people are innovators, creators, builders and leaders of the future. But they can transform the future only if they have skills, health, decision-making, and real choices in life."

In real what venues are we providing to the most vibrant blood aged 14-20? Many from them are begging on streets, some are involved in pity and even harsh crimes, a lot are in the grip of cheap drugs, rest are lost with no proper guidance. A difference between extremist groups and our legally elected representatives is that while the former are committed towards imparting the knowledge of Jihad to any and every young blood they are able to tap, the latter are busy in promising well-being, but turn blind and deaf when a 12 year old girl with a begging bowl knocks the door of their bullet-proof cars. Why even a single child of India is allowed to wander on roads, is a question I am seeking an answer to. In case the issue is with high fertility, what is holding you from instigating population control drive? If the issue is lack of schools and skill development centers, what is not allowing you to open a basic vocational institute in every possible corner that can impart teachings on being a blue-collared worker at least? Mind you, though we need more IITs and IIMs to produce world-class engineers, managers, innovators and entrepreneurs, but prior to this, we need venues to train the untrained on how to perform basic labor jobs, after all, more people are required to build ports, railway lines, water/ sewage pipelines and other construction works that can foster progress of Indian industry and economy.

The irony is that nobody wants to talk and discuss work aspects for youth between 14 to 20 years and blue-collared factory and construction based work. Every one of us wants AIIMS, IIMs, medical institutes and if not these, we want diploma courses, short-term programs, on-the-job trainings, but all of these are accessible to those who have certificates from school, what about the ones who for any reason could not attend basic school sessions, will they be left to invitations from criminal gangs, extremist groups or beggars' association? Employment creation for the youngsters who remained the target of bad destiny till the age of 14 or so years is also the responsibility of the government; and if you say that they themselves are liable for their condition, open a school in each and every corner to cater the need of rising population, force the ones not attending by any possible means and support families for whom they stay out of studies, unwillingly. We have been fighting against child labor practices since decades, but do we realize that UNICEF suggests that poverty is the underlying cause of child labor? Prior to gifting a book to every child, we will need to ensure grains in every household, the scarcity of which leads to their engaging in work. I hold consensus with banning child labor below 14 years of age in any and every industry, be it hazardous or non-hazardous, but I also expect my government to ensure that not even one child is left out from the Right to Education, forcible inclusion of children in schools and making parents/guardians liable in case of non-adherence to be added in the RTE Act.

Only option that seems viable in the present scenario that cannot be changed overnight is creating employment and developing infrastructure simultaneously. Design programs and make arrangements to take every child above 14 years of age to basic skill learning centers where a 1-2 month course can make them a productive asset for infrastructure development companies. You would all agree that a hand carrying bricks from one point to the other is better than a hand with a begging bowl or a knife, or a hand that seeks pity benefits and subsidies from governments the entire life.

"You cannot help men permanently by doing for them what they could and should do for themselves." – Abraham Lincoln

(Posted on blog on 25 February, 2015)

□

They Need Books, They Need Work

It is a common saying that the youth of a nation are the backbone of economy. We all have heard our national and state leaders advocating the fact that the prosperity and viability of India is much dependent on the young blood. Do they talk about the same youth who have knowledge, outlook, and educational degrees; however no jobs. Or, do they address the little ones who walk through the compartments of trains begging for pity cash, which is then used for buying drugs and alcohol? Step out of your house and the very next moment you would come across the young brigade harassed at every stage, with nil backing from the government.

While on one hand, girls are not allowed to enter the world; the born ones fight at every level to maintain dignity and arrange for food. You can often see little boys, with their parents involved in disguised employment, and you can be sure that a day would come when they too would become a part of the same milieu. A report predicts that every third youth of Punjab is trapped in the curse of drug addiction, while the governments and the leaders are busy projecting the newly built flyovers. The irony is that the political men too know the vitality of the young blood in nation-building; however no labors are being done to exploit this immense power.

The Right to Education was seen as a key measure that could at least ensure that the little ones would have adequate knowledge and academic aptitude. Visit a tea stall near your office, or a local restaurant around your home, and you would realize the real picture. The hands which should have a pen and a book are busy cleaning glasses or arranging for the helicopter landing of any powerful political leader. Yes, we are moved; however no one dares to take a step ahead. And when we talk about the limited resource capacity of India, why do we oversee the fact that the prime resource, which is our upcoming generation, is being wasted to the core.

To be precise, more than 8 million children in India have no other option than to waste their crucial childhood days at firework factories, restaurants, and even as disguised home maids. As per the reports of distinct NGOs, Delhi is home to more than 50 thousand street children, who spend mornings to late evenings as beggars. Same is the condition in Mumbai, where out of 37 thousand street children; more than one-fourth are not even able to arrange for food for the day. Miserable to note, reports reveal that around 10 percent street children are severely addicted to drugs and alcohol. Plus, active involvement in criminal activities is a common scenario.

None of the ministries has ever been concerned to even take a minute note of this drastically ill position. The Right to Education Act strives for every child of age 6 to 14 to have compulsory access to school and the accountability lies with the state governments. Lack of coordination among distinct ministries and deficient willpower of state governments have caused millions to writhe. It is to be realized that since most of the street children come from backward castes, they must be accorded with all the services destined explicitly for this category. Rescuing of street children and ensuring education, food, and above all, dignity is the prime need of the hour.

The primary authority that could help India fetch the maximum out of the youth is the policy-makers. While the election manifestos are flooded with blossoming prospects for unemployed, the 5-years term of almost every government has proven hopeless. I expect a lot from the new union government, which is being headed by a personality who has been tested at numerous times and has proven his capability. Mr. Modi, who realizes that the Indians have voted for pride and prosperity in the 2014 polls, will have to come up with visionary plans and workable solutions that can save the little ones and can enrich the ones looking for work.

A lot can be done. Compulsory and I recommend forceful measures must be taken to ensure that none of our little ones is saved from being a part of the education system. Along with, the standards of our teaching system will have to be reformed in view of prevailing global trends. Counseling of parents is necessary too. Jobs will have to be created by allowing quick inflow of funds and easy commencement of new ventures. Technological domain is to be strengthened by importing technical know-how to render our youth with essential expertise. Bare promises will now not be accepted and I believe that Mr. Modi would surely have a concrete plan of action.

(Posted on blog on 5 July, 2014)

□

Prostitution in India – Though Unnoticed, but A Grave Concern

What would you say about the development model of your country when you witness a 12 year old girl awaiting a car late in the evening, which would take her to a place where she would be forced to serve the lust of multiple men? The decent and reputed section of our society neither pays any heed to nor is concerned in any manner with the humiliation of such women. Rarely I see any articles or comments that highlight this issue; however when national dailies are filled with luring advertisements of massage parlors proposing any and every service, I comprehend the acceptance and demand of this trade. Let me make you aware of a few figures.

Of more than 3 million sex workers in India, approximately 35 percent are below the age of 18 years. While the Right to Education Act promises compulsory education for children of this age group and the Child Labor (Prohibition and Regulation) Act prohibits child labor below the age of 14 years, which law or custom is favoring such harassing deeds? Vital to note, The Immoral Traffic (Suppression) Act of 1956 does not prohibit prostitutes to offer services privately. The Act is now amended to The Immoral Traffic (Prevention) Act, which limits; however does not comprehensively favors the end of prostitution in India (the trade is thus not unlawful).

Vending of girls and women by close relatives, neighbors, and even by acquaintances is a common scenario. Dishonest hopes of marriage, untrue promises of work, unplanned meeting with a pimp, and an urge for quick and easy payouts are a few reasons that back the coming in of girls and women in flesh trade. For sure, lack of proper work prospects, unbearable poverty, unhelping educational services, and the never-ending lust of men are the real factors that are liable for such downgrading of our society. Uncontrolled population that survives on limited resources is one of the most fundamental causes that add to the severity.

The Sonagachi in Kolkata, G.B. Road in New Delhi, and Kamathipura in Mumbai are places that are known to all owing to their fame and approach to lure men. Are the state governments, police officials, social workers, and the so-called leaders of communities blind to not have noticed uncountable places of prostitution in almost every part of the country, where sex workers are coerced to trade their body for pity cash? Even those, entering this business on their own aspiration, seek help to overcome the day-to-day murdering of dignity. Rarely do we see the police take any severe action, which too is often due to lack of cooperation by sex workers.

When we talk about educating every child, providing basic necessities to every household, ensuring security, and such other fundamental advancements, why do we disremember those young girls and women who spend sleepless nights and appalling days to content the lust of men? Are we ever concerned about the countless episodes of rapes that take place inside the brothels every day snatching away the most precious belonging of such women-'dignity'? What about those guiltless lives that commence from such brothels and witness the evil happen right from the very childhood days? Questions are many, but hardly anyone cares.

Not that complicated it is to salvage girls/women from this reprehensible practice and connect them to the common group. State governments and the policemen, along with support of the general public can bring in the much-needed variation to the lives of deprived females. Above all, uncontrollable lust of man has to now die (an easy way can be meditation, yoga, and faith towards the divine God), or will have to be killed. Females looking for quick money will have to understand that the pride of womanhood shall not be put at stake. Let us not overlook the fact that prostitution is not just related with the misery of sex workers, but is also adding to the unproductivity of men and boys trapped in this enticing world of sin.

Lastly, we must also not oversee the acceptance and prevalence of this trade since centuries. Accept it or not, prostitution has been an integral part of our society since ages, which means that complete prohibition is somewhat unmanageable. However, coerced flesh trade is a curse. Plus, the coming in of underage girls in this trade is unpardonable. Besides curbing these two evils, organizing legal prostitution shall be the new government's mission, which appeared to be lacking in the former governments. The law makers must ensure comprehensive execution of the laid down laws, along with assuring secure and easy exit to those who are willing to quit.

Places like Netherlands and Germany have put forth a model, wherein the trade has been regulated by the law of the land. Vital to note, in 2002, Germany passed a law that removed general prohibition on flesh trade, which permitted prostitutes to attain usual work contracts-An attempt towards bettering the lives of sex workers. Though Indian culture and social norms do not allow clear approval to this practice, can we disremember the episodes of Amrapali and Nagarvadhu, which existed in the ancient India? None of us can deny the fact that absolute suppression of this trade is just a dream. Indeed, the policies and regulations of the government need to be stringent enough to restrain the evils of child prostitution and forced trade.

And when we know that total eradication of prostitution from our country is next to impossible, some workable measures are the need of the hour. A skilled committee can be bestowed upon with the responsibility of outlining the limits and rules this business. The committee shall also establish the link between organized flesh trade and drop in instances of rapes, if any. Remember, we cannot ever justify that with easily accessible paid sex services, rapes can be lessened. Involvement of personalities from the religious, corporate, and political sphere in rape cases proves the fact that people who can uncomplicatedly hire prostitutes are not invulnerable to commit rapes. Both evils are equally immoral hence a deep study of the matter is looked for.

(Posted on blog on 17 July, 2014)

□

Women Empowerment can Deliver much more than Just 'Safeguarded Women'

In case only laws were all that we needed to fortify the presence of every human, we would have achieved a socially and economically balanced position way back. The irony is, however, that despite so many laws aimed at the betterment of underprivileged, handicaps, women, and such other overlooked members, India is still scuffling with all those ages-old disparities and setbacks. I have always emphasized a very elementary fact that economy is the second name for any society; without apt means to live and prosper, you cannot deliver social contentment. Post the Delhi gang rape incident, the government hastily rolled out new set of rules, but the desired outcomes have rarely been attained until today. For that matter, cases of rapes and molestation have rather increased. This is because we find easy solutions but never pay heed to the roots of the issue. The IT and BPM industry, one of the most women-friendly domains, employs merely 30 percent women in their total workforce. Then it is not that hard to conclude what is the statistics in other paid workplaces, rural parts of India being the worst.

Isn't that very simple? Men relish all that freedom, security and growth because they have always been at the epicenter of the economy. Indian women have been restricted to homes and those who work are suppressed. Bring women to work, make them a part of the economy, a contributor and sharer. The underlying fact with respect to ever-high number of crimes against women is that though our media and films have freely used the stamina of women, the society and economy still craves for their part in evolution. Then again, bringing more and more women to workplaces is dependent on the quality of services viz. education, laws, and special perks that we can provide to our women. Having talked about these key essentials many a time, let me today focus on what all paybacks can we fetch by endorsing women involvement in the economy. The trend nowadays is though predictive that with the youth workforce of India, we will be able to see more and more value addition and creativity in our economic structure, unless we recognize the forte of women contribution, the race will be half won.

Let me begin with a simple to understand notion. More economic participation brings more economic demand, which in turn calls for more economic participation. Isn't that an easy addition to the GDP? With inclusive partaking of women in the country's fiscal domain, I can assure a minimum 2 percent upsurge in our growth rate. Then is another equation, with more and more women working, addition to retirement savings would boom, hiking the much-needed social security savings, thus bringing down the funding gap of the government with respect to such welfare schemes. Gender pay unfairness is a concern, believe it or not. Males are usually considered more reliable; hence with an increase in women engagement in management, this disparity is likely to curtail. Risk taking and risk management an issue? Why not play safer then; studies reveal that the females in any society are more risk-aware, can take more risk-prone decision, wisely. For those who disagree with studies, at least give it a try, let us then analyze results.

IT start-ups have amused many venture capitalists. This means that the doors for wise innovations is open; then why not call people from diverse areas, who can bring in all-new concepts within the group. Since same groups are leading those high-profile cabins and board rooms, Indian corporates are rarely coming up with those out-of-box ideas. The society and the workforce of today's India have a reformed perspective towards work and workplace. More and more people want to work with organizations that are socially accountable and are delivering a real value-addition. Sooner than later, as have the IT and BPM sectors realized, corporations will need to be focused towards gender equality. Should I also advocate the well-known equation of any economy, that with more people increasing their monetary holdings, investments will thrive, thus bringing in women in this scenario is indispensable. Then are the social pluses, which will range from more and more education drive among females and carried forward to children of these working and more informed women. Crimes will drop down since demands will be met with ease, women-centric wrongdoings would trim down too.

Yes, this good-looking picture is not that easy to achieve, nor is the same that tricky. It just calls for broadening our mindsets and realizing the fact that women are no less. The legislatures and women advocators have to think beyond making for-women laws and have to extend labors in calling for their enhanced participation in the economy. With all these dowry and rape laws that rather than safeguarding women have become a weapon, in many cases, to humiliate blameless men and families, we even today are what we always have been, aimless. I was pleased to hear that post the Uber rape case, cab companies are focusing on hiring female drivers, but are we not late and narrow to have realized the power of women? The Companies Act, 2013 also mandates a woman on the board of companies, but where are the means to make so many desired women directors talented and responsive towards the corporate needs of today? Schemes for direct recruitment of women in few reserved occupations, special incentives for companies that allow flexible working hours to female employees and educating conservative clusters on autonomy of women can ease the way to real women empowerment. Lesser bank interest rates and tax holidays for women entrepreneurs will boost up their share. Rest, education, access to toilets, easy reporting of grievances, and such other basic rudiments will play their part.

(Posted on blog on 29 December, 2014)

□

Women –
What They Deserve and What They Get

Indian women deserve far more than what the society is offering them. While on one hand we feel proud to have women like Kiran Bedi and Mother Teresa; the everyday instances of molestation, eve-teasing, and rapes call for urgent attention. We respect our mothers, sisters, and wives; however when it comes to respecting the sisters of others, we are somewhat biased. And then we say 'the society is not safe'. Aren't we the part of same society? Concerns are many and I believe every one of us knows the answers. Then why isn't our cities and villages secure for women? A lot was expected after the 'Nirbhaya' instance; however nothing changed.

From birth till death, a woman plays numerous roles. And, at every such stage the surrounds are distinct. I will talk about how the life of a woman can be rendered dignity and resourcefulness. Four pillars that can adhere to this duty are parents, teachers, government, and the society at large. The men-led society of India undertakes the illicit task of discrimination right from the birth, and many a times even before that. Female child is often looked as a debt and is not allowed to live. And when they live, girls are provided with lesser perquisites as compared to boys. Hence, the change has to take place at the very first stage-Parents.

Next is the role of teachers. When properly educated, it is a known fact that any woman can supersede men. Hence, appropriate education facilities, along with aptly equipped education centers are the need of the hour. Post this is the crucial role of the government in ensuring that women are not discriminated in terms of work prospects. Inclusion of a woman director in the Board of companies is a brave step towards this. However, government's accountability doesn't end here.

Security at workplace and at home, and even at roads and in buses/ trains, stringent legislation, and quicker judiciary process will add to the justice to women.

The most crucial pillar is the society. It now doesn't even shock anyone when the new channels are flooded with rape instances and acid attacks-Have we accepted this? The recent back to back molestation in U.P. and the laid back attitude of the state government and the police system reflected how unaffected are we. Acceptance is not the solution; rather reforms and tough measures are needed sooner than later. Those involved in molestation shall not be given even a single opportunity to escape. Much is expected from the state and the union government who have been entrusted with the task of securing secured and honorable life for all.

What has been happening in the U.P. and other parts of the nation is disgraceful and needs to be stopped anyhow. Even women have to understand their responsibilities and the power of Indian judiciary. Silence will no way serve any purpose. I am quite sure that the U.P. Chief Minister, Mr. Akhilesh Yadav would not allow any misuse of power and the accused will be punished. Lastly, the police will have to be fair, vigilant, and above all ethical while dealing with such circumstances. Together we can surely put an end to the ills of our society, and the women of India can be delivered with the conditions that are favorable and prosperous.

In the end, I will share a worry that is vital to note. The Indian heritage is one of its own and excessive westernization would create grave imbalance. Indian women must too realize the centuries-old Indian culture and rituals that encompass embedded integrity. Extreme exposure and unjustifiable relationships are too the root causes of this grave issue. Let me clarify that I in no way repel transformation; however upper limit of every aspect shall be paid heed to. Another area of concern is the prevailing access to porn websites that in no way are adding to either the evolution or the dexterity of India. Herein, self-realization by women will be the key.

I would advocate the adaptation to western ethics only to the extent they are not detrimental to Indian heritage. And when we favor the infusion of western norms, let us first understand the viability of our legislative and judiciary system that is incapable to stand at par with European standards. Hence, the foremost concern must be to uplift the standards of our key wings viz. legislative, political, and judiciary, prior to thinking of following the fashion trends of European nations. Lastly, the Indian censorship board for films shall also take a note of prevailing unwarranted sexual content. All this can lead to an enhanced living place for women.

(Posted on blog on 10 June, 2014)

□

Religion and India

Is Secularism at a Crossroads?

India was always a haven of religious tolerance from time immemorial although it has been only during the last 67 years of its existence as an independent nation, free from the colonial yoke, that Secularism has been the nation's official policy. Sanatana Dharma of ancient India did not discriminate between people of different faiths, whereas it has always envisaged the whole world as a global family (Vasudhaiva Kutumbakam).

The lesser known Tamil poet, Kaniyan Poonkundranar, of the Sangam Period (3rd century BC to 4thcentury AD) always viewed the whole world as his dwelling place and all those residing in such a vast homestead as his kin. He outrightly rejected the division of mankind into different categories and emphasized on the universality of all men.

In addition to the prevalence and popularity of lofty thoughts such as universal brotherhood, India has given birth, throughout its long history, to several major religions like Buddhism, Jainism and Sikhism, which have coexisted in total harmony with Sanatana Dharma. Zoroastrianism (Parsi religion) which was uprooted from its birthplace of Persia consequent upon its persecution by Islamic fundamentalists, took shelter in India and has been doing well for itself till today.

Secularism and the Hindu Psyche

There is a popular belief among non-Hindus worldwide that Hindus are tolerant, calm, harmonious and peace-loving people. The 17th century French philosopher Voltaire was a strong votary of this belief. He was of the view that the West was indebted to the East for the latter's most precious gift of the Vedas. He regarded Hindus as a "peaceful and innocent people, equally incapable of hurting others or of defending themselves". He was himself a supporter of animal rights and a vegetarian. He acknowledged that the Hindus' treatment of animals showed "a shaming alternative to the immorality of European imperialists".

Hindus are the first ones who would readily agree with Voltaire's pithy assessment of their nature. Never in history have they waged a war on a State or people, within or outside India, in the name of religion. Bound by tall insurmountable mountain ranges and hostile terrain on the North and by sea on the other three sides, Hindus had lived in total harmony and led a cloistered, contended and peaceful life, free from external threat, for a fairly long period of time in history.

Native religions like Buddhism and Jainism never posed a serious threat to Hinduism, which assimilated the salient features of those religions and emerged as an inclusive body of faith. By doing so, Hinduism deflected their challenge to its unrivalled spiritual supremacy in the subcontinent. The influence of Hinduism in East Asia was achieved by means of cultural and trade diplomacy and never by military campaigns. This situation lasted till the 12th century when Muslim invaders struck at the heartland of Hindustan and changed the rules of the game.

Arrival of Islam

The killings, desecrations, lootings, pillages, forcible religious conversions and, above all, the religious intolerance exhibited in the form of massacre of tens of thousands of Hindus and followers of other native faiths who had refused to abandon their religion and convert, had been unimaginable and incomprehensible for the Hindus who had always considered their own survival and that of their religion as a case of mind power over matter. Hindus had always considered that life on earth was truly ephemeral in nature and that the soul was on a perpetual journey, not bound by concepts of time, place or physical constraints, to a state of self-realization or liberation.

Conquest of the hearts and imagination of people of other religions, atheists and agnostics, entirely on the strength of their own religious ideology, was their preferred form of interaction with people who were not on the same page as they were. Winning over someone to their side by the might of the sword and preventing the flock from going astray by instilling the fear of torture or death was downright repulsive an idea that had no place in the lofty principles and beliefs that the Hindus cherished. Hinduism does not promote or talk of proselytization. Nor does it mandate its followers to 'spread the word of God'.

Advent of Christianity

Christianity made its advent in India in a big way in the 17th century with the arrival of the European traders and colonialists. The spread of Christianity in India was achieved using a mix of factors like force, deception, state support, inquisition and persecution of Hinduism and other native faiths.

Resilience of Hinduism

The combined might of the Mughal Empire and European colonialists could not wipe out Hinduism despite the horrendous genocide wrought by the Muslim invaders, arguably the biggest and the worst of its kind in living memory, inquisitions by the European colonialists, and large numbers of mass conversions of Hindus forcibly carried out from time to time.

What is the secret of the survival of the Hindu religion, especially when its followers are a tolerant, peace-loving and harmonious people, not known for a wily war craft or Machiavellian statecraft? It was their unflinching faith in their Dharma, which they believed would protect them so long as they sincerely observed it, that enabled them to carry on despite the odds, hardships, unwarranted criticisms, ridicules, humiliations and downright hostility and massacres.

Secularism in Post-Independent India

Even after India attained independence from British rule, the minority religions of Islam and Christianity found a fertile ground for growth in the country under the patronage of the State in the name of Secularism, which is an official policy of the Indian government. Freedom of the individual to practise the religion of his choice was guaranteed by the Constitution. Different religious groups were granted the rights to profess and propagate their faiths among the people, run their educational and religious institutions as per their religious tenets. Muslims have been allowed to have their own personal law under Sharia.

Islam was planted forcibly on the Indian soil by Muslim invaders and Christianity by European missionaries and traders. Aggressive means and methods such as propagation and conversion, which had been unheard of in India till the advent of these religions, were adopted as marketing strategies. In the normal course, tribals and people of other weaker sections of the Hindu community living on the fringes of society were targeted for proselytization. And in certain cases, people of entire villages were converted.

Being a totally unorganized religion, Hinduism never believed in keeping its flock together under a central command. In fact, followers of Hinduism living in different parts of our country have always enjoyed the freedom of offering prayers and worship to the deities of their choice in conformity with the unique and individualistic cultural practices of their regions. Having never been subjected to the straight jacket of religion earlier in their life, they were systematically lured and enticed with pecuniary benefits and, not infrequently, coerced through societal pressure into converting to the new religions.

Pseudo-Secularism

Congress, Communists and other Opposition parties have proved adept at playing vote bank politics and playing the reservations card among the Dalits, OBCs and other socially and economically weaker sections among the Hindus. The nexus of the Congress-led parties who profess Secularism but actually promote pseudo-Secularism for their own narrow and selfish political ends on the one hand and the religious and political organizations of Islam and Christianity with a vested interest in promoting those religions on the other, has been unfairly targeting BJP for pursuing a 'saffron agenda' and flagrantly promoting the interests of Hinduism.

In their attack on BJP, RSS and the other Hindu organizations like the VHP and Bajrang Dal, the Main Stream Media (MSM) has willingly played a big role by supporting these pseudo-secular parties. Although BJP is in power at the Centre and is committed to defending the interests and improving the welfare of the Hindu community, as it forms the main plank of the country's demography, the party is hamstrung by the limitations imposed by the Constitutional provisions and the cruelty of numbers in the Parliament.

Resurgence of Hindu Pride

With the BJP-led National Democratic Alliance coming to power in India, there has been a major shift in the perception of the Government of India with regard to its policy on Secularism. Since BJP has strong moorings in the Hindu organization of the RSS, the Sangh Parivar units like the VHP and the Bajrang Dal have felt upbeat and have accordingly initiated activities to give shape to their theological ideas and beliefs. This in turn, has given impetus to calls for construction of Ram Mandir at Ayodhya, 'Love Jihad', 'Ghar Wapsi', etc, with BJP MPs like Yogi Adityanath and Sakshi Maharaj vociferously supporting the calls.

In the meantime, politically appropriate statements had to be issued by BJP leaders and spokespersons to undo the damage caused by these calls. Sadhvi Niranjan Jyoti, who is a Minister of State in the Modi Cabinet, made a controversial remark about Opposition parties, which was perceived to be communal in nature. Subsequently, in the face of a strident protest from the Opposition parties, she retracted her statement.

Another raging controversy that is currently being debated in political circles is the issue of passing legislation against conversion. Prime Minister Modi, who has asked BJP leaders not to make statements out of turn, has himself maintained a stoic silence over the controversial statements issued by his party colleagues and has preferred to focus on matters of development and administration.

Although his silence has been criticized by leaders of the Opposition parties as well as political commentators, Modi has steered clear of all controversies. His strategy has been to avoid controversies that could give rise to communal confrontations, while also keeping his partymen in check and not allowing them to aggravate the situation. Fortunately, this strategy has paid off. However, it may appear that the BJP has lost some of its cutting edge as a progressive party totally focused on developmental programs. In contrast, Congress and its allies have continued to play the communal card rather than projecting economic and social policies for the development of the country and its citizens.

Some sections attribute BJP's inability to win a single seat from the Kashmir valley in the last Assembly elections to the loss of its cutting edge. But, given the unique position of the State of Jammu and Kashmir in national politics, BJP's inability to persuade the people of Kashmir valley to pin their faith on the national party in the face of hostility from the local political parties and terrorist activities by extraneous forces, was not totally surprising. BJP may still need to cross some impediments before it is able to convince the people of Kashmir that their future is safe only when there is a seamless transition of the State from the insular politics currently being practised to the mainstream national life, a source of immense strength and national pride.

'Sickularism'

Although Secularism is an Article of Faith for BJP as the ruling party of the country, it cannot help noticing the steady erosion of credibility of the doctrine in the Indian context. With the export of terrorism by the country's hostile and meddlesome northern neighbour, Pakistan, which has been sheltering and actively supporting a host of jihadist elements, and the terrorist organization Islamic State already casting its ugly shadow on Afghanistan and Pakistan, the people of India have reasons to have fears over the inability of the ever-so-brittle doctrine of Secularism to unite all sections of the people, cutting across religious and communal barriers.

This has been made further hollow by the scheming and conniving Opposition parties by playing to the gallery with pseudo-Secularism and promoting their vote bank politics, in the face of terrorism at home as well as external threats from sinister international forces. People, at an individual level, are already contemptuous of and highly cynical about India's experiment with Secularism to the extent of their coining a new word 'Sickularism' in the Social Media to replace the pseudo-Secularism that is being practiced in India currently.

Secularism for Unity

The fear of the people regarding the inadequacy of Secularism, no matter how ill-founded it may prima facie appear, requires to be collectively addressed by the Society and the Government. We should not continue to live in a state of denial and believe that everything is hunky-dory between Secularism as a political doctrine on the one hand, and the political and social life of the people on the other. While establishment of a theocratic State, a Hindu Rashtra, is a theoretical alternative, in practise such a step would be highly unrealistic and not at all viable, especially with large numbers of non-Hindus living in the country.

A really viable alternative would be to make Secularism a truly flawless and non-partisan doctrine, which does not promote bitterness among the people of the majority community and those of the minority communities. To this end, it has to be ensured that Secularism, in its true sense, is wholeheartedly accepted by all political parties as an inviolable political doctrine. For this purpose, a national dialogue would have to be organized with the participation of all political parties.

At the religious and communal level, there has to be an exercise for arriving at a consensus among different religions and faiths regarding a Uniform Civil Code. A national referendum, with equal participation from people all over the country, would be able to forge the conflicting viewpoints of the people at large. In brief, a total divorce between Politics and Religion is a sine qua non for the nourishment of Secularism for the unity of the people and territorial integrity of the country as well as for making the parliamentary system of democracy, which India has consciously chosen for the development of the country and progress of its people a success.

Given the demographic situation of the country and the geopolitical realities of the global war against terrorism, probably Secularism cannot be wished away by India at this juncture. All the same, the political and social conditions of the country have to be improved and made congenial to make it possible for Secularism to snugly dovetail with the system in place. Consigning Secularism to the dustbins of history for the faults in the system and lack of will to administer the doctrine dispassionately would not be much dissimilar to throwing the baby away with the bath water.

Furthermore, tolerating 'Sickularism' as is practised today in silence, much to the vexation it has caused to the psyche of the majority community, would not be in the long-term interest of our nation. Because doing so would be tantamount to covering up the nation's shame with a fig leaf of appeasement of the minorities. In fact, the Central government and the state governments in our country should never leave any room for any kind of appeasement or any type of discrimination based on caste, creed or religion. 'One for All and All for One' should be adopted as the nation's credo to complement the current lofty eternal truth 'Satyamev Jayate'!

(Posted on blog on 17 August, 2015)

□

Why Ram Mandir in Ayodhya is Crucial, Inevitable

History has lessons for us, to realize that furthering religious persuasion can be for two reasons, either to oppress and win over other faiths, or to ensure well-being of ours in view of assaults on members of our community. Many can say that exodus of Kashmiri Pandits and construction of Ram Mandir in Ayodhya or for that matter, drop in number of Hindus in Bengal, withdrawal of criminal cases that were filed against members of a particular community by the UP government are unrelated occurrences, but isn't there something in common, and that something has a bearing on the lives of the followers of a faith that has remained long-neglected in the era of so-called secular politics, for appeasement of minority religions of India. Law of the land is inescapable; hence hasty decision in the sensitive and centuries-old Babri Masjid-Ram Janmabhoomi dispute will only lead to more disorder, law for the construction of Ram Mandir at the disputed site cannot be passed unless Rajya Sabha approves, but can or should this be postponed for long?

It will be sensible if this is perused basis rational, historical and archaeological facts and indeed the sentiments of any of the communities seeking custody of the disputed land will find the last place. Excavations by the Archaeological Survey of India, conducted in three distinct years, 1970, 1992 and 2003, found flawless evidences specifying that the site under question had a large Hindu complex, and be it the Rama temple or a Shiva temple, the pilgrimage was that of the Hindus. In 1788, the year when it was reportedly the first time that someone defied the rightfulness of Babri Masjid, Joseph Tiefenthaler, a missionary and notable European geographer, advocated that the Masjid was on the birthplace of Lord Rama. Since then, many honorable courts, learned researchers and a wide array of historians have backed the presence of a Hindu temple at the site, which was demolished by one of the Mughal emperors, conspicuously, Babar or Aurangzeb. In one of the most timeworn judgments, the Faizabad District Judge, in 1866, said that the Masjid built on land which is sacred to Hindus is an unfortunate event, but cannot be reversed since more than 3 centuries had passed and it was too late to accord justice to Hindus.

Uprightness forbidden because of a long interval! And since then, in the name of India's rich secularism, communal harmony, fairness to all religions and such other captivating phrases justice to the followers of Lord Rama has been kept miles away. Now, this does not validate what occurred in December 1992, on the 6th the Masjid was brought to the ground by Hindu devotees, I will not use the word 'hardliners' since the same is more apt for extremists, but the postponement of justice was the real cause of the agitation and accusing some leaders or Hindu groups is like finding an easy course to delay this movement further and gain political mileage in the so-called religiously-affluent India. In 2005, terrorists attacked the site and targeted the provisional Mandir, and who can forget the 2002 Godhra case, which left Hindu pilgrims in fumes and resultant deaths in the rage that they were returning from Ayodhya.

Tens of thousands of casualties have ensued until today, and the unfounded debate by our legislators alleging that religious accord is above any structure, be it a Mandir or a Masjid, has only kindled the subject, has ridiculed the death of those killed in many riots over this issue and has left us in a state where vulnerable-appearing Hindus and Hindu groups alleged to be hardliners by self-styled secular governments are an easy target to oppression and blame. Now that we have seen a paradigm shift in the way our country is run by administrators post the 2014 Lok Sabha elections, is it wrong or unwarrantable to expect a judicious solution of the Ayodhya dispute, also because the attached word 'dispute' with Hinduism's most sacred site 'Ayodhya' is completely unmerited. For if the Mecca is an undisputed place of worship for the Muslims and Jerusalem the holiest site for Christians, are the Hindus extreme in seeking an undoubted accordance of Hinduism to Ayodhya?

Don't we know why even realistic demands by Hindus are turned down, why extremism is the name accorded to any movement seeking justice, why even in the wake of exact facts and evidences minorities are acquitted and why there exists a wide gap in facilities for minority factions and Hindus? Perhaps it is the rule of politics and diplomacy that is to stay forever, for every king needs public backing, and this comes best from the ones who are lesser in number but adamant to mark their presence. To be precise, in India, one community relishes superfluous bonuses, which would not have been probed had it not been at the stake of another community. Such equations kill the very essence of our democracy and Constitutional framework that further equality and justice.

After the judgment of the High Court, which is stayed by the Apex Court, it is apparent that the very existence of a Hindu temple at the site is totally undisputable, had it been so, the demolition of Masjid would be the only substance taken into notice and the 2/3rd part would never be given to Hindu plaintiffs. Also, the present government grasps the delicacy of this subject, Ram Mandir being a nerve center of Hinduism and its followers, but the need is to deliberate this topic scrupulously minus deferral and diplomacy. For the time being, until the BJP attains majority in the Upper House, at least debating the legislation for erection of Ram Mandir at the site and conveying the same in the Lower House is expected. BJPians are not to disremember that Ram Mandir in Ayodhya was a promise they made in the very initial days of forming the party, and Hindu votes backed them substantially in making it to the topmost echelons of Indian politics.

The Supreme Court stayed the verdict of the High Court saying that split of land was never demanded by any of the disputing parties; status quo has been ordered, and this is a chance to stand up again in the court with substantial evidences and findings to ask for a decision in the favor of Ram Mandir. Believe me, unless this matter is put to end, a decisive one, politics and appeasement will just result in suppression of both Hindus as well as Muslims, Hindus exposed to greater risk since many political parties rest on Muslim votes during polls. Then why allow interminable defeat of justice and Hindus? In judicious sense, and also to corroborate your claim for Hindus' well-being after series of downfalls, Ram Mandir is crucial, inevitable.

Having said that bringing of uniform civil code, erection of Ram Mandir and annulling of Article 370 of the Constitution demands at least 370 seats for the NDA in lower house, BJP president Amit

Shah has flashed a new debate. Uniform civil code finds place in the directive principles of state, an addition made to steer clear of its actual implementation by the then Nehru government and all know of the gift, Article 370 by PM Nehru to J&K. These may need Constitutional amendments; hence 2/3rd majority in the lower house; however Ram Mandir cannot be delayed owing to this deficiency. Indeed, apt valuation of present conditions to assure that harmony and national security is not compromised by the erection of Mandir is undeniable. All in all, we cannot allow our descendants to be engaged in this turf war like we have been since centuries, let peace prevail with the construction of Ram Mandir in Ayodhya.

(Posted on blog on 11 August, 2015)

□

BJP and the Kashmir Imbroglio

Though Kashmir has always been an integral part of India as any of its other territories, the state has always been inextricably linked with our country's foreign policy on account of the unwanted presence of an extraneous factor – Pakistan. In an ironical turn of events in the history of Indian subcontinent, Pakistan, which had steadfastly refused political equality to the people of its own Eastern Wing, and subjected them to one of the most horrid military onslaughts in history that resulted in the birth of Bangladesh, albeit with the active assistance and support of India, has been harping for the 'independence' of Kashmir.

Bitter wars have been fought by India and Pakistan over Kashmir. Colossal amounts of money have been spent on financing these wars, setting the economies of both the countries back by several decades. While enormous amounts have been spent by both the sides on oiling the war machine, other losses in terms of human lives have been incalculable. Furthermore, rancor runs so deep between the two countries that bilateral relations have been irreparably damaged.

Pakistan, the Spoiler

To make matters worse, Pakistan has been waging a proxy war against India in the absence of a full-fledged war, apparently in the hope of keeping up the sagging morale of their civilian population that started despairing long ago over their government's failed policy of 'liberating' Kashmir from India. Notwithstanding the fact that Pakistan had captured parts of Kashmir by military might and deception immediately after partition of the united India in 1947 and installed a puppet government in the Pakistan-occupied-Kashmir, the authorities of Pakistan have realized the futility of their foolish endeavor to wrest the rest of Kashmir; but find it impossible to let go of their pet obsession for Kashmir which forms the keystone of their foreign policy.

If ever they give up their claim for Kashmir, they would have to shift focus to the economic and social development of their own people. This indeed would be a formidable, nay, impossible task for a country which has unsuccessfully experimented with democracy, off and on, during the course of its six decades of independence. Even when it had been possible to hold elections and a democratic government was put in place, all the time it was the army that was in real control of the levers of power in Pakistan.

In short, because of a political atmosphere controlled by an unholy nexus between the Army, ISI and corrupt politicians, democracy could never take deep roots in Pakistan. In fact, having become a level playing field for the Taliban, Al Qaeda, and a host of terrorist organizations of all shades and hues, and a convenient place of refuge for terrorists like Hafiz Sayeed, Dawood Ibrahim and others, wanted by the Government of India, Pakistan has proved to be an ideal launching pad for terrorist activities against India.

Propped up by the US with vast quantities of economic and military aid to enable its ally to play a major role in the global war against terrorism, Pakistan has diverted and subsumed all the assistance in furthering its military might at the cost of its social and economic development. Caught in the crossfire between the subversive and seditious activities of various terrorist groups and self-defeating policy of an all-powerful military and ubiquitous intelligence agency, Pakistan is today a failed state, a rogue one at that. The bleatings of Pakistan, with feet of clay, laying claim in international for a over Kashmir had never sounded more hollow, than now.

Kashmir and the Average Pakistani Citizen

Internally, in a political atmosphere that can only be described as a sham, policies of the State have always been the prerogative of the ruling clique, with the people of Pakistan having no say whatever in the matter. Not to make too fine a point, it would be presumptuous to believe that an average Pakistani citizen who is an unwary victim of the despicable political and security situation in his own country, would ever care as to whether Kashmir continued to remain a part of India, became a free country or became a part of Pakistan any more than which morally or ethically corrupt political dispensation ruled his country.

Kashmir and the International Community

Much to the discomfiture of Pakistan, the people of Kashmir enjoy political freedom to decide their own political destiny in local elections as well as elections to the state legislature and the nation's parliament, just as the people of any other state of India. This has vindicated India's stand in the eyes of the international community that Kashmir is truly an integral part of the country not merely because India says so, but because of the ground realities obtaining in Kashmir.

UPA Government and Kashmir

To understand the game plan or policy perspective of the current government in Delhi on the Kashmir issue, it would be necessary to appreciate the basic difference between the Narendra Modi government and that of his predecessor. The policy paralysis which had afflicted the Manmohan Singh government during its second stint (2009-14) had permeated India's foreign policy. This had inevitably led to a stalemate in the settlement of the Kashmir issue. The UPA government's Janus-faced stance mentioned below is a case in point.

We had been telling Pakistan and the rest of the world that Kashmir is an integral part of India. And rightly so. But, what had we been telling the people of India, including those of Kashmir? That notwithstanding the fact that Kashmir was an integral part of India, it enjoyed a special status in terms of a separate Constitution it had, distinctly different from that of India. Now the question is why should there be a separate Constitution that gives Kashmir a special status different from the rest of India of which it has been an integral part?

Circumstances leading to this anomalous situation date back to 1947, when India was partitioned and it constitutes a well-documented fact of history. After over 60 years of independence, the question which begged an answer was whether this was a permanent arrangement; if not, why hadn't the situation been reviewed? Was India ever going to do it? What had been preventing the people of Kashmir from integrating with the mainstream India with their special status thrown overboard? Neither the Manmohan Singh government nor the ones preceding it ever had an answer.

It would not be too uncharitable to point out that the powers in Delhi simply lacked the gumption or political nerve to address the issue and had kept it in cold storage! Notwithstanding its political will, the NDA government led by Atal Bihari Vajpayee was, on its part, not in a position to address the issue due to lack of a solid majority in the Parliament; it did, however, try its best to bring Pakistan around to the negotiating table without any success.

Kashmir and BJP

The time for addressing the Kashmir issue had never been as propitious as now in the history of free India. This is on account of the fact that currently BJP is in an unassailable position at the Centre. BJP has the political arithmetic right (the party, with Narendra Modi at the helm of affairs, has already demonstrated that it is capable of managing the numbers in the Rajya Sabha) and political conviction in consonance with its ideology, to go for the jugular of the issue. The broad parameters with regard to this issue pan out as follows:

- With its very existence hanging precariously in peril, it is far from likely that the Nawaz Sharif government in Pakistan would address the Kashmir issue for a meaningful and realistic resolution. That Pakistan's house is not in order, and therefore, renders that country incapable of taking the initiative is to India's advantage. This should, however, not be allowed to degenerate or dissipate by having discordant notes from different sources within India. All political parties should have a consensus, the bottom line of which should be "Kashmir is an integral part of India and its territorial integrity is not subject to compromise". The consensus should be declared India's national policy, binding on all individuals, parties and movements and legally enforceable.
- Kashmir is a bilateral issue which is to be settled between India and Pakistan, without the involvement of any other country, or extraneous agency from either country.
- Individuals, political parties or movements in India seeking separation of Kashmir in clear violation of the government's policy on Kashmir, should be imprisoned on charges of sedition, and disqualified from participating in any further political activity.
- To this end, an immediate review of Kashmir's place in India's political system, its Constitution and the special status accorded by the country's Constitution should be undertaken. This would

evidently cause much chagrin among certain sections of people or groups in Kashmir. Necessary Constitutional amendments and laws should be introduced. Only by having such a firm and irrevocable policy can India hope to have an unassailable position at talks with Pakistan. A divided house would weaken India's position.

Repeal of Article 370

Understandably, BJP has not yet placed the question of repealing Article 370 of the Constitution that vests Kashmir with a special status on the top of its political agenda. It should, however, be taken up sooner rather than later.

The contentious Article has not helped the people of Jammu and Kashmir in any way. It has only helped the mealy-mouthed wastrels with a feudal mindset among the politicians in the state to strengthen their stranglehold over the governance of the state. J&K has regretfully remained a backward and corrupt State, with no economic development and a high incidence of unemployment.

Cut off from mainstream India, thanks to Article 370, the state has become a hotbed of terrorist activities. Fight against terrorism in the state has been made more complicated, with the obtrusive Pakistan generously exporting terrorism. The state has witnessed a lot of violence and bloodshed besides an exodus of an estimated 700, 000 Kashmiri Pandits. With the introduction of a new government, with BJP as an alliance partner, the stifling political backwardness of the state may be expected to be on the wane.

The regional political parties in the state such as the National Conference (NC) and the People's Democratic Party (PDP) and major opposition parties in the country are vehemently against repeal of the Article because of vested interests. Their argument is that the Article is the only Constitutional link between J&K and the rest of India; therefore, if the Article were repealed, J&K would no more be a part of India. People of the state should realize that this line of argument is fallacious and cannot be sustained.

The state is at a crossroads. Winds of change have been blowing all over India, heralding better times for the Indian economy. People of J&K should wake up to the new reality, shun their self-serving politicians and latch on to the new resurgent India so as not to get further left behind in India's march to progress and prosperity. It is high time they realized that fibbing over legal and technical aspects of an Article of the Indian Constitution, which had, in any case, been created on a very temporary basis and has outlived its purpose, will be an exercise in futility.

Winning Over the People of Jammu and Kashmir

Now, it is imperative for the BJP to win the hearts of the people of the state and capture their imagination. This would become feasible by ensuring good government and clean administration not only in the state but in the entire country. For starters, it should expose the separatist leaders in the state for the men of straw they really are.

For undertaking the political exercise delineated above, a steely vision and iron will are required. Today, Narendra Modi is the only Indian leader who has the popular mandate and political sagacity to rise up to the occasion and unravel the Kashmir imbroglio. Only after this seemingly improbable mission is achieved, would Kashmir emerge as a truly integral part of India in all senses of the term, safe from the grubby hands of the avaricious neighbor, Pakistan.

(Posted on blog on 14 July, 2015)

□

BJP and Hindutva

Hindutva or Hindu nationalism has a special resonance for every true citizen of Hindustan or India (also known as Bharat) whose heart beats for his motherland. He proudly wears it as a badge of honour as it makes his life more meaningful and purposeful. Hindutva also gives Bharat a unique and respectful place among the comity of nations. Patriotism sans nationalism would be tantamount to love for one's country without the collective self-esteem of a people or a yearning for a unique and distinct cultural identity which is rightfully the core ipseity of a people. Hindutva is the binding force that brings and blends together people of different regions of our country, known for its rich divergence of ethnic, linguistic and sartorial identity.

Hindutva and Hinduism

Hindutva per se does not imply that a person subscribing to this ideology necessarily has to be a member of the Hindu religion. It is a common core value of every patriotic Indian, irrespective of his religious or spiritual proclivity. It is a coalescing agent or factor that enables the cohesion of all patriotic Indians of varied backgrounds and beliefs into a united people to make the task of nation-building feasible. However, India being his own birth place as well as that of his religion, no Hindu (in the current context, the usage of the term Hindu is restricted to refer to a member of Hinduism) faces at any point of time the predicament of having to choose between his loyalty to his religion and his motherland.

For a Hindu, his religion and motherland are happily and inextricably intertwined and loyalty to both comes naturally and spontaneously. In fact, a Hindu would find nothing more absurd or far-fetched a proposition than to have to choose between his country and religion. The same is the position of a member of any other religion that emanated from India such as Buddhism, Jainism or Sikhism or a faith like Zoroastrianism which was given refuge by India in the face of religious persecution.

Hindutva and other Religions

That said, what about those religions of foreign origin, which were implanted on the Indian soil with the advent of the Turko-Central Asian marauding forces or European colonizers? Or could the question be dismissed outright or swept under the carpet as one of hypothetical or improbable a scenario or situation where one is torn asunder by loyalty to one's country and loyalty for one's religion? This kind of a paradoxical situation might have been considered ludicrous or contemptuously shrugged off in a different national or international scenario as existed till a few years ago; but not in today's changed circumstances, which have thrown up a melting pot of religious extremism and shifting territorial borders, resulting in an unholy mix of strife, terror, bloodbath and gross violation of human rights on a scale seldom witnessed in history.

We have already been privy to unfortunate and deplorable instances of recalcitrant religious elements in our own country, including some Members of Parliament, being vocal about their holding their religion in primacy in preference to their national identity. This kind of rabid religious fundamentalism could, if not checked right at the initial stages, become widespread among the members of the particular community either out of fear for a religious diktat by the Clergy or on their own volition out of misplaced values and beliefs.

Nationalism and Patriotism

It is in such extraordinary circumstances or during challenging conditions that Hindutva stands out and shines like a ray of hope and guides one in a crisis or dilemma in national life or service to the nation. Loyalty to the motherland is the supreme virtue of every patriot. Religious or cultural affiliation could not be allowed to be a rigid impediment in the way to loyalty to motherland. It has to be tweaked or pruned to the extent of shaping it to complement one's patriotism.

Promotion of Yoga

When Prime Minister Narendra Modi recently spearheaded the

cause of Yoga and its promotion on a never-before scale to enable it to assume a truly international stature, all right-thinking citizens of our country rallied around him, with the exception of some skeptics and naysayers who included religious fundamentalists and the Main Stream Media (MSM), acting at the behest of vested interests. The thrust of opposition was that promotion of Yoga was intended to further the cause of BJP's 'saffron agenda' and that Yoga militated against the religious sentiments of minority communities.

The detractors saw a Trojan horse in Yoga and a sinister design behind the move that was actually meant to promote a purely non-religious component of Indian culture. The fact that Hinduism had embraced Yoga, which contributes to the development of physical and mental discipline, thousands of years ago and immensely benefitted from it was beside the point. A similar move by people of other nationalities and faiths would equally benefit all sections of humanity as in the case of Indians in general and Hindus in particular.

Several member-countries of the UN, including Islamic countries, which were members of the OIC (Organization of Islamic Cooperation), supported the resolution to adopt an International Yoga Day while the detractors within the country of origin of Yoga sulked, opposed, protested and boycotted the effort and its celebration. This was a clear case of religious affiliations and extraneous considerations blatantly working together to thwart a unique manifestation of Hindutva.

Opposition to Hindutva

With BJP wedded to Hindutva, which is an official policy of the party, every move by the BJP government at the Centre in the direction of promotion of Hindutva comes under scanner by the Opposition parties and the MSM, which do not pass an opportunity to harangue the government and the ruling party with the charge of communal bias. When the government announced December 25th, which is the birth anniversary of former Prime Minister Atal Behari Vajpayee, as Good Governance Day and declared it a working day for the government, it was bitterly opposed on the grounds that the government's move would dilute its significance as the day of Christmas and hurt religious sentiments of Christians.

In fact, it was wrongly argued that the government's move constituted a deliberate bid to push down the status of equality of religious minorities, guaranteed by the Constitution, notionally by a notch, with scarce regard to the religious sentiments of the minority Christian community. The fallacy of this argument stands exposed by the stand of members of the Christian and Islamic communities and others who bitterly complained against the ban of beef imposed by the government of Maharashtra, in deference to the wishes of the majority Hindu community, at the end of a due legislative process that had lasted several years.

The champions of beef eating, comprising primarily Muslims and Christians, demanded that their right to eat the food of their choice be upheld, in utter disregard to the sentiments of the Hindu community, which considers cow a sacred animal and worships it. How could it be gainsaid that the religious sentiments of minority communities be respected and celebrated and those of the majority community damned?

Votebank Politics

It is an unfortunate fact of history that all the governments at the Centre that had preceded the present NDA-II government (with the exception of AB Vajpayee-led NDA-I government, which was severely hampered on account of lack of numbers in Parliament) lacked a vision. Nor were the economic progress of the country and social development of the people their priorities of governance. Whenever the Congress Party was in power, either on its own or at the head of a rainbow coalition, it had strived, with single-minded devotion, for the perpetuation of dynastic rule and consolidation of economic gains and political power for the ruling elite, with total disregard to the welfare of the people at large. To this end, the powers that be misused the vote bank strategy.

Minority religious communities were viewed as vote banks, which the government took great care to appease by pandering to the smallest of their whims and fancies. This reprehensible approach of causing an artificial schism among the people of the country on religious lines, was inherently inimical to healthy and wholesome governance, and should have sounded alarm bells for the majority community. But the shrewd manipulators of power had their own answer to the situation to pre-empt such a possibility. They divided members of the majority Hindu community too – on the lines of caste, which caused artificial fragmentation of the society. This clever ploy prevented consolidation of votes of the majority community into a single sizeable bloc unlike in the case of minority communities. In short, politics was not really the sum total of its parts.

Appeasement of religious minorities in the name of Secularism and endless grant of reservations to certain sections of the majority community in the name of social justice, and pitting the leftout sections of the majority community against beneficiaries of the government's vexatious reservations policy were the cardinal principles of those who had grabbed power when the country attained independence by virtue of their predominant position in a certain stream of the movement for independence. Not surprisingly, Hindutva figured nowhere in their scheme of things.

In fact, Hindutva was anathema to their brand of politics. They used it as a bugbear for scaring the minority communities with the possibility of a ‹saffron wash' and manipulating their support at the polls. With the coming to power of the BJP and its allies in May 2014, it was time for standing the votebank politics of Congress on its head. This needed, however, to be done gradually and in a systematic manner without giving cause for undue criticisms and doubts among BJP's supporters and well-wishers, of indulging in vindictive politics instead of focusing on good governance.

Sops and Concessions

India is the only country in the world in which a State where a minority religious community is living predominantly and has been allowed to have a special status and its own Constitution. The unique position of the State of Jammu and Kashmir is not congenial in the long run to the idea of members of various religious communities in the country living together peacefully in harmony as was envisaged by the founding fathers of Bharat. We should neither have wheels within the wheel nor can afford to have the people of Kashmir living in an island for much longer. It is not unlikely that the current state of affairs would lead to at least a section of the people of Kashmir, already living with a closed mindset, wanting to drift away from the mainstream nationhood of Bharat. That kind of a situation could be forestalled only by the exposure of the people of the valley to the successful application of Hindutva in the rest of the country for its betterment.

Uniform Civil Code

The people who are practising Islam have been allowed to have their personal law in terms of Sharia. It is evident that the Muslim personal law is unfair to the womenfolk of the community in matters of marriage, divorce, inheritance of property, etc, which does not augur well for their equal treatment with men. Unfair treatment of women and gender discrimination albeit with the sanction of religious tenets of the community are not tenable in a secular country like India. The Constitution was changed, when the courts in the Shah Bano case ruled that a secular nation must have only one law, and not separate religious laws. Islamic religious and educational institutions were promised a policy of non-interference.

This situation calls for a drastic change in the form of a Uniform Civil Code, cutting across all religious communities without exception. There has, however, been a recent landmark judgment by the Supreme Court in the case of a Christian lady fighting for rights as her own illegitimate child's guardian. While granting the lady the rights, the Court did not take cognizance of certain tenets of Christianity cited in support of the case against her claim. It further stated that there should be a Uniform Civil Code in a country like India, and religion should be kept away from law. We may hope that the judgment will prove to be a milestone in BJP's quest for a Uniform Civil Code.

Hindutva and the System of Education

In keeping with the spirit of Hindutva, senior leaders of the BJP have been appealing for the need to inculcate a sense of pride in youngsters for the Indian culture, customs, traditions, values and languages as against the current trend of aping the West. A true sense of appreciation of Hindutva is feasible with a factual and unbiased depiction of Indian history in text books, which would instill a sense of pride amongst our youngsters with regard to the past glory of our country and an urgent need for its resurrection.

Indian history as has been rendered by the yesteryear colonial masters with a vested interest, either completely neglects the bravery, valour and patriotism of true Indian heroes who fought the marauding forces of invaders and colonialists or portray them in poor light vis-a-vis the alien warlords in a winner-takes-all account of history. A review of our education system with the strong underpinning of Hindutva is the need of the hour. If in the process of achieving the goal for betterment of life of the people and resurrection of the lost glory of the country, a few toes had to be trodden on, it would still be worth pushing the envelope.

(Posted on blog on 20 July, 2015)

□

Criticising Hindutva, is 'No Solution'

"*Since the election, religious minority communities have been subject to derogatory comments by politicians linked to the ruling Bhartiya Janata Party (BJP) and numerous violent attacks and forced conversions by Hindu nationalist groups, such as Rashtriya Swayamsevak Sangh (RSS) and Vishva Hindu Parishad (VHP).*" – The US Commission on International Religious Freedom (USCIRF)

My Reply-Ask your soul, if the secularism and religious liberation that you are endorsing today is in true sense the genuine manifestation of our liberal code of conduct? Is the Hindu group RSS truthfully the oppressor of minority? Is it as wide of the mark for a not-for-profit association, working as the savior of humans during natural disasters, to halt the crooked conversion of vulnerable Hindus to other faiths? Dear United States, I could effortlessly count at least five recent cases of religious intolerance in your country that were aimed at Hindus, Muslims or Sikhs and their places of devotion, but just to portray ourselves as 'seculars', we do not come up with report cards for other nations and their respective heads. The words in the beginning of this writing have faultily judged India's competence and will to deal with matters related to faiths and followers, and also have ill-criticized the role of Hindu groups.

Though I am not their spokesperson, let me assure you that the vandalizing of churches and attacks on Christians in India were by a collection of men who we can term as anti-social and perpetrators, but cannot link them to any particular organization. And just because groups like RSS and VHP project themselves as pro-Hindu, this does not imply their proximity with extremism or religious prejudice. Indeed, they know how to deal with religious intolerance, not by way of picking up swords or guns, but by fortifying the presence of the vulnerable and exactly analogous is what they are endeavoring. Coming to the allegation on the Indian government regarding incidents of religious fanaticism on Christians and Muslims, it is severely immature to denunciate an effective leadership solely on the basis that it is backed by considerable Hindu votes. The government's delivery in the flood-struck J&K, where more than half the population is Muslim, was as flawless as are its labors in quake-ridden Nepal and during Indians' rescue from Yemen.

India's RSS, VHP, BJP or any other pro-Hindu group is as 'Secular' as were Sir Winston Churchill and George Washington. The purpose is not to suppress any religion or its followers, however, fortification of our faith is an obligation and we ought to take notice of the same.

Now that we are all either a Christian, a Muslim, a Jewish, a Hindu, or affiliated to some other community, let us live with this fact, and in the finest and most peaceful manner possible protect what has given us identity. Answer to questions like 'what should be the modus operandi to save all faiths' is quite uncomplicated, non-violent too, unless perused in the diplomatic way, as is being done globally, just in the wake of endorsing fake secularism and to hailstorm unmerited perks on minorities in respective countries.

Let me take you not very far in the history; I will recall 'The Holocaust', genocide of millions of Jews by the Nazis, which was more or less the depiction of world's divide on account of religions, ethnicity and other beliefs. I must also tell the western world that though the term Holocaust is allied with the murder of six million Jews during 1940s, my country, India, witnessed, what we can call an outright carnage of humans and humanity during Islamic India, when Hindu temples were ruined, women raped and abducted, and tens of millions of followers of Hinduism were brutally eliminated; wasn't this sheer religious intolerance? The mockery is that this slaughter isn't talked about much, and in today's world, with associations like UN and Human Rights Commission, and with democratic, republican and secular form of states, only minority groups can relish the right to justice and equality.

The more you blindly endorse one and the same status to all faiths and their respective followers, the more you are preparing for another 'Holocaust'. And shall I not say that we are undergoing the same if we collectively count the number of fatalities across the world in the name of religion and fanaticism? How many incidents should I sum up, the

Charlie Hedbo of France, the 9/11 of the US, the 26/11 of India, the Peshawar school bloodbath of Pakistan, the 2005 London Bombings; the list is incessant, and the manner we are dealing with radicalism is bound to embrace the killings of more and more innocents. Nations, specially the developed ones, may have attained nuclear armament but were you individually or even collectively able to halt the beheading incidents by the Islamic extremist group ISIS? Aren't these a mockery of your alleged valor, and also a slap on the face in the context that you assuredly promise well-being to your citizens?

The bitter fact, that every social and political leader of the world is aware of, but rarely does anyone declare in the public is the escalating population imbalance in almost every part of the world, where Islam can be seen as many steps ahead to other faiths. Over the next 20 years, Muslim population is predicted to grow twice as fast as the growth of non-Muslims and by the end of 21st century Islam would become world's leading faith with 35 per cent of world's population as Muslim. Presently, Islam is the most prevailing religion in Asia and many scholars believe that the United States has been issuing false and reduced count of number of Muslims in the US. Let me also reiterate facts that are openly accessible to world leaders. During the 1990s, 12 million more people embraced Islam than Christianity; in the US, more than quarter of Muslims are converts and it is estimated that around 20, 000 non-Muslims embrace Islam every year in America. Projections based on the study of population growth say that by the year 2050 Muslim population would be the largest in India, surpassing even that of Indonesia.

If at all Muslims are growing at a much faster rate, there shouldn't be havoc. But, the study of worldwide extremism suggests that there is something to feel nervous about. And it isn't the Holy book, Quran; it is rather the misinterpretation of its tenets, which is the real cause of the uninterrupted rise of Islamic terrorism. There exists not a single reason to doubt human and ethical values of Muslims, but I am afraid that if we tend to cover up flaws of a cluster of Muslims, 'the fanatical ones', we will end up witnessing the destruction of the world. Conversion of non-Muslims cannot go unnoticed and if at all it does, be prepared for yet another era of suppression of Hindus, Christians and others at the hands of radical Muslims, the Islamists. I don't baselessly stimulate Hinduism; Hindu ancestors, who always remained eminent and were never categorized in the corrupt wave of secularism or communalism, gave us many possessions to cheer. Hereunder is an extract from one of Swami Vivekananda's speeches which concludes who is a Hindu.

"Mark me, then and then alone you are a Hindu when the very name Hindu sends through you a galvanic shock of strength. Then and then alone you are a Hindu when every man who bears the name Hindu, from any country, speaking our language or any other language, becomes at once the nearest and dearest to you. Then and then alone you are a Hindu when the distress of anyone bearing the name Hindu comes to your heart and makes you feel as if your own son were in distress."

Dear west and the people accusing us of 'Ghar Wapsi' (re-conversion of non-Hindus to Hinduism), you may need re-worked statistical report on how the number of Muslims and Christians in India amplified so dynamically only owing to conversion of Hindus by Christian Missionaries and Islamic Madrasas. If at all you are the authentic promoter of communal harmony and equivalence of all faiths, talk about enactment of Uniform Civil Code in India, endorse population control measures for all Indians and ask for a strict law against faith conversion of vulnerable families.

(Published in Organiser magazine in Vol. 66, No. 46, 17 May, 2015 edition)

□

Ferocity Against Minorities Displeasing, but Accusing Hindus is no Answer

You will agree to this-We are in the grip of ages-old evils, have been unable to deliver a state with zero-tolerance towards violence and one that is just for all communities not because we lack the intent and will, but for a simple reason that we never diagnose the issues faced by our society in an unbiased way that could pave way to improvement. We try to suppress, exaggerate and also set aside concerns depending on how much profit can we extract from a happening, a happening that sees vandalizing of religious buildings or brutality against people of one caste/community or furtherance of one community at the stake of another. And by 'we', I am not just referring to politicians and spiritual leaders, this word grips us all, we are sometime a news channel which for want of sensation portrays an incident in a completely deceptive manner, at the other time we are a source of rumors, and sometime we are part of the crowd that follows these political and religious 'contractors' for want of special privileges. The attack on a church under construction in Haryana and the vicious crime involving rape of a 72-year old nun in West Bengal deserve punishing of the convicts, guarantee of future safety, framing of tougher laws, but no blame games and diverging from the actual topic.

Something that hurt me the most after coming across the rape incident in a convent school is the politicization of these shameless and unforgivable cases. While addressing a crowd from the platform of her car, Mamta Banerjee, the CM of WB, did not hesitate a bit prior to naming her political rival BJP for what occurred. When I was expecting a sense of shrewdness, at least from some leaders of the AAP, their spokesperson and a former journalist (hence expert in playing with words) was quoted as saying that PM's show of concern through words has become a routine after the members of Hinduism-fortification groups crush law and order promoting religious intolerance. The Congress, which in the name of 'spying' on Rahul Gandhi was obstructing the working of Indian Parliament now has a new card, and in this endeavor they have found supporters in the form of TMC, SP, JD(U) and other opposition parties. Isn't it sad? The accused of the rape case are still not behind the bars, a liability which the state police of West Bengal should have served without delay and if not, the CM of the state must have summoned the police, rather than tackling with such a sensitive manner on lines of polls due in the state in 2016.

The irony is that we create an instant hype of any incident for a day or two and then discard it completely. May be because our political leaders extract all benefits from such anti-secular events in a day by hampering the working of Vidhan Sabha/Lok Sabha, by holding marches and protests, and the public feels they are being heard, but the blame-game does not allow any improvements, on the contrary, time that was to be utilized for planning is killed, resources are wasted. At time when other parties are accusing the present central government of backing anti-minority deeds, what if the government indicts opposition parties of upsetting brotherhood by deliberate acts for political gains? It is true that in our country, any authority can claim any nonsense, accuse the other of harshest crimes, can announce any verdict publically and thus develop a detrimental state of affairs when sometime Hindus, sometime Muslims and at other times Jaats, Pandits, SCs, Sikhs are blamed for an attack by a group of three/four men on another community. 'Divide and Rule' is as effective policy today as was decades ago, and until the general public changes the way it perceives happenings, this policy will remain a vibrant tool for ruling in the hands of our corrupt politicians, though not all, but many.

Another mockery of our democracy and secularism is that while allegations on Christian missionaries and Madrasas of inducing religious conversions are condemned by most of the political parties and social reformers, unconfirmed charges on Hindu groups give chance to these men to cry of foul conduct by the BJP government. Not at all will I try to shield any political party by my writing, but yes, the central government of this country, which has a clear mandate for next 5 years, a mandate to eradicate poverty, unemployment, under-development and communal hatred, if is stopped dishonestly, I will never remain silent. Criticizing policies of the government in no way means a 'no-questions-asked liberty' to obstruct working and growth; when we know that WB rape incident and the vandalizing of church in Haryana are crimes and criminals ought to be punished, we shall ask for arrest of the wrong-doers, not blame the union government of endorsing anti-secular activities. The police of the states are answerable, the letdown rests on the shoulders of the state rulers, not on the PM. Repeated failure of law and order is now a usual scenario in West Bengal, Didi, however, is busy diverting her MPs from normal conduct of Parliament to creating disorder and affecting an operative and productive Parliament session.

This is an appeal to all my countrymen-To pave way for development politics and to cut down communal politics, we are to prove that we are united despite being from dissimilar castes and communities. Let us challenge real forces that promote communal violence and hatred, rather than blindly following the so-called self-acclaimed protectors of secularism.

(Posted on blog on 19 March, 2015)

□

Directive Principle, 'Prohibition of Cow Slaughter' be Centrally Regulated

Directive Principles of state policy are not enforceable by any court; however the makers of the Constitution laid these guidelines to assure that free India becomes a just place for even the weaker section as well as for agriculture and animal husbandry. While the past governments paid heed to some of these principles viz. free education to all children aged 6 to 14 years and advancement of minority and backward sections, the area that craves for government's courtesy is the directive principle, 'The State shall endeavor to organize agriculture and animal husbandry on modern and scientific lines and shall, in particular, take steps for preserving and improving the breeds, and **prohibiting the slaughter of cows and calves** and other **milch** and draught cattle.' Many of us do not even know that there is no law that explicitly forbids consumption of beef and legislations governing slaughter of cattle vary from state to state. The country, where Hindus form the majority and for whom cow is a symbol of strength, generous giving, abundance of earthly life, and sacredness, embraces states that do not at all restrict slaughtering of cattle; we rank 5th in world in terms of beef creation and 1st in terms of exporting; now that is a clear breach of trust with Hindus. The story isn't old when a couple of senior IPS officers of the state of UP could trace a link between cow smuggling and funding of underworld and anti-national activities.

The concern which finds a due place in the Constitution of India is not a matter of worry for the politicians, may be since they are more anxious about minority votes. It is in the open; many states ban shipping of animals across state borders, but cows are regularly shipped to states with lesser or nil restrictions on slaughtering; several thousands of cow slaughterhouses operate in India, unlawful ones are at least ten times in number as compared to the legal ones. In the state of Andhra Pradesh, the brutality can be noticed with the fact that the state has only 6 licensed slaughterhouses; however more than 3000 of such places run unlawfully and produce thousands of metric tons of beef. Then are the perks associated with the production and exporting of beef; in the year 2012-13 export earnings from processed meat were close to INR 18, 000 crore. Isn't it weird that in a Hindu-dominant country, the food processing ministry had announced subsidies of INR 15 crore to modernize abattoirs? Then, while in Europe and Australia, stunning animals prior to their being slaughtered for food is a compulsory norm, India has no such norm, and backed by the demand of Gulf countries that insist on Halal meat, most of our beef production is without stunning, thereby meaning killing of a conscious living being.

Protectors of law are very well aware of the rampant abuse of animals during transport and slaughter; they are overloaded in trucks and are transported abruptly without food and water. I was speechless to witness a video showing some young men pinching the tail of a cow in such a manner that it was forced to move into a small car, post which was taken for slaughter and feeding. FIAPO, Federation of Indian Animal Protection Organizations, complains of letting off of vehicles carrying cattle by police officers thus cheering unlawful slaughter just for the sake of a few pennies. Aren't we then letting a person kill the faith and morality we have been carrying since ages? Let me share a few more numbers. According to India's livestock census, India consumes 300 million cattle, and 185 million sheep and goats every year. Despite setting up various committees and expert groups to look into the critical question of banning cow slaughter in India, we have been promoting schemes like Pink Revolution that provides subsidies and tax breaks to owners of slaughterhouses and exporters. The advocates of this law say that officially only buffalo meat, with 11 lakh tons of shipments in 2012-13, went out of the borders of India; however it is broadly known that abattoirs consider no difference between buffalo and cow, the latter being exported illicitly.

I can reiterate the words of our present PM who wanted a Green and White Revolution in India. The condition is warranting also because our total cattle population fell from 204 million to 199 million between the 1992 and 2007 livestock census. Isn't it shocking that in the state of UP where Uttar Pradesh Prevention of Cow Slaughter Act,

1955 bans slaughter of cows and considers the same as cognizable and non-bailable offence, more than 5, 000 cows are taken to unlawful slaughterhouses every month to be butchered? Same is the case with other states. Findings reveal that root cause of slaughter of milch cattle is the unnatural conditions under which animals are kept for milk production in urban areas, while economic necessity is the reason behind slaughter of dry animals. Way out can be what many other countries have followed, which is removal of cattle from cities and arranging milk supplies from rural parts of India. The same would also boost the development of cattle and dairy industries. Let me also quote the words of the Cattle Preservation and Development Committee appointed in 1947, which read as, *'This Committee is of the opinion that slaughter of cattle is not desirable in India under any circumstances whatsoever, and that its prohibition shall be enforced by law. The prosperity of India to a very large extent depends on her cattle and the soul of the country can feel satisfied only if cattle slaughter is banned completely and simultaneous steps are taken to improve the cattle, which are in a deplorable condition at present.'*

Isn't it undeniable then that there is a pressing need of a **central law** on the subject of slaughtering of cows, Goddess of Hindu groups, and superseding of all state laws with respect to slaughtering of cattle? A **department/ministry for cow protection**, functioning under the union government, can also be thought over. Provisions for maintenance and care of serviceable and unproductive cattle and for development of feed and fodder are desired; Gaushalas and Cattle Protection Societies and Salvage Centers be encouraged.

(Posted on blog on 9 January, 2015)

□

Abide by the Constitution, Streamline 'All' Faith Conversions

You can term this either as the basis of our existence or as the root cause of our varied opinions, but 'religion' will never lose its authority and influence. It many a time is so sensitive that thousands lose their lives owing to clashes and is sometime so immaterial that persons from same community do not think twice while slaying one another. Isn't it true that you can defame the father in the presence of his child, but the same child will become a rebellion in case you defame the religion he belongs to? Let us not fall into the argument of which religion is the firstborn or which one is the supreme. The makers of our Constitution explicitly gave freedom to pursue any religion to the citizens, and we must all respect the ideology. This is something that makes us stand a step ahead and be proud to call India our motherland. Also true is the fact that genuine faith conversion is neither prohibited under the Constitution nor in any of the laws. But what is authentic and what constitutes to being unauthentic is a tough question to answer in the absence of any national law on faith conversion. Lured and forceful conversions have happened in the past, the irony however is that they were not conversed in the Parliament as was the Agra one since they saw Hindus convert their faith. Does this not mean that we have let one of the most penetrating issues disturb communal harmony and hold real development?

In the present scenario, a person accused of forceful or lured faith conversion is booked under the Sections 295A (Deliberate and malicious acts, intended to outrage religious feelings), 153A (promoting enmity between different groups), and 505(2) and 505(3) (Statements creating or promoting enmity, hatred or ill-will between classes) of the IPC.

The Agra dispute is being handled in the same manner and now when the converts are alleging that they were misled and lured with perks, the 'reconversion' or 'home coming' drive of Hindu groups has come under observance. Was it so wicked on the part of the organizers to bring back Muslims under the shadow of Hinduism, who at some point in time in the history had converted to Islam? And if this is, why isn't there an explicit law of the land that should aptly differentiate between what is allowed and what isn't? It is so uncomplicated to bring any of the organizers under the heat of law post any religious conversions by claiming that the converts were coerced or were enticed to change their faith. Let us get real please, and a bit more prudent. How will someone determine as to whether the converts of Agra knew what the ceremony meant, and who can deny the possibility that they changed their statement owing to political and religious pressure? Secularism in India is more of anti-Hindu now rather than anti-communal.

The worst part was the warning by one of the opposition leaders that the Agra instance can result in communal riots. One thing is sure, political groups, and especially regional ones, backed by either of the communities/castes will use this as a way to gain mileage and rarely will anyone think of honest endeavors to check such setbacks in future. The talk of the town now is the upcoming event announced by the VHP which is likely to see as many as 6, 000 non-Hindus reconvert their faith to Hinduism. The duty of the state is to validate whether the scheduled episode has bona fide consent of probable converts and if this is the case, then deploying policemen to stop this happening in the name of likely disturbance of communal accord is unlawful. Haven't we heard of instances when the Christian missionaries lure underprivileged rural residents with money and other perks for persuading them to embrace Christianity? Who funds these associations, or for that matter, aren't some Madrasas being funded by illicit elements to encourage Hindus part with their faith? But since the present incident relates to alleged defeat of the minority, the Parliament has been made a combat zone by opposition legislators.

Uniformity is what we need when it comes to such a sensitive substance. Conversions backed by coercion and/or luring have to be curtailed sooner than later. Plus, to make it tough to blame the organizer post honest conversions, reporting of any such incident to the local authority, say one month in advance, should be a compulsory norm. It cannot be denied that reporting of such faith conversions in advance may invite harsh attempts aimed at the probable convert from people of his/her present faith. The need to frame a well-defined conversion law, able to prevent any forcible/lured faith conversion and misuse of allegations for violence over conversion organizers, is indispensable. Religion is a complex subject-matter and cannot be handled by dirty and aimless protests in the Parliament. A pure secular nation, India, cannot allow any funds from overseas flowing with a view to disturbing the sacred balance of communal accord. In the same context, let us also not disremember that the essence of our Constitution lies in freedom to any religion, hence faith conversions should not be prohibited, rather be streamlined. Be it any political party in the center or in the state/s, and be the same 'secular' to the core, any infringement with the fundamental right to freedom of religion should be curbed.

Constitution is supreme and the basis of our democracy. The makers had the wisdom of considering what was to be made a part of this binding literature, but can we deny that they too were political men, had some ambitions, and also the immense pressure to make all castes and communities contented. Isn't Article 25 (1) of the Constitution, which says 'Subject to public order, morality and health and to the other provisions of this Part, all persons are equally entitled to freedom of conscience and the right freely to profess, practice and propagate religion', an evidence of same. The word 'propagate' means 'spread and promote widely', which boils down to inducing people convert faith. While a few true secular leaders opposed the inclusion of this word, the Congress was least bothered. This was something that accorded extended life to what had happened during the Mughal reign and the British rule, where Hindus were converted to Islam and Christianity. Many backward and poor Hindus of Andhra Pradesh, Bihar, Jharkhand, and Chhattisgarh have been lured using foreign funds by Christian missionaries and mass faith conversion ensued. Hindu groups, with lacking means, were helpless to avert.

Vote-bank politics and the command procured by regional political parties will never make it possible to get rid of the word 'propagate' from the Constitution. But, when Hindu groups are legitimately bringing converted Hindus back to their faith, allegations of luring and coercion are baseless. And to avert any real luring and coercion, we would first need to collate the data as to how many Hindus were decoyed to convert by the Christian or Muslim groups, and then deploy such labors that can forbid these episodes in the future. A law on faith conversion has to be wide-ranging, superseding any and every of such law presently adopted by states, which however are being disputed in the Apex Court for allegedly being unconstitutional, and above all, the same has to be equitable and justifiable to all religions. Never forget that religion and belief in God is an attribute which makes a person lead a path towards righteousness and development of all. When the same is disrupted or is taken away by illicit endeavors, the person loses any vision towards growth or empowerment. For a poor family, which is vulnerable to such acts, the only motivation and strength is their religion and God. Protection of same, hence, is the foremost duty of the rulers. Political men should learn that religion is to relish and worship, not a weapon to get hold of power.

In the end, let me also cite a petition which is presently under consideration in the honorable Supreme Court and requests for extension of Scheduled Caste status to Dalit converts who have embraced Christianity or Islam. Isn't that understood that if the converts were honest enough during conversion, they would have known that nothing as 'untouchables' exists in Islam or Christianity? And if the only reason for conversion, as they allege, was the appeal of the other faith, why then look for pity statuses and perks post conversion? It is evident that a fraction of converts to Islam either hunt for the freedom of multiple marriages or the state-backed benefits extended to Muslim or Christian minorities. Tell me, what shall be the underlying aim for faith conversion?-Of course, to be more near to the so-called Almighty of the new faith. Why then look for added perks in the society. A central law on faith conversion, as discussed above, must consider this and should bar any perks to converted ones which are available by the grace of Constitution or laws of the land to the inherent ones. It is evident that unless a vigorous law checks such dishonest transformations, India would witness more and more conversions and ensuing damage of national uprightness, especially Hinduism.

(Posted on blog on 14 December, 2014)

□

Scuffling with the Misfortunes of Destiny – Kashmiri Pandits

19th January 1990, it has been 25 years now that thousands of them escaped what could have been their brutal assassination in the name of Jihad and supremacy. If you want to feel the endless pain of this cluster, allow someone to displace you from your house, take over your possessions that you collected with immense labor, and then make you struggle to get started from the scratch. Promises of the government and condolences of politicians and social activists are not even a trivial support for someone who faces the challenge of re-establishing the family from the very basics. We have been assuring the population of better education and health services, but what about the ones who are clearly the sufferers of displacement in the name of faith and terrorism? Right to property, right to dignified and safe life, all become baseless for people who become victims of forced migration and harassment. What on earth have our governments been doing when it is evident that Kashmiri Pandits, who constituted almost 15 percent of the valley population until 1947 and 5 percent until the year 1981, are now a mere part of the valley with some 800 families, which live in a physical, mental and social trauma, without even a moment of what we call 'dignified life'. Live a day with that fear, that harassment and that denouncement, and then will we realize the agony of those who are being consoled since decades but real measures for their advancement remain far than achieved.

Kashmir valley has been a place of conflicts since long and past governments have cared about a community that form the majority, yet even their ruin is known to all. Subsidies and perks have moved to the valley from New Delhi, but have we been able to deliver peace and economic expansion so far? And greater is the distress of this small cluster which remains beside the point for both the state government of J&K and the central government. What we call as the 'worst massacre in Kashmir history', the 19th day of January 1990 saw thousands of Kashmiri Pandits flee from their homes to escape death. While the nation was preparing for an economic recovery in 1991, many of the families, displaced from the valley, were on roads with no hopes of recovery. The past governments could not realize that the state which has always been referred to as 'Heaven on Earth' has turned into a graveyard of innocents and hell for the inhabitants. Though misfortune has seen no difference between a Hindu and a Muslim in the valley, the sorrow of Pandits has remained concealed and unheeded, owing to political and vote-bank equations. The faith that has been the occupant of the valley since ages and even prior to when the Muslim rulers motivated heavy influx of Muslims is today weak and vulnerable to severe troubles, even in the presence of heavy military shield.

Time has seen coerced conversion of Kashmiri Hindus, and literature is flooded with all kinds of brutalities on this group only because the state has abundance of Muslims and also of people who in the name of Jihad want the valley free from Hindus and even from the dominance of the Indian government. The resolution passed by the United States Congress recognizes that since 1989 more than four lakh Kashmiri Pandits were either murdered or forced to move from their ancestral homes. Extremely worried over the cases of mishaps by the Indian army in Kashmir that sees Muslims being harmed for no valid reason, why aren't the governments equally concerned about the rapes, murders, and other violent activities to which Hindu civilians are subject to in the name ethnic cleansing of the valley by terror outfits like JKLF, Hezb-ul-Mujahidin and others? And the irony is that even the Muslim populace, who are not in consensus with this so-called cleansing, face similar cruelty from terror groups. While talking of the notion of all-inclusive development and work prospects for all, the governments often overlook apparent victims; however they deserve the courtesy of rulers prior to all other benefit-seekers. When we talk of reformed way of living for Indians, add Kashmiri Pandits to the top of the list of wounded and deprived.

It is crystal clear. If you are honest rulers, have the guts of executing the promises you make to the general public, give them their homes back, return them peace and their very right to dignified and safe life. The position of the J&K government formation is unclear but the verdict of voters is not the same this time, and the center is being managed with a new energy and a much greater devotion. In this light, the Kashmiri Pandits are hoping a change of circumstances in the valley and the return of their right of living in their ancestral houses. In the past six decades, Kashmiris, Hindus as well as Muslims, have seen mass killings, with lakhs of them losing lives, becoming widowed and orphans, and thousands missing from homes and while in custody. Sh. Atal Bihari Vajpayee, one of the most capable rulers India have seen, had promised peace and safe homes to Kashmiri Pandits in 2003, and also reassured them of a rehabilitation policy. The dream of this veteran leader remains unattained due to political troubles, and is a challenge for the new wing of the BJP. The manifesto of the BJP for 2014 general elections talked about 'return of Kashmiri Pandits to the land of their ancestors with full dignity, security and assured livelihood'. It also promised good governance, infrastructure, education, healthcare, job opportunities and better quality of life to the people of the valley. It is time to deliver, fulfill the promises made.

To bring peace, giving away the right over Kashmir, which has been India's jewel since centuries, is like paving way for invaders to ask for more provinces; Kashmir is the part and also a responsibility of India, making it a safe and developed place is an undeniable liability. Kashmiri Pandits have been overlooked for a long time now; their rehabilitation is much-urgent, an obligation to be pursued sooner than later.

(Posted on blog on 19 January, 2015)

□

If within the Limits of Law, No Attempt to Save the Religion is Immoral

'Dharma' is the basis of our existence. Even if you deny the actuality of God, you cannot rebut the moral values as advocated by our religious books. 'Bhagavad Gita' or 'Quran' are a guide not just for religious practices but also for our social behavior, our understanding of right and wrong and our sustainable growth. These holy books teach us the value of morality and justice. Religion in no way divides humans; however it is the misconception of translators that many a times leads to communal differences. Nevertheless, Dharma must be followed and the teachings must be adhered to. Plus, any illicit endeavors to harm the Dharma shall be retaliated cogently.

'Love Jihad' is what they have termed it and is what that has become a sensitive concern in the parts of the U.P. The two words combine to present a delicate form of Jihad, which boosts men of the Muslim community to target girls belonging to non-Muslim communities for conversion to Islam. Herein, the young girls are approached lovingly and many a times sympathetically with a view to reassuring them to part with their religion and adopt Islam. The instance when the non-Muslim girl of Karnataka married a Muslim boy of Kerala was when Love Jihad was accorded a solemn thought. The police said 'Love Jihad was a campaign with no substance'.

In no way am I attacking any religion; however I am concerned about the religion I belong to. And I wholeheartedly believe that our (India's) religious multiplicity is what that makes us feel proud and contented. I am, however, concerned when I hear people alleging that the actions of RSS and other Hindu-backed associations are dividing the nation on communal lines. Is the attempt of the RSS wherein their cadres would tie 'Rakhis' on the hands of Hindus with a vow to safeguard the religion against any illicit attacks an unethical or unlawful measure? The recent incident of Meerut should not be hyped; however the underlying issues must be resolved.

It is to be remembered that the Kerala police in October 2009 reported that there were strong reasons to suspect concentrated attempts to convince non-Muslim girls for conversion to Islam post they fell in love with a Muslim boy. Now, there is a very thin line of demarcation between 'conversion to Islam' and 'organized conversion to Islam'. We very well know that voluntary religious conversion is legal in India; however what would you say about an organized setup wherein Muslim boys are encouraged by community leaders to deceive non-Muslim girls by offering them pity perks like false love, corrupt money, or better prospect of finding real God?

Love sees no boundaries and serves as a pure bonding between two humans. Marrying person of a dissimilar community is not forbidden in India; however no religion can have the authority of cheering organized love and conversion. This is what the RSS realized and thus has come up with a campaign of tying Rakhis so as to make certain that the Hindus are not enticed by untrue representations. The endeavor of the RSS is well within the limits of law and hence cannot be alleged as immoral. It is just that a few of our politicians do not escape any chance of appeasing particular groups. Now, sensible and prudent verdict of the common man is much-needed.

(Posted on blog on 15 August, 2014)

☐

Ill-advised by Extremists, Muslim Youth in Grip of Sorrow

He was, I can't say whether he will resume this again, an aspiring engineering student, his father is a doctor, though a shattered man now, and his sister is a doctor too in one of the renowned hospitals of Mumbai. Along with Areeb, three other men from more or less same backgrounds fled to Iraq to fight for the terror outfit Islamic State of Iraq and Syria (ISIS), after they were persuaded by the radicalism and so-called Jihad. Isn't this something similar to extending money to Ponzi schemes in want of unsure returns? This is however somewhat unalike because the persuaders promise these 'heavenly returns' not in this world, but in the lap of so-called terror-loving Almighty. Easy it is to control the mind and emotions of the youth by telling them that members of their community are being beleaguered around the world, that their sisters and daughters are being molested, that westernization would mark an end to their following, and that bringing every human under one shadow is the direction of Allah. Otherwise why would a young doctor, with a loving wife and dependent parents tie a bomb around his waist and along with him would kill hundreds of other guiltless humans? Now is this not similar to those self-styled God-men who relish the best of material perks and in the sidelines ask pupils to stay away from amusement? We have so many cases and exposures to learn from.

Prior to Areeb's move to Iraq, they say that he shunned his cellphone, condemned her sister for watching TV, which according to him promoted nudity and filthiness, and even left a letter censuring his family. A few days later he and his friend called home to ratify that they have picked up arms for the support of ISIS and also claimed that even their families would go to 'heaven' for their deeds. The heaven that Areeb observed then was a disguised place where youth from distinct parts of the world were educated on dark side of Jihad and were motivated to fight against all others who are 'dissimilar', even if they are blameless. The stimulus, however, disgraced in a few days and this young man from Mumbai realized that this may be a pathway of death, but surely not of heaven. It then became pressing for the man to escape such unfounded acts and be a part of the same old world that promotes education, patriotism and harmony. Lucky enough, Areeb is back in the town, his father thanking the Indian government and the NIA, but those three men from the same Kalyan in Mumbai and countless others from different parts of the world are bound to pursue the path of destruction, which I can bet all of them would have realized was the most ludicrous blunder of their lives. But once you are up for radicalism, there isn't any road for return; you die either as an outcome of counter action or due to internal rivalry/betrayal.

How does a country prosper or an economy nurture? No government alone can reap the fruits of betterment, hence individual labors are indispensable. Now those, not a part of nation-building, are keeping the settings unmoved, while many others are deteriorating the pace of development alleging that either their share is being curbed by others or this is a revenge for harassment that men from their community faced. Should I also then pick up an AK-47 and kill that person who disrespected my father when his bicycle hit the person's superfluous car? Justice is always hunted for by common men in the democracy from those rulers and adjudicators who are expected to check social and economic prejudice. Many a time uprightness is curbed but this does not allow anyone to harm those who had no role in the unjust. And in case you are so willing and sturdy to make the society an unbiased place, why not study law, administration, or for that matter be a part of the political structure, and then fetch justice which would not serve only your purpose, but will also prosper the lives of million others. The youth and others who abandon their social and economic accountabilities and purse the path of brutality and devastation aren't extracting any benefits for the members of their community, but are dragging them towards a dark future, a future where helpless widows and orphan children, with no economic agility, will be forced to pick weapons, hold bombs around their waists and destroy the present and future of many others.

The separatists in the J&K and many other fragments of the world have been talking of taking the men of their religion to the doors of prosperity and nimbleness. Why then all these terror-backed states are just homes of deaths, famine, rapes and social and fiscal volatility? Is the youth of India so dumb that we cannot assess the difference between two nations, India and Pakistan, the former where radicalism is curtailed and the latter where the same is endorsed; or for that matter, countries like U.S. and U.K. where religion is far superseded by human values and respect? Shouldn't the people of J&K question the philosophy and working mechanism of separatists and former CMs who have lots and lots of hate words to speak but had no valor to save the state from the ruins of flood? Are the dwellers of the state living in peace or is the noise of mortars and fires making them spend horrendous and sleepless nights? The young engineering student, Areeb is in the custody of the NIA and an FIR may be filed under Unlawful Activities (Prevention) Act. Other three men of Mumbai are living a disastrous life and may one day attain the 'death' as promised by their educators, but 'heaven and other heavenly pleasures' will never fall in their baskets. To Indian youth – India seeks your labors, your will and your love for the nation and its inhabitants. If you want to pursue any duty, pursue the one enlisted in our Constitution, the duty of serving the homeland.

It was and would never be the aim of any lawfully formed government to suppress the wellbeing of the minority community of India. Though the past governments shouted at the peak of their voices that secularism will be chased as directed by the Constitution but special perks and subsidies in the name of betterment hasn't helped, and even the minority realizes this. For sustainable growth, one cannot be 'dependent', but needs to be 'participative'. And does this word 'dependent' even sound honorable? Why not then be one of the pillars in the success of India, and for the same being an army man is not the only option, rather any economic activity, small or big, with bona fide commitment is what the nation demands. Lured by extremists and separatists, the youth can only be subjected to fatalities and setbacks. On the other side, however, is the road that though seeks labors but is full of contentment, peace and honor. This may be my personal view but is also the view of administrators of other countries and fiscal experts that presently India is one of the most favorable investment destinations around the world owing to the commitment of present rulers. Funds are coming and so are the opportunities, not just for a particular section, but for us all. A Muslim youth in Delhi, working as software engineer and a Muslim girl in the Indian army are examples to follow. Also the learning from Areeb's return is worth paying heed to. His indoctrination was through internet, followed by teachings of Quran for 20-25 days. 20-25 days! 20 days to make a vibrant and aspiring youth disremember lessons on harmony! Final call is yours, my friends.

I believe that everyone must be in agreement with the views expressed by Pope Francis on his return from Turkey that he understands why Muslims were offended by many in the West who automatically equated their religion with terrorism. He also suggested of a global denunciation of terrorism by Islamic leaders, which will help majority of Muslim population. As far as I see this, unanimous voice in favor of peace by these leaders will also change perception of all towards Islam. Claiming that they aspire for community's good, Islamic leaders, be them the religious, political or academic ones must condemn any deeds aimed at inciting Muslim youth in favor of radicalism. It is sure that with an end to violence, the world will be a more secure, hence a prosperous place.

(Posted on blog on 1 December, 2014)

□

Syed Ahmed Bukhari, Stop Mixing Religion and Politics

I am writing not because I wanted a supervisor of the property of the Waqf Board, the Shahi Imam, Syed Ahmed Bukhari, to invite the flag-bearer of India in the ceremony that would see yet another appointment for the position of 'successor to Shahi Imam', but because the 'politics' involved herein is not what that the Indians thought of while voting in the 2014 general polls or legislative polls in Maharashtra and Haryana. Isn't it very obvious that to run your political career in a country like India, you just need to either blindly support one religion or suppress some other community without reasons? So, 'conflict of interests' with one or the other religions is what you need to relish the fruits of 'power'. To be a community leader, just drive back a politician who does not biasedly favor yours. Then ask your community to favor the leader who promises biased courtesies for your religion, and this goes on and on. We thought this would end with the subject-matter of development and inclusiveness, but some people rarely learn.

Honorable Delhi Court, in one of the cases against Syed Ahmed Bukhari, said, 'It is very surprising and shocking to see the police force not able to execute the NBW issued against Bukhari. Such inaction against Bukhari is intolerable.' This came because Delhi Police has been for years not able to arrest the accused, Syed Ahmed Bukhari, citing communal tension-Politics herein too. Let me tell you that an 'Imam' is an Islamic leadership position and the person entitled shall lead worship services and provide religious guidance. In case you are confused as to what the current Shahi Imam aimed at while promoting SP in the UP legislative polls and Congress in the recent general polls, try finding lessons on politics in religion and religion in politics. The main mosque of India, Jama Masjid, is the property of the Waqf Board and Imam Bukhari is just an employee of the Board, as ruled by the honorable Delhi High Court. And when Imam is all set to pass on the baton to the new generation, I believe that at least a respect was expected for the topmost position holder in the democratic republic of India.

But the Shahi Imam did not consider his words twice when he urged that the present PM is anti-Muslim and is responsible for riots, hence he cannot be invited to attend the ceremony at Jama Masjid on November 22. In the era, when the current rulers of India are putting all labors for inclusive growth, such cases tell that we can hardly overcome the bitterness of communal gap. Alleging the PM liable for massacre of Muslims, did the Imam notice what this message means to the people of this community, living not only in India, but even in other countries? Interestingly, the son-in-law of Syed Bukhari was an MLC of Samajwadi Party, who resigned when Bukhari accused Mulayam Singh Yadav for being unfavorable to Muslims. The Imam, shouldn't we believe, has more to do with politics than religion? Then for this sake should he have not respected the peers? And when he says that the entire Muslim community is unsupportive to the PM, I wonder who casted the votes in Gujarat and general elections when the BJP secured seats in even Muslim-majority constituencies? For sake of power, please stop mingling religion and politics, else I am sorry we will have no other option than to look beyond religion.

To the news houses, yet another 'hot topic' has emerged for prime time debates. The leaders, from each side, are justifying their stands; however no gain is being secured by the country. Aiming for cleaner Ganga, financial inclusiveness, bettered industrial sector and such other constructive goals, the Indian PM, I believe, should pay least heed to matters that are initiated with the intent of gaining communal appreciation and nothing more. To some extent, religion and politics have been separated from one other by the Indian voters in the recent polls; however much more of such verdicts are needed for complete parting. Asking for Modi's apology, who has been adjudged blameless by the SIT, on what happened in the state of Gujarat in 2002, the religious leader must, prior to anything else, co-operate with the police and the Court for the case pending in his name. To news houses-Indians' aspirations have taken a shift and so is much-needed from you all in case we want the youth to witness a prosperous tomorrow.

To general public-Our religious sentiments do not run the economy, a capable administrator does this job; hence your support for the right is sought for.

Lastly, to the person; who disrespected the democratically elected Prime Minister of India, a leader holding primary Constitutional position; India and Indians' would not raise the value of any such misdeeds, and to promote your political and religious career, better shift to a place wherein the citizens approve such detrimental views. It is clear that the political acceptance within your community, your father Abdullah Bukhari, carried when he managed to mobilize people to vote out Congress government of Indira Gandhi, lacks in you, but for the same, India cannot allow you to burn the fire of communal hatred or to disrepute a leader chosen by the mass. No right to freedom of speech can tolerate this.

(Posted on blog on 31 October, 2014)

□

Are They Warning, or Are They Planning For Riots?

Either the words of our so-called secular leaders are meaningless, or they mean a lot. The general elections of 2014 have been a spectator to baseless allegations, absurd announcements, and above all unabashed warnings. It is an established fact now that the polls of 2014 are 'for-Modi' or 'against-Modi'. Political groups other than the BJP have no agenda except for warning the general public of the aftereffects of Modi's win. And, these aftereffects as predicted by the leaders of Congress, SP, BSP, JD (U), and TMC are a forbidden way to threaten people. Such absolute shame of our political structure and the measures adopted by leaders to get hold of support could not have been foreseen by the Constitution makers.

What does the Congress leader, Rahul Gandhi mean when he foresees mass killings in case the Modi-led government comes into the picture? On what basis are the leaders of distinct political entities declaring Narendra Modi as the person accountable for what happened in 2002? Have our leaders disregarded the findings of the Special Investigation Team set up by the Supreme Court that confirms that the then CM of the state had no mala fide role whatsoever? To fetch support and to get hold of power, our political leaders have crossed every probable limit of humanity as well as governance. And when these leaders foretell the consequences of Modi's win, they seem to be preparing of some conspiracy.

'The entire nation will see massive destruction, blood, and oppression if Modi comes in power'. This looks more like provoking certain groups to bring in unlawful state of affairs with a view to disturbing communal harmony. Can the Congress answer as to which group can be held responsible for the massacre in Rawalpindi in the month of March 1947 when 5000 Sikhs were slaughtered. Wasn't the Congress the most dominant group when millions of Sikhs, Hindus, and Muslims were massacred in 1947? Or for that matter the riots of 1969 in Gujarat, Moradabad riots in 1980, Nellie massacre in 1983, and the anti-Sikh riots of 1984. Which political party was administering the nation and was accountable for maintaining law and order when the nation witnessed these hardhearted days?

Declaring BJP and Narendra Modi as the ones who would promote communal detestation, the SP chief Mulayam Singh forgot to take a sneak peak at the facts and figures of the state which his party rules. As per the data presented by the union minister of state for home, RPN Singh, UP was the home to every third communal clash in the country during the first ten months of 2013. In 250 reported incidents of communal violence, 95 people lost their lives and 313 were injured. Ever since, UP has been the key center of communal revulsion under the reign of SP. Favoring a particular community, the state government is often charged with the allegations of backing the Muslims so as to ensure that the party does not lose the vote share. Who can forget the incident when the Allahabad High Court prevented the UP government from withdrawing cases against Muslims accused of terror outbreaks-An endeavor to appease Muslim voters.

The BJP, which has been declared as a clear winner of the 2014 polls by every pre-poll survey, would not just have to bear the pressure of the economic chaos created during the decade long ruling of the UPA, the party will also have to remain vigilant of anti-social elements who can bring in communal disturbances to deceive the general public. Is it so hard to foresee the fact that our political groups which have left no stone unturned to lure the minority castes can even go to the extent of harming the constituents of these communities to prove what they are warning people of? Politics is a dirty game. Surely, the hangover of being in power is tough to part with. The leaders who have disremembered the declining GDP and agricultural growth, and the ever-rising unemployment and inflation are stuck to just one factor-Secularism.

And these advocates of secularism know every trick of exploiting this factor and fetching votes. The constituents of the minority community have to move a step ahead to put an end to this fake secularism. Though you may retaliate this, however the fact is that the places with large number of members of the minority community have always been the center of conflicts. The vulnerability to disturbances at these places is high on the basis that the political as well as the community leaders have the requisite know-how to play with the minds and sentiments of the minorities. What can be done? Rather than being lured with pity favors, the general public has to pave way for all-embracing prosperity and harmony. Let us become the supporters of economic and social opulence. Let the tricky leaders know this time that we have learnt from past incidences and will not accept discrimination in the name of secularism anymore.

(Posted on blog on 5 May, 2014)

□

India, Together with the World

Is India Prepared Enough to Fight a Full-Blown War Against Terrorism?

Terrorism has been growing unabated the world over since the late 20th century. It has been used as a tool or weapon seldom by nation states but largely by ragtag terrorist outfits or ideologically-motivated groups of fighters against stable regimes in countries like Israel, India, USA and Russia. Of late, those who resort to terrorism call themselves freedom fighters or jihadists and are motivated by the ideological conviction of throwing occupation forces of colonial nations out of the lands that they claim belong to them by right.

They consider the USA their arch enemy and have been hitting and hurting the American interests and strategic assets practically all over the world, including the mainland US. Some of the terrorist outfits such as the Islamic State (IS) have, in a wide overreach of their unbridled ambition, declared the establishment of a Caliphate in parts of Syria and Iraq. The IS dreams of expanding its suzerainty over the entire West Asian and Gulf areas as well as several European, African, Mediterranean and South Asian countries, including sizable parts of India.

In their operations, they adopt medieval and barbaric practices like committing brutal and indiscriminate killings, rape, slavery, destruction and desecration of places of worship of conflicting and minority religious groups. They also enforce fastidious religious edicts dating back to medieval ages on pain of excruciating death or incapacitation not only against opposing armies but amongst the civilian population of the enemy countries as well. They have already committed numerous war crimes against humanity like ethnic cleansing, genocide, cultural cleansing, etc. The brutal onslaught of their inhuman terror attack is still on in full swing.

War on Terror

The War on Terror declared by the then US President George W. Bush in October 2001 following the devastating terror attacks on key targets in the US by Al Qaeda, for hounding out the Al Qaeda leaders and cadre and bringing the rule of the Taliban in Afghanistan to an end, was drastically toned down and brought practically to a halt, after success was partially achieved, by President Barack Obama in 2013. President Obama acknowledged that it was more pragmatic and prudent to selectively carry out military attacks on selected targets of terrorists rather than fight a global war on Terror as a tactic.

The US and its allies are currently engaged in a fight against Al Qaeda and the Taliban in Afghanistan. USA's ally Pakistan has not, however, been fully committed in the fight against the Taliban and Al Qaeda and has been doing far from enough to restrain and control the assorted groups of terrorists much to the chagrin of the US. Separately, the US, along with its NATO and non-NATO allies, has been fighting a war in Iraq and Syria since 2013 against the IS in addition to a war against the regime of Syrian President Bashar al-Assad. Russia has, in a show of defiance to the US dominance in the region, come out in support of President Assad and joined the fray by mounting intensive aerial attacks against IS in Syria, causing immense damage to the enemy.

Defence Preparedness

Defence preparedness must be a country's topmost priority as it is critical for the very survival of any nation state. In this context, given India's geographical location and the complex nature of its political relations with its neighbours, especially China and Pakistan, our country is required to be on the alert all the time. After attaining independence in 1947, India has already fought five bitter wars with Pakistan and China. While some were won by us, the others were either inconclusive or downright disastrous. None of the wars brought the nation prosperity or material gain. They were not intended to.

Those were wars that we had to fight at enormous costs to defend the country's territory and save our nation's honour. Besides, the armed forces have to be on the alert practically all the time, with barely any let-up, on account of the countless numbers of border incursions, indiscriminate shootings from across the frontier without provocation, military conflagrations, skirmishes, flare-ups and standoffs likely to degenerate into warlike situations. Thus, high defence preparedness is an inescapable deterrent not only in conventional warfare but also in the war against terrorism.

The current defence budget of our country is a whopping Rs 250,000 crore. Moreover, the BJP-led NDA government has been giving topmost priority for the modernization of the armed forces, equipping the forces with the most modern weapons and equipment, refurbishing the ageing fleets of fighter aircrafts and warships and tweaking the DRDO for indigenous defence production. Notwithstanding the fact that India is not a superpower with an inexhaustible supply of resources to spend on the protection of its territory and strategic assets as well as the lives and property of its citizens at enormous costs, our country has been making steady progress in its defence preparedness.

Pakistan and Terrorism

Dismayed over its failure to take on India in traditional warfare, Pakistan considers terrorism a genuine weapon to be used for resolving its feud with India. Pakistan-occupied Kashmir has turned out to be a fertile ground for the breeding of terrorists. Uneducated and unemployed youth are recruited, indoctrinated and trained in carrying out terror attacks by Pakistan's intelligence agency and army. They infiltrate into India by crossing the border, under the cover of fire from Pakistani troops.

These terrorists are heavily armed with guns, explosives, fake Indian currency, etc supplied by the ISI and the Pakistani army. They establish contacts with the disgruntled separatist elements and mercenaries in the Kashmir Valley, with whose help they manage to spread on to different parts of India. The aim of these jihadist elements is to carry out terror attacks, kill or maim innocent people and cause damage to the political fabric of the country. Destabilizing the political system of India and creating chaos in the orderly life of its citizens are the goals of the terrorists.

Objective of Terrorism

The target of a terrorist is not a professional army nor its objective victory in a war. The target is the civilian population, and the aim is to make them freeze into inaction and make the nation bleed. A series of explosions is carried out in a metropolitan city within a short span of time, causing the death of scores of defenceless and vulnerable people in a densely populated area, thus rudely interrupting and throwing the daily routine of the survivors of the mayhem out of gear. The idea is to show off the ability of the security forces to protect the citizens of the country in poor light.

For instance, a commercial airliner is hijacked, and hundreds of passengers are held captive and demand for the release of some militants held in a high-security prison are put forward. The entire nation plunges into gloom and uncertainty and wonders what is going to happen next. Irrespective of the final outcome of the standoff between the terrorists and the law-enforcing agencies, the tension and uncertainty created by the incident are what the terrorists want to achieve in the long run. The release of the incarcerated militants is a short-term goal. Similarly, on the eve of festivals and national holidays, people are advised by the police authorities to avoid crowded areas, be alert and watch out for suspicious-looking persons lurking around and suspicious-looking objects lying about.

The need to be on a perpetual state of alert causes the joy and euphoria of hanging around in the public fizzle out and render the festive atmosphere fall flat like a cola without the fizz. Public places surcharged with an extremely sanitized atmosphere, and crawling security agencies, in the uniform or plainclothes, are the last places that one wishes to visit on a holiday and spend quality time in the company of family or friends. When the holiday is finally over, instead of reliving moments filled with fun and frolic and looking for doing it again, one heaves a sigh of relief and shudders at the thought of the horror that could have resulted if things had gone wrong in case of a terror attack, which was very much on the radar of possibility but mercifully did not occur.

Prime Minister Modi's Initiatives

No sooner had he been elected as the Prime Ministerial candidate of BJP in the 2014 Lok Sabha elections, than Narendra Modi demonstrated his proactive stance in mending fences with Pakistan. He invited the Prime Minister of Pakistan along with Heads of other member countries of SAARC to his inauguration. In the one-to-one meeting that he had with Nawaz Sharif, he made it abundantly clear that his Government would give no quarter to acts of terror on the Indian soil by Pak-trained militants. He also insisted on the expeditious trial of the terrorists involved in the attacks carried out in Mumbai in 2008.

Simultaneously, he made a positive gesture by agreeing to host talks between the two countries at the level of Foreign Secretary. This was followed up by another pro-active measure by his agreeing with Nawaz Sharif in his meeting in Ufa, Russia, to host talks on terrorism at the level of the National Security Advisers of the two countries in August this year. Due to the recalcitrant behaviour of Pakistan, the talks did not materialize on either occasion. This was entirely because of the obduracy of Pakistan, which was not willing to discuss terrorism and was keen on the leader of its delegation being allowed to meet the Kashmiri separatist leaders before the scheduled talks commenced.

India would not allow Pakistan under any circumstances to cross the new red lines, talks or no talks. There has resultantly been a standoff on India's peace initiatives. To make matters worse, Pakistan has been lambasting India for allegedly instigating and abetting acts of terror in Balochistan! Pakistan's NSA, Sartaj Aziz, went to the extent of threatening India with Pakistan's nuclear weapons.

Pakistan in a Bind

On account of the fact that Pakistan had already carried out 192 ceasefire violations until July 29 this year along the international border in Jammu and Kashmir resulting in significant civilian and defence casualties, Chief of Army Staff General Dalbir Singh Suhag pointed out that a very high level of operational preparedness at all times had become part of India's strategy as there was recognition that the swift, short nature of future wars was likely to offer limited warning time. Meanwhile, his Pakistani counterpart threatened India with 'unbearable damage' in the event of a war.

Notwithstanding Pakistan's brandishing the threat of a nuclear attack from time to time, India has already demonstrated its capability of striking at the terror elements that take refuge in other countries, by successfully carrying out a short and swift commando operation in the jungles of Myanmar earlier this year. This has resulted in Pakistan feeling all the more threatened of the terror network that it has been assiduously building on its territory coming under a similar deadly attack by Indian forces.

A measure of tremendous importance taken by Prime Minister Modi was to formally conclude and finalize the Land Border Agreement with Bangladesh as this measure would enable the authorities to monitor the situation of infiltration of undesirable elements into India – a vital step in the war on terrorism. The cyber laws need to be tightened, and punishment for violation or infringement made harsh by the government to ensure that terrorists do not succeed in using the internet and social media for propagation or recruitment purposes.

Addressing Global Terrorism

In his recent visit to the US in September this year, Narendra Modi had meetings with US President Barack Obama, British Prime Minister David Cameron and French President Francois Hollande, and they discussed global terrorism, among other things. He pointed out in these meetings as well as his address at the UN that terrorism was a global phenomenon that had an adverse impact on practically every country without exception. And no country was immune to this threat, which India had been battling for four decades now. Modi also pointed out that the time had come for the international community to speak with one voice on this issue and adopt the long pending Comprehensive Convention on International Terrorism, which had been delayed because of the disagreement on the definition of terrorism. Modi's views were met with agreement from his interlocutors.

Pakistan's Counter-Charge

Pakistan has claimed that it has handed over to the UN Secretary General dossiers purportedly containing details of alleged Indian interference and also support for terrorism in Balochistan and Karachi as well as the links between its security and intelligence agencies and the Tehrik-e Taliban Pakistan, especially in FATA. Pakistan's representative at the UN accused India of using the "terrorism bogey" for stalling the bilateral dialogue between the two countries.

Rubbishing Pakistan's four-point formula for peace, External Affairs Minister Sushma Swaraj asserted earlier it was ready to discuss all the issues if the neighbouring country addressed "just one" point of ending terrorism emanating from there. She also referred in her address to the perpetrators of 26/11 Mumbai attacks who have been roaming around freely in Pakistan and urged the world community to ensure that countries providing finances, safe havens and arms to terrorists "pay a heavy price".

People's Role in the War

While India government is thus fighting its case against terrorism at the international fora, the people of the country would do well not to lose track of their own role in the ongoing war on terrorism. Eternal vigilance is the price that every nation has to pay for liberty. Unless the people are attuned to the developments in this regard on the international front and are psychologically prepared to play their part, the government's efforts in this regard would remain incomplete. The responsibility that weighs with the people assumes greater significance because of the fact that the onslaught of the terrorists has dangerous religious connotations capable of causing a rift in the society along communal lines.

Hence, for the common man the need of the hour is to be vigilant and combine it with the ability to identify the troublemakers without deliberately offending the susceptibilities of the peaceful and law-abiding citizens of any of the communities. It would be a good idea to form area-wise citizens' peace committees to act, strictly in coordination with law-enforcement agencies and not on their own as loose cannons, to act as the eyes and ears of the said agencies and report cases of suspicious activities of strangers or residents suspected of involvement in cases of inciting violence, money laundering or such unlawful activities.

Regular meetings of police authorities with community leaders and representatives of political parties could help avert instances of irresponsible behaviour by irascible elements, inflammatory speeches, etc. Local friendship associations could be formed with the participation of youngsters from all communities to forge a healthy understanding between the communities. It must be ensured that religious festivals and functions are peacefully organized to avoid situations where potential terrorists could cause trouble and create explosive situations.

Contingency plans should also be put in place for managing the situation in case of a terrorist attack, without allowing rumours to spread and the situation to get out of control. These are but a few of the baby steps that members of every residential area should be able to adopt. Above all, complacency should be nixed and replaced by eternal vigilance.

Are We Doing Enough?

No amount of preparation is enough to keep such a large country as India with a huge population, given the idiosyncrasies of the system and the society, out of harm's way all the time. But all of us can rest assured that the current BJP-led NDA government is closing the gaping holes in the system and chinks in the defence armour. Bits and pieces are falling in place in our country's preparations, slowly but steadily. And surely, we will overcome the odds and win the war. There is no choice.

(Posted on blog on 29 October, 2015)

□

The Highs and Lows of India-Pakistan Relations

Pakistan's shenanigans leading to the last minute cancellation of the National Security Adviser-level meetings with India, which had been scheduled for end-August this year, portended the fate of the negotiations and were a part of the high voltage drama that preceded the ominous denouement. Pakistan's announcement, calling off the talks, came neither as a surprise nor as a shock. India had already called Pakistan's bluff when it made the ground rules for the talks abundantly clear. India would not acquiesce to the importunate demands of Pakistan for the expansion of the scope of the talks beyond terrorism and for its envoy to be allowed to meet the Kashmiri separatist leaders during his visit to Delhi for the talks.

Pakistan called off the talks purportedly on the grounds that talks, if held on India's "preconditions", would serve no purpose, making it obvious to India and the rest of the world that the only "purpose" it had in mind was the appropriation of the whole of Kashmir, part of which has already been under its forceful occupation. Pakistan would be ready for talks at the NSA-level or, for that matter, at any level, only if it is convinced that the talks centered around what it considers as the "core issue" of all talks between the two countries viz. Kashmir.

Terrorism as a Tool

Ironically, talks or no talks, Pakistan considers the use of terrorism as a low-intensity weapon fair and square. Whenever India has protested against acts of terrorism orchestrated on its soil by its Western neighbour and ceasefire violations by the latter's troops, Pakistan has turned the table on India by feigning to be the real victim of the aggression and terrorism. Divided by the Shia-Sunni religious schism that has fuelled a spate of mindless violence with alarming regularity, which has already claimed the lives of thousands of its own people, Pakistan has been a fertile breeding ground of ragtag outfits with an extremely narrow religious orientation and unbridled political ambitions.

Such militants have regularly and frequently trained their guns against India with aid and assistance from Pakistan's Inter-Services Intelligence (ISI) agency and army. After infiltrating into India and creating mayhem and death by striking at vulnerable civilian targets, the terrorist elements sneak back to the safe haven of Pakistan, where they lie low till they embark on the next round of assault on Indian targets. Pakistan has not hesitated to accuse India of instigating and abetting terrorist activities in Balochistan and being the perpetrator of the border violations.

Kashmir-centric Policy

Pakistan has never shied away from thumping its chest over its nuclear-power nation status and daring India to use its military might against it. This has been the pattern of events, marked by Pakistan's unhelpful and unacceptable response to initiatives by India to discuss outstanding issues between the two countries. It is evident that Pakistan's policy about India has been simple – Kashmir-centric. It is hardly interested in easing of trade restrictions or the improvement of people-to-people relations, like in the consular, sport and cultural fields. Any reference by India to the export of terrorism by Pakistan meets with stiff resistance and negation from the latter. Furthermore, Pakistan has not hesitated to vilify India of trying to act like a regional superpower against its smaller neighbour.

Birth of Pakistan

The chequered relations between the two South Asian neighbours have witnessed many a conflict and upheaval over the years. The birth of the theocratic nation of Pakistan was the inevitable fallout of a diabolical plot foisted on India, poised on the threshold of independence from a colonial past of two hundred years. It was the outcome of an unholy nexus of the outgoing colonial forces, which were none-too-happy about the prospects of the emergence of a strong united India on the one hand, and fundamentalist religious elements of the sub-continent with a warped mindset that wanted to carve out a geographical niche where they could perpetuate their medieval religious dogma and procrustean value system, on the other.

The cataclysmic events that led to India's partition, marked the most tragic and portentous moment in the post-colonial history of India, having taken a toll of over a million lives and hundreds of thousands of broken homes, migration of over seventeen million people between the two countries and the consequent loss of home and hearth, constituting the most horrendous human tragedy of a colossal scale seldom witnessed in history.

Pak-occupied-Kashmir

Immediately after India's partition, Muslim tribal militias entered the border of the Princely State of Kashmir and tried to secure large areas for Pakistan. They were actively assisted in the bid by regular Pakistani troops. In the ensuing conflict, the Indian Army came to the rescue of the Princely State's forces at the request of Maharaja Hari Singh, who entered into the Instrument of Accession with India. After a prolonged war and protracted negotiations, a cease-fire agreement was signed by the two countries under the watch of the United Nations.

As per this agreement, Pakistan was required to withdraw its forces, both regular and irregular. It allowed India to retain a minimum strength of its forces in Kashmir to maintain law and order. Further, on the compliance of these conditions, a plebiscite was to be held to determine the future of the territory. However, Pakistan managed to takeover roughly two-fifths of Kashmir while India maintained the remaining three-fifths. There has been no headway on the Agreement since Pakistan has been unwilling to withdraw its troops although insistent on the plebiscite, which is a non-starter.

Replacement of Wars by Terrorism

Overall, the two neighbouring countries have fought three major wars and an undeclared war, besides being involved in numerous armed skirmishes and military stand offs. Till date, wars and armed conflicts have not helped in the resolution of the Kashmir logjam. Nor is either country looking at war as a viable option in the changed scenario of both the countries being in possession of nuclear weapons. The prospect of a nuclear warfare has worked as an effective deterrent on both the sides. There has consequently been a military standoff with no peaceful solution in sight to the vexatious problems bedevilling the relations between the two countries ever since their emergence as sovereign free countries in 1947.

Meanwhile, India has witnessed a steady stream of insurgents from across the border infiltrating into its territory with the sole aim of causing grievous body blows to the Indian polity. Notwithstanding the heavy casualties and damage caused to the smooth functioning of their economic and social life, the Indian people as well as the political and defence establishments, have emerged much stronger and successful in their resistance against the nefarious activities of the terrorists and covert military operations of the Pakistani intelligence and army.

Unresolved Issues and Disputes

Besides Kashmir, there have been other unresolved territorial claims by Pakistan such as over Siachen Glacier and Kori Creek that have been put on the back burner, with primacy accorded to the vexatious Kashmir issue. Pakistan has been stubborn in its demand for the resolution of the "core issue" of Kashmir, without relenting to withdraw from those parts of Kashmir which had been illegally occupied by its forces in 1947.

In 1949, close to one million Hindu refugees from the then East Pakistan, fleeing from extortion and persecution by the Pakistani authorities, had flooded West Bengal and the other Indian States. Following talks between Prime Minister Jawaharlal Nehru and his Pakistani counterpart Liaquat Ali Khan, a pact was signed between the two sides which provided for the return of hundreds of thousands of refugees to Pakistan. Furthermore, there are unresolved disputes over apportionment of water, arising from the Indus Waters Treaty, which governs the rivers flowing from India into Pakistan.

Terror Network

Frustrated by its failed military bids to forcibly capture Kashmir, and inability to drum up sustained international support for its case, Pakistan seems to have reconciled to the idea of keeping up the pressure on India, by mounting terrorist attacks under cover by its army. While playing the role of ally of Western powers in their war against global terrorism, and receiving billions of dollars worth of economic and military aid in return, it has been allowing scores of transnational terrorist outfits to thrive and flourish on its soil.

Some of the terrorist organizations created and nurtured by Pakistan include Hizb-ul-Mujahideen, Harkat-ul-Mujahideen (previously known as Harkat-ul-Ansar), the Haqqani network, Lashkar-e-Taiba, Jaish-e-Mohammad, and scores of other organizations. The aim of these organizations is to create mayhem and instability in India and its neighbourhood, terrorize the civilian population, make the State machinery vulnerable to change in perception of a terrorized civilian population and drain the resources of the State in the process of keeping its security forces perennially alert.

Former President of Pakistan Asif Ali Zardari acknowledged in July 2009 that the Pakistani government had "created and nurtured" terrorist groups with the aim of accomplishing its short-term foreign policy goals. An analysis published in 2008 by Saban Centre for Middle East Policy at Brookings Institution depicted Pakistan as the world's "most active" state sponsor of terrorism, including aiding groups. For the past so many years, Pakistan has aided quite a good number of terrorist groups, which have been fighting against India in Kashmir. Over and above this, it has also been a major sponsor of Taliban forces fighting the US-backed government in Afghanistan.

Acts of Terror

Pakistan could not reconcile to the good work being done by India in Afghanistan for the latter's stability in political, economic and social sectors. It could not accept an enhanced level of bilateral relations between India and Afghanistan and has been using every available opportunity by covert means to thwart the coming together of these two nations. The Indian embassy in Kabul became the target of a suicide bomb terror attack in July 2008. The US intelligence officials indicated that Pakistan's powerful Inter-Services Intelligence agency had planned the attack.

Although Pakistan tried to deny any responsibility, US President George W Bush reportedly confronted Pakistan's Prime Minister Yousuf Raza Gilani with strong evidence. Bush also warned Gilani that in the case of another such attack he would have to take "serious action". In May 2014, four heavily armed men carried out a terror attack on the Indian Consulate in Herat, Afghanistan, on the eve of Prime Minister

Narendra Modi's oath-taking ceremony to which Pakistan Prime Minister Nawaz Sharif had been invited. There was incontrovertible proof of ISI's involvement in that attack.

Similarly in December 2001, an attack on the Indian Parliament by four terrorists from Lashkar-e-Taiba and Jaish-e-Mohammad was foiled. This incident brought these two countries to the precipice of nuclear war. Moreover, an unsuccessful attempt was made on the Legislative Assembly of Jammu and Kashmir in November 2001 by terrorists trained by the ISI. In November 2008, 10 Pakistanis who were members of Lashkar-e-Taiba carried out a series of 12 coordinated shooting and bombing attacks, which lasted for four days across Mumbai. They killed 164 people and wounded at least 308.

Ajmal Kasab, the sole terrorist who was caught alive, tried and executed by hanging, was a Pakistani national. He had confessed to the involvement of the ISI in the dastardly attacks. These are some of the landmark acts of terror carried out by Pakistani terror outfits that are financed, trained and supported with materials and logistics by its intelligence agency ISI and Army. Despite copious documentary evidence of its involvement and complicity provided by India and widespread condemnation of these incidents by the international community, Pakistan is yet to act on India's complaints against the masterminds of the mindless violence, who are roaming freely in Pakistan.

Dawood Ibrahim, Hafiz Saeed and Zaki-ur-Rehman Lakhvi are some of India's most wanted terrorists who have taken shelter in Pakistan. In 1999, an Indian Airlines aircraft bound for Delhi from Kathmandu was hijacked to Kandahar in Afghanistan. Maulana Masood Azhar, a dreaded terrorist who later became the Head of Jaish-e-Mohammad, was released from their custody by the Indian security agencies in return for the passengers of the hijacked aircraft. Despite India's repeated requests for their extradition, Pakistan has either been saying that those terrorists are not in that country or complaining of lack of sufficient evidence to be able to take legal action against them. It is a clear case of Pakistan not wanting to act against its own interests. Currently, there are two Pakistani terrorists in Indian custody who are undergoing legal proceedings for infiltrating into India for carrying out acts of terror.

High Points

It has not always been a case of the Indo-Pak relations going south all the time. Occasionally, there have been high points too. There have been several attempts to improve the relations, like the Shimla Summit, the Agra Summit and the Lahore Summit. Confidence building measures were initiated like the Ceasefire Agreement of 2003 and inauguration of a train service by the name of Samjhauta Express between Lahore and Amritsar in 1976; and inauguration of a bus service between Amritsar and Lahore in 1999 by the then Prime Minister Atal Behari Vajpayee who travelled by the bus to Pakistan on its inaugural run. Another bus service connecting Amritsar with Lahore and Nankana Sahib was started in 2006.

Prime Minister Modi's Initiatives

Prime Minister Narendra Modi had invited the Heads of Government of all SAARC countries, including Pakistan, to his oath-taking ceremony in May 2014. He had a meeting with visiting Prime Minister Nawaz Sharif during which Pakistan was urged to cease terrorist activities in India, expeditiously conclude the cases of terrorists involved in the 2008 attacks in Mumbai and extradite all the terrorists wanted in India.

The meeting was to be followed by Foreign Secretary-level talks, which were cancelled by India at the last minute on account of Pakistan's unyielding obduracy about its envoy meeting Kashmiri separatist leaders. In July 2015, Prime Minister Modi met Nawaz Sharif in Ufa, Russia, on the sidelines of the Shanghai Cooperation Organization Summit. During the meeting, the two leaders agreed to have, among other things, talks at the levels of their National Security Advisers and Directors General of Military Operations. Narendra Modi also accepted an invitation to visit Pakistan in 2016 in connection with the upcoming SAARC Summit.

Pakistan's Failure

Despite the agreement between the Heads of both the countries that there would be official level talks, and the 2008 Mumbai terror attack trial would be expedited by Pakistan, there has been no headway in the de-escalation of tensions. On the other hand, relations have nosedived on account of incessant terror attacks from across the border since 2011 and repeated violations of the border by the Pakistan Army. The inability of Prime Minister Nawaz Sharif to take on the ISI-Army nexus and present a concerted case of Pakistan at talks is contributing to the continuance of the stalemate. In the meantime, a determined India has scored a marked victory by showing its adversary the new red lines, which are not to be crossed.

Strategy for Taking on Pakistan

India's efforts during the past seven decades to resolve outstanding issues bedeviling its bilateral relations with Pakistan have so far proved futile. During this period, the Government of India has tried out various policy measures and strategies to counter Pakistani terrorism and to bring to an end the undeclared war that its western neighbor has been waging on the borders right since its inception. Though none of them has yielded any positive results, the current NDA government has not given up hopes yet. However, Prime Minister Narendra Modi's initiatives to hold talks – the first time at Foreign Secretary level and then at NSA-level – were scuttled by Pakistan, both the times at the last minute and on technical grounds.

It has now become obvious that Pakistan's initial acceptance of the proposals for talks and the subsequent act of pulling out of the peace process by insisting on meeting separatist Kashmiri leaders and extrapolating the scope of the talks agenda, were part of a carefully choreographed put-on act for stealing India's thunder at the peace initiatives. Knowing well that it would have been pinned down on the mat at the negotiations on account of its complicity in hosting, promoting and equipping terror networks working against Indian interests, Pakistan took the easy way out and stayed away from the talks.

Till such time as another peace initiative is mooted by India, Pakistan would continue using cross-border terrorism as part of its asymmetric warfare. This strategy of Pakistan is untenable and has to be exposed and defeated by India with an effective counter-strategy of its own. Although neither India nor Pakistan could afford yet another war in the changing world of shifting geo-tectonic political plates, Pakistan's recalcitrance and obduracy pose a conundrum that India has the unenviable task of unravelling. Pakistan has already committed 192 ceasefire violations along the international border in Jammu and

Kashmir till July 29 this year at the considerable cost of civilian and defence casualties.

Chief of Army Staff General Dalbir Singh Suhag stepped in and pointed out that quite a high level of operational preparedness has now become a part of India's strategy as there is recognition that the swift and short nature of future wars are unlikely to offer adequate warning time. Although the Pakistani Army Chief has warned India of "unbearable damage" in the case of a war, implying a nuclear attack, Pakistan's braggadocio stood already exposed when it had threatened India earlier too, off and on, of its nuclear might. The last time this happened was in August this year when Pakistan's NSA, Sartaj Aziz, had said that Pakistan was a nuclear power capable of taking care of itself.

Pakistan's excessive reliance on nuclear weapons and repeated threats to use them flow from that country's internal weaknesses on account of rampaging unemployment, slow economic growth, surging religious intolerance, unabated rise in extremism, perennial conflict between various power centers and the country's inability to match India's strength in conventional warfare. Pakistan's threat to use nuclear weapons is, therefore, to be treated as no more than empty bravado on the part of a failed state, teetering on the verge of an implosion, fully aware of an assured massive retaliation bordering on that country's virtual obliteration, which it cannot afford. In the above backdrop, India should draw up a multi-dimensional strategy incorporating diplomatic, economic, political and military modes to rein in Pakistan from resorting to any adventurism against India and to impress upon it to do more to curb terrorist activities emanating from its soil.

Diplomatically, India should press on with negotiating the terms of peace through diplomatic channels and flag meetings of the army personnel, for a total cessation of border incursions and export of cross-border terrorism and handing over of the terrorist elements wanted in India. If that does not yield the desired results, India should not hesitate to downgrade Pakistan's mission to consular status and even oust Pakistan's ambassador. Meanwhile, India can also contemplate economic sabotage by making its trade ties with Pakistan conditional to the latter delivering on terrorism.

Politically, India should expose Pakistan by highlighting how the latter has been consistently sponsoring terrorist organizations, funding terrorist activities, spreading hatred between communities and violating ceasefire norms. By doing so, India would be in a position to change the narrative about this conflict and convince its international backers that there is no "India-Pakistan problem". Rather, it is only a Pakistan problem as this country has now become an epicenter of terrorism. And unless the international community accepts this truth and joins hands to force Pakistan to abandon terror, nothing is going to change.

Simultaneously, India can explore the scope for resorting to military options such as pounding of terrorist training camps in Pakistan-administered Kashmir and in other territories across the border, which is posing a serious threat to India's border zones by short and swift operations using drones and unmanned aerial vehicles (UAVs). This multi-dimensional strategy seems to be the only way to deter Pakistan from continuing with the undeclared war it has been waging against India for almost seven decades now.

(Posted on blog on 15 October, 2015)

□

Prime Minister Narendra Modi's Landmark Trip to Ireland and US

From Vedic Land to Ireland

What could be more befitting for an Indian Prime Minister who is proud of the rich spiritual and cultural heritage of his country than to be received in a country in the Western hemisphere to the chant of Vedic hymns by children of that country? The warm reception accorded to Narendra Modi at Dublin on September 23 with the graceful Vedic recitation by Irish children marked an indelible moment in the bilateral relations between India and Ireland. This in turn made the hearts of the 26,000 strong Indian community in Ireland and that of every patriotic Indian at home, swell with pride at the recognition accorded to the undisputed leader of the modern Indian nation as the proud inheritor of a glorious past of Vedic civilization.

This thoughtful gesture of his Irish hosts was accepted with his customary élan by the Indian leader with a quip about the champions of pseudo-secularism in India! Taking a dig at the so-called secularists back home, Narendra Modi said if anyone had welcomed him in India by reciting Sanskrit slokas as was done in Ireland, then pseudo-secularists would have created a hue and cry by raising questions concerning the country's secularism.

Bilateral Relations Reset after Long Hiatus

When Prime Minister Modi met his Irish counterpart Enda Kenny in Dublin, the two leaders reviewed the bilateral relations between their countries and exchanged views on regional and global issues of common interest. The visit was expected to provide an excellent opportunity to bolster the economic ties between the two nations as there are clear complementarities between their flagship programs, in particular, Skill India and Digital India, and Ireland's proven educational institutions. Other areas that have scope for closer cooperation for mutual advantage are information technology (IT), smart agriculture and food processing industry.

From the East Coast to the West

On the successful conclusion of his one-day Irish visit, Narendra Modi proceeded to the USA, primarily for addressing the UN General Assembly session at New York, a traditional annual exercise. He combined this with a visit to the Silicon Valley that he took by storm. He summed up the effect of his US visit as one that demonstrated "extraordinary depth and diversity" of India-US relationship and also said that a lot of ground had been covered during the visit.

Earlier, at the 'India-US Startup Konnect 2015' program and later at the 'Digital India' dinner at San Jose on September 27, he spoke of how a nation of 800 million youth below the age of 35 years was eager for change; had the energy and drive to pursue it; and, the confidence to achieve it. He also spoke of how when each of the 500 odd towns of India created ten startups and each of its 600,000 villages produced six small businesses, on a regular basis, the country would create an enormous economic momentum and generate a vast number of jobs. He also described the vision and the spirit behind the Digital India Program thus: to use technology to transform governance, eliminate barriers to opportunities, empower our citizens, deepen social change, impart scale and speed to development, improve delivery of services, customize services for specific groups, design affordable products for the poor and build a more sustainable future for our planet.

Above all, he said he saw technology as a means to empower the people and as a tool that bridged the distance between hope and opportunity; and that social media connected people on the strength of human values and not identities. Referring to the India-US partnership as the defining partnership of the century, he pointed out how it could advance and further prosper in the two countries – from creating infrastructure to services; from manufacture of products to human resource development as well as from supporting governments to enabling citizens and promoting digital literacy.

Digital India is a vast cyber world of opportunities open to a joint partnership. Welcoming the launch of the India-US partnership schemes that would support India's mission, he assured the assembled technology entrepreneurs that the schemes would not trap their creativity in long government procedures. He assured them that the Indian Government was already into reforming its regulations and processes with the aim of making it easier to start and do business in India.

Leaders of Industry

Prominent leaders of industry who called on the Prime Minister included Satya Nadella, CEO of Microsoft; Sundar Pichai, CEO of Google; John Chambers, Executive Chairman of Cisco; Tim Cook, CEO of Apple; and Paul Jacobs of Qualcomm. In the meetings with the leaders of industry, there was a clear discussion on how these iconic companies could contribute to the Prime Minister's flagship program, Digital India and Skill India. Tim Cook of Apple expressed great desire to be a partner in the Digital India initiative, which he thought was a transformation initiative and a game changer for India.

G4 Summit

PM Modi's program included his participation in the G4 Summit in which he mentioned that the reform of the Security Council within a fixed time frame had become an urgent and important task. He pointed out that the Security Council should include the largest democracies of the world, major locomotives of the global economy as well as voices from all the major continents. This particular measure will carry greater credibility and legitimacy and be more representative and successful in addressing the challenges of the 21st century, he added.

UN Sustainable Development Summit

Addressing the UN Sustainable Development Summit, Modi outlined the poverty eradication schemes of his government and stated that India was fulfilling its responsibilities as a development partner in Asia and Africa and also with small island states from the Pacific to the Atlantic. He dwelled on the subject of climate change and stated that when nations spoke only of climate change, there was a perception of their desire to merely secure the comforts of their lifestyle. It was while speaking of climate justice that nations demonstrated their sensitivity and determination with regard to securing the future of the poor from the hazards of natural disasters.

It was important, he said, to focus on solutions that could help nations reach their goals. Nations should forge a global public partnership to harness technology, innovations and finance in a bid to put affordable, clean and renewable energy within the reach of all. Equally important for nations to do was to look for changes in the lifestyles of their people that would make the world less dependent on energy and more sustainable in its consumption.

It was quite important to launch a global education program that would prepare the next generation to protect and conserve Nature. He expressed the hope that developed nations would fulfill their financing commitments for development and climate change, without placing both of them under the same head!

UN Summit on Peace Keeping

The Prime Minister attended the UN Summit on Peace Keeping in New York where he reiterated India's commitment to the ongoing and future peacekeeping operations. Earlier in a meeting with UN Secretary-General Ban Ki-moon, he called for a change in the manner in which decisions are being taken concerning peacekeeping operations where large troop-contributing nations like India were not consulted adequately enough before peacekeeping missions were authorized. This was despite the fact that cumulatively India has been the largest contributor to international peacekeeping operations.

Back-to-Back Talks

At San Jose, Narendra Modi had three back-to-back meetings with British Prime Minister David Cameron, French President Francois Hollande (Bill Gates was a surprise visitor at the meeting with his inputs on climate change), and US President Barak Obama. He discussed with them issues like climate change, terrorism in general and the Comprehensive Convention on International Terrorism in particular, UN Security Council reform and India's desire to become a member of the four export control regimes, starting with the Nuclear Suppliers Group (NSG) and Missile Technology Control Regime (MTCR).

On UN Security Council reform, President Obama reiterated the support that he had publicly articulated in favour of admitting

India as a permanent member of the Security Council. Now that the inter-governmental negotiation process was going to start, how India and the US could collaborate on that front was also discussed by the two leaders.

On the issue of climate change, Modi reiterated that India's commitment to environmental conservation was second to none. India was prepared to play a leadership role on this subject. Modi said that India had sought permission to declare its **intended nationally determined contributions** (INDCs) on October 2. The deadline was October 1, but October 2 being the birth anniversary of Mahatma Gandhi, who was passionately committed to the cause of environment, and was also a champion of sustainable development, India's declaring its INDCs on October 2, would add a very significant moral dimension as well to its commitment.

There was a broad appreciation for this point of view, with all the three Western leaders appreciating India for declaring its INDCs and combining it with the observance of Mahatma Gandhi's birth anniversary. India has since fulfilled its commitment on October 2 and vindicated its principled stand in the matter. On the substantive issue of climate change, Modi made it very clear that the prevailing mood of negativism cannot be a useful factor as the world prepares for the crucial negotiations of COP 21 to be held in Paris this December.

He said rather than just putting pressure over caps on emission targets, it would be far better if there is an active agenda that enables countries to opt for more sustainable development paths by providing them with finance and with the requisite technology. That was the path India had been advocating. He also outlined his own ambitious agenda for 175 gigawatts of renewable energy and the steps that he had initiated to reach that goal.

There was also a discussion on some of the very innovative ideas that India had taken in this field. There was further discussion on how more such innovative ideas could be found so that the whole debate on climate change went along the path of a positive agenda rather than a negative one. President Obama was very forthcoming in the matter and said that he totally accepted the point that developing countries needed to be provided with the right technologies.

In this context, he referred to the solar panels and said their prices had gone down in the US because of which they became more easily affordable for developing countries. He said this became possible because of a conscious decision on the part of the US government to make these technologies inexpensive.

Modi called terrorism a global phenomenon that had an impact on each and every country without exception; no country was immune from its threat, which India had been battling for four decades. He said the time had come for the international community to speak with one voice on this issue and resolve the long pending finalization of the Comprehensive Convention on International Terrorism, which had been held up because of the disagreement on the definition of terrorism.

Modi also spoke of India's aspiration for membership to the four export control regimes. There was broad support from all the three interlocutors who stated that they wanted to see India as part of these non-proliferation regimes in view of its impeccable track record in this particular area. Apart from discussing issues of concern common to the three interlocutors, Modi separately discussed with them matters of bilateral interest concerning their respective countries.

Social Media Interface

Narendra Modi visited the Facebook headquarters on September 29 where he was received by Mark Zuckerberg and Sheryl Sandberg. Modi wanted to know how social media could be used for giving greater coverage to the Indian government's social program such as Swachh Bharat, etc. Later, at an event at the Town Hall, Modi answered various questions on the role of social media and some personal questions pertaining to his early life, the role of his mother in his life, etc. The Q&A session was fraught with poignancy and nostalgia on the part of the Prime Minister, which gave the audience rare insights into the leader's personality, making the occasion quite momentous and unique.

Modi visited the Google headquarters where he was received by Eric Schmidt and Sundar Pichai. Larry Page, co-founder of Google, was present too. They showed the Prime Minister three or four of their top technologies like Google Earth, the Iris project, Knowledge Panels, Project Loon, etc. Eric Schmidt said he was very excited about the Prime Minister's initiative to bring Digital India to every corner of the country.

Modi evinced keen interest in Google's flagship project, Project Loon, which is aimed at bringing internet access to hitherto unserviced areas that have no internet signal at all. Google is doing a pilot project in Andhra Pradesh, the idea being to target rural areas that still do not have internet penetration. Modi felt this could be a very, very significant innovation to help with rural connectivity. The Google top brass said if internet access is expanded, then 160 million people could be lifted out of poverty. So, the Prime Minister immediately felt the usefulness of the application of Project Loon for areas such as long distance education, rural schools, telemedicine, etc.

There was a discussion on the project that Google was now doing in partnership with the RailTel to offer Wi-Fi connectivity at 500 railway stations in India. Starting with Mumbai Central, the project, the biggest in the world, would roll out to 100 railway stations. There was also a discussion on the possibilities of Google technologies for the agricultural sector in terms of developing an algorithm, etc.

Mega Event to Fete the People's Leader

After visiting Facebook and Google Inc headquarters on Day 2, Narendra Modi was accorded a grand reception at SAP Center, San Jose and he addressed a mega event at the San Jose Convention Center that was attended by 18,000 people. In a way, this was the West Coast trying to outdo the East Coast, which had a similar privilege last year. If the rockstar reception of 2014 at Madison Square Gardens, New York had been in anticipation of the tasks that Modi had set out to accomplish as the newly-elected Prime Minister, the latest one at San Jose was in clear recognition of his wowing the world in his inimitable style with his ambitious schemes and ingenious programs for good governance during the past sixteen months.

Suffice it to say that the Prime Minister's candid question at the event as to what the audience thought of his performance and acquittal of a blemishless and corruption-free personal conduct, was more than amply answered by the deafening chanting of his name by the 18,000-strong exultant audience. Narendra Modi started off his address by paying tribute to Shahid Bhagat Singh on the latter's birth anniversary and finished his speech by announcing a good news – that Air India would be commencing a non-stop flight from Delhi to San Francisco in December. He also said that the mission of his government was JAM – 'Jan Dhan' bank accounts for all, Aadhaar unique identity card and Mobile Governance.

The rest of his speech was devoted to the accomplishments and achievements of his government, besides being interspersed with patriotic fervour. He also paid heartfelt tribute to members of the Sikh community who had migrated to the West Coast in the 1940s to work as farm labourers and founded the Gadar Party that campaigned for India's Independence from colonial rule. Praising the role of the Indian diaspora on the West Coast in making a mark not only for themselves but also for India with their technical expertise and professional prowess, he spoke of how the rest of the world was looking upto India as the most outstanding performer among the BRICS group of nations. He reassured his captive audience that the 21st century was going to be universally acclaimed as the century of India.

He disowned all credit for the transformation of India's fortunes and recognition at international fora like the World Bank, IMF and rating agencies like Moody's and attributed it to the 125 crore people of India. Rubbishing all talks of "good terrorism" and "bad terrorism" (by Pakistan which he did not name), he seized the occasion to reiterate India's stance on terrorism and urged the UN not to lose any more time in coming down heavily on what has now become a global phenomenon. Meanwhile, he struck a positive note and emotional chord in the audience by stating that he viewed the exemplary collection of so many illustrious Indian nationals on the West Coast not as Brain Drain but as Deposit of Brain which could turn as Brain Gain for their motherland's economic transformation at the appropriate moment. The crowd rose as one man to express in unison its solidarity with PM Modi.

Roundtable on Renewable Energy

Prime Minister Modi attended a roundtable conference on renewable energy, which saw the participation of international experts and authorities on the subject as well as Nobel Laureates and academics. The participants felt India had the potential to emerge as the clean energy capital of the world. And with electricity storage becoming inexpensive, clean and renewable energy will soon become a viable and affordable energy option. On his part, Modi emphasized India's commitment to realizing the vision for 175 gigawatts of clean energy. He said there was massive scope for investment in the sector, for example through the railways, where 100% FDI had been made admissible. He also gave an overview of initiatives already undertaken by his government in the area of renewable energy.

Bilateral Meetings

The Indian Prime Minister had separate bilateral meetings with his counterparts from Bhutan, Nepal, Sri Lanka, Sweden, Cyprus, Egypt, Palestine and Mexico and a brief meeting with Prime Minister Kenny Anthony of St. Lucia.

Interaction with Indian Diaspora

While in New York, Narendra Modi met a broad section of the Indian American diaspora. He also had separate interactions with members of the Sikh community and with some other persons of Indian origin. Some other personalities who called on Prime Minister Modi were Governor of California Edmund G. Brown and Salman Khan, founder of Khan Academy

Accolade for the PM

The personal involvement, understanding and tireless interest displayed by Prime Minister Modi in the schemes and projects for eradication of poverty and digitalization of India, were a tremendous source of inspiration for the American corporate honchos and technology entrepreneurs who are vying for a piece of the great Indian business pie. This US visit of Narendra Modi, second as Prime Minister, turned out to be a resounding success just as his first one of last year. It made everyone wonder yet again as to what made Modi stand out as the most popular and successful Prime Minister of India.

It was undoubtedly his ability to combine the down-to-earth qualities of modesty about his past, which was evident in his interactions with global leaders and corporate honchos, pride in the spiritual and cultural ethos of India and political pragmatism vis-a-vis the Hindutva ideology of his party. All these allowed him to have no constraints about doing business with capitalist and theocratic nations.

This in turn, seems to have made his interlocutors at the international fora more receptive to his ideas and initiatives in comparison to his predecessors. For instance, Jim Yong Kim, President of World Bank said that Prime Minister Modi's reforms have had an enormous impact on the way the world looks at India. This was no mean compliment by any standard, not even by the standards of the Congress Party, which had lashed out in animosity by denigrating the Prime Minister's visit as a mere fashion show!

(Posted on blog on 9 October, 2015)

□

The Untold Story Indians can never Forget

England ruled over India for almost 200 humiliating and punishing years, a period that must remain etched forever in the annals of our country's trajectory. In our entire history, we haven't witnessed more horrific massacres than that committed by the English over us. Having reached our land driven by their outright and shameful greed of profiteering, the English used every opportunity to exploit our ancestors and treat them like subhumans. That England did so even in China fuelling the opium wars, the drugs being grown by the English in the Indo-Nepal border region and trafficked in China, is another testimony to their brutal past.

India, as a nation, and we, as a people, must always remember this past and learn from it. India was plundered by the English, our women raped, our wealth looted and our people treated as slaves. The English even took many of our ancestors to faraway lands like Fiji, Guyana, Suriname, Trinidad and Tobagoto use them as indentured servants and slave laborers. They separated many families and destroyed the harmony in our society. In their sadistic lust for power, the English killed hundreds of innocent Indians in incidents like the Jallianwala Bagh massacre. The ultimate suffering they caused was through the Cabinet Mission plan announced on May 16, 1946, which led to promulgation of another alternative plan on June 16, 1946 that eventually led to the partitioning of India into Hindu-majority India and a Muslim-majority Pakistan.

The second plan's implementation caused the 1947 riots and bloodbath resulting in the death of lakhs of people. This happened mainly because the English imperialists felt it wise, as the ruling power, to sanction the breaking apart of our country. Divide and conquer was their tried and tested strategy through which they unleashed genocide upon our people. It is in the memory of those Indians who were killed, cremated and buried during the partition days as well as those who were humiliated, tortured, murdered and desecrated by the English Empire, that I write this article. In 1947, the English imperialists left behind a bankrupt India, a nation torn apart and a people subjugated and broken. We Indians should never forget this humiliation because a nation that fails to learn from history is doomed to repeat it.

It is no wonder that England always favored Jawaharlal Nehru, an Anglophile with his background of English education, as the man they could easily influence and control, directly or via proxies like Edwina Mountbatten. But the English were scared of leaders such as Sardar Vallabhbhai Patel and Netaji Subhash Chandra Bose. No surprises then that Sardar Vallabhbhai was not chosen as India's first Prime Minister, despite winning elections from majority of the provinces (Nehru didn't win even from a single province), whilst Subhash Chandra Bose was made to disappear from the scene altogether.

Since Nehru's ascension, England always exerted considerable influence over India, from behind the scenes. Even Indira Gandhi was educated in England. We all know Rajiv Gandhi was enrolled at Cambridge University. And Rahul Gandhi worked in London for two years, and still likes to go there to celebrate his birthdays. Thus, through the Congress party, England always managed to retain some semblance of control and power over India, since the Congress party hierarchy had its assets, its lives and its secrets in the hands of its benefactors, the English. We wouldn't be surprised to learn that even MI5 and MI6 kept dossiers on Congress Party leaders in a bid to exercise control over them.

Today, England faces a very different reality: a resurgent India and an increasingly confident nation that is striving to emerge as an economic leader internationally. And for the first time since independence, India has in absolute majority a nationalist ruling party in power that has no ties to England, and is not beholden to them in any manner. InPrime Minister Narendra Modi, we have a true son of the soil, a man who grew up, studied and has always stayed in India. In fact, none of the current top leaders in India's ruling party has had any background of education or familial ties in England. Nor does India purchase any weapons of war from England. So what does a nation like England do in such a case, habituated as they are to feeling superior, and treating us Indians as inferior subservient slaves?

Given the recent turn of events, it can be inferred that England is trying to interfere again, and weaken India's nationalist Bharatiya Janata Party (BJP). It seems that the English are resorting to some dirty tricks, shamelessly trying to hurt our governance and our security, and thereby threaten our national interests. And they are trying to indirectly blackmail us through their media. Here, let me give you two recent examples.

Rupert Murdoch is the leading media tycoon in England. He is also one of the strongest supporters of the Conservative Party that governs England today. His newspaper, The Sunday Times, recently published a scandalous article in a bid to denigrate our Foreign Minister Sushma Swaraj. Through this article, the newspaper attempted to create a media furore aimed at embarrassing India and our government. It would not be unreasonable to assume this was England's way of hinting to our government that before our Honorable Prime Minister's official visit to London scheduled in November this year, he better realize that England can always make life difficult for his government. As a patriot, this underhanded move via The Sunday Times to malign India's honorable Ministers disgusts me. And it should definitely offend every true Indian.

When this particular scandal petered out with more and more people realizing that India government had done nothing wrong, England threw another bombshell. Leaking some police interviews of some alleged members of Pakistan's Muttahida Quami Movement in London, England claimed via the BBC(though unsubstantiated by facts on the ground), that India was funding MQM, and by proxy, our government has been helping the party create unrest in its stronghold of Karachi. Such dishonest and deliberate leak of patently false and unjustifiable rumours can easily be something out of the play book of the dirty tricks department of the English Government and its intelligence agencies.

This rumour has the potential to easily sabotage efforts of peace between India and her neighbour, and it can have adverse impacts on generations in South Asia, a home to over 1.5 billion people. It may also lead to India being isolated and branded as a nation that interferes in the domestic affairs of its neighbours. But more importantly, it can even eliminate hopes of a peaceful coexistence between India and Pakistan.

England, through these leaks and disclosures, thus contrived to humiliate India and also tried to weaken our country's international standing, whilst desperately trying to make us look like sponsors of domestic terrorism in our neighbouring country. And this false propaganda of England took place conveniently, just before cases against Zaki-ur-Rehman Lakhvi and the Jamaat-ud-Dawa (JuD) were being brought up, apropos the Financial Action Task Force (FATF).

England almost succeeded in creating a wedge between India and China at the FATF meet, thereby deviating the focus from the path of tranquility and this was very aptly highlighted by our Honorable Prime Minister. Worse still, England tried to weaken our hands in negotiations with Pakistan on the sidelines of the just-concluded Shanghai Cooperation Organization (SCO) summit in Ufa, Russia, where Shri Narendra Modi met Pak Prime Minister Nawaz Sharif. England has thus directly threatened our national security policies and objectives, which is indeed a very serious matter.

Whilst highlighting the treachery of the English government in their desperate bid to regain control over us, we should not be too surprised. After all, they have exercised unbelievable control over the Congress party, which has ruled India for the maximum number of years after our country attained independence in 1947. Here, I would like to make two more important observations before I conclude this article.

England has never given us any reparations for the loot and plunder of our nation which they had resorted to for almost 200 years. Not even once they have offered to compensate us for the murder of millions, unlike what they insisted from Germany in the treaty of Versailles and again from Germany after the Second World War. And while Germany had to apologize repeatedly for the genocide by the Nazis, not once has England, either through her Head of State, the Queen, or through her Head of Government, their Prime Minister, ever apologized to India.

In fact, England hasn't even offered to apologize. If Germany apologizes repeatedly even today for its past, how arrogant must these English imperialists be to never apologize to us for the brutality England unleashed on us during the 200 long years it ruled India. Let us seriously think about it for a moment! Perhaps England felt that Indian lives were cheap, and the heinous crimes of its citizens were glorious.

Perhaps they still have the hubris to think that we natives, the colored people, don't deserve an apology. Perhaps they feel India doesn't merit apology for the rape, pillage and plunder she had suffered at the English hands. Undoubtedly, England's arrogance has no boundaries, and all this while England continues to blackmail us. They want to weaken our position before our Prime Minister visits London in November this year. Perhaps they want more business and are indirectly putting pressure on us to buy their military weapons.

Perhaps they still feel they are our imperial rulers, just like Queen Victoria had conveniently declared herself Empress of India in order to promote herself higher amongst the royalties of Europe. Or perhaps England just feels the need to try everything to humiliate the ruling nationalist political party in India today, in a bid to make it more compliant like the Congress Party to England's wishes. But the new India should never bend, and must never fall for such a horrifying and arrogant behavior of the English.

India must insist on an apology from the English government. We must be careful until we see true remorse and humility from England. We must be wary of England's use of media to promote false propaganda and spread lies with the aim of defaming our government. India should insist on England returning to us what was originally ours – like the Kohinoor Diamond as well as other national treasures and artifacts, which they had looted from our country.

Meanwhile, we should never forget the sacrifices of Mangal Pandey and Rani Laxmi Bai, of Chandrashekhar Azad and Shaheed Bhagat Singh, and of our other brave souls who had consistently fought the tyranny of English. Their names must remain glorious in the annals of our history, as those who fought the tyranny of the English to free us from the yoke of slavery. And we must always remember our past, for the same may be getting played out today, driven by England's evil designs to subjugate India's rising power and strength. Jai Hind.

(Posted on Bharat Niti portal on 1 August, 2015)

(Posted on blog on 27 July, 2015)

□

Foreign Policy Initiatives of Prime Minister Narendra Modi

India's foreign policy was till recently like a family heirloom, known more for its sentimental value than intrinsic worth or craftsmanship, passed on by successive generations to the next in line. Consequently, rigidity was its underpinning. Perhaps, the fact that India got freedom through a largely bloodless struggle deluded our leaders into believing that war was passé in the post-World War II era and that our neighbouring countries would understand India's language of love and peace, being in awe of the moral stature of the country that had produced the Mahatma, Apostle of Peace. As a result, there was hardly any scope for maneuvering in our foreign policy in the face of realpolitiking in a world of shifting tectonic plates of geopolitics.

Product of Nehru's Romantic Global Vision

A product of Western education of his times, India's first Prime Minister Jawaharlal Nehru was reconciled to taking over the governance of India rather as a Mughal-British legacy than as an inheritance of thousands of years of unbroken history of Bharat. Eventually, every tenet of his foreign policy such as non-alignment, Panchsheel treaty, nuclear non-proliferation, peaceful and fraternal relations with belligerent neighbouring countries miserably failed. Consequently, both our northern neighbours – Pakistan and China – back stabbed India and have continually dared to make intrusions into our territory posing existential threats to the country, apart from one of them brazenly exporting cross-border terrorism.

Border disputes with China and Pakistan have remained festering wounds since Nehru's time. None of the Indian prime ministers who succeeded Nehru were strong enough to address this problem.

Eventually, India's foreign policy exercise centered on vacuous proposals of talks, negotiations, dialogues, and so forth. Despite endless rounds of Biryani diplomacy and Cricket diplomacy, and exchanging of gifts of Alfonso mangoes, and cultural troupes, there was no headway in our border disputes either with Pakistan or with China. Matters became more complicated for India with the disintegration of the USSR, a tried and tested ally that had stood by us through difficult times. Non-Aligned Movement (NAM) became passé. Our foreign policy had the fundamental flaw of being too rigid to address emerging new threat factors like global terrorism, religious fundamentalism and regional hegemony.

Enter Narendra Modi

With the arrival of Narendra Modi on the scene, there was a paradigm shift in international perception about India's position at the diplomatic high table. Across the world, he was considered a hardliner, representing India's Hindu nationalist party, the BJP. The world had expected, not without much trepidation that Modi will strike uncompromising postures and assume precipitous positions in heady shows of diplomacy, which were already in full flow in the region. In short, they had expected the new prime minister to be a rabid politician and a poor diplomat.

Diplomatic Coup

However, Modi surprised the prophets of doom and naysayers both within and outside the country by scoring a diplomatic coup at the very outset of his assumption of office by inviting the Heads of Government/Heads of State of all SAARC countries to his swearing-in ceremony. The event was a grand and solemn occasion, the biggest of its kind our country had ever witnessed. It was also indicative of the new government's resolve to renew and further strengthen India's bilateral and multinational relations with the regional players as also its readiness to operationalize new ideas within the parameters of the institutional mechanisms already in place, without trenching into major policy benchmarks. The event was rightly acclaimed as a mini-SAARC Summit. It clearly highlighted the Foreign Policy priority, which the new Indian government accorded to the neighbouring countries.

Pakistan

The toast of the occasion was Pakistan Prime Minister Nawaz Sharif. His willingness to do business with India, despite opposition from the hawkish elements in his country, augured well for peace in the region. This was a positive trend and it was welcomed by all right-thinking people and major political parties in both the countries. In his meeting with the Pakistani leader, Modi categorically told Sharif that export of terror by Pakistan was not acceptable and must end and that the perpetrators of the 26/11 terror attacks in Mumbai, who were hiding in Pakistan, must be brought to book without any further delay; and India was unhappy at the slow pace of trials against the perpetrators of violence.

Sharif was also told that Hafiz Sayeed, the master mind of the terror attack, should not be allowed to go around Pakistan at will and say whatever he wanted, about India. He was further informed of India's concern about the militant attack on India's Consulate at Herat, Afghanistan, by Lashkar-e-Taiba, and its expectation that such attacks would not recur. The rules of the game under the new Indian Prime Minister were clearly spelt out.

Extension of a hand of friendship at Modi's inauguration was followed by India's invitation to Pakistan to participate in the Foreign Secretary level talks in August 2014. However, the talks were later called off by India following a breach of diplomatic protocol and a political red line by the Pakistan High Commissioner in Delhi who invited separatist Kashmiri leaders for consultation on the eve of the proposed Foreign Secretary level talks. India told Pakistan in unambiguous terms that as long as the latter continued to indulge in wanton undiplomatic acts of meeting and talking to separatist elements despite the disapproval of the India government, they could forget talks with India.

These developments on the Pakistan front clearly demonstrated India's willingness to find a comprehensive solution to its problems with that country through peaceful means, but not at the cost of Pakistan's pusillanimous stand of reneging on the inviolability of the diplomatic and political red lines. Being subsumed in its numerous internal problems and with its inability to hold meaningful talks with India and being unable to bleed India without getting grievously hurt itself, now Pakistan finds itself in a bind. That is India's biggest advantage today and that is because of Modi.

China

With no sign of an end to the logjam in sight over the festering and contentious border issue between the two major South Asian powers, the China conundrum had defied an easy solution, and had been conveniently but unwisely kept by the previous Indian governments on the back burner. Modi, however, took it on headlong immediately after taking over office. Conceding that this is a complicated and old problem, he is all for addressing it with care and deliberation. He is highly critical of the way India had been allowing China in the past to dominate our country across international policies and has been unequivocal in his assertion that there would be no compromise on India's interest.

His recent visit to China and the Chinese President's visit to India last year were indicative of Modi's commitment and willingness to do business with China. He is all for the deepening of our bilateral relations with China and believes that a tactical approach should make this possible. Far from being overawed by the edge that China has over India in its economic development, he advocates showcasing of its strengths by India, as China has been showing off Shanghai to the world.

Wary of its ambition of regional hegemony, he took a broadside against China while on a visit to Japan last year and stated that currently one gets to see everywhere an 18th-century expansionist mindset: encroaching on another country, intruding into others' waters, invading other countries and capturing their territory.

In an oblique reference to China, he said this mindset should be left behind. He touched on the South China Sea in both the ASEAN-India Summit and the East Asia Summit organized last year, reiterating the importance for all actors in "following international law and norms on maritime issues". Furthermore, poaching in waters of the Indian Ocean by the Chinese Navy was not allowed to go unnoticed. Close and timely interaction with the new regime in Sri Lanka by the Modi government was a well-orchestrated exercise in damage control, which was quite unlikely under the previous Indian governments, especially the one which had preceded the present one.

The key components of Modi's China policy include keeping China at bay in its game plan of gaining supremacy in regional leadership by strengthening India's military might while simultaneously increasing political equation with other regional players including Sri Lanka; keeping the option of meaningful dialogues at political and operational level to resolve the border disputes; and engaging China in matters of economic and cultural cooperation. All these are aimed at deftly turning the tables on Beijing.

Neighbourhood Policy

Modi's foreign policy is focused on improving relations with neighbouring countries in South Asia. One of the major policy initiatives taken by the Modi government is to shift the focus back on its immediate neighbours in South Asia. Even before becoming prime minister, Modi had hinted that his foreign policy would actively focus on improving ties with India's immediate neighbours. Apart from inviting the Heads of Government/Heads of State of all SAARC countries to his inauguration, he asked Indian scientists, during a launch event at ISRO, to endeavor and develop a dedicated SAARC satellite to share the fruits of technology like tele-medicine, e-learning, etc with the people across South Asia in a bid to complement the currently operating Indian Technical and Economic Cooperation (ITEC) Program in the region.

Make in India

One of the main items on Modi's agenda during his visits abroad has been his 'Make in India' program, an aggressive economic push aimed at reviving the ailing manufacturing sector by encouraging global companies to set up their manufacturing facilities in India. The program is aimed at job creation and skill enhancement, while maintaining high quality standards and minimizing the adverse impact on the environment. The initiative hopes to attract capital and technological investment in India, and also increase GDP growth and tax revenue.

Act East Policy

Relations with its East Asian neighbours have always had a special resonance for India. It is a foreign policy priority for the Modi government. The government's 'Look East Policy' dating back to 1992, was tweaked by Modi to give it an aggressive thrust in the form of 'Act East Policy'. Unveiling the new policy at the ASEAN Summit in

Myanmar last year, Modi highlighted specific recommendations to advance ASEAN-India economic relations over the next few years, including establishing a special purpose vehicle for project financing, building information highways and inviting ASEAN countries to participate in India's ongoing economic transformation. Modi's recent visits to Mongolia and South Korea were an exercise in stepping up the actualization of the Act East Policy.

United States of America

In the meantime, Modi also scored another diplomatic coup – this time by inviting US President Barack Obama to be the Chief Guest at India's Republic Day anniversary functions on January 26, 2015. During Obama's visit, India and the US broke the seven year old logjam and operationalized their landmark civilian nuclear deal, besides deciding to jointly produce military hardware including Unmanned Aerial Vehicles. In what the US President termed as a 'breakthrough', the two sides cleared hurdles pertaining to the liability of suppliers of nuclear reactors in the event of an accident and the tracking of fuel supplied by the US.

The two countries have also decided to hold regular summits at increased periodicity as well as to elevate the Strategic Dialogue to a Strategic and Commercial Dialogue. The two sides stated that India and the US agreed to elevate their long-standing strategic partnership and each step being taken to strengthen the ties was a move towards shaping international security as well as regional and global peace. The US President extended his country's support to India's inclusion in the Nuclear Suppliers' Group as well as induction in the UN Security Council as a Permanent Member.

Bangladesh

Meanwhile, Narendra Modi visited Bangladesh on June 6 and 7, and signed as many as 22 agreements, thereby opening up a new chapter in the relations of the two countries. For the first time since independence in 1947, India has agreed upon a clear demarcation of its porous borders with a neighbouring nation by signing the prickly Land Boundary Agreement (LBA). To give one illustration of its historic significance and how it dramatically alters the destines of the two South Asian nations, LBA has brought cheer to over 50, 000 virtually stateless people living in the enclaves of the 4, 096-km long India-Bangladesh border by giving them a national identity.

Furthermore, Modi announced a US$2 billion Line of Credit (LOC), for use in infrastructure, power, health and education projects. The LOC is expected to create 50, 000 jobs in India and provide a big boost to project exports from India and help Indian companies. This will, in turn, give the 'Make in India' scheme a shot in the arm. Bangladesh, on its part, stands to benefit with big ticket investment projects expected to follow suit. Two Indian companies have reportedly committed a combined investment of US$4.5 billion for setting up power generating projects in Bangladesh. Another agreement provides for creation of two Special Economic Zones (SEZs) in Bangladesh exclusively for Indian companies. This would encourage Indian companies and give both countries a way to address the yawning trade deficit.

There was also a clear breakthrough in the maritime trade sector with the signing of an agreement that allows Indian cargo vessels to use the Chittagong and Mongla ports. The Chittagong port was developed by the Chinese and forms part of their 'String of Pearls' ports in the Indian Ocean Region. There is a belief among political analysts that although it is ostensibly a commercial port as of now for all practical purposes, it could any day be used by China for strategic purposes. For India to gain access to the Chittagong port is a big achievement both in economic and strategic terms. Moreover, it is perceived as an expression of building up of greater trust between Bangladesh and India, more than ever in the past.

Meanwhile, the Coast Guards of the two countries have signed a MoU that envisages combating human trafficking, smuggling and circulation of fake currency notes – a sore point in the bilateral relations of the two countries. Another outcome of the visit is increased cooperation between the two countries in terms of rendering better and faster consular services to their citizens. India will open two new Consulates in Sylhet and Khulna while Bangladesh will open one in Guwahati. In another exercise that directly benefits and thus has a special resonance to the people of the two countries, Modi and Sheikh Hasina flagged off two buses.

These bus services – Kolkata-Dhaka-Agartala and Dhaka-Shillong-Guwahati – will link West Bengal to three North Eastern states of India via Bangladeshi capital Dhaka. This has been hailed as a historic moment in the bilateral relations between the two countries and a milestone in the people-to-people diplomacy. The bus service will bring India's northeast closer to the rest India and provide the people of Bangladesh access through India to markets in Bhutan and Nepal.

Thus, this visit of Modi to Bangladesh has accomplished a good deal of tangible results across a wide range of developmental sectors such as connectivity, power, ports, education, health and investments in an act of political sagacity to the mutual benefit and satisfaction of the peoples of the two countries in an atmosphere of bonhomie and cordiality, not to be seen since 1971 when they had jointly fought a common enemy.

In a nutshell, the visit has given a new orientation to the India-Bangladesh bilateral relations in the form of 'Nouton Projonmo – Nayi Disha' (New Generation, New Direction), as the joint declaration issued at the end of the visit was called. PM Modi likened the Land Boundary Agreement to the coming down of the Berlin Wall. He availed of the opportunity to affirm India's support to Bangladesh in their joint fight against terrorism with the securing of the border. The successful visit portends the coming down of more regional Berlin Walls. That is the 'nayi disha' in which India proposes to traverse under Modi's foreign policy with new orientation.

Summing It Up

Well, these are some of the more pronounced Foreign Policy Initiatives of Modi, which promise to stand India in good stead in our country's aggressive bid to assume a more assertive role in the world of international politics and diplomacy. The highpoint of Modi diplomacy is his out-of-the-box thinking and fresh orientation to aspects of special interest to India. Needless to say, much more could be said, with the entire world panning out for a mention. But due to space constraints we shall leave it for another day.

(Published in weekly magazine Uday India in Vol. VI. No. 43, 27 September, 3 October, 2015)
(Posted on blog on 12 June, 2015)

□

Indian Ocean – Checkmating China

Currently, the Indian Ocean is a hotbed of conflicting interests for the two major South Asian political and economic rivals viz India and China. While India rightly looks upon the Indian Ocean as its backyard with tremendous strategic importance, China has thrown down the gauntlet in its bid to claim political and commercial hegemony and naval supremacy among the countries of the Indian Ocean region.

Riding on a burgeoning volume of international trade and a booming military might, it has been on a spree of acquiring strategic assets in the form of ports in many countries across and beyond the region and setting up bases, like in Bangladesh (Chittagong), Sri Lanka (Hambantota), Seychelles, Pakistan (Gwadar), Kenya (Lamu) and Tanzania (Bagamoyo). Called the 'String of Pearls' by Western sources, these ports would purportedly enable China to secure its commercial interests in the procurement of raw materials and sources of energy for its energy deficient economy.

A likely scenario to emerge over the years in the Chinese scheme of things is that the dependence of the world on crude oil will increase manifold; keeping pace with the demand in oil will be the control of China over the Indian Ocean. It has accordingly aligned its foreign and defence policies to ensure its economic success the world over and emergence as a market leader.

Naval Bases

Although China claims that the underlying motive of the Pearls of ports is purely an economic one viz to ensure its maritime interests for energy security, the current ground realities in the Indian Ocean throw up a different kind of indicator, making the communist country's intentions appear far from innocuous. China has set up electronic intelligence gathering facilities on islands in the Bay of Bengal, and funded construction of a canal across the Kra Isthmus in Thailand. It has entered into a military agreement with Cambodia and has been building up forces in the South China Sea.

The Gwadar deep sea port in Pakistan provides China with a 'listening post' from where it can monitor Indian activities in the Arabian Sea. China can patrol the Indian Ocean sea-lanes for its security of shipments. It has a naval base on Hainan Island that can hold submarines, which pose a major threat to the US, but could be a threat to India too. China has dismissed reports of any plans of creating military bases overseas, but Chinese maritime strategists such as Shen Dingli advocate the need for China to set up overseas military bases.

China would not fight shy of protecting its energy imports that pass through the Indian Ocean. Nor is it comfortable with Washington and New Delhi being the security providers in the region. Inability to sustain troops in the region would leave a chink in its armour, which would mean that China's energy imports would be highly vulnerable in the event of a military standoff with either the US or India.

Being already embroiled in maritime disputes with several countries in the South and East China seas over the ownership of islands, China is wary of the possibility of the Indian Ocean waters becoming another contentious area at some point of time in the future; in the absence of an effective blue-water Navy to protect its commercial and political interests.

Ruffling Indian Feathers

China has raised India's hackles by docking submarines at the port of Colombo in Sri Lanka. India's concerns have been further raised by the expansion of Chinese maritime powers with the development of aircraft carrier battle groups. Currently, China has the largest aircraft carrier in Asia. And alarm bells rang when Chinese nuclear submarines carried out patrols in the Bay of Bengal. The possible presence of Chinese nuclear missiles so close to its coastline was a matter of utmost concern to India's nuclear deterrence.

India and the US

The first salvo of a resurgent India under the Narendra Modi government in response to a belligerent China's ambitious maritime agenda being aggressively pushed forward by that country was fired soon after Modi became Prime Minister and visited the US in September 2014. Prominent among the issues discussed by the Indian leader with President Obama was maritime security of all nations to peacefully carry out their trade activities in the Indian Ocean.

During the visit of President Obama to India in January 2015, the two leaders reaffirmed "the importance of safeguarding maritime security and ensuring freedom of navigation and overflight throughout the region, especially in the South China Sea". They also called "on all parties to avoid the threat or use of force" in maritime disputes. China sharply reacted to an India-US joint statement referring to the disputes in the South China Sea, saying that only the countries involved in the disputes should work together to resolve the problems.

"At the current stage, the situation in the South China Sea is generally stable and there is no problem with navigational freedom and freedom of flights, " the Chinese Foreign Ministry spokesperson said. According to political observers, Modi perceives a greater role for India in Asian affairs in pursuance of his policy of 'Act East', coinciding with Obama's own pivot to Asia policy. Events after Modi assumed office as Prime Minister, have contributed to bringing India and the US toward a consensus on China.

India and Japan

During his August 2014 visit to Japan, Modi and his Japanese counterpart reaffirmed the importance of upgrading and strengthening of defence relations between the two countries in their strategic partnership. Keeping a wary eye on a rising China, the two leaders agreed to accelerate talks on the possible sale of an amphibious aircraft to India. The coming together of the two countries in matters of strategic partnership was seen by political observers as a bold initiative on the part of India and Japan to redefine the balance of power in the region and counter the ambitious expansionist policy of China.

India's Extended Neighbourhood

India has extended its neighbourhood beyond the South Asian region where it has its presence in the Southeast and Indo-Pacific region. The Southeast Asian states have evinced interest in India by playing an active role in the region to counter the dominant Chinese position. India in recent years has strengthened its relations in the Southeast Asian region in pursuance of its 'Look East Policy' launched in the 1990s and reinvigorated and renamed under the Modi government as 'Act East Policy'. India has integrated the Pacific in its extended neighbourhood concept. It has signaled that its Act East Policy was not limited to Southeast Asia, but goes beyond that to Australia and other Pacific Ocean nations.

India is not interested in taking on China in a direct confrontation. However, Chinese imperialist designs may succeed in uniting the countries of the Southeast Asian region. China would not be inclined to bargain for such a situation as it would be difficult for it to contend with. Any alignment of interest in the region would significantly affect the balance of power, posing serious consequences for all nations. India's growing technological advances (with the launch of Agni-V) has placed it amongst an elite group of nations. This in itself has far-reaching consequences for the States in the region.

Strengthening Bilateral Relations with Island Nations

With a view to countering China, India has upgraded its military ties with Maldives, Madagascar and Myanmar in the Indian Ocean and with Singapore, Indonesia, Thailand, Vietnam, Taiwan, the Philippines, Australia and Japan. India has also enhanced its economic and security relations with South Korea, Japan, Taiwan, Vietnam, Singapore, Indonesia, and Australia.

In order to counter China's naval presence in the Indian Ocean, India has its naval presence in the South China Sea and the Pacific Ocean. Malaysia launched defence cooperation with India by signing a memorandum of understanding in 1993. Defence cooperation between the two countries has been revived in 2008. Since then India has had a substantive military mission in Malaysia, focusing on training pilots and air force personnel.

Singapore has emerged as the closest security partner of India in the East, given its critical location in the Strait of Malacca at the confluence of the Pacific and Indian Oceans. Thailand is holding joint naval exercise with Indian Navy and under the comprehensive MoU signed in 2005 they are regularly conducting exercises in the area adjacent to their international maritime boundary lines. India is increasing its defence cooperation with Indonesia after the related cooperation agreement of 2001.

Australia and India concluded a pact on joint naval exercise in 2005 and a more comprehensive memorandum of understanding on maritime security cooperation in 2006. And during the visit of Prime Minister Kevin Rudd to India in November 2009, both sides agreed to enhance their defence interaction, with a special emphasis on naval cooperation. Furthermore, India has signed agreements to develop infrastructure with two Indian Ocean countries, Mauritius and Seychelles in their two islands – Agalega and Assumption.

India and Maldives

Despite its geographical proximity to India and having historically been within India's sphere of strategic influence, Maldives has increasingly been strengthening its relationship with Beijing. Chinese investments in the Maldives have increased over the years, ranging from housing projects to other infrastructure projects such as building roads and airports. This has become a major cause of concern for New Delhi.

India and Seychelles

Location of Seychelles and its proximity to the coast of Africa makes it a lucrative option for Beijing to establish a naval base in that country. China is already participating in anti-piracy operations in the Gulf of Aden and has growing economic interests in Africa. However, India and Seychelles share close military ties as New Delhi helps the island nation secure its EEZ by presenting surveillance aircrafts and patrolling ships.

India and Sri Lanka

The previous government of Mahinda Rajapaksa appeared fairly

China-friendly, awarding many infrastructure development projects to Beijing. The Maithripala Sirisena government is now reviewing all Chinese investments in the country, especially the US$1.5 billion port city project. The Sirisena government has also reassured India that such "incidents, from whatever quarter, do not take place under our tenure".

India and Mauritius

As Mauritius looks to attract investments from China, India is stepping up its game by providing a 1, 300-tonne Indian-built patrol vessel, the Barracuda, to Mauritius to help the island nation protect its coastline. While India may not indulge in any China containment policy, New Delhi realizes it is absolutely crucial to reengage with these islands and secure its strategic interests in the Indo-Pacific region.

China's Stated Position

While affirming that it has no plans to set up naval bases in the countries of the Indian Ocean region, China has warned that the Indian Ocean could end up "as an ocean of conflict and trouble" if countries like India, the US and China itself failed to engage with each other more constructively as their interests begin to overlap.

India's Call

This is an opportune moment for India which has achieved political stability under Narendra Modi's leadership to expand trade with China and to go all out for the settlement of the border issue. With support from regional countries and associations, India can play a decisive role in the region and the world. To this end, it is imperative that India take pro-active measures to engage China in dialogues for settling its long standing border disputes with that country. It is an established fact that China would only involve itself in any meaningful exercise of resolution of disputes when the adversary nation is politically stable, economically vibrant and militarily formidable.

India should strive and acquire the required edge under the present dispensation in the country and emerge as a strong enough partner nation, to do business with China. Needless to say, despite the Western orientation of India's foreign policy in recent times, India should accord top priority to its own interests while dealing with a militarily and economically stronger China which views the West with suspicion. And acquisition of an early Permanent Member status in the United Nations Security Council would set India in the same league as China, which is an essential prerequisite for checkmating the latter in the Indian Ocean.

(Posted on blog on 22 June, 2015)

□

PM Modi to Revive Indo-China Historic Bonding

India and China are no different, be it the liability to serve massive population, or the legacy of being world's leading economies prior to American or Russian advent, or the inherent conservative approach of the society, or even the non-authoritative structure of polity where China's communism and India's democracy are examples for the world to follow. Also is the similarity that lies with respect to relations between the People's Republic of China and the Republic of China (Taiwan), and India's relations with impish Pakistan. As per a recent survey, 80 per cent of the China's population was contented with the working of the communist government and the unprecedented win of the BJP in 2014 validates Indians' support to the present Modi-led government. The fresh era of politics and economy in both the countries commenced in the 1940s, in China after the admission of defeat by the Empire of Japan in the Second World War, and in India post the outgoing of the British Raj. Even the economic downtrends in both these emerging economies were managed by welcoming market-oriented and liberalized economy.

When the Indian Prime Minister, Narendra Modi, would meet his counterpart, Xi Jinping, on his first visit to China, on the top of his agenda, likely subjects would be the trade deficit, the ever-prevailing boundary dispute, India's stand on the Asian Infrastructure Investment Bank promoted by China and indeed a dialogue with Chinese entrepreneurs to convince them to Make in India. Now all these may be very much significant in their respective backgrounds, the trade deficit that soared to USD 36 billion in the FY 2013-14 and is likely to cross USD 60 billion in the coming two years if the imbalance in trade remains unaddressed is to be accorded the uppermost priority.

It is expected that the Indian PM would ask for corrections in the Asia-Pacific Trade Agreement so as to lower the trade barriers for Indian exports, but along with, novel avenues of bilateral ties with tough-to-deal-with neighbor are to be found. Remember, it was Atal Bihari Vajpayee's distinguished approach that led to appointment of Special Representatives for clearing up of LAC dispute; on similar grounds, it will be Modi's acumen that can address trade deficit in a never-thought of manner.

A basic that explains this wide gap between India's trade with China is that the Chinese exporters have tapped the segment of Indian market where our indigenous producers have been unable to focus. PM must stress the need of a balanced bilateral trade and in the current scenario, which indeed is unsustainable for India, China must extend respite by way of raising investment and pooling resources on technical terms. While we export a few primary commodities to China, we are in receipt of technology-intensive products. I feel that unless China realizes the fact that the two Asian giants are to grow in chorus, it will rarely serve any need even if we secure easy entry of Indian pharmaceuticals, IT, tobacco, rice or any other commodity. Import of mobile phones from China accounts for more than USD 5 billion every year and the same is likely to swell if Chinese giants like Xiaomi and Huawei aren't enthused to participate in the Make in India drive.

PM Modi must emphasize on the historic ties between both countries that range back to more than 2000 years, and also how India extended cordiality by accepting PRC as the lawful government and putting an end to our affiliation with Republic of China. It was a shared effort by India and China in the Second World War that ceased the evolution of Imperial Japan; however China's growing strategic relations with India's topmost rival, Pakistan and also the incessant incursions of Chinese military into our soil have been an unpleasant position so far. A vivid orator, Narendra Modi, will not escape mentioning a noteworthy bond, the Silk Road that aided the spread of Buddhism from India to parts of East Asia. Though it seems hard at this point in time to bid peaceful farewell to the boundary dispute, for which both nations have a dissimilar interpretation, by persuading China to fortify economic ties, the controversial dispute and tensions at the LAC can be lessened.

China and India are the most sought for investment locations for foreign investors, and there is no wrong in saying that India has taken a lead in the past few months. China's economy and GDP growth rate are not to see smooth road in the upcoming days, but in India, investors' outlook is firmly bullish. Modi's country is to out pace that of Jinping's in 2015 and the gap would amplify in 2016; hence China is to see India with a reformed perspective now, by allowing our exports to flow freely in their market, and also refrain from dumping cheaply priced goods in the Indian market. When it is estimated that the bilateral trade would touch USD 1 trillion by the year 2050, no single country can expect undue favor in this agreement. The world economy, as per the forecasts of IMF, is not to show any sizable advancement and will grow just 3.5 per cent in 2015. Taking note of all the said forecasts, it is constructive that the world's manufacturing hub, China and the IT hub, India take a mutual step towards development.

By all odds, the foremost call of integration may come from India-China consensus on 'One Belt One Road' initiative of Xi Jinping that will lift multinational economic progress with land based Silk Road and water based Maritime Silk Road. Asia and Europe are to be integrated via infrastructure development and cultural connections, and the parts of planned route will pass through south India that calls for Indian backing to the project, but not without studying strategic impact of India's encirclement. The Trans-Himalayan Economic Zone of co-operation with Nepal and Bhutan seeks New Delhi's involvement; a suspicion is cast over China's intents; however Indian cannot abstain from partnering with China so as to unfold economic windfalls in Asia and Indo-Pacific. In all views, this is a fascinating topic at time when PM Modi too knows bonuses of integration, reflected from his 'Bharat Mala' blueprint, a road network of about 5, 000 km.

Diplomacy and keeping the enemy or even the ally guessing are tactical approaches in running a government. Though the border dispute did not result in any bullet been fired for over a quarter of a century, as said by the Indian PM to the TIME magazine, China has cautiously played mind games with India over the years, USD 50 billion pouring for China-Pakistan economic corridor that would also pass through the PoK and steady military aides to Pakistan reveal this. India has an edge as well; Japan and Vietnam are eyeing India as a responsive partner, these nations being wary of China's attitude in the South China Sea region. Plus, Tibet is an aching concern for China and India's strength lies in countering China-Pak affection by varying its tactic, which has so far remained in favor of China to appease the dragon by former Indian leaders. Along with, second and third leg of PM's tour will be South Korea and Mongolia, nations with cold relations with China. Using diplomacy, perhaps, can keep Modi at the same level as Xi.

Let's be assured that PM Modi will revive the historic Sino-Indian bonding with his Midas touch and President Jinping will be equally friendly. China's pro-Pakistan era and India's era of troublesome trade deficit are to see a long-term break to allow the two Asiatic giants exploit available prospects in the global market, effectively and unitedly.

(Posted on blog on 12 May, 2015)

□

Pakistan, and Section 370 – A Tough Outlook

Was it right on the part of the previous union government to not even bother about simplifying relations with a neighboring nation? Despite many calls from Pakistan, the UPA and UPA-2 PM did not care even once to share the expectations of India. Nor did the previous government take any sturdy actions to curb terrorism in India, which has a concrete association with this neighboring nation. The all they did was to sit, watch, tolerate, and express sympathy. However, the picture is quite distinct now. With a buoyant administrator of the state, India now looks for new alternatives and renewed outcomes.

Mr. Modi was quite clear of his stand to invite the Pakistan's PM on the occasion of his swearing-in. The next day saw a constructive meet, wherein the Indian leader shared his expectations from the nation that shares close vibes with India in term of history and culture. Terrorism and the attacks of 26/11 were a key part of the agenda of discussion, and it was unmistakably conversed that India would not tolerate any terrorism that finds its roots in Pakistan. Surely, the Pakistani PM too wants cordial relations with India; hence the dialogue can be expected to reap enhanced consequences.

We need to learn from our past experiences that silence cannot serve any purpose. When you want the circumstances to progress, actions are compulsory. And it is sure, that the new leader acknowledges this fact. It is evident-If you want to secure cordial and peaceful relationship with Pakistan, you have to take a stand. The PM of Pakistan, too deserves applaud, who crossed the barriers of domestic differences with respect to his visit, and took a vital step towards the harmony of two nations-Something, that even the past Indian PM, Mr. Manmohan

Singh could not do even when called officially to attend the swearing-in of Mr. Nawaz Sharif.

Next is the most sensitive subject-matter that has grabbed the attention of the entire political family-Section 370. I believe that the BJP and RSS are fairly clear about their intentions. Mr. Modi while addressing the general public during his campaigning persuasively advocated a transparent discussion regarding the deliveries of this Section in terms of prosperity that the residents of J&K have secured. And, is that so wrong? In a democratic setup, outcomes shall be reliably assessed and correction actions, if required shall be taken. And, when the center of discussion is the fortune of the mass, nothing is forbidden.

It was astonishing to hear the comment of the J&K CM, wherein he has warned the BJP to either forget the revocation of Section 370 or J&K as the part of India. I would call this pure dictatorship. It is to be remembered that the inclusion of Section 370 was temporary considering the then prevailing circumstances. A revision, therefore, is the need of the hour. Plus, when the said Section was for the betterment of the state and the residents therein, actual delivery of this has to be analyzed. Mr. Modi, though, has not revealed his actual outlook over this vital subject; I am sure that this capable leader would resolve the prevailing concerns.

(Posted on blog on 29 May, 2014)

□

The 'Common' Indian

Why the Disaffection Over OROP?

Legacy Inherited

One Rank One Pension (OROP), a matter crucial to the welfare and self-esteem of retired defence services personnel, has been an extremely contentious issue that has been tearing at the heartstrings of the nation for quite some time now. The bitterness felt by the principal stakeholders of the issue was an unenviable inheritance of the BJP-led National Democratic Alliance (NDA) from a host of governments, which had preceded it during the past three decades. Surprisingly, the previous governments had done practically nothing to redress the grievance of the veterans regarding lowly pension rates.

Although the principled stand of BJP on the issue had been well-known since even before the Lok Sabha elections of 2014, the retired defence services personnel resorted to protests and vociferous outbursts of outrage over the continued indifference of the successive governments over the years. The nation watched in disbelief and amazement the virulent attack undeservedly mounted on the Narendra Modi government that had, in reality, been sympathetic to the cause all along. The NDA government's action in the matter had been characterized by the measured steps characteristically taken in an unhurried, yet steady pace, befitting the tremendous import of the issue. It had warranted a close examination of the financial, administrative and legal aspects of the matter, which had been kept in the cold storage, nay, doghouse, for all these years.

The impatience of the veterans, who felt there was hardly any forward movement in the matter, grew by the day. They were instigated by the Opposition parties with an axe to grind and a highly irresponsible section of the mainstream media that believes in sensationalism rather than objective reporting. As a result, all these assumed darker shades resulting in a deplorable sense of despondency and despair all around.

To make matters more confounded, the layman wondered, bemused and blissfully oblivious of the subterranean course of bureaucratic measures set in motion, over the apparent lack of action despite promises on the part of the government.

Discontentment Continues

Eventually when the NDA government announced its momentous decision to implement the One Rank One Pension scheme, there was a mixed response in store. While the government's decision came, by and large, as a welcome relief measure for the veterans' camp, there were discordant notes and murmurs of discontentment over the nitty gritty too. Although considerably scaled down, the bitterness and rancour have refused to die down and continued to vitiate the atmosphere.

No Jubilation Over Decision

Now that the storm, which had been ominously brewing up has blown over with the announcement of the government's decision to implement OROP, where is all the jubilation, the hoopla and the celebration over the good news? Shouldn't the nation which had been slamming the uncomplimentary treatment meted out to that honourable section of the society and pride of the nation, namely the veterans, be all jubilant over justice having been done at long last and simply go agog? Leaving aside the veterans, who still have a few dodgy points of the OROP scheme for the government to look into in further detail, what has been holding back the nation? And what has been preventing the Opposition parties and the more difficult sections of the mainstream media, from falling all over themselves in congratulating the veterans and complimenting the government?

Why the continuance of the sore note? Has it become a characteristic trait of our nation to be grumpy about giving credit where it belongs and paying compliments for a good job well done? How quick we were in rising in criticism! How ruthlessly we castigated the government for its laid-back attitude and lackadaisical approach to the sterling issue! How vociferous and unequivocal we were about justice for those who protect the country's borders with their lives! How condescending we were about the merits of the issue and restoration of the glory to the meritorious veterans! Why are we still sore and sulking? What are we still fretting and fuming about? Not to make too fine a point, is it not the time for our nation to sit up and self-introspect to get a drift of the disaffection over the issue of OROP?

Political Opportunism

Notwithstanding the tremendous amount of empathy that the entire nation has for the cause of the defence services personnel, the Opposition parties, the common man and the army veterans seem to have viewed the whole issue from a very biased standpoint and perspective. Does it not remind an impartial observer of the classic Indian parable of a bunch of persons with impaired vision touching and feeling about different body parts of an elephant and trying to describe the animal in totality. The Opposition parties, for instance, had absolutely no concern for the enormity of the issue or the intimidating nature of the challenges ahead in implementing OROP, given the ground realities of the nation's economy.

The Congress party and its allies, which had been in power for most of the period during the last three decades of the pendency of the issue, had kept OROP on the back burner. This obviously happened because the implementation of the scheme against multiple odds had meant no political dividends, and they did not consider the defence services personnel a constituency worth cultivating. Now that they are themselves in the political wilderness, they are clutching at straws in the wind for dealing a broadside at the NDA government and found in the OROP issue a handy political weapon for doing so.

The stance of the Congress and its allies in the matter is not based on any political or ideological conviction about doing the right thing, but it is totally a matter of political opportunism, pure and simple! Hence, their abortive attempt to steal the thunder from the government by making false claims about having taken the decision and doing all the commendable work themselves! The hollow ring of their claims has, however, been too deafening for the people not to notice. Consequently, the Congress and its allies stand exposed in the eyes of the masses for not only doing nothing when they were in power but also for underwriting the NDA government's creditable performance in the matter out of spite.

Sensationalism versus Defence Outlays

As regards those sections of the mainstream media that are given to playing up issues for the sake of sensationalism, the issue is still a burning one. They have been whipping a dead horse by talking about how an ungrateful nation has all along ignored the welfare of its soldiers who have unquestioningly served the country with sweat and blood in extreme conditions and daunting circumstances. Countless numbers of columns and blogs have already been written, with more on the way, about how niggardly our soldiers are paid during their service and post-retirement in comparison to their counterparts in developed countries like the US, UK, France and Japan. Such columns and blogs have also ranted about how a nation, which does not pay its Army well, has no moral right to send it to fight wars.

Our soldiers not only fight wars with the enemy across the border, but are also called in to help with relief measures whenever there is a natural disaster at home and, at times, in a neighbouring country like Nepal. All the more reason why they should be treated like the real heroes they are and all their demands met! While doing the comparison along sentimental lines, one conveniently forgets how it does not add up to make much sense to compare the pay structure and pensionary benefits of an Indian soldier with those of his counterpart from a developed country for obvious reasons such as economic viability, the nature of duties performed, etc.

Besides, having never been a colonial power, India has never sent its troops abroad to fight wars like their counterparts in the Western world except for peacekeeping operations as part of the UN Peace Keeping Forces. The only exception to this was the brief role they played as Indian Peace Keeping Forces in Sri Lanka during Rajiv Gandhi's premiership. Furthermore, India has never started a war with a neighbouring country unlike Pakistan or China, which are given to military adventurism and hegemonic ambitions. Guarding the borders along a harsh land terrain of 15,200 km and a 7,517 km long coastal line, is undoubtedly no mean task, requiring maintenance of a standing army with 1,325,000 active front line personnel and 2,143,000 reserve personnel.

India's defence budget is a whopping Rs. 250,000 crore per year, in addition to which the retired defence services personnel are paid Rs. 60,000 crore every year by way of pension. With the announcement of OROP, an additional annual expenditure of Rs. 12,000 crore is added to the defence outlay. These are not just statistical figures but the kind of price that the nation has to pay for safeguarding its frontiers from external aggression – during times of relative peace, with countless numbers of border incursions thrown in!

Sentimentality

For the people of the country, in general, neither the costs involved nor the challenges faced by the government in implementing the scheme, constitute a matter of concern. Meeting the demands of the defence services personnel, who are an eternal source of inspiration and symbol of patriotism for the crores of awestruck people of the nation beholden to the heroic soldiers, is not only a matter of sentiment and passion but also a means of redemption of its gratitude. Moreover, it is also a sign of its rewarding of supreme patriotism worn on the sleeve by the war veterans as proudly as the shining medals of honour won for valour in wars. In such circumstances, pragmatism tends to take a back seat.

More Categories to Follow

The veterans are still protesting over the perceived inadequacies of the terms of the scheme like the periodicity of the revision of pension rates and the rates of pension. While the review of the pension rates is due every five years as per the scheme, the veterans are demanding an annual revision. Besides, the protestors are demanding that pension be fixed at the highest pay of the rank in which one retires whereas the pension payable as per the approved plan is the average of the highest and lowest rates of the rank pay, with protection to those who are drawing the highest rate. Furthermore, the month from which OROP becomes effective is July this year. The protestors are demanding that the scheme be implemented with effect from April this year. Thus, there is no dearth of points of discord with nary a care to mounting additional costs of implementation!

The possibility of the paramilitary forces and law enforcing agencies like police personnel of different States demanding OROP is becoming more and more distinct and pronounced like ominous dark clouds gathering on the not-too-distant horizon. The question arises as to how justified or fair it would be to treat the soldiers who safeguard the country's borders from the external enemy as a superior category, the demands of which are to be met at any cost without hesitation or reservation, in preference to the law enforcing agencies that safeguard the integrity of the nation from the evil designs of internal and external enemies? No doubt, the defence services workforce have a shorter duration of service in comparison to the personnel of the law enforcing agencies, due to which they are deprived of the benefits of periodic pay revisions.

Furthermore, there are other differences too, which set the soldiers apart as a special category. But differences in the retirement age and service conditions pale into insignificance when the contrast stops at that. Because there is no comparing the employees of the law enforcing agencies with defence services personnel in the matter of valour and selfless service which both the categories of staff display in their respective spheres of operations in the service of the nation. As in the case of defence services workforce, application of OROP to the law enforcement agencies could not be linked to the expenditure outlays for reasons of sentiment. Yet another government sector wanting OROP is the Railways, the personnel of which have made the demand some time ago.

Less Government, More Governance

How dramatic, if not devastating, an effect will the spiraling costs of implementation of OROP to the complete satisfaction of the protesting defence services personnel, have on the country's budget? Where can the line of distinction be drawn between different government services in applying OROP? Are the people of the nation ready to take on additional taxes in future budgets to meet the demands of the swelling tribe of government personnel demanding OROP? In the clamour by more and more government department personnel demanding OROP, and the snowballing of expenditure outlays to meet these requirements, has the nation forgotten all about the droughts and famines and the consequent hardships and suffering of the farmers all over the country?

How far is our nation prepared to go to meet the demands of the defence services personnel, law enforcement agencies and similar workforce in the government machinery without compromising its obligation to other economic and social sectors? Is the nation not committed to the basic tenet of good governance enunciated by Narendra Modi before and after the Lok Sabha 2014-15 elections – less government and more governance? Where do we draw the red line of less government? Now is undoubtedly one of the moments of reckoning, which every nation on the right course of progress and development faces to be able to answer the daunting questions.

What is obvious, in any case, is that the nation should collectively decide its response to the culture of protests, demonstrations and rallies, and not leave it to the government which is meant to give clean governance which, in turn, brooks no interferences. The nation should not buckle under pressure. Nor should the government allow itself to be sucked into the quagmire of non-developmental expenditures. Having traversed thus far, it is probably time to bring the issue to a swift conclusion and move on in quest of productivity and progress with no interferences, a condition very vital for good governance.

(Posted on blog on 6 October, 2015)

(Posted on Bharat Niti portal on 24 October, 2015)

□

Swami Vivekananda – A Soul Who Enshrined India, Every Indian

Many view him as a scholar, many as a philosopher, many as a spiritual leader, for me, he was a guide, a guide who nobly exhibited the road to principled life, a life worthy enough for the society and the economy even. We cherish the lives of our sacred Gods and worship Him for the want of eternal fortune. Present, however, not just demands our remembrance of God, but also seeks our works devoted to the world we live in, for the progress of humans and humanity. Swami Vivekananda endorsed those elementary moralities, which if followed by every human on earth, would reverse all the evils. National Youth Day, as cherished on the 12th of every January, the birth day of Swami Ji, was declared in 1984, with the Government quoting, 'It was felt that the philosophy of Swami Ji and the ideals for which he lived and worked could be a great source of motivation for the Indian Youth'. Three decades of this 'Youth Day' and abundance of literature with the ideals of Swami Ji, however, aren't ample for the young blood of the country to live up to the path displayed by this esteemed soul; just because the passion of patriotism lacks. Not all of us are guilty; not everyone has disremembered the vitality of Karma, but in a country drowned in curses, fractional labors cannot be ample.

Motive is not to write the same words that are accessible to us all in the libraries and over the internet, the aim is to let people realize that past has done what it could have, now we have to live the present, shape a robust tomorrow. Whenever the legacy of Swami Ji is talked about, many of us affiliate him with furtherance of Hinduism, Gita, Vedanta, and Yoga. Do we remember that this person travelled thousands of kilometers and delivered hundreds of lectures emphasizing that service to God can be rendered by service to mankind? The person, who lived for just 39 years, the age when many of us are busy arranging for just our own families, was able to move the entire world with his awareness and approach towards life, towards religion and towards Karma. What if he had accepted the lucrative and honorable positions offered by the Harvard University and Columbia University? He turned down the proposals saying that his duties at the university would conflict with his obligations as a monk. His duties were to persuade the youth to work for the advancement of humankind, and the book 'Karma Yoga', which embraces his lectures on the significance of 'work and duty', tells us that this form of yoga is nothing other than dedicated mental discipline that allows us to carry out our services to the world, as a path to enlightenment.

I have much more to tell, his delivering of thoughts at the platform of the Parliament of World Religions in Chicago in 1893, his founding of the Vedanta Society of New York that promotes holiness and social service, his founding of the Ramakrishna Mission for communal welfare, and his advices to the followers to be holy, unselfish and to hold Shraddha, being some of them. On the occasion of Youth Day, however, I will confine my writing to his much-treasured work, the Karma Yoga. Youth of India has the highest sharing in the country's population and hence bears the liability to take forward the pluses and overcome the minuses of the society. Yet again, I would synonymize country with economy; economic dexterity and equal income dispersion can turn any stressed country into a prosperous one. Shouldn't I then also relate economy with the amount and eminence of labors done by the workforce; the same has a very deep linkage with the Karma Yoga as described by Swami Ji and holds that each one is great in his own workplace, showing us the path to attaining our goals through Karma, and advising us that non-attachment is complete self-abnegation. Swami Vivekananda's life and works have plenteous for the youth to study and imbibe in their doings, but the real essence lies in execution, to put it right, in honest and generous execution.

There is so much to be done; so much for yourself, your family, your country, and for the entire world. For yourself, spare some time and think what are the aims that you have always dreamt of and why haven't you attained them until now; nothing is above your approach and courage, defeat all the hindrances then. For your family, think for a while how your parents fulfilled their duties and what now their expectations from you are. For the country, think of what all are the bottlenecks, why your contribution is indispensable and how your partaking can bring a revolution. Swear not to be idle when time demands work, swear not be silent when situation demands retaliation, and swear not to be desirous when you know that resources are for all hence everyone has to be the recipient. It's time to live up to the legacy of Swami Vivekananda, as for afterwards we would complain of old age factors affecting our throughput. Get a book of 'Karma Yoga' authored by Swami Ji and know the secret of work, know how we help ourselves, not the world and that the path to enlightenment is service towards the whole world. He was an influential orator, a renowned writer; his writing 'Bartaman Bharat', a Bengali language essay, was a simple message to all the readers to honour and treat every Indian as a brother irrespective of whether he was born poor or in lower caste.

To all my young friends and also to India's future shoulders- The country seeks your active partaking in the path that can lead to sustainable evolution and dignified life for all. Unify all the scattered drops of energy lying within and aim for a better India, just to all and heaven on earth for all, indeed, achievable through devoted Karma.

"All power is within you; you can do anything and everything. Believe in that, do not believe that you are weak; do not believe that you are half-crazy lunatics, as most of us do nowadays. You can do anything and everything, without even the guidance of any one. Stand up and express the divinity within you." – Swami Vivekananda

(Posted on blog on 12 January, 2015)

□

Banning Porn Websites and Search Engines in India

Individual versus Society

With the possible exception of a recluse living in an otherwise uninhabited island or in such an improbable scenario outside the pale of human civilization all by himself, nobody is living in a world of his own where one could say or do things or act exactly as one pleases without a care or thought to the sensibilities of others. Every individual is a link in a chain that forms a society, with every single unit having its bearing on the whole. A society is a group of individuals and more. People's thoughts, ideas, concepts, ideological contributions and behavioural pattern make a society much more than the sum of its parts. They also contribute to the evolution of the society. As a higher body, these constituents are responsible for and responsive to the collective need of keeping the society the august organism that it is.

When thoughts, ambitions, aspirations and goals of individual members of the community, especially the younger segment are lofty, like during the Independence Movement, there will be an upsurge in the collective will of that society. This leads to an uplifting and productive period, conducive to that country's betterment and progress. During such periods, which are often marked by the appearance of a Mahatma or a visionary with outstanding leadership qualities, the nation makes bold strides in the creative fields of arts, science and spiritual development. On the contrary, when the cultural moorings on which society is based are shaken, decay sets in, making the collapse of the stature of that community only a matter of time. In short, while the society provides for the individual's personal liberty and freedom of expression without which the evolution of that community is not possible, the individual owes it to the society to conduct his affairs in a responsible and restrained fashion. This is to ensure that his conduct does not impinge on the society's fundamental and basic tenets of decency and decorum.

Indian Society

In India, where the society had traditionally been conservative down the centuries, the Western culture that started making inroads along with the wonders of information technology, paved the way for the horrors of cultural and moral decay. It is an indisputable fact that the cultural mores and acceptable norms of conduct and behaviour in India in matters of public display of affection and adult entertainment are at variance with those of the West countries and elsewhere.

An unrestrained and unorganized influx of data and informational material, which are crass and indecent in nature, are a risqué factor that is capable of playing havoc with the moulding, shaping and development of feeble minds. As they have been designed to cater to the base or animalistic instincts in humans in the name of entertainment, adult or universal, they need to be blocked by the society for ensuring a healthy lifestyle of its members, conducive to the collective welfare of that community. Without trying to sound too moralistic or pontificating, it may be safely said that sleaze, smut, obscenity or vulgarity should find no quarters in a civilized society.

Porn and Exploitation

It is hard to imagine a world where the participants in the put-on acts depicted in porn movies, clippings, etc seen on the porn sites on the internet lack self-esteem and willingly demean themselves by enacting the scenes of depravity. Without getting into the gory details, it may be safely claimed that the participants are either economically or otherwise exploited and forcibly pushed into crossing the Rubicon. Today, pornography is a multi-billion dollar industry. It thrives and flourishes on abominable vices and crimes such as human trafficking, modern day slavery, extortion, human rights violation, particularly concerning children and women, drug peddling, etc. It is a sinister and murky world of purveyors of sleaze and depravity who view the humans they prey upon as mere commodities in their money spinning operations.

They work in close cooperation with underworld dons who undertake to lure in easy prey for their shoddy services, launder black money and keep competing adversaries and snooping law enforcing authorities out of the beat. Money making is the only aim of the purveyors of filth and the churning out of a never-ending stream of sleaze and smut for those on the lookout for lasciviousness their sole occupation. Their gateway to a lucrative pornographic industry of easy pickings is strewn with the early casualties, of attributes such as innocence, honour, basic human decency and faith in fellow human beings. And the victims are not only exploited but also coerced into falling in line. Even in economically advanced Western countries, we see the sorry spectacle of helpless governments unable to crack down on the spectre of grooming of innocent schoolgirls who are sexually exploited, blackmailed and then pushed into a fate worse than death. Surprisingly, such countries even include France and the UK, which have become a cauldron of heterogenous cultures that don't merge but stick out like sore thumbs.

That the governments of such countries choose to remain inactive is a matter for deep self-introspection for the concerned societies. They don't initiate action owing to fear of antagonizing the minority migrant communities, which are fertile breeding grounds for such evil crimes. But an undeniable fact is that pornography industry is often the fountainhead of sex-related crimes and attendant violence, which are absolutely unjustifiable and unacceptable in any civilized society. On the one hand, the internet is a wonderful medium of information and knowledge, and it has shrunk the world to the amazement of humanity. However, this same internet acts as the conduit of the wares of the purveyors of sleaze, and it has overdone its bit by transcending all norms of decency and decorum and features the ugly underbelly of human behaviour and conduct.

Sample the Evil

Aside from the evil practices employed in the porn industry, how pornography has overwhelmed the young and vulnerable segment of the Indian society and brought it under its outreach is a matter of grave concern for parents and the community. According to the findings of a survey conducted by 'Rescue', an NGO that works on social issues, over 3 lakh students in Chennai aged in the age range of 16-21 years watch rape videos every day. Among college students, 44% watched 18 videos of violent porn, rape and gang rape every week. For 84% of those in the age group, porn is an addiction, just like drugs.

Recommendations

Abhishek Clifford, CEO of 'Rescue', who is also a statistics lecturer in London says now no one can deny the link between youngsters watching rape and porn videos and the ever-increasing figures of violent rape and abuse in India any longer. The survey has also found that 62% of those students who watched rape videos wanted to do it in real life. Even if 10% of this lot act on their desire, it will produce 1,300 rapists each year, Clifford points out. Based on the survey, members of 'Rescue' have put forth some recommendations. They include: incorporating cyber ethics in the first and second year syllabus of college students; installing porn-blocking software in cyber cafes as they tend to provide easy access to pornographic material; and creating awareness among parents about the psychological impact of porn and how easily their children can access it.

Evils of Porn

Pornography is addictive, especially in the case of adolescents whose minds are not adequately developed. Regular exposure to uncensored adult material, replete with untrammeled passions and unbridled violence, is capable of tricking young minds into cultivating wrong notions about man-woman relationship. Apart from robbing the innocence of the viewer, such dubious visual experience could result in extreme trauma, shock and psychological setbacks. It can also severely alter the concept of gender objectivity and adversely affect the way individuals view others, especially members of the opposite sex. This could lead to a situation where young men and women who work in close proximity with each other and married couples develop a cock-eyed view of the commonalities and differences of perception about each other's gender.

Healthy respect for emotions, feelings and sentiments on the part of one's partner in a beautiful man-woman relationship for which there is no scope or room in porn, could give way to lust and urge for gratification of animalistic instincts, primeval cravings and primordial perversions. Such a situation could eventually lead to skepticism and pessimism towards concepts such as platonic relationships and beautiful friendships between members of opposite genders. There could be an unhealthy atmosphere of mistrust and animosity in educational institutions and workplaces. Corruption of a pristine mind at too early a stage in life is pernicious and is likely to make one lose focus on the development of creative faculties and progress. In short, young men and women are likely to go astray, and get sucked into the treacherous and uncharted waters of extreme gratification of sensory perceptions.

For and Against Porn

Some defend pornography, saying that critics overreact and that porn may act as an outlet for aggression. Liberal thinkers are per se against curbs and restrictions on individual freedom for a lifestyle of one's personal choice, such as accessing porn on the internet. There are others who believe that pornography is immoral, could ruin relationships and perpetuate sexism, besides falling foul with religious norms and tenets. While both the sides have their own arguments, based on logic, reasoning, beliefs and facts, no government could play mute spectator to the phenomenon of pornography affecting the individual and the society. It must take a call on the issue and take appropriate measures to curb the menace of porn before it gets out of control and cause irreparable damage to the cultural fabric of the country.

Censorship and Ban

Indian culture has a rich diversity with strong underpinnings of regional, linguistic and faith-based beliefs and value system. There is a common thread of Hindutva running through our culture notwithstanding the differences of perception on the part of people in different communities in the manifestation of creative art forms. It cannot be denied that ours is a country where the woman is not only respected but revered too, as female worship predominantly features in people's religious and spiritual beliefs. The importance of family values is of tremendous significance. As such, the need for movies and other creative art forms to be temperate in their artistic expressions cannot be overemphasized as their impact on the viewers is immense. Hence the need for censorship in the absence of which obscenity, vulgarity, obscurantism and violence could run roughshod over the viewer's sensibilities.

When art and mainstream cinema is subjected to censorship, how could pornography, to which more people have access to, within the precincts of their home than the viewers of movies, be allowed to skirt censorship? In the absence of a self-auditing mechanism, porn on the net has to be subjected to rigorous filters. The resultant product has to be in conformity with strict control measures and exacting standards before it is allowed to reach the viewer. Complaints from viewers about breaches of regulations and excesses should be subject to review of permission to the net service provider. Sites on child porn, taboos, incestuous relationships, demeaning of women, violence and other unnatural acts must be banned. A comparative study of measures initiated by the governments of other countries to regulate or proscribe porn on the internet may be undertaken for designing an appropriate policy for India.

Action by Government

The NDA government has taken upon itself the task of regulating and organizing the availability of risqué material on the internet, citing threat to public morality. With a shot-in-the-arm directive from the Supreme Court, the Department of Telecommunications had on July 31 via a discreet order directed internet service providers to block access to 857 websites and search engines that were providing an unrestricted flow of porn material. They were found violating Article 19(2) of the Indian Constitution. The said Article imposes "reasonable restrictions" on the exercise of free speech, particularly in instances concerning decency and morality. However, in the face of a stiff and sustained pressure from the mainstream media and criticism, the restriction had to be partly lifted. The ban on the sites featuring child porn still continues.

Meanwhile, in the second fortnight of September 2015 the Supreme Court Women Lawyers' Association (SCWLA) has filed an intervention application in the apex court seeking a national policy on the issue of pornography, framing of guidelines as well as initiation of strict measures to curb the growing menace of child pornography. The SCWLA has expressly sought blocking of all porn websites claiming that pornography "corrupts" the mind of the younger generation and provokes them to commit crimes against women and children.

In its endeavour to bring about a complete stoppage of porn in all its vicarious and pernicious manifestations, the Central and state governments should press their agencies and continue to examine ways and means, for the collective good of our Indian society. These efforts should be in tune with the commitment to the preservation of the Indian culture and notwithstanding the grandstanding of liberal thinkers harping on the personal liberty of the individual. Thus, the Central and state governments should be determined in their bid to prohibit pornography and need not be apologetic about the viability of the drive to achieve the laid-down goal. The following are some measures that could be taken up for consideration:

- A battery of intellectual luminaries, community elders, spiritual gurus, representatives of organizations that work for women's and children's welfare, and representatives of the parent-student community could be engaged for launching a nationwide campaign for creating awareness of the evils of pornography.
- A media blitzkrieg could be considered to give the movement visibility and high profile.
- Some real-life cases of individuals and organizations who have successfully battled the pornography dragnet could be illustrated and feted.
- A nationwide contest may be conducted for launching a catchy logo with wordings like "Say No to Porn".
- A drive could be initiated to enlist volunteers who come forward to express their opposition to porn and spread the message of the government's determination to eradicate porn.
- Prohibitory orders and censorship laws could be made more stringent to send a dire warning to internet service providers.
- Cyber laws should be strengthened to fight cases of pornography on the same lines as treason.
- Above all, the real life panacea of Yoga could be promoted to combat the evils of porn.

(Posted on blog on 30 September, 2015)

□

Caste Based Reservation System – Until When?

In case you have never witnessed a payee of our reservation system, who exceeds many from the unreserved category in terms of economic prosperity as well as opportunity, my writing is of no use. When many justify the merits of our caste based reservation system, can anyone from them substantiate that the perks of reservation flow only to the needy? Since inception, our so-called progressive reservation system has been an area of controversy; however with a view to get hold of power none of the political groups seems to favor any constructive changes. With 15 percent for SCs, 7.5 for STs, and 27 for OBCs, the General category strives with just 50 percent.

The very inception of this futile caste based reservation system can be related with distinct representation provided for Muslims, Sikhs, Christians, and Dalits by Ramsay MacDonald in 1932. Known to all, this was a part of the 'Divide and Rule' policy, which was protested by Mahatma Gandhi; however gained support from the face of Dalits, Dr. B.R. Ambedkar. The subsequent development of this absurd proposition can be comprehended with the fact that the percentage of SC employees in the Central Government Class I category augmented from 1.18 percent in 1959 to 10.12 percent in 1995, while from 2.38 percent to 12.67 percent in Class II.

'When is our nonsensical reservation system further enlarged' is not that tough question to construe. The Maharashtra Government has recently announced 16 percent and 5 percent reservation for Marathas and Muslims, respectively enhancing the total reservation to 73 percent, which means mere 27 percent for the General category; despite the fact that many from this category are far more underprivileged than members of reserved castes. 'Vote Bank Politics' is all that has never allowed the politicians and governments to look beyond castes and communities, and make available paybacks to real seekers, the truly underprivileged ones.

The Supreme Court of India has consistently laid down the principle that reservation for any category can only be permissible in case backed by relevant data and evidence that can justify the need for reservation. On the contrary, the state government of U.P. announced reservation in promotions in the year 2007, with a view to get hold of the votes of particular castes. Challenged in the court of law, the measure was declared unconstitutional. Same was the case when the Central Government's vote-oriented announcement of sub-quota of 4.5 percent for minorities was stayed by the Election Commission for violation of the model code of conduct.

The very addition of the favors granted to particular castes in the Constitution of India can be understood as the underlying basis of this grave concern. The makers, though were conscious of the then-prevailing backwardness and lack of opportunities for the backwards, did not pay proper heed to the milieu when members of these castes would unjustifiably profit from this setup, while the real underprivileged would rarely advance. For sure, the untenable caste based reservation system has to be replaced with reservation based on economic status of the family. Not few, comprehensive amendments to laws and procedures is the pressing need of the hour.

(Posted on blog on 13 July, 2014)

□

Modernization and Westernization are Not Synonymous

Westernization is nothing but embracing the culture, ideas, lifestyle, values and guiding principles of the west by communities from other geographical locations.

But, isn't it all within? Moody's has lately upgraded India's sovereign rating outlook to 'Positive', which previously stood at 'Stable'. The reason cited by the rating agency was perceptive and constructive measures taken by the Narendra Modi-led government in past months, and same factors are to attract more and more foreign fund inflows to India. Let's now dig some soil and pull out facts about economic richness of the country as embraced in the history of this world. Indus Valley Civilization is said to have initiated the economic history of our country, then by the Maurya Empire, followed by classical civilizations of Rashtrakutas and Western Gangas, and it was during this phase that we had the largest economy in the world up until the 17th century and the rise of the Maratha Empire. The accounts of historical facts approve that India was the richest economy in the world and our dominance was led by the personal shrewdness of rulers and traders, political unity and unbroken security.

Why I have cited these details and will quote a few more is for the reason that we are, more or less, scrutinized basis the global parameters, ranging from contribution towards world's GDP growth rate to sentiments of investors towards us, and a minute elevation of us in these ratings makes us feel assured, relaxed. Have we turned so global that in case we are termed as one of the most promising emerging countries of the world, we tend to forget our opulent past, the caliber of our forefathers and the way they made not only India develop, but the global trade until the 1700 AD depended substantially on South Asia's master, India? In no way can this discussion lead to or justify complete self-dependence for the purpose of attainment of goals ranging from wider employment prospects for the youth and prosperity of agriculturists to empowerment of women and education for all. But 'dependence' cannot be a thorough and unanalyzed adaptation of western socio-economic and political concepts and philosophies; rather it is just getting what we are deficient in, for say nuclear arsenal from France and Canada, and evolving ways for making India a flag-bearer in the contest of universal development.

Now when the current PM has linked development with environment, it is crucial to see when we would unlink development and westernization. Sensible appraisal of the past will be the key to initiate the revolution for India's true social and economic growth. The decline in Indian industry was much palpable during the colonial period, the time, when in the 19th century much of the world was undergoing industrialization, but India lagged behind. Technological innovation was the basis of the lead that European nations were able to take; India being an agriculture-dependent and a low wage country trailed. The turning points, however, came when entrepreneurs like Jamsetji Tata, a visionary who setup TISCO with tactical arrangement with the British that any surplus production will be procured by Britain, paved way for technical skill enhancement and adequate pays to industrial laborers. Today, if we stay restricted to just the western paradigm or the feat of Bill Gates or theories of communism by Karl Marx, we might not prudently judge the needs of the Indian socio-economic and political spheres, also, we may invite long-term damages in desire of short-term advancement on the global parameters of growth.

Call it 'Bhartiyata', 'Hinduism' or anything else; the bottom line is that the brains, arms and hearts of India are capable enough to take the country to new echelons of success without relying on the notion of blind westernization, rather by inventing novel concepts and making resourceful use of our assets, tangible as well as intangible. So if today, we assess the development of our women as per the benchmarks set by EU countries or the U.S., or we measure the level of climate change in accordance with the limits set by the WHO, and find ourselves as progressive, the tasks remain half-done. Where are the national parameters that in my view can even be harsher than the global ones, but they would carry and remind us of the rich past that was able to cater to the demands of the Indians; we have, however, failed to deliver these since decades owing to our political and communal weaknesses? Shouldn't we crave for deep analysis of the commerce and technology world-over, absorb the pros, yet for the real betterment of our craftsmen and small-scale businessmen, discover and revive our old but tested methodologies so that wage earners do not lose jobs, available entrepreneurship is fully utilized, and the center of production be cottages, farmlands and homes, not mere factories.

On one hand is the model of the west, where consumption and value of commodities determine progress of economy, while on the other was Indian theory of contentment. There is no harm in studying the pluses of the west and procuring resources that aren't easily available within the borders. New alliances, pacts and consensus must be a part of the foreign policy of the government; along with, however, the hidden Indian pluses and apparent minuses are to be worked out. In the wake of human rights, activists of the west placed humans above all, above the remaining living beings, but the principles of ancient as well as modern India differ, on basis that cows here are considered divine and though humans are to be cared about the most, this cannot be on the cost of other creatures, an example set by the Maharashtra government which recently banned beef consumption. What good are human rights if they supersede core human 'values' like love, help and sympathy? What good could be throat-cut competition, self-concentrated pricing policies, sub-standard production, and use of muscle-power and caste-equations in winning over an election?

Believe it, by the grace of the Almighty, we have all the resources that add to build a developed nation. Manpower, capital and acumen, we aren't lacking in any of these. In fact, lacking is the national pledge, pledge to use unity and uprightness as the drivers of our growth and supremacy. Today, the socialism and communism as advocated by minds like Karl Marx and Joseph Stalin, and adopted as a philosophy by many countries, has lost its essence in the dust-storm of corruption and self-centeredness. To regain the title of being the richest country, we are to exploit core Indian values and philosophies. A philosopher, teacher and strategist, Chanakya authored Arthasastra and is credited as the mind who played the most pivotal role in the establishing of the Maurya empire; a lawyer, freedom fighter, and social and political activist, Mahatma Gandhi who stands tall in London's Parliament

Square; Mother Teresa; Dr. Abdul Kalam; Vinoba Bhave; J.R.D. Tata, and a few of those names that are evidences of our aptitude; I hope that the government would turn today's youth in the similar direction, and the blind motive of westernization will be superseded by intellect endeavors and exploitation of indigenous resources.

India's intellects' obsession of the west finds its evidence in why the man who laid the foundation of political integration of India, Sardar Patel, is compared to Otto Bismarck, the man who united Germany in 1860s; the irony is that Shakespeare was and is never termed as Kalidasa of the Great Britain, or Napoleon as Samudragupta, the military genius, of Europe. Let me very clearly and fearlessly advocate adopting of Indian values and richness as guiding principles for our future actions, in contrary to blind following of the west. 'Development, Modernization and Westernization can never be synonymous.'

(Posted on blog on 12 April, 2015)

□

Do Not Punish Innocent Men in Pursuit to Women Empowerment

I have collated some facts, which though are uncomplicatedly accessible to all of us but we hardly care for the other side of the story, after all we are pro-women. In 2013, the High Court of Delhi observed that women were using fabricated rape cases for personal crusade, harassment, extortion and forcing men to marry them. This year, a leading news house reported that two-third of total rape cases filed in Delhi in 2013 involved consenting couples, with the parents accusing male of rape. In the month of October this year, the Delhi Commission of Women released a report, which revealed that out of 2753 complaints of rape filed between April 2013 and July 2014, only 1287 were found to be genuine. Here is the most dramatic one. In 2010, the Delhi High Court overruled a man's appeal to drop a false rape case filed against him, saying that this was to ensure that the complainant, a female police employee, is indicted for the deceitful case; the woman in the case had reached an out-of-court settlement with defendant. Same is the case with cases of dowry, and the Apex Court in 2010 directed the government to revise Section 498A of the IPC in view of rising numbers of false/exaggerated grievances against male partners and their relatives by women. Why then the alleged accused, who never have committed such crimes, live in the state of despair since the common public regard them as deemed-guilty.

In past couple of days, I went through a number of news, but these two were where I had to stop and meditate. The first is the Human Rights Watch report which talks about overcrowded mental rehabilitation centers where women are mentally and physically abused, and a hope to escape is nil. The report is titled 'Treated Worse than Animals' and I would want all those craving for women empowerment to read the same once. In the second one, which is almost the most sensational news of recent times, two sisters have emerged as 'Mardanis', having taken a hard call on suspected eve-teasers. The act of heroism is also caught on camera and the video has gone viral. They used hands, legs and belts to make sure that what they say happened to them shall not happen to any other girl. In the present milieu, I too was moved with such bravery and for a while considered the girls as a role model, wanting other girls to learn from them a lesson on retaliation against evil. Today, when we are unhappy for crimes against women anyone who turns out to be a protestor, whether truthful or not, becomes an iconic figure. The other side of the Rohtak case is that the row was over seats and the girls can clearly be seen using foul language. Those who valued the bravery must be watchful now when another video of them thrashing a man, and fresh witnesses in the bus instance have come forward saying that the girls weren't molested. The media also has now shifted its stand realizing the sensational twist and the 'staged' acts of bravery are being tested. I also could not apprehend the logic of our media which published the news of the brave-heart girls at the very first page on the first day; however now, when the contradictory to girls' statement facts have come up, the news makes less relevance to media houses.

Now, with a few female workers at my workplace, I am a scared man. On top of this, they report to me at day's end with tasks done, the same makes me vulnerable to cases of molestation and harassment. And I am not the only one. Men at reputable positions, be it in the corporate, politics, media, or sports, face the threat of being dragged into cases of woman assault. The mockery is, even the common 'man' is at the risk of being detained, beaten up, and defamed in the public, just because the groundless search for women empowerment is on. What's wrong, him? Women have repeatedly been victim to domestic violence, dowry, eve-teasing and rapes. This indeed calls for empowering the woman of India, but in the pursuit of the same, haven't we disremembered that the words empower and power are very dissimilar to one another. While empowering would mean enabling, powering someone would mean assigning someone surplus powers that may even supersede the laws of the land. Why then we treat extremists differently? They too at some point in time in history were assaulted by the society, why otherwise someone would tie a bomb around his waist and blow himself up? But this is forbidden, forbidden in every book of religion, society, politics and even our sensational media. On the contrary, 'no questions asked' policy is followed in case a woman allegedly beats a male who is later blamed for harassing, eve-teasing and even raping.

To the seekers of women empowerment-I am not in favor of any anti-women law or for that matter against furtherance of women. The simple notion that men and women shall be treated alike, however, is crushed when we allow a woman employ unlawful measures even in cases where justice can be realized under law. Certainly, investigation by police was the solution in the Rohtak case, not abrupt rewards to girls or debarment of the accused men from army. Isn't it an evident suppression of justice, when only the reporting media is held as evidence and the ones truly breaching law are imprudently declared lawful? When the honorable courts of India have comprehended the abuse of women protection laws, the government should take prompt rectifying measures. The solution rests in fortifying police administration and easing the way for filing sincere grievances, and herein a man and a woman are to be considered alike. Just like law and righteousness are alike both for rich and poor, it shall be for men and women. Yes, bettering the conditions of women, deprived of basic rights is the liability of us all and has to be pursued with extravagant labors. But, in want of hasty development of our women, let us not overlook what we claim, 'Nature has made man and woman alike.'

One thing is sure, unless we put an end to the 'no questions asked' rule when it comes to a female accusing a male of molesting or harassing, real enablement of women will never be attained, as a day would come when retraction would reach such heights that these complaints will not be paid heed to. Were the media reports ample to adjudge the men in the Rohtak incident guilty? When did we turn so proactive, or shall I say hasty? The real irony is that Indian laws are so contradictory that when the legalized age for sexual activity has been regarded as 18 years, obviously with mutual consent, a girl can still accuse the male of sexual annoyance even when mutual consensus and age factor are in place. What will you say about cases when a female wakes up post 5 or 10 years of alleged harassment, where at most of the occasions the real motive is to extract fiscal perks or to defame a person on instigation of his opponents? Isn't it easy for a female to say 'He used me under a promise to marry' and drag the person to the misery of lifetime? Promise! Why do we need the Indian Contract Act then? Was the girl not at fault when she made it, or shall I not say 'relishing' with the man before marriage and in some cases even with a married man?

The loopholes of our laws are placing Indian men at risk, high risk I say, even for the male lawmakers and law protectors. Just recently, the honorable Chief Justice of India has set up a two-judge Social Justice Bench to speed up cases involving missing children and such other social evils. This move is appreciable and the man of acumen should also consider as to where we all are heading in our visionless pursuit of women enablement. How can the guiltless parents of a male be defamed and detained just because the daughter-in-law alleges that she was asked for dowry? Why are we consenting to out-of-court settlements in cases of sexual harassment and are allowing false complainants to extract their ill motives? Rape is a crime and how can such settlements render the same guiltless? What's wrong with the Khap Panchayats then? Improving the laws by making them so stringent and by adding severe punitive clauses for filing false complaints/retractions in cases of sexual assault is the pressing need. Media, politicians, and indeed the common man have to be wise enough while giving verdicts during such cases. Never forget that you can be at the painful end one day.

To all women-My intents for women empowerment are as pure as they should be for the sake of security of my daughter, wife, and all other women, reflection of the same are my blogs, 'Need to Empowering Indian Women' and 'Women-What they deserve and what they get published on March 4, 2014 and June 10, 2014 respectively, but I am equally thoughtful when it comes to shielding my son, father, and other men from any illicit attacks, as evident from my blog, 'Deemed-Guilty Before Judicial Judgment' published on 27 September, 2014. An overlooked fact that the society needs to realize is that along with the alleged accused, women associated with that man, his wife, daughter/s, and female employees are equally punished and forced to live a miserable life. Helpless in correcting the laws of India, I still have a piece of advice for my friends-Use CCTVs at places of meet with females. Better proactive than a rapist, agree?

(Published in weekly magazine Uday India in Vol. VI, No. 41, 13-19 September, 2015)

(Posted on blog on 4 December, 14)

□

Infuse 'India' in the Heart and Soul of Every Indian

While going through the controversial subject of extremism, I learned how militants use religion as a weapon against mortality. Having read that the terrorists, who crushed the civil order and slaughtered hundreds of guiltless in Mumbai on 9/11, were given lessons on using heavy weapons and adjusted-history on brutality with the men of a particular community, I realized that extremists are far more tactical and strategically-adept than those who urge for global peace. They corruptly play with the minds of new blood, turn them into destroyers, and steer clear of adverse outcomes. I then hunted for any group in India which, I thought, would be linked with conveying lessons on national service and patriotism. Luckily, I came across an arm of the Indian Army, The Territorial Army, which enrolls civilians and provides them prospects to receive military training and thus creating a reserve force that could back the regular army, when circumstances warrant. Pleased was I and looked for admission. Then were the admissibility criteria, which only permitted 'gainfully employed' civilians possessing a graduate degree. But that did not let me down as I am 'eligible'. The 'criteria', however, urged me to pen few thoughts.

Why at all is this necessary?

Those who designed study curriculum would have had considered an authentic fact that unless you inform the kids of the nation about the contributions and sacrifices of worthy Indians, the sensation of reverting what we fetch from nation's soil cannot be expected. Poems on Rani Lakshmi Bai and chapters on India's struggle for independence were not for adding knowledge of science but for adding patriotism to kids' approach. But, 'busy and tough life' we call it, that fades away all lessons and we just want our police, army, politicians, and activists to pursue the path of national service. Tell me, as a common man, scuffling for better work and living prospects, am I relieved of the duty of serving my nation? And if your answer is 'No', then why am I found polluting the roads, bribing the officials, discarding the laws of the land, and employing any and every trick for the betterment of 'my' house? Civilians, in any nation, far outdo the number of government employees, hence nation-building is lacking without the common man's partaking. And then, when I imagined 125 crore 'Indians', with India in their heart, I foresaw cheerful and prosperous households as an outcome of equal distribution of national wealth.

Milieu in other nations

I could find a hefty list of countries, which engage civilians in enforced military training for a year. The youth is infused with a sensation to serve the nation, whenever the time demands. Along with, punctuality, use of weapons, and coordination are what that the youth learn at the very early age of their lives. Norwegian Parliament has lately adopted amendments with a view to extending obligatory military services to women of Norway. 'Conscription', as the world terms it, denotes compulsory enlistment of citizens in some sort of national service, which most often is the military service. Post serving the 'active duty', the recruits are transferred to 'reserve force'. Even in the U.S., males between 18 and 25 are mandated to register with the Selective Service System, which helps to keep a track of persons available during crisis.

Indian setup

Having discussed the Territorial Army wing of Indian Army, I have shared the option of being a part in national service, however, only a few can avail the same. Unemployment rate in India is above 3.5 percent; hence this cluster becomes 'ineligible'. Next, with the pressure of serving private and government jobs, how many of the employed ones can opt for the same? Graduation degree is another binding clause. Presently, the Territorial Army has strength of 40, 000 first line and 160, 000 second line troops. Do you think this is acceptable for a country with second highest population in the world?

Suggestions

It is evident that achieving a model similar to 'compulsory military service' will not be a feasible option in India. But, infusing 'India' in the heart of every India is indispensable if the PM is aiming for inclusive support. You would agree that the teachings we learn in schooldays fade away with time. Herein, the need is to deploy one army personnel at all educational institutions, public or private, for the purpose of teaching a lesson each day on national service until grade 12th. Plus, post High School, one hour of essential quasi-military training should be added to the learning course. Lessons on obedience, realism, physical activeness, handling tensed situations, readily accepting the call for national service, and 'India first' must be made obligatory. National Anthem and Constitution of India, biographies of national heroes, and vitality of contribution towards country must be a part everywhere. And when all educational institutions are talked about, taken into account should also be privately-run local schools and madrasas.

With 'India' in every Indian's soul, betrayal and brain drain will not find any place. Plus, the youth will become much more responsible post undergoing military training. India can then expect loyal, participative citizens, readily available for national service.

(Posted on blog on 31 October, 2014)

□

Indian Holiday System – Detrimental to Growth

When I look at one of the calendars at my workplace, a hefty list embracing 34 holidays seems soothing enough. Those red dates in the month are looked upon by most of us as relaxing and cheerful days. Being a secular nation with abundance of religions and customs, India is one of the most liberal countries in terms of work-offs. And if I will ask you the underlying cause for a specific holiday, most of us will search for the same on Google. Then why not search for number of public holidays allowed in nations that rank above us both in terms of GDP growth rate and Human Development Index. Sorry to say, but we would all welcome a declared paid holiday on 'Ravidas Jayanti'; however only a few of us know about his contribution towards the society. Moreover, the exact motive behind declaring some days of the year as public holidays is unknown. Did we want just a reason to take some rest from work, or did we want the public to realize the meaning of such days when a prominent person was born or a critical event took place? Tell me justly, do we ever recall the teachings of great Indian men while relishing offs?

Anyways, we rarely care to remember the ideals of Mahatma Gandhi on the 2nd of every October; however, yes we plan the fun activities for the day weeks before. The Human Resource Management modules these days advocate 'People First' principle, wherein all workplaces must provide a harmless and enjoyable milieu to employees, incentives for innovation, recognition for traveling the extra mile, and breaks from work to maintain lasting interest. I can understand the role of the initial three concepts; however either we have misinterpreted the concept of breaks from work or we are willingly allowing the productivity to hamper. The new '5-days' working culture became popular with the advent of IT and BPM sector. And then we have those 'Monday Blues' with feelings of anxiety and the 'Friday Fever' with the enthusiasm of the weekend. Yes, the same could have been an acceptable theory in case we valued the 'Work while work and play while play' idea. But are Indians, or more precisely, most of the Indians, ready for this model?

As per the directions issued by the Department of Economic Affairs (Banking Division), Indian banks relish 15 public holidays, which embrace occasions and celebrations for all the religions prevailing in the nation. Sunday is a universal rest-day. But, the local shops of any locality and even the multiplexes/supermarkets work 24 × 7 × 365. Yes, they make profits, the workforce enjoys work, and the contribution to national GDP is eminent. But how do they manage such work culture? Rotational shifts, fun at work and roster offs balance the tough job and employees' expectations. Even the IT and BPM industry calls the workforce for extended shifts and variable week-offs to manage the demand-supply equilibrium. In the public sector, however, the list of 15 holidays is abruptly enlarged by respective state governments in view of public appeasement. Not rare are the instances when political parties with specific vote bank declare public holidays on days which are of prominence to only a small cluster. Loss of business? – Who cares.

We repeatedly hear about caste-based reservation system and caste-based rallies (most common in states like U.P. and Maharashtra), but no one talks of caste-based holidays which are consistently eating up our viability. FYI-The BSP-led state government of the U.P. declared October 9, the death anniversary of party's founder, Kanshi Ram, as a public holiday; however the SP-led government cancelled the same after assuming power in 2012. And the irony is that not even a trivial percentage of state employees or school children knew why they were off from work on October 9. Is someone caring for nation-building, or is everybody busy in luring the vote bank? Shouldn't the government at the center revoke all such negative powers of states? If you take away all Saturdays and Sundays, public holidays, and paid casual/sick leaves, almost every wage earner in India works even for less than 200 days. And then we wander for development. Adding to the curse is access to social networking websites, personal emails, messages, and calls during work hours. Isn't banning the same while work lawful? Remember, until we take up our work as a fundamental social duty, we can never anticipate success.

As per the BBC, every bank holiday in the U.K. costs the U.K. economy £2.3 billion. In India, when the bank employees opted for strike against a change in the Banking Laws Bill, ASSOCHAM estimated per day loss to the economy as INR 15,000 crore. We know that the banking system is the backbone of our economy. Same is the case with other public departments which are set up for the sole purpose of uplifting the economy. The common men, most of whom are free from work liabilities on Sundays, face a condition of distress when every public office, be it the local municipality or a nationalized bank, have their doors closed. Imagine how weighty would be the detriment to the economy when apart from the statutory 15 public holidays, even most of the states have framed their own Industrial Establishment Holidays Acts, wherein firms are directed to declare a paid holiday for specific days, which most of the times are of regional connotation. The milieu is alarming as even during working hours, we deliver sub-optimal outcomes.

It is evident that offs from work are legitimate only to the extent they do not hamper productivity. Herein, declaring only the three days of national importance as statutory holidays and allowing five other optional days for paid leaves can be a workable notion. The optional holidays can be cheered by the employee on any of the days listed, which must be days of prominence. Yes, the culture of '5-days' can be followed; however, the public offices must be made accessible 365 days a year. This can be done by employing extra workforce for Saturdays and Sundays, and also by effecting the variable week-offs system. Possibility of extending the working hours of public offices to 9 pm can also be established. Businesses seek approvals from the government departments, the general public hunts for easily accessible state offices, and the inter-state trade looks for same holiday policies in all states (specifically banks). The new government will have to find ways to cut down the evils of hefty holiday-list and to let the economic environment breathe zealously. Of course, the pain of a common man wandering to pay bills and to file documentation in government departments on Sundays is also to be paid heed to.

The month of October has gifted a lengthy holiday spell to most of the Indians wherein from the 2nd till the 6th many offices would observe paid holidays. As many as 8 holidays on weekdays in a month and then you have those Saturdays and Sundays again. To all-While we are pledging for a cleaner India this October 2nd, let us also give a deep thought to the concern that is hurting our throughput and development to the core. This vow is a must – "My nation needs my labors, urges for my commitment, and seeks pure work while work; Yes, I am ready to deliver, I am ready to serve my motherland."

(Posted on blog on 2 October, 2014)

□

Deemed-guilty before Judicial Judgment

The essence of justice says that every person is innocent unless proven guilty. And the authority lies with the judiciary to adjudge a person guilty of an offence. My purpose of writing will become evident in case I quote the instance of a father and mother affirmed shamefaced to have killed their daughter. And you know the names. Since 2008, and all through the passing years, the media, the police, and those news-bite experts did not leave any stone unturned to make the general public believe that the parents were the slayers. It was in November 2013 that the special CBI court proclaimed the association of parents in the brutal crime; however the public was certain to the core as the verdict was many a times pre-announced by the police and media. Can you fail to recall those reincarnations by the media houses based on the theories projected by the police where they alleged the murdered girl's sensual connection with the male house-help? We all remember a veteran BJP leader's pure acquittal in the Ayodhya and in the multi-crore hawala case. Then why blame him of prejudicing the investigation by political stimulus?

This is just one of those cases where the probable offender is deemed-guilty basis the unsubstantiated equations proposed by the police and media. The recent is the much-hyped Badaun case, which if you will search is listed as '2014-Badaun gang rape' in the Wikipedia. The CBI, however, has established zero evidences for sexual assault. And in case the discoveries come true, what about those detained men who would re-live their public lives; however with a tag of deemed-rapist? 'Breaking News', which most of the times comes from 'sources', makes every endeavor to validate whatever is stated. Just lately, the CBI reported to the court that the agency could not establish any connection between mala fide activities and a highly regarded Indian entrepreneur in the Coal-Gate scam. Now, would the same CBI or the media houses that adjudged the industrialist as guilty pay for the losses incurred in the business owing to a blow to his reputation? No. Post such failures, none of the probing agencies stand liable for harms to the acquitted.

Bloomberg has claimed that the evil of 'paid news' is decomposing Indian democracy. It is now quite easy to ruin the public life of any individual by bribing either the police or a media house. Considerable to note, post the toughening of rape law in 2013, acquittal rate in rape cases has gone as high as 75 per cent. But would these 75 per cent be able to lead a normal and reputable public life owing to the sensational claims made by the police in many of these cases ending with declaring the apparent offender as guilty? The list of such cases is not exhaustive and ranges from violations linked with murders, corruption, rapes, and cheating. And extending from shattering the public life to sullying the business/career, the outcomes take away even the basic right of a person to lead a cherished and peaceful life. The catastrophe does not end here. A deemed-guilty even when led free by the court remains a suspect in any of the wrongs that subsequently happen. What a wretched conclusion of our Constitutional rights and privileges.

The most vulnerable to this obscenity are the renowned individuals viz. the politicians, businessmen, film stars, and bureaucrats. Politicians were once considered as men who for the service of the mankind and economy abandon their personal lives. In the Indian political setup, however, with many politicians held as suspects in scams and crimes the general public regards the entire community as cheats. Same is the case with corporate houses, the crucial leaders of which are named in police/CBI charge sheets, leaving the hard-earned business reputation at stake. Our bureaucracy is usually acknowledged as the most crooked wing; however, the list of bureaucrats declared guilty by the court of law is noticeably trivial. And the common man, who has every right to be respected in the society, is deprived of all such honors once he is charged with misconduct, many a times even without any substantial evidences. The ones, able to get out untainted, are blamed to have prejudiced the judiciary with misuse of political power or money. The gravity is severe and hence Indians' Constitutional rights ask for some quick actions.

Holding of press conferences the same day when the case is recorded in no way makes sense. The investigating agencies, with their rushed disclosures and verdicts, rule out the accused as guilty there and then. The enduring part is played by the media and the accused has no other option than to live in a state of anarchy. More flavors are added by the lawyers of both sides who voluntarily give news-bites to press. To my valued government officials-Sir/Madam, the public appreciates your devotion towards work; however premature exposes leave the accused in dejection. Appearances on TV are not that important, the reputation of the accused, however, is a life-long earning. All of us know what happens in the search operations of IT Department when the eager officials adjudge cash and gold holding as illicit, but later findings find the same as untainted. The public standing of any 'deemed-guilty' is what we all need to preserve, always.

Let me share an incident where an NGO filed a petition with the Delhi High Court over sharing of information with the media by the investigating agency in Delhi serial bomb blasts case. The petition said, 'Delhi Police is leaking info claimed to be obtained by them in the course of interrogation into a case to the media and the manner in which the media publishes the same, apart from being defamatory in nature, also affects the fundamental right of the accused to a fair trial.' The Court not just issued notice to the Centre and the city police, but also said, 'It is a serious issue. Such press conferences go beyond giving information to hamper the investigation. You are an investigating agency. Don't you know how to preserve evidences?' It is thus evident that apart from damaging the repute of the accused, Indian investigating agencies also leak substantial information during press releases, or shall I say hurried press releases. Forget justice or fair trial in the particular case, such immature acts even lead to additional detriment.

Now, either the new rulers or the Apex Court of India should step in at the earliest. Infringement of rights listed under the Constitution is apparent in such conditions; hence firm guidelines have to be established to prevent further breach. Investigating squad, lawyers in the ongoing suit, media houses, and other government officials must be directed to preserve the findings of the case, which are prone to take twist and turns subsequently. Press releases by police and re-creations by media are not to be allowed unless one of the courts of law adjudges the defendant as guilty. The other side of the coin though demands flow of facts in the public domain; however this can only be said in case of proven facts. Little knowledge is a dangerous thing-An old proverb says.

(Posted on blog on 27 September, 2014)

□

Right to Contempt can never be Fundamental

"Mandir Gurudware Bhi Hain Yahaan
Girija Ka Hai Ghadiyaal Kahin
Mullah Ki Kahin Hai Azaan
Ek Hi Apna Ram Hai, Ek Hi Allah Taala Hai
Hum Sab Bharatiya Hain, Hum Sab Bharatiya Hain"

The lines above may sound unfamiliar and unheard of to many Indians; this is an extract from the National Cadet Corps Song 'Hum Sab Bharatiya Hain'. 'Unity and Discipline' is the motto of NCC, a tri-services voluntary organization engaged in the mission of instilling discipline and patriotism in Indian youth. Now, let's also take into cognizance an entirely opposite occurrence, where some so-called learned and intellect citizens of India did not think twice prior to their act of contempt of court, the Supreme Court of India, in the matter that involved execution of a terrorist. Discipline and patriotism, the former with respect to obeying the rulings of courts and the latter relating to holding every person charged of proven sedition as an enemy of oneself, saw deep decline, something that has substantiated, yet once again, that crime, judicial rulings and politics will always remain dyed with the colors of religion and caste in India.

As a general citizen of India, most of us relish the right to speak against rulings of courts, despite being fully aware that the time consumed in deciding any criminal case in our country is prolonged, not because of lack of judicial expertise, but because it is our inherent ideology that a wrong-doer may escape punishment, but an innocent never be penalized. In other cases, the Supreme Court may take into account such contempt; however since we are gifted with a

Constitutional right to freedom of speech and expression, we regard ourselves free to criticize judgments in the public and in debates over news channels. In the recent incident, shall I ask as to how many of those who censured the verdict of the court had comprehensively read the judgment? Did you actually know as to how many accused were held guilty in the 1993 bomb blasts case, how many are still behind the bars, how many have been acquitted and why Yakub Menon was the only one to be delivered with death penalty? Unaware of facts, in the name of so-called humanitarian relief, and in some cases, for want of publicity and political perks, a few of us never mind going against the most trustworthy wing of our democracy, the judiciary.

But, patriotism and unity hasn't died utterly yet. On the same day when the guilty was hanged, one of the most cheered Presidents of India, Late Mr. Abdul Kalam, was also being bid farewell. Though news channels were busy broadcasting the 'sensational' hanging of a person found guilty of conspiring against the nation, real citizens did not escape the chance to pay reverence to the people's president. Since many intellects and eminent personalities from politics and film industry too backed the idea of commuting the death penalty of the guilty as they allege that the court's verdict was on 'merely the confessions of other accused', news houses saw immense profits and TRP in debating this subject rather than devoting maximum time to showcase contributions of Late Mr. Kalam, which would have inspired the Indian youth to aim for India's prosperity than to challenge court's verdict with full valor and weak specifics.

Not all can be blamed, yes many news channels also discussed the former president's ideology; however in the prevailing conditions where we cannot afford anything less than 'sheer commitment' towards nation-building, the episode of the hanging of a guilty shouldn't be debated to such extent. Of course, no one can deny that deliberations regarding the applicability of death sentences in India are necessary, as such debates pave the way for legislative and social corrections, confining to just one case for this cannot be justified. Let us go back to from where we started, 'the motto of NCC'. Most of us have not been a part of this exercise; at least an insight into the belief of the NCC is much needed. Unity cannot be thought of unless we begin connecting ourselves with the pillars of democracy; faith in the verdicts of our courts is indispensable. They have upheld our Constitutional rights, were the key in striking down sections of various Acts that infringe our privileges. In the same context, discipline is attainable if we are ready to stop politicizing matters of national integrity and security, India will become a nation of happy people with us being devoted to national service and economic betterment.

Here, it is unequivocally evident that the word 'Secularism' has taken an all-new connotation in India, even perpetrators of bombings and treason are evaluated basis their religion. A leader of one of the political parties of India and self-acclaimed guard of Indian Muslims linked death penalty of Yakub Menon with his being of Muslim origin-sheer contempt of true secularism and judicial competency of India, and also of the entire Muslim community. The media too saw this as a golden opportunity to increase viewer base, even when they realize how minorities are brain-washed during such cases by arguments over national television, this is similar to ISIS propaganda of radicalizing the youth by exploiting social media. Rarely did any news channel inform the general public that the court based its judgment on substantial evidences that proved Yukub Menon's key role in planning of bombings, arranging finance, and yes, he may not have placed bombs on the very day, but this was to escape being caught, so they misused vulnerable youth for the same. It is not the time to find which news channel is owned by men of which political group, this is time when we, the viewers, rethink as to what we shall view and thus make perceptions and conclusions.

It is also time that we realize that Right to Contempt of Court, even by way of debates, isn't and cannot be fundamental. For news channels, they are to introspect and make necessary amendments to the way news are handled, discussed and broadcasted. 'Sensation' is to be replaced by 'Sense' and 'Sustainability'. Let us all look deep within ourselves and make corrections in view of the song of NCC, some lines are hereunder.

"Hum Sab Bharatiya Hain, Hum Sab Bharatiya Hain
Apni Manzil Ek Hai
Ha, Ha, Ha, Ek Hai
Ho, Ho, Ho, Ek Hai
Kashmir Ki Dharti Rani Hai
Sartaj Himalaya Hai
Sadiyon Se Humne Isko Apne Khoon Se Pala Hai

Desh Ki Raksha Ki Khatir Hum Shamshir Utha Lenge
Hum Shamshir Utha Lenge
Bikhre Bikhre Taare Hain Hum Lekin Jhilmil Ek Hai
Ha, Ha, Ha, Ek Hai
Hum Sab Bharatiya Hain"

(Posted on blog on 1 August, 2015)

□

Inflated Prices and the Absurdity of Middleman

Surely, we have been effective so far in guaranteeing the perfectness of our market. Restricting monopolistic forces to the minimum, we have delivered an environment wherein consumers have wide choices with possibility to select the product that suits the pocket. Post the economic crisis of the 90's, liberalization was the most talked about subject matter. Participants augmented with the minimization of entry barriers, which on one hand lifted the pace of economic growth, while on the other helped entrepreneurs exploit their vision. What, however, was the key intention of eliminating monopoly and flooding the market with abundant multiplicities? With the upsurge in the number of producers, it is expected that the consumer would be delivered with reasonably priced goods.

Have we in real sense accomplished this goal? Let us consider a few real instances. Schools have been demanding colossal hike of fee on the grounds that modern infrastructure, which includes smart classes, upgraded faculty and enriched study environment, calls for additional charges. The irony, however, is the work opportunity with a smart class manufacturer wherein the marketing personnel have to ensure concentrated sales of company's product. Medicines, which are a key constituent of our expenditure budget, call for extensive promotion by medical representatives, which in turn inflates cost for the end-user. Adding to the curse is the commission extended to doctors for prescribing medicines of a particular producer. You must have comprehended my purpose of writing now.

Products/services prior to being delivered to the end-user pass distinctive channels of production. From procurement of raw materials to winning the customer, several value adding phases make a product what it should be. However, the value addition ends at the instance when finished goods are ready for being retailed. Post this stage comes the most challenging phase-Earning customers and adding revenue. The task is handled through distinct marketing channels that include advertisements, in-person visits, cold calling, and online promotion. The necessity of these channels is inevitable because of the fact that competitors are many; however users of a specific product/service are limited.

Though the old rule of economics suggests that the price of any commodity in a perfectly competitive market depends on the demand and supply variance, this however comes into the picture post the cost is already inflated due to marketing expenses. Rather than talking endlessly on the topic of inflated prices due to elevated outlays on marketing, which is often the cause of extraordinary rates for medicines, school books, clothing items and almost every second purchase we make in a day, I will talk of some measures that can curb the curse and can ensure that the end-user pays what truly is justifiable.

Marketing expenditures can be measured as a percentage of the rate charged to the consumers. To ensure that this fraction does not exceed a tolerable level, the ratio, in consensus with the specific industry embracing units producing similar kind of product, should be pre-defined. The upper limit can be determined by analyzing the needs for promotional activities in every distinct industry. Thus, separate industries producing dissimilar products can have unlike statutory percentage beyond which the outlays on marketing shall be forbidden.

Within the ambit of statutory audit of financial statements, adherence with marketing expenditure norms shall be certified for curbing any upward deviations and for guarding the wellbeing of the consumers. Non-allowance of the portion of expenditure incurred above the pre-defined limit as deduction under the IT Act and stringent disciplinary actions can add to the impact. The measure would serve two purposes simultaneously, one, this would restrict the inflating of prices for the end-user, plus, business units with limited resources (small and medium sector enterprises) would not be outshined by giant market players.

Along with, wide-ranging utilization of the online platform can be of enormous help. For every product type, each and every producer's particulars shall mandatorily be available in a columnar and comparable arrangement through a webpage run and monitored by the government. From the quality standards followed to the durability of the product, this comprehensive data shall be accessible to all with a view to facilitating easy and educated purchases. Non-participating producers with respect to adding produce details to the database shall be penalized. With a reduction in the price of commodities, these measures would also restrict corporate corruption linked with procuring resources from known agents in lieu of illicit personal paybacks.

(Posted on blog on 27 April, 2014)

□

Transforming Social Interactions and Behavior—The Social Media

Exchange of user-generated content via technologically-driven platforms can be understood just as the foundation of social media. Today, this has crossed almost every possible boundary and has allowed users to exchange information, modify it, assess it, and above all respond to the information in a completely dissimilar manner. Indeed, social media has transformed the social conduct of humans and has in turn added much more value to decisions. Awareness and feedback are traveling and crossing borders, with enormous impact on consumers' buying preferences, voters' voting preferences, and in fact on the overall outlook of the society.

Time has certainly changed from when you could just read a writer's views in a daily newspaper and had no means to raise any questions or send across any feedback. Social media has accorded voice to every participant and hence has enhanced the reliability of the content. In case you disagree with the facts or perceptions of the content-generator, prompt response can be sent across which shall be accessible to every reader. Certainly, any perception cannot be closed-ended. Social media has brought people a step forward, wherein ease of participation in discussions has opened new ways for responsiveness and widely-accepted conclusions.

Easy access to the desired piece of information, availability of comments and feedback from others, and real-time sharing are the pluses that social media has brought in. Truly, the world was never so contracted, as it has become post the evolution of platforms that have allowed users to generate content, upload it from anywhere, make people notice it, and in case it is worth noticing, then to be paid for the good work. Ranging from Facebook and Twitter to e-commerce websites viz. Flipkart and Snapdeal, users are free to post comments and reviews, which in turn many a times modify the frame of mind of the subsequent reader.

Not just restricted to social networking sites as we believe it to be, social media embraces blogs and microblogs (Twitter), news networking sites (NDTV), and content communities (YouTube). Who could have thought of a day when businesses would spend huge cash on marketing their products and services in the social media? The underlying fact is the ever-high traffic with respect to number of users, along with number of active contributions in dialogues and the impact of such activities on the behavior of the user. From political groups to corporate houses, everyone wants an online presence so as to ensure noticeability and acceptability.

True is the saying that every revolution has a few minuses too. The society has witnessed cases when sharing of misleading content via the social media ignited the fire of hatred in many parts of India and caused communal displeasure. On the contrary, the freedom of speech and the power to share thoughts that have been extended to the society by social media are something to cheer about. Users are the ultimate power-bearers, hence shall recognize the potential and the opportunities. Today, my voice is free to flow, can fetch feedback from readers, and has the supremacy to drive social behavior in a far more constructive manner.

(Posted on blog on 3 July, 2014)

□

Censorship of Films, TV Programs and Ads to be Strengthened

Development and right to express are allied. Be it a common man, a politician, a film maker or a press reporter, every human has a fundamental right to express thoughts, and the same is appreciated by the Indian Constitution. Unobstructed speech paves way for all-inclusive betterment and furtherance of unnoticed groups. Hasn't press reports revealing corrupt behavior of politicians and bureaucrats, films like 3 Idiots and Mother India, and public protests such as the one in mid-1970s, the Sampoorna Kranti by Lok Nayak Jayaprakash Narayan and the one by activist Anna Hazare, the movement for Jan Lokpal Bill aroused the conscience of millions of Indians? The flaws of any society and its political and economic structure cannot be remedied unless voices of people are allowed to flow freely. There, however, exists a distinct aspect as well. A press report that presents a suspect as guilty, a film that surpasses the limit of religious tolerance, and a movement that beats the intentions of law are as much detrimental as is the corruption of our governments and cases of women harassment. Truth, a basic requisite for the functioning of democracy, must prevail, but unethical and anti-social is what that should not be allowed to propagate in the name of freedom of speech.

I, in my former article, 'Deemed-Guilty before Judicial Judgment', have emphasized on how media houses relish their freedom of expression overlooking the fact that innocent men face the heat of society as a result of their misreporting and manipulating of details. A controversy has lately sparked in India over the release and broadcasting of a film, which, according to some religious groups, embraces disreputable facts regarding God and alleged God-men. This isn't new and we have all seen suppression of freedom of speech in the past in the name of hurting of communal sentiments and accord. Accept it; India is a community-rich nation and such large number of religions and languages not just make us different from other nations with respect to secularism, but also in terms of social equilibrium and tolerances. Some of the religious clusters protest even genuine movement of expressions, but the other side of the coin is that a few film makers too cross the limit of forbearance, outcomes being adverse to our shared consensus. Protests and right to free speech both have certain boundaries and these binding limitations make these two yield positive returns. Then the need is to diagnose few basic issues related to our freedom and to cure them.

This is a bit challenging; in case the government bans release of films and press reports that exceed the level of religious/social tolerance, the news and film makers would cry unfairness and clampdown, on the other hand if such adverse expressions are allowed to flow freely, the secular and social balance of India comes under vulnerability. Then we also have some clusters which come into action promptly when a not-so-kind media is released. These groups leave no stone unturned in disturbing communal equilibrium, asking for ultra vires demands, and damaging the public property. There have been, in the past, instances when state governments have taken tough stance on the release of films that are not in accord with the so-called secular thoughts of religious leaders and some political ones too. Why can't these political parties and religious leaders judge the purity of many television series that amenably promote vulgarity and nudity? Isn't that obvious, to make big news, retaliate something big, no matter the trivial ones are more harmful. Most of the programs that are aired on Indian television are an adaptation of a popular overseas' series, they run and control the minds of Indian viewers, but have we ever thought over the difference in culture and religious scope between India and U.S.?

Sony Pictures stalled the release of a film owing to warning by North Korea since the leader of the country was made a part of the film; the stepping in by the U.S. President, however, furthered the release and as a retaliatory measure the U.S. has imposed some economic sanctions against many North Korean government agencies. Similar approach with problems related to suppression of freedom of speech lacks in India and the same can be attached to vote-bank and caste-based politics. I would not approve or condemn the retaliation by Hindu groups of a recently screened film; however it has been seen that in cases of alleged hurting of minority sentiments, many political groups respond hurriedly. To put to rest any prejudiced verdicts, the key is to make the Censor Board so capable, responsive and commanding that any of their conclusions should become binding. Electronic media in India runs in a strange manner where some reports and films are objected just because they are not in consensus with a few groups, while those films, advertisements and TV programs which in every possible way play with the ethical and moral values of India are allowed to air freely. Now that everyone knows what those surrogate TV commercials of Music CDs of hard drink producers mean and aim at, the authorities are still silent. Tally the revenues of such companies from the music CD division and compare if that division is capable to handle such lavish commercials on TV. I am sorry, but even after searching for these music CDs in super stores, I wasn't able to get one since they are never on sale. On similar lines are the commercials of elaichis by the manufacturers of tobacco.

Television, films, advertisements, and news reports are the most heeded substances. It is then very crucial to accord some sort of norms that shall be adhered to in the wake of religious richness and centuries-old culture and values of the Indian society. Need is to fortify the Censor Board of Film Certification by adding in it members holding acumen from distinct faiths. Post the Censor clearance, state governments cannot be allowed to stay the release of any film, save in conditions that are exceptionally nerve-racking, and which if held judicious should restrict the release round the nation, not in just a state or two. In the era where televisions have such high viewership, contrary-to-Indian values programs cannot be endorsed. A Censor Board for Television broadcast is much-needed in the light of wide access to satellite TV. Plus, TV commercials that are deceptive and promote forbidden goods are to be stopped with immediate effect. Press Reports that convict a suspect are the killers of right to dignity and thus should be regulated. It is imperative to realize that in the name of religious copiousness, honest endeavors and freedom of expression cannot be hindered, but the same also cannot be permitted to overdo the parameters of forbearance. The ultimate aim of all censorship boards should be to ban any forbidden endeavors that can disturb communal harmony and/or Indian values and ethics, be it by way of films, TV programs or commercials.

(Posted on blog on 5 January, 2015)

□

Financial Inclusion of the Underprivileged – The MFIs

The finance and investment sector cannot justify its social and economic dexterity unless the needs of the underprivileged sections of the society are addressed to in a comprehensive and apt manner. We have been talking about poverty, discussing about the ways to overcome this curse, and adding abrupt measures as tools for betterment of the poor. To name a few of these tools, food and employment security schemes deserve a special mention. However, what purpose do these schemes solve? Ways have to be identified that are enduring and promising. Inclusion of India's seven microfinance institutions in the list of world's top 50 Microfinance Institutions (MFIs) is not just encouraging, this also evidences that endeavors are being made in the appropriate direction.

Banks, which serve as the backbone of any economy, procure savings from household and allocate these funds in form of credits to reliable borrowers. However, the poor and those unable to provide collateral for the credit rarely benefit. This is where the microfinance institutions step in, recognize the needs of the deprived section, and extend funds. The term 'microfinance' refers to relatively small credit, savings, insurance, and other financial services, which serve exclusively the economically deprived sections of community. In India, to undertake the task of attending the financial sector needs of the poor, several delivery models have emerged, though every of these have their own limitations.

Let us discuss a few. SHGs (Self Help Groups) comprise of members from similar social strata and aim at pooling small savings of the households and extending funds out of these deposits to the member/s of the group. The Federated Self Help Group model is an extension of the SHGs in a way that multiple SHGs are brought together and then pooled funds are rotated within the enlarged group. Next, are the Gramin Banks that serve the needs of rural finance with attributes like low transaction costs, no collateral, and repayment in small and short intervals. Co-operative models too contribute in a way that human and financial resources are united and the group manages its own fiscal needs.

Microfinance institutions, a source of finance for the poor are heterogeneous groups registered as NBFCs, societies, trusts, or Section 25 companies. Turning out as the most proficient source of financial inclusion of the underprivileged, MFIs too suffer from multiple drawbacks. The foremost is the restricted outreach in a manner that these institutions serve the needs of the women on priority considering them as potential and reliable borrowers and savers. Next comes the high level of interest rates that demotivate rural inhabitants to borrow. The interest rates are high owing to the fact that MFIs rarely receive any subsidized credit and hence recover their costs of operations from the borrowers. Another concern is the focus of MFIs on poor in the rural areas with almost nil measures for the urban poor.

Client retention, high costs of transactions, credit defaults, delayed payments, frauds, weak loan collection procedures, and geographical factors are some other prominent bottlenecks in the functioning. It is vital to note that studies in the MFI sector reveal that core poor are rarely being served with the any real benefits. The states of Bihar, U.P., Jharkhand, Madhya Pradesh, Orissa, Uttaranchal, and Chhattisgarh, which embrace almost 53.5 percent of poor in India, hold only 23.6 percent share of the total microfinance outreach in India. Another fact is that the average amount of funds extended to the members of MFIs and SHGs is not more than INR 4000, which rarely can serve the financial needs of the section.

The government and the authorities will have to come up with workable solutions for the sector, sooner than later. The priority task can be defined as setting up of a regulatory body for the MFIs, which currently are under the purview of state governments. Another key task is to educate the beneficiaries of the programme with regards to their prospects for credit, along with enlightening them about the repayment parameters. Plus, balance has to be ensured in terms of micro financing in rural and urban parts of the nation. It has to be realized that almost

41 percent of the population is deprived of banking facilities. Thus, measures like MFIs will have to be pushed with elevated pace and synergy. The Micro Finance Bill, which has been rotating from one department to the other for approval now calls for urgent sanction.

(Posted on blog on 13 May, 2014)

□

This 26th Jan-Re-live the Values of Our Constitution

What made the Union of India Republic of India? Which literature declares India to be a secular, socialist, sovereign and democratic republic? Which is the source that assures all Indian citizens equality, justice and liberty? And where are the structured principles, rights and duties of people and government laid? This cannot be just a piece of writing; this cannot be just another book in our libraries or just another subject in school syllabi. The Indian Constitution is much more, at par with our religious books and the sayings of our religious leaders. It wasn't on the 15th of August 1947 that Indians gained freedom; it was on the 26th of January 1950, the date when the Constitution was adopted, that in true sense the people of this nation were assured of fair and dignified life, free from the clutches of interference, unjustified authority and disparity. Today, we are free to elect our representatives, are free to move and work in any of the states of India, are free to express, and are free from any perpetual supreme authority, all backed by a literature, which if studied and abided to diligently by all citizens and their representatives in the administrative setup, will better not only the Indian society, but also our economy, environment and political structure.

Freedom from foreign rule or autocracy is not absolute and reasonable unless explicit guiding principles promising right to honorable life are in place. This is why the rulers of free India felt the need of a supreme law that should set out the fundamental rights and duties of citizens and lay down the framework for separation of powers and directive principles for governments. Any law that contravenes with the prescribed norms of the Constitution cannot stand, thus ensuring that the citizens of India would forever remain protected from the glitches of corrupt politics. Then will it be so wrong to say that our Constitution holds no less prominence than our Gita, Quran or Bible, and that along with motivating the new generations to adopt the sayings of these religious literatures, they should also be awakened to imbibe the Indian Constitution? This means that Constitution cannot be just confined to a subject in the education module, it has to be accorded much more importance, such that the learnings from this never get faded in our memories and our day to day actions are in complete consensus with the utmost law of the land. Would you not agree with the truth that merely anyone of us recalls the lessons on Constitution that we get in our school days and what about those who even lack elementary education? Are we then not unaware of our rights, our obligations and our liabilities towards the nation?

We celebrate the 26th day of every January, but for most of us it is just another holiday. We know that a Constitution embracing our privileges exists, but what exact those rights are, we rarely know. We, from news sources, come to know that someone has challenged an unconstitutional act of the legislature/parliament in the court of law, but why the same is alleged to be void ab initio, we hardly detect. Constitution is the very basis of our lives and being acquainted with even the minute particulars as contained therein is all that necessary to realize our sense of duty. While we cast our votes and then expect from our representatives to make good the living conditions, should we not also be well familiar with the political setup of India, with the notions of separation of powers, directive principles of state policy, elections, emergency provisions, and trade and commerce? Remember, the functioning of the governments and the conduct of our representatives should be in line with the norms of the Constitution; hence any misuse of power is ultra vires. When we expect them to be honest at work, should we also not play our part in the process of nation-building, and the same is attainable if we adhere to the fundamental duties of all citizens as enumerated in the Constitution.

We are the world's largest democracy and are ruled by the longest written Constitution of any sovereign country around the globe, but lack of awareness and hunger of what we deserve has held us back.

From politicians to bureaucrats and from religious leaders to general public, every person on the soil of India should be aware of what the Indian Constitution expects from us all. Directive principles, though not enforceable by any court of law, should be the guiding codes for every government. A few overlooked aspects such as cow slaughter and uniform civil code are to be paid heed to sooner than later. Then are our fundamental duties that ask us to uphold and protect the sovereignty, unity and integrity of India, and to strive towards excellence in all spheres of individual and collective activity so that the nation constantly rises to higher levels of endeavor and achievement. Fundamental rights embrace right to equality, right to freedom, right against exploitation, right to freedom of religion, cultural and educational rights, right to property and right to Constitutional remedies. The honorable Supreme Court has adopted the view of the fundamental rights and directive principles being harmonizing with each other, one supplementing the other's role in aiming at the sole goal of establishing a welfare state by means of social revolution. Isn't it very clear then that all that we expect from the society, political leaders and economy are there in our Constitution, which makes the same the most supreme piece of literature in India?

For those who haven't read or have disremembered the lessons on this guiding principle, this 26th January go through at least the Fundamental Rights, Directive Principles and Fundamental Duties as encompassed in the Constitution. The dream of 'Better India, Just for All' can come true in case our works compliment the dictums of our Constitution. To all-Try to place a copy of the Indian Constitution at your homes and offices; better we are when aware of the supreme directive that establishes the rule of law and not the rule of man, provides against encroachment on the individual's right and preserves the political institution against political whim or caprice. One thing is sure-26th Jan, 15th August, and 2nd October cannot be just another holiday from work or study, these days are the genesis of free India, they remind us the command of honesty, truth, and of the common man, who has all the courage to change the circumstances, it is just the will and spirit that lack. If we promise to change any one wrong each year on these days, it would not take long for the Indian society and economy to prosper and be a world leader. The Parade of 26th Jan is a symbol of unity and synchronization; let us then be an Indian, not a Hindu, Muslim, Jaat, Pandit, Shia or a Sunni. From the core of my heart, Happy Republic Day!!!

(Posted on blog on 25 January, 2015)

□

Police and Public – Why a Gap Subsists?

Unless warranted, a common man would never want/dare to exchange any words with a policeman. And the two words, 'want' and 'dare', elucidate everything. In a democratic setup, wherein we are free to elect our representatives, who in turn are accountable for appointing personnel so as to guarantee security and justice to all, how can even a trivial form of autocracy find any existence? The police force, who has been delegated the task of protecting citizens' rights and helping them in any and every possible manner, seems to have disremembered the very preamble of existence. Let us try and find the underlying causes of this critical gap.

What is the basic dissimilarity between dictatorship and democracy? While in the former, the protectors of justice follow only the directives of the ruling authority; in the latter, the guards of law work under the guidelines laid down by the law of the land, treating all citizens, whether rich or poor, alike. Then what shall we think of the prevailing scenario of our country, wherein the guardians of law, our policemen, rarely care for the common man and adhere to just what is directed by the MPs, MLAs, and other political personalities? For sure, until our police force becomes uncomplicatedly accessible to the general public, the purpose of democracy is not met.

Not for even a day are our newspapers free of any biased/unlawful conduct of the police. While in many of the news, the report ends with the note that the police have not yet registered the case, in the others we read about the laidback outlook of cops. It is easy to debate over the instance of rape or acid attack; however the pain of the victim, which further enhances when she approaches the police to get the complaint registered, is hard to even imagine. Or for that matter, when a poor villager moves to the police station to list a complaint for a stolen bicycle, he often senses absence of any justice, when the cops abuse him without listing the complaint.

The motive of my writing is not to uncover the sad instances of unfairness yet again. However, when we are anticipating for high GDP rate, enhanced work prospects, dipped prices, and lowered interest rates, let us also focus on a basic need-certain and unbiased security of all. Why at all has this need arisen is not a tough question to answer. The management of the police force lies more or less with the political leaders, who quite often have their distinct vote banks. The policemen, even when they move towards doing the right thing, are stopped by the power holders. Next is the greed of fetching unauthorized perks in lieu of helping the common man.

And accountable for such a decline is the common man too. It appears easy to escape penalty by bribing a policeman, which in turn sets an evil and unstoppable trend. Tell me honestly what is the first thought that comes to your mind when you break law-For sure, bribing the guardians of law. Indeed, unless the police force is freed from the day to day political snooping, nothing much can be expected. Herein, the directives of the Supreme Court regarding setting up of state security commissions to curb undue pressure of politicians, fixed tenure of police officers, and transparent appointment of police heads, have to be executed by all the CMs sooner than later.

(Posted on blog on 27 July, 2014)

□

Dexterous Electoral Process

One Should Vote-Who can Deliver Prosperity and Dignity

Polls of 2014-Leaders endeavoring to fetch the requisite numbers, voters too are motivated towards extending support to those who represent honesty. The upcoming Lok Sabha polls are not the same as always. Anna's movement against corruption, the gathering for 'Damini', and the rise of a new political group that alleges to be the most uncorrupt have definitely uplifted the political milieu. Leaders, for the very first time, are stressing the need to eradicate corruption. 'Integrity' is the factor that everyone is talking about. Is honesty the only aspect that can bring in the reforms and revolutions we are looking forward to? With a new group of people representing themselves as history-makers and the most sincere candidates, what shall be the approach of the voter? Remember, not everyone alleging to be God can be followed. Honesty is never through words, it calls for acts. Now, what shall the voters consider?

As declared by the Constitution, we have considered India as a secular and sovereign state that unites diverse religions, cultures, and communities-A fact we feel proud of. Along with defining and laying down the principles for the formation of the Government, our Constitution also defines the responsibilities of the elected Government. Prosperity of all is a part of this, which in turn calls for equivalent distribution of income, alike prospects of employment, and policies aimed at betterment of society as a whole. Shall we not consider India as an Economy then? – An economy that shall aim at maximizing profits and providing the dignity of being employed to all. Definitely, this shifts our basis of understanding to a distinctive ground. Will mere honesty-alleging candidates be competent enough in handling such a large-scale economy that is accountable to billions of citizens? Yes, we want to shut every door for corruption; however other vital factors shall too be paid heed to.

What should we expect from our political entrepreneurs? Vision, administrating capabilities, unbiased attitude, and swift decision-making potential can be the answer. This reminds me of the incidence when the nation was struggling from economic crisis in the 90s and the then Finance Minister, Dr. Manmohan Singh initiated liberalization of industries with a view to providing broader investment and capital prospects to privately-held ventures. The outcomes were surely favoring. Aptitude and ability to comprehend the global economic conditions are what make a leader an entrepreneur. As voters, we must consider the fact that we are a part of an economic society. Prosperity follows fiscal viability. The Constitution has recognized the vitality of employment and states that the dignity of every citizen is backed by the capability of earning livelihood. The status of being an economy is thus inseparable.

Should we then consider just the alleged-honest candidature, or shall we weigh our candidates on factors including intelligence, economical awareness, vision, and governance capability? Remember, governance is not that easy. The one, who is the most honest of all, can't surely be the most capable administrator. Diplomacy is inseparable to leading. While we are part of a nation with multiplicities of castes, we also represent a nation that comprises of groups that look forward to perquisites without pains. The voters can with no trouble be influenced by promising materialistic benefits and policies favoring their particular community. The instability of past Union Governments is the outcome. The resultant outcomes are inflation, corruption, misuse of investigating agencies, and special packages to particular states. Voters, remember, we all constitute to build a nation and the prosperity of the nation would mean development of all.

Are we aware of the fact that private sector investment has dipped consistently since 2007, the figures of Sensex and Nifty aren't promising, and the Indian currency reached its peak against U.S. Dollar a few months ago? Nomura, a prominent global financial institution, considers that the Modi-led Union Government in India would boom investments; the rupee would stand below 60 per dollar by June 2014; and the Gross Domestic Product of India will be above 6 percent in the financial year 2015-16. Though my words could be seen as favoring the Prime Ministerial candidate of the BJP, my sheer motive is to let voters recognize the urge of a stable economy. The voters, along with measuring the candidates on grounds of integrity, must also look forward to extending support to leaders that can bring in economic reforms at the earliest. Plus, never forget, governance demands sacrifices, diplomacy, and an unfair attitude at times. Administrating India is complex. The one who can deliver prosperity and dignity for all shall be voted for.

(Posted on blog on 18 March, 2014)

□

Are Minority and Backwards Just the Voters?

An SP leader, post the outcomes of the 2014 polls, claimed that even the Muslims who were adored with manifold perks did not favor the party. Subsequently, a few of the schemes that were announced to lure the minority were rolled back. Mayawati accused Muslims to have taken a wrong route since the BSP came up with nil numbers. And the Congress blamed the BJP of enticing all the Hindu voters who, with a view to oppose the Muslim voters, voted in bulk for the BJP candidates. When would anyone bother to ask the real concerns of the much-talked about 'minority', which is the actual sufferer of the 'Secular' approach of political groups?

I believe that the word 'secular' comes up with an altogether distinct meaning when talked about in the Indian scenario. Herein, the one who treats all religions alike is not secular, rather the one who promotes or even talks of promoting any minority community is considered to be a true secular. The synonym 'anti-communal' is what that has been accorded to this word. For sure, if you think or endeavor to endorse the Hindu community, you are being communal in India. And in case you just take part in a few dialogues with the community leaders of Muslims you will be allowed to claim yourself as a true secular.

The Sachar Committee, which was appointed in 2005 by the PM to report the real condition of Muslims in India, revealed the social, economic, and political backwardness of the community despite uncountable measures adopted by the governments in more than past 30-35 years. Though the coming in of a minority-favoring government enhances the feeling of security among Muslims, in real sense, the living conditions rarely advance. It is quite known to all that the so-called secular political groups make every attempt to make the minority community realize that they are backed by the government in all the wrongs they commit.

While on one hand, most of the Hindus prefer preserving acceptable detachment from Muslims; the political groups on the other hand talk of promoting the wellbeing of this community till the votes are in their favor. Indeed, the essence of the word 'secular' has been manipulated in the country that is home toalmost every prevailing religion in the world. None of the political leaders is worried about the countless tailbacks; rather 'Ponzi' schemes declaring extraordinary returns are announced every other day with a view to fascinate Muslim voters. According to a recent finding, Muslim women are far educationally backward than the SCs and STs.

Until the political groups and their so-called secular leaders discontinue considering Muslims as a mere vote bank, the circumstances can hardly progress. Plus, a vital role has also to be played by the members of this community with respect to appreciating and favoring real development. A K Antony, heading the committee probing the underlying reasons of Congress' disaster, has recently set the political arena on fire by claiming that too much appeasement of the minority was what that caused the Congress to pack bags. Again, no one seems to be worried of the facts revealed by the Sachar Committee, which begs for factual betterment of the minority.

Lastly, alike is the case with backward castes, which once were coddled for being key voters for particular political groups; however with time focus shifted more towards the minority voters. Vital to note, the percentage of underprivileged from among the Hindu backward castes as well as the non-reserved castes is far more than the percentage of minority under the poverty line. And acknowledged by all is the fact that our senseless reservation system enhances the living standard of only the capable backward families, whereas the really economically deprived families, no matter from general or the reserved category, rarely fetch any paybacks. Time urgently calls for comprehensive reinvention of the definition of secularism and backwardness.

(Posted on blog on 4 July, 2014)

□

Realize Your Crucial Role in Nation Building Before it is too Late

Did you ever count the number of hours you spend in real productive activities? Or, did you ever notice how much engaged you are with social networking applications, election discussions, IPL fever, and instant messaging services? While we are busy counting the drawbacks of our political leaders, the likes and comments on our new feed, and the declining economy of the country, we never care about our contribution. This is where we lack and thus create an environment where the nation can hardly prosper.

It has been our tendency to blame the leaders, managers, and authorities for deficiency of better work prospects. What about our personal contributions towards nation building? Though we never assess our participation in the economic development, we collectively define the roadmap to nation's glory. Post watching an IPL match, we are busy criticizing the team structure and the bowler who wasn't able to contain runs. And then, we are ready for the next match.

From past many months elections have been the subject-matter of our discussions. Offices, government departments, and even colleges have developed into premises of dialogues where every other individual has a distinctive opinion. We analyze the past deliveries of the government, and discuss future political assumptions; however are least bothered with the fact that our productive time is what we are sacrificing. Though our active participation is the need of the hour, this should not hamper the economic prosperity of our organizations.

Better governance is what we all aspire from the national leaders; however we fail to contribute our stake. Involvement of personnel in political discussions during working hours is not that can help the nation achieve the desired GDP. Individual businesses participate in developing products and services that collectively represent the country's GDP growth; hence this in turn demands honest and time-bound delivery by the professionals. Above all, we rarely follow time promises. If the meeting is scheduled at 10, we pre-suppose it as 11. Was this 1 hour productive, or were we busy checking our cellphones for any new notifications from social networks?

Lesser attention towards official work and execution of personal tasks and family commitments is a trend in most of the employees working in state/central government departments and public sector undertakings which has led to decline in the performance of these crucial pillars of economy. Plus, features like job security and negligible accountability have enhanced relaxation among government employees. Punctuality is assured while non-productive activities; however when it comes to reporting at office we are usually late. Small businesses and proprietary firms often witness the in-charge reporting late and that too followed by engagement in private obligations during working hours. With a supervisor carrying laid-back attitude, what can be expected out of workers?

Early mornings and late hours during nights are spent on web applications that are sure to make profits for their own, however rarely add to nation's productivity. And, the aftereffects of our conversations too add to our lessened working hours. Behavioral factors that include pleasure, sorrow, fear, and anger are ignited post our visit to social networking webpages and messaging applications. A typical professional who attends office for eight hours loses uncountable hours in such activities, which subsequently adds to the decline in efficiency and thus hampering the overall business output. Above all is the fact that we are least bothered.

Ever thought why western countries were able to realize better outputs despite five-day working culture? Work during work and play during play. That also implies no official phone calls during play hours. This is what that helped the professionals attain glory that we aspire of. Though we are in the phase of adopting the five-day work culture, sturdy commitment during working hours is a basic necessity. Why do we overlook the fact that our individual hard work is the key to prosperity, personal as well as mutual? Political parties have too comprehended the non-workaholic attitude of citizens and hence have come up with policies that promise everything for nothing.

Wake up. Other side of the coin demands that the employer too shall restrict bothering personnel post office hours except in pressing circumstances. Sooner we realize, in a better tomorrow we are. My purpose of writing is restricted to helping individuals realize their role in the collective prosperity of the nation. In no way, I disagree with the usefulness of social networking platforms and active participation of citizens in political discussions; however definite time should be allotted for such activities making sure that working hours are exploited to the maximum helping the nation deliver better GDP, cost-effective and revenue-rich industries, and of course superior employment prospects.

(Posted on blog on 17 April, 2014)

□

Are We Ever Allowed to Elect Real Talent?

Trends do vary with time. Really? We have read about the kings passing over their reign to the descendants. India expected much from the Constitution that allows any Indian citizen to be a part of the parliament/legislative assembly; however for decades, the country is being taken care of by the same families although with distinct participants. We have witnessed instances of a former Chief Minister of Bihar handing over the administration of the state to his spouse; sons and daughters being passed over the representation in the Parliament; political groups led by particular families; and above all, the elevated curses of price rises and unemployment.

What does democracy in real sense mean? The expression 'of the people, for the people, and by the people' has 'of the people' a bit tensed and misplaced in India. The word 'people' in this context means the general public, which has not inherited power/politics and is rather the most capable to run the administration. Indian MPs and MLAs are though elected through the ballot system; we could rarely find candidates with nil political background coming up with any equations. This means that corporates shall never employ raw candidates, and the task of policy making shall lie only with the descendants of the CEO, CFO, or the Chairman.

A change has been sensed. The general polls of 2014 did make a few transformations with prominent descendants including Farooq Abdullah, Milind Deora, Sachin Pilot, and Jitin Prasada losing their seats, which however can be related with the wave of Mr. Narendra Modi wherein the Indians did not vote for any party/leader, however, voted for change. SP's only five seats won by the family members prove that even how strictly we decide to change; India would not stop welcoming the kings and their descendants. Are we so deficit with respect to aptitude and talent? And if no, then why the policy makers aren't chosen by merit in India?

I read somewhere that two-third of our recently elected MPs, aged below forty-five have their near ones in the arena of politics. And when we talk about the Indian National Congress, a political group that played a key role in India's liberation, almost every young MP has inherited the position from either of the parents. The trends are almost similar with the YSR Congress, Samajwadi Party, TDP, and most of the other political groups. Though real talent be awarded, excess is alarming. And it is evident that unjustifiable trend of dynasty politics has not delivered any paybacks. Post decades of democratic setup, Indians scuffle for basic necessities.

We can expect some workable solutions from the PMO, which has clearly indicated strict end to family favors in government departments/ministries. With a Prime Minister who attained success by placing a step over every single level of the ladder, India can expect trends to vary now. Much also depends upon the voters, and even the political leaders who have no aspirations above the prosperity of the family. I suggest that the Constitution of all political groups must be altered to add a clause with inclusion of new members on the basis of merit and aptitude. For how long would the Indian talent stay out of the most vital administrative role?

(Posted on blog on 14 June, 2014)

□

The Curse of Polls—Words of Leaders

What happened on the 8th of April 2014 showed us the real picture of politics, and leaders' approach to seek support. A cabinet minister of the state who is bestowed upon with the responsibility of governance did not even think twice prior to saying that a particular community helped the nation win the war of Kargil. Categorization of army men on the basis of religion can be looked upon as the most disrespectful and illicit way to gather votes. SP chief Mulayam Singh has recently justified the discontinuance of death sentence for rapists alleging that 'boys are tend to make mistakes'. And, so are our politicians.

What drives politicians to deliver such speeches and yet escape any punishment from the commission that stands responsible for fair and free elections? Let us quickly remember a few instances that corrupted the face of democracy. Who can forget the provocative speech of the All India Majlis-e-Ittehad-ul Muslimeen MLA, Akbarudin Owaisi. The intention was clear-Support on communal lines. Other noticeable, yet shameless incident was when the Congress candidate from Saharanpur, Imran Masud was found delivering a note in public that was intended to provoke the residents against the prime ministerial candidate of the BJP. While we are travelling to a world of tomorrow that talks about human rights, integrity, and respect for all, a separate line of politicians are still carving their way to the Parliament on communal lines.

Yes, the diversity of this nation may be the reason why our representatives are prone to exploit such ways; however, the protection of our richness should what they must aim at. What can you expect from other leaders of a political group, the President of which alleges community leaders to safeguard the split of votes to other parties? While we choose our leaders to bring in prosperity and open new ways of earning livelihood, our MPs and MLAs are least bothered. They have so far realized the fact that the residents of this nation are less attentive towards development and more focused towards gaining personal benefits. Let's now come out of the instances of MNS leaders resorting to violence against the migrants from other cities and a senior leader of the Congress, Beni Prasad Verma calling a prime ministerial candidate a 'goon' and party's president his slave.

It is necessary to uncover the factors that have led the leaders take a safer route towards agitating communal sentiments, and yet escaping any penalties. The voters, to whichever community they belong to, are never hesitated to welcome additional benefits for their religion/ caste while keeping the other communities' interests at stake. It is so uncomplicated for the religious and political leaders to lure voters with perks and with statements that rank their community superior to the others. On the second hand, the EC has always been lenient and inattentive towards the speeches that agitate communalism. At least a single instance of cancellation of the candidature is the need of the hour to set a stringent example.

The Army officials played an eminent role in defining the principle that anyone who fights for the country's pride is an Indian and no division on communal lines will be allowed. Voters too must encourage leaders to follow such footsteps and must curtail any of their attempts to fetch votes on basis of communal hatred. Let's term this pure process of selecting a deserving and capable representative a 'competitive test' rather than a 'battle-ground'.

(Posted on blog on 11 April, 2014)

□

Leaders Unruffled to Violate EC Model Code of Conduct

While every second news update on our televisions relates to politics, every third, nowadays, relates to the violation of model code of conduct. What makes leaders so stouthearted that they publicly challenge the laid down standards? Considerable to note, two eminent codes under the model code of conduct read (1) No party or candidate shall indulge in any activity which may aggravate existing differences or create mutual hatred or cause tension between different castes and communities, religious or linguistic, and (2) Criticism of other political parties, when made, shall be confined to their policies and programme, past record and work.

I remember the incidence when a minister in the MP state government was slapped with a notice for disregarding the model code on October 18th 2013. He was accused of distributing money during campaigning and criticizing the EC code of conduct in public. The next news I heard was his 6th consecutive win in the state elections. Shocked was I; however the incident was soon overlooked. The question that strikes is 'Is EC incapable of ensuring stringent actions against such violations, or does EC let such infringements occur?' Surely, the state is critical and calls for immediate rectifications so as to uphold the integrity of the process of electing public representatives. Mentioned hereunder are a few straight and severe violations followed by a conclusion.

It was uncomplicated for NCP chief, Sharad Pawar to advice voters to erase the ink mark and indulge in illicit voting both at Santara and Mumbai constituency. Later, Pawar claimed that his statement had a tinge of satire. The defilement, as usual, occasioned for an off-the-cuff warning by the EC. The SP leader motivated supporters not to care about the EC's model codes during elections as the state is run by the SP and hence any cases against violators would subsequently be withdrawn. The inclusion of special treatment of cases against Muslims by judiciary bodies in the manifesto of AAP has crossed every imaginable limit of infringement.

Other prominent incidences include Sonia Gandhi's appeal to the Muslim leaders for ensuring that the community votes do not split, Meghalaya's CM Mukul Sangma misusing the public transport chopper service during the campaign for Daryl Momin, Raj Babbar extending the stipulated time during his roadshow, and Kejriwal violating the code by not seeking prior police approval for his roadshow in Gujarat. As per PTI, nearly 55, 000 complaints were received by the EC till 19th March for model code violations, not a figure to be proud of.

What is expected out of a Constitutional body that is responsible to ensure fair and unprejudiced process of voting? Definitely, the EC has to stand tough and make its sturdy presence felt. Swift cognizance of defaults must be guaranteed followed by severe penal actions. Political leaders and parties must not only be warned of their violations, the violators must be debarred from contesting. Defined strategy and laid down procedures are the need of the hour. To uphold the honor of the democracy, the EC has to part with the laid-back attitude and has to deliver examples that can threaten those who are fearless of laws and authority.

(Posted on blog on 4 April, 2014)

□

General Elections of World's Largest Democracy – India

Hundreds of languages, multiple religions, and distinct castes and cultures proudly represent the nation, India. With a view to streamlining and strengthening the ruling, the Constitution makers defined the structure of Government, the mode of selection of members of the Parliament, and their duties and responsibilities. With the passage of time, the nation's political environment witnessed the rise of political parties that are backed up by particular religion/caste. This definitely led to realistic development of every sphere of society; however undue favors to specific castes can also not be overlooked.

Counting and listing down the achievements of the nation in the past seven decades post independence is not easy. We can surely recollect the incidences when representatives from distinct religions were bestowed upon with the task of governance. The Muslims who are considered to be in minority with respect to the overall population represented the post of President at three different times. The nation also was a spectator to the incidence when a catholic lady forfeited her Prime Ministerial candidature and favored the appointment of a Sikh Prime Minister. Shouldn't the nation be proud of the fact that the Speaker of the Lower House of the Parliament is a woman, while that of the Upper House is a Muslim? The verity that a woman succeeded a Muslim President who contributed enormously in the scientific glory of the nation is considerable to note.

How many of us know that India has been the largest economy in the world for 1500 of the last 2000 years? Diversity has been the nation's strength. We have seen India becoming home to Americans, Syrians, and natives of distinctive countries. Also, the Zoroastrians when forced to quit their homeland created their homes in this nation. Do we feel proud of the verity that the religions, Hinduism, Sikhism, Buddhism, and Jainism were born in India? The leaders of religions must know that India is the second largest Muslim nation on earth – wherein they are an inseparable part in the prosperity of the economy and infrastructure. Recall the fact that the Jewish have been the residents of India since the Romans burnt their second temple. Also, the nation has been home to Dalai Lama and even the Government of Tibet in exile.

Hurdles have been many. When terrorism shattered the root of mankind on one hand and on the other the religious leaders created gaps, all-inclusive development was complex. The facts are still favorable. The economy of India has been lifting 40 million residents out of poverty every year and promises to deliver middle class standards to majority of the population by the year 2025-Feel proud to be a part. Above all is the fact that more than $1/10^{th}$ of humanity herein is ready to vote-An inspiration to most developed countries. More than 700 million votes are ready to direct the upcoming governance of the nation. The pace of growth has surely been lessened by factors that include corruption, lack of infrastructural facilities, criminalization of politics, biased policies of the Government, lack of accountability, and lack of women empowerment. The upcoming general elections would definitely witness the agony of the residents towards these factors. The political party, which will be bestowed upon with the responsibility of forming the Government at the Centre should be vigilant to ensure uniform prosperity of all. The nation has viewed thriving implementation of measures that have helped reviving the economy. Let us believe that the upcoming years would bring in the much-awaited and stricter reforms. Let us also remember that we can be a part of this by being a voter and not a petitioner.

(Posted on blog on 26 February, 2014)

□□□